How to Live the Good Life

In
New York
By the
INTREPID
NEW YORKER

Tory Baker Masters
&
Kathy Mayer Braddock

To Philip, Charlie and Sam
You are growing up to be true Intrepid New Yorkers.
We are so proud of you.

Library of congress cataloging-in-publication data is available upon request

ISBN 0-9653080-0-6

First Edition

Printed in Canada

For more information about The Intrepid New Yorker contact us at:

The Intrepid New Yorker, LLC
1230 Park Avenue
New York, NY 10128

212 534-5071
212 534-7499 fax
www.intrepidny.com
email: info@intrepidny.com

DISCLAIMER FROM THE INTREPID NEW YORKER

No fees were paid or services rendered for inclusion in these pages.

A word of caution: Over time, businesses do change hands and the quality of goods and services can improve or decline dramatically. We will continue to update this list as we update our book. **In the final analysis, however, you have to be your own best judge of quality.** In addition, our facts have been checked and rechecked-services offered, payment method, location, telephone numbers, etc.-but it is always a good idea to make a phone call before visiting a particular business or service to make sure their status has not changed.

Table of Contents

THE SUBURBS DECIPHERED

HOW TO OPERATE LIKE A VIP
ON A POOR MAN'S BUDGET

THE BEST OF THE BEST

Introduction

For those of you who have been anxiously anticipating The Intrepid New Yorker, *THE SEQUEL*, it has finally arrived. Your patience is being rewarded with a guide that we believe is smarter, more germane, and broader in scope. We have spent the six years in between guides covering a lot more ground – literally, expanding our information base beyond Manhattan Island to include the NY tri-state suburban area within a 75 mile radius of Central Park. And for invaluable insights into the how's, why's and where's of living **the good life in a mega-metropolis of extreme terrain,** The Intrepid New Yorker has its customers, in particular, to thank.

Those customers are the hundreds of relocating executives and their families who we have helped settle within the NY tri-state area over the last decade. The Intrepid New Yorker Partners – Tory Baker Masters, Kathy Mayer Braddock and Sylvia Ehrlich – have virtually lived through the process with each and every one. What you may not know is that we are first and foremost, tri-state relocation consultants who help individuals, corporate executives and families successfully recreate a life here, not just find a home. To that end, we take them by the hand, and walk them from the information gathering and orientation stage, through the home, community search and then help them settle in. No matter how much money or clout can be thrown at this process, the search for direction, resources and answers is a mind-numbing experience, without expert guidance.

Over and over again, we have helped CEOs as well as entry-level professionals acclimatize to our world-renowned high cost of living. We've showed them how to come out ahead in the real estate game, negotiate the fiercely competitive and bureaucratic school system, and pinpoint the right community out of hundreds with divergent lifestyles, culture, commute, taxes and housing costs. **With this guide, *Living the Good Life In NYC,* The Intrepid New Yorkers' intention is to help newcomers and veterans alike, to minimize trial-and-error and the uphill "feel" of the day-to-day. This book dares you to declare yourself without hesitation, an Intrepid "tri-state" New Yorker!**

Acknowledgments

Thanks go to the many New Yorkers who work hard to make this city a better place to live in and who opened their doors wide to us to help with our research. Thanks go to a few people who worked so hard and so long to help us produce this new edition: Daryl Stern for her inspiration and contacts, Kurt Metzler for his design expertise and patience, Helaine Silver for her great ideas, Sheri Wolfe and Melissa Stoller for their great research capabilities, George and Isabel Shattuck for their on-going interest, Sylvia Ehrlich, our partner, for her amazing support and suburban insights and to Howie Masters, who is our greatest champion.

Tri-State Area

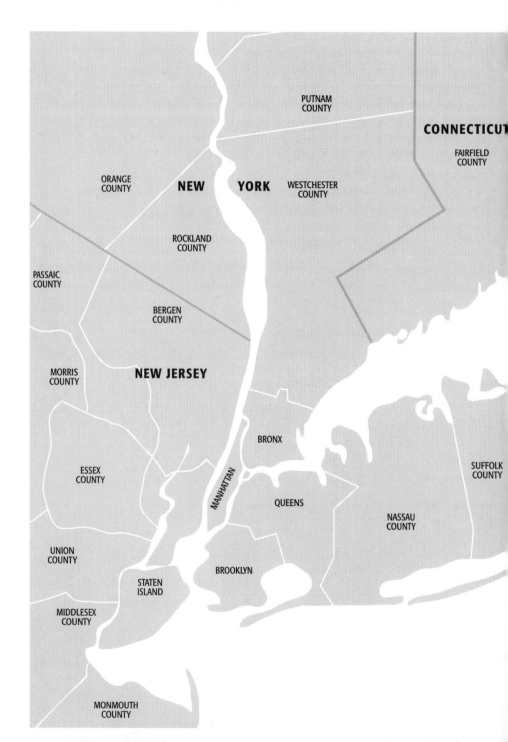

Upper Manhattan

Harlem

Central Park

Upper
West Side

Upper
East Side

Midtown West

Midtown East

Garment
District

Murray
Hill

Flatiron

Union
Square

Gramercy

Lower Manhattan

GETTING YOU ON YOUR WAY TO THE GOOD LIFE

2 **The Intrepid New Yorker**

YOUR STARTER RESOURCE KIT

PERCEPTION VS. REALITY

The perception about NY/tri-state living is that the pursuit of happiness is a constant uphill struggle and New Yorkers are all Davids trying to slay the tri-state Goliath. The truth lies, first, in the perverse passion New Yorkers have to one-up each other on the size of the dragon they slew that day and second, that New Yorkers don't want to admit that they really don't need weapons, just smart tools, to tame the beast.

Consider this chapter as your starter kit to the pursuit of happiness. It includes The Intrepid New Yorker's three keys to living successfully in our city and the tools that will help advance the process.

SOLUTIONS: YOUR THREE KEYS

1. Knowledge
Is the first key to the city — it puts you in the driver's seat.

2. Assertiveness
Comes from knowledge and knowing that you have rights, options and support...to get what you want out of this city, exactly the way you want it.

3. Instincts
There is no better guide to successful living in NYC than trusting what your instincts, common sense and personal comfort level tell you. In a city of passionately opinionated New Yorkers, you need to heed your own internal guide.

SOLUTIONS:

There is essential reference information you should have at your fingertips. New Yorkers would spend far less time completing tasks if they had access to important information and services right from the start.

ESSENTIAL REFERENCES FOR DAY-TO-DAY COPING

The Yellow Pages
It isn't just an excellent guide for finding services and products. It

also includes information you can't do without like seating charts to theaters and sports stadiums, Manhattan and vicinity overview maps, detailed maps of Manhattan neighborhoods, subway and bus maps, emergency numbers, area codes throughout the U.S., Manhattan ZIP codes and post office locations.

The White Pages
It also contains an emergency care guide, the blue pages of government listings, and zip codes.

Business to Business Yellow Pages
This is a very important publication to be aware of. It is a special yellow pages for finding products and services used by businesses. It gives New Yorkers much greater access to a wide range of products and services at lower prices. The Business to Business Yellow Pages lists all the wholesalers and manufacturers, not the retail stores. New York City is the East Coast mecca for all wholesalers and importers for everything from clothing to food to toys. Not all sources will sell to the consumer, but many will, so it is worth the search. As we said earlier, the catch is that you will have to buy in bulk—but often the minimum required order isn't as big as you might think.

Here's how to get it: By calling your local telephone business office, which is listed on your monthly bill. They will ship it to you free of charge.

800 Directories
Most people aren't aware these directories exist. They have a consumer version and a business-to-business version. This is what they offer:

• countrywide 800 numbers
• "800" catalogs and gift ideas
• mileage charts to and from every major city
• calorie charts
• weights and measures chart
• interest rate and discount tables

Here's how to get it: Call (800) 426-8686. You can request the consumer 800 directory for $12.99 and the business-to-business 800 directory for $19.99 or both for $26.99. American Express, Visa, and MasterCard are accepted.

Official Airline Guide
This is a must if you travel a lot. This publication puts you in control of how you get to your destination and how much it is going to cost. You will no longer be at the mercy of one ticket agent or one airline.

The pocket version is a monthly and offers you every possible connection of flights on every airline in and out of every major airport in the country. It costs $96 for a one-year subscription.

The desktop version offers you every possible connection of flights in and out of all major airports including the smaller airports. You can get one that also includes all airline fares, and you can subscribe on a monthly or bimonthly basis. The price starts at $299.

Here's how to get it: Call (800) 323-3537.

Zagat Restaurant Guide

This is simply the best restaurant guide to New York. You can get it at almost any bookstore.

"We Deliver"

This is a neighborhood guide to restaurants that deliver, and comes complete with menus. This guide covers the Upper East and Upper West Side.

Here's how to get it: Call (212) 288-4745.

NOSHNEWS

NOSHNEWS is a quarterly publication that focuses on a different New York neighborhood. Call 212 222-2243 to subscribe.

The Big Apple Visitor's Guide

It's not just for the tourist. It will tell you everything you need to know about what is happening year-round in this city, including:

- seasonal calendars of all activities and events occurring in New York
- a New York hotel guide with room prices
- a city map
- shopping information
- coupons for stores, hotels, and restaurants

Here's how to get it: Order a copy from The New York Convention and Visitor's Bureau, Inc. (New York & Co.) at (212) 397-8200, at a fee of $4.95, or go in person to the Times Square Information Center, at 229 West 42nd Street, to obtain a free copy.

Michelin Guide

This is one of the best overall guides to New York City for veteran and newcomer. You can purchase it at any major bookstore. It includes:

- a restaurant locator
- a hotel locator
- a cultural attractions locator
- an overall sports and recreation locator
- all necessary maps
- seating charts of arenas and theaters

The Green Book
This is a book put out by the City of New York on all government agencies and services, and lists whom to call depending on what particular assistance you need. You can find anything in this book from places to apply for a permit or license, a list of all foreign consulates, and municipal parking lots, to school boards, golf courses, and real estate information sources—you name it.

Here's how you get it: Call City Books at (212) 669-8246 or go to City Books at 1 Centre Street, Room 2223, in Manhattan.

Books Published by City & Company
City & Company publishes a host of books about Manhattan and its boroughs. Subjects range from "City Baby: A Resource for New York Parents from Pregnancy to Preschool," to "A Short & Remarkable History of New York," to "New York's 50 Best Wonderful Little Hotels." Call City & Company at (212) 366-1988 for a complete list of books, and for information on where you can purchase them.

PERIODICALS
The New York Times - daily
Wall Street Journal (Friday weekend section)
Daily News - daily
Paper Magazine - weekly (latest rends)
Crains - weekly
NY Observer - weekly
New York Press - weekly
New York magazine - weekly
The New Yorker - weekly
Time Out - weekly
The Village Voice - weekly

MUST HAVE WEBSITES
WWW.NEWYORK.CITYSEARCH.COM
A great over all New York site to get you the information that you need.

WWW.CI.NYC.NY.US
New York City's official Web site tells you where to file complaints about daily problems of city life. Its mission is to provide the public with quick and easy access to information about New York City's agencies, programs, and services. It also provides a guide to programs in city parks and recreation centers, as well as other sports and recreation events.

WWW.DIGITALCITY.COM

Digital City has listings of community events, as well as links that lead to information on dining, movies, news, sports, culture, employment, and real estate, to name just a few.

WWW.EXPATEXCHANGE.COM

A free virtual community for expats of all nationalities, living in over 140 countries. The site's country peer support networks enable expats to share advice and meet others in overseas locations.

WWW.NEW YORK.ORG

Links you to many important New York web sites.

WWW.ALLNY.COM

Super source guide for all of New York. Includes information about what is happening around the city: nightlife, cultural events, shopping, what to see and where to go.

WWW.NYC.COM

A good New York City information site. Has general but up to the minute information on nightlife, clubs, food, schools, job opportunities and real estate.

WWW.NYTIMES.COM

The New York Times online. This site includes archives, real estate, travel and tourist information, neighborhood guides and a complete entertainment section.

WWW.MTA.NYC.US

The transit site for the best routes, maps, schedules and general transit information for getting in or out or around the city. It includes Metro North schedules and information about Connecticut.

WWW.EDIFICEREX.COM

A great site highlighting the best of New York.

HOTLINES

Call 911 for Police, Fire and Ambulance Emergencies

All numbers are Area Code 212 unless otherwise indicated. All numbers listed below are answered 9 to 5 weekdays unless otherwise indicated.

ANIMALS

ASPCA

American Society For The Prevention of Cruelty to Animals
876-7700

Animal Bites / Nuisance Complaints

Bureau of Animal Affairs,
NYC Dept of Health
676-2483

Animal Emergency Care
Animal Medical Center
838-7053
Open 24 hours;
phone calls 9 a.m. to 11 p.m.

CONSUMER COMPLAINTS AND SERVICES

Better Business Bureau
Public inquiry and complaints 533-6200

CUSTOMER COMPLAINTS

NYC Dept of Consumer Affairs 487-4444

DRY CLEANING

Damaged and lost items 967-3002

MOVING AND STORAGE COMPLAINTS

Interstate Commerce Commission........................1-800-832-5660

New York State Department of Transportation 718-482-4816

CRIME

Crime Victim Hotline
Non-profit Metropolitan Assistance Corp 417-5160
24 hours a day

Police Emergency Number.....................................911

Police Headquarters
24 hour number for precinct referrals 374-5000

Sex Crime Hotline
Sex Crimes Unit, Police Dept. 267-7273
24 hour service staffed by female NYPD detectives

DAY-TO-DAY INFORMATION

Time
Automated system with the exact time 976-1616

Weather Forecast
National Weather Service.....................................516-924-0517

Weather, NYC...976-1212

DISCRIMINATION COMPLAINTS

NY State Division for Human Rights 417-5041

ELDER CARE

Department for the Aging
Referral Lists of agencies and transportation
services...442-1000

Meals on Wheels information................................442-1000

Alzheimer Center and Long-
  Term Care Services
  Advice for families
  obtaining care 442-3086

Health Insurance Information,
  Counseling and Assistance
  Program, Answers to questions
  about Medicare and
  Medigap 333-5511

Catholic Charities of Manhattan
  Counseling and Referrals..371-1000

Catholic Charities of Brooklyn
  Counseling and Referrals..718-677-9848

Self-Help Community Services
Counseling and Referrals.....971-7600

Jewish Board........................212-586-5770

New York City Self Help Center for every
affliction from alcoholism to breast cancer

Jewish Association of Services for the Aged
  Counseling and Referrals...................273-5210

ENTERTAINMENT
Cultural Affairs Department
  Hotline.................................643-7770

Parks and Recreation Department
  Current events 360-8111

SPORTS PHONE
Schedules, scores, supplemental
  information 976-1313
                                                     976-2525

FIRE
Emergency Number 911

HEALTH AND MEDICAL CARE
Ambulance Emergency Number 911

Animal Bites
Bureau of Animal Affairs, NYC Dept. of Health 676-2483

NYC Dept. of Health Bureau of
  Communicable Disease....................................788-4204

Dental Emergencies
First District Dental Society 573-8500

Emergency..573-9502

IF YOU DON'T HAVE ACCESS TO AN ENCYCLOPEDIA, YOU MAY WANT TO CALL YOUR LOCAL LIBRARY'S REFERENCE DEPARTMENT. THEY CAN ANSWER JUST ABOUT ANY QUESTION YOU HAVE OVER THE TELEPHONE. FOR HELP, CALL THE NEW YORK PUBLIC LIBRARY AT (212) 340-0849, THE BROOKLYN PUBLIC LIBRARY, AT (718) 780-7700, OR THE QUEENS BOROUGH PUBLIC LIBRARY, AT (718) 990-0714.

Department of Health Central
  Complaint Bureau 442-9666

Doctor Referrals
New York County Medical Society, AMA 684-4670

Doctors on Call...737-2333
                                                                     718-238-2100

Poison Control Center
NYC Dept. of Health...764-7667

24 hour service 340-4494

Suicide Prevention
24 hours a day 532-2400

24 hours a day 673-3000

7:30 to 12 midnight 718-389-9608

HOUSING

Electrical and Steam Emergencies
Consolidated Edison 683-0862
  24 hour service

Gas Leaks
Consolidated Edison 683-8830
  24 hour service

Heat Complaints
NYC Housing Preservation and Development   960-4800
  24 hour service of the Central Complaint Bureau

INCOME TAX

Federal Tax Information
Manhattan, Bronx
  Brooklyn, Queens and
  Staten Island..1-800-829-1040

Federal Tax Forms
24 hour number 1-800-829-3676

New York City and State Information....................718-935-6000

New York City and State Tax Forms
24 hour number 1-800-462-8100

LIBRARY

New York Public Library Information 340-0849

Manhattan, Bronx, Staten Island
  Reference Service 340-0849

Brooklyn Reference Service..................................718-230-2100

Queens Reference Service....................................718-990-0714

Branch Locator 930-0800

MARRIAGE LICENSES
NYC Marriage License Bureau 669-2400

MOTOR VEHICLES
Alternate Side of the Street Parking Regulations
NYC Bureau of Traffic Operations 225-5368

Car Lockouts
Locksmith...362-7000

Highway Emergencies
NYC Department of Transportation.......................225-5368
  24 hour service

Licenses and Registration Information
Motor Vehicle Department, New York State 645-5550
  7:30 a.m. to 4:00 p.m.

Parking Violations Help Hotline
NYC Department of Transportation.......................718-422-7800

Towed Away Cars
NYC Bureau of Traffic Operations 788-7773

OMBUDSMAN
Complaints, City Agencies
Office of City Council 788-7100

Complaints, State Agencies
New York Department of State 417-5776

Consumer Fraud
NY State 487-4293

Mayor's Action Center
Receives calls about NYC problems and
  complaints 788-7585

POST OFFICE
General Information 967-8585
  8:00 a.m. to 8:00 p.m., Saturday 8:00 a.m. to 4:00 p.m.,
  closed Sunday

SANITATION AND GARBAGE
Complaints
NYC Department of Sanitation 219-8090

Noise and smell complaints 718-699-9811

Environmental Action Coalition
Recycling..677-1601

Unsanitary Conditions
Restaurants...442-9666

STREET MAINTENANCE

Potholes
NYC Department of Transportation........................768-4653

Streetlights
NYC Bureau of Electrical Control 669-8353

Water Mains, Sewers
NYC Department of Environmental Protection
   24 hour service 718-600-9811

TELEPHONE

AT&T
Equipment service and complaints 800-526-2000

Bell Atlantic
24 hour repair 890-6611

Wiring service and complaints 800-722-2300

TOURISM AND TRAVEL

New York City Information
New York Convention and Visitors Bureau 397-8222

New York State Information
New York State Department of
   Economic Development.....................................803-3100

Vacation Information
Recording after 5:00 p.m.....................................1-800-225-5697

Traveler's Aid Services
Metropolitan Assistance Bureau 1-800-225-5697
                                               202-647-4000

TRANSPORTATION-AIRPORTS

Airports
Port Authority of NY & NJ 1-800-AIRRIDE

John F. Kennedy International
Information 718-656-4444

Lost and Found..718-244-4444

Parking Information and Conditions.....................718-244-4444

Complaints 800-498-7497

LaGuardia
Information 718-476-5000

Lost and Found..718-533-3988

Police Desk..718-476-5115

Parking Information..718-533-3850

Newark
Information 973-961-6000

Lost and Found/Police Desk.................................973-961-6230

Parking Information and Conditions......................973-961-6000

Buses

Lost and Found (NYC Transit Authority)................212-712-4500

Bus Schedules (NYC Transit Authority).................718-330-1234

Port Authority Bus Terminal Information 564-8484

George Washington Bridge Bus
    Terminal Information 584-8484

Greyhound/Trailways Bus Lines...........................1-800-231-2222

Ferry

Express Navigation..800-BOATRIDE

NYC Department of Transportation Bus &
    Ferry Information...225-5368

NY Waterway...800-53-FERRY

Staten Island Ferry 718-815-BOAT

PATH (Hudson Tubes)
Travel Information 1-800-234-7284

TRANSPORTATION-RAILROADS

Railroads

Staten Island Rapid Transit..................................718-966-7478

Amtrak (Penn Station) 582-6875
                                       800-872-7245

Metroliner Reservations (Penn Station)................800-523-8720

Metro-North (Grand Central) 532-4900
                                       800-METRO-INFO

Long Island Railroad (Penn Station) 718-217-5477

New Jersey Transit (Penn Station) 973-762-5100

Subways

Lost & Found (NYC Transit Authority) 712-4500

MetroCard 638-7622

Subway Schedules (NYC Transit Authority) 718-330-1234

Taxis

Complaints (NYC Taxi and
    Limousine Commission) 221-8294

Lost & Found (NYC Taxi and
    Limousine Commission) 302-8294

Transit Authority Customer Service Office

Complaints about service.....................................718-330-3322

MANHATTAN ADDRESS LOCATOR

The following formulas for finding street and avenue addresses in Manhattan are elaborate and absolutely worth knowing. Crosstown street numbers follow a more-or-less set pattern, avenue street numbers are much more complicated and doing the math before heading out can save you quite a bit of time in locating a particular address.

East and West Side Avenues

To determine the cross street for an address on an avenue, follow the following formula:

Take off the last digit of the building number

Divide the remainder by two

Add or subtract the number given in the chart below

Avenues A,B,C,D ....Add 3
1st Avenue ....Add 3
2nd Avenue ....Add 3
3rd Avenue ....Add 10
4th Avenue ....Add 8
5th Avenue – Up to 200 ....Add 13
5th Avenue – Up to 400 ....Add 16
5th Avenue – Up to 600 ....Add 18
5th Avenue – Up to 775 ....Add 20
5th Avenue – From 775 – 1286
  (cancel last figure) ....Subtract 18
6th Avenue / Avenue of the Americas ....Subtract 12
7th Avenue – Below 110th Street ....Add 12
7th Avenue – Above 110th Street ....Add 20
8th Avenue ....Add 10
9th Avenue ....Add 13
10th Avenue ....Add 14
Amsterdam Avenue ....Add 60
Broadway – Above 23rd Street ....Subtract 30
Columbus Avenue ....Add 60
Convent Avenue ....Add 127
Lenox Avenue ....Add 110
Lexington Avenue ....Add 22
Madison Avenue ....Add 26
Manhattan Avenue ....Add 100
Park Avenue ....Add 35
West End Avenue ....Add 60

Central Park West and Riverside Drive do not fit into this formula. To find an address on Central Park West, divide the house number by 10 and add 60. To find an address on Riverside Drive, divide the house number by 10 and add 72.

Crosstown Streets

A good rule of thumb to help guide you on crosstown streets is to remember that 5th Avenue is the dividing line between East and West, all numbers start at 1 and increase as they move further away from the center in their respective directions. For example 25 West 42nd Street would be between 5th and 6th Avenues while 25 East 42nd Street would be between 5th and Madison Avenues.

East Side Crosstown Streets

Fifth to Madison and Park: 1 to 99; Park to Lexington: 100 to 140; Lexington to Third: 140 to 199; Third to Second: 200 to 299; Second to First: 300 to 399; First to York: 400 to 499.

West Side Crosstown Streets below 58th

Fifth to Avenue of the Americas: 1 to 99; Avenue of the Americas to Seventh: 100 to 199; Seventh to Eighth: 200 to 299; Eighth to Ninth: 300 to 399; Ninth to Tenth: 400 to 499; Tenth to Eleventh: 500 to 599.

West Side Crosstown above 58th

Central Park West to Colombus: 100 to 199; Colombus to Amsterdam: 200 to 299; Amsterdam to West End: 300 to 399; West End to Riverside: 400 to 499.

> NEW YORK IS A WALKING CITY. EVERY 20 BLOCKS FROM NORTH TO SOUTH IS ONE MILE. MOST NEW YORKERS CAN WALK THAT IN ABOUT 17 MINUTES. PSYCHOLOGICALLY, NEW YORKERS HAVE A HARDER TIME WALKING EAST TO WEST BECAUSE THE BLOCKS ARE TWICE AS LONG AS THE ONES THAT GO NORTH TO SOUTH.

24-HOUR SERVICES (OR CLOSE TO IT)

D = deliver

AIR CONDITIONING SERVICE

AIR COOLING ENERGY • (212) 982-2488

24-hour emergency service. After-hour rates are $85 per hour. You usually need a service contract for their around the clock aid but they often make exceptions to this rule.

CLEANER

MIDNIGHT EXPRESS

Long Island City • (212) 921-0111 • D
They pick up and deliver in Manhattan up until 8:00 P.M. Turnaround time is 24 hours.

COMPUTER AND COPIER SERVICES

KINKO'S • Locations Throughout the City

Twenty-four hour computer rental, xerox, and fax service.

THE VILLAGE COPIER • Locations Throughout the City • D
Twenty-four hour xerox and fax service.

DRUGSTORES (WITH PHARMACY)

DUANE READE
2465 Broadway (91st Street) • (212) 799-3172 • D
224 West 57th Street • (212) 541-9708 • D
1279 Third Avenue (74th Street) • (212) 744-2668 • D
378 Sixth Avenue (Waverly Place) • (212) 674-5357 • D
Open twenty-four hours, including pharmacy; no delivery after 6:00 P.M.

Waverly Place is only open until 12:00 A.M.

GENOVESE DRUG
1299 Second Avenue (68th Street) • (212) 772-0104 • D
Open twenty-four hours, including pharmacy;
no delivery after 6:30 P.M.

RITE AID • 146 East 86th Street • (212) 876-0600 • D
2833 Broadway (110th Street)* (212) 663-3135 • D
282 Eighth Avenue (24th Street) • (212) 727-3854 • D
Open twenty-four hours, including pharmacy;
no delivery after 6:00 P.M.

Call (800) RITEAID for more store locations, hours and information.

DRUGSTORE (WITHOUT PHARMACY)

LOVE DISCOUNT • Locations Throughout the City
Open till 12:00 A.M.

ELECTRICIAN

ALTMAN ELECTRIC • (718) 681-2900
Twenty-four hours a day, seven days a week. Emergency service costs $95 per hour after 4:00 P.M.

GAS STATIONS

AMOCO
1599 Lexington Avenue (102nd Street) • (212) 289-7399

EXXON • 2040 Eighth Avenue (110th Street) • (212) 864-5003

MOBIL
309 11th Avenue (30th Street) • (212) 594-1515
718 11th Avenue (51st Street) • (212) 582-9269
Open twenty-four hours.

MESSENGER

SONIC AIR COURIERS
33-02 48th Avenue, Long Island City • (718) 786-6862
Twenty-four-hour service.

NEWSSTANDS

GEM SPA • 131 Second Avenue (at 8th Street) • (212) 529-1146
Open twenty-four hours.

POST OFFICE

JAMES A. FARLEY POST OFFICE
421 Eighth Avenue (31st and 33rd Streets) • (212) 967-8585
8:30 A.M.—6:00 P.M.

All services except registered mail and limited services for packages. Twenty-four hour window service is available for stamps, express mail, priority mail, parcel post, and money orders. (212) 330-4000. Twenty-four-hour Touch-Tone answer line.

RESTAURANTS

AROUND THE CLOCK CAFÉ
8 Stuyvesant Street (Third Avenue and 9th Street)
(212) 598-0402
24 hours Thursday – Saturday, till 3:00am Monday – Wednesday, till 4:00am Sunday.

COFFEE SHOP
29 Union Square West (16th Street) • (212) 243-7969
American-Brazilian food and a full bar that never stops.

CAFETERIA • 119 Seventh Avenue (17th Street) • (212) 414-1717
Although it's name suggests differently, Cafeteria serves really good New American food 24/7 with hip décor and waiters. A great place to go late night when you're all dressed up...or even when you're not.

CARNEGIE DELI
859 Seventh Avenue (55th Street) • (212) 757-2245
A New York institution for overstuffed sandwiches and Classic NY Cheesecake open Twenty-two hours a day, 7 days a week, 365 days a year.

EMPIRE DINER
210 Tenth Avenue (at 22nd Street) • (212) 243-2736
Twenty-four-hour Americana.

FLORENT * 69 Gansevoort Street (two blocks south of 14th Street at Ninth Avenue) • (212) 989-5779
Open twenty-four hours on weekends; until 5:00 A.M. weekdays. Re-opens at 9:00 A.M.

Moules-frites are always served at this meat-market hot-spot. New York's only late night French bistro.

KIEV • 117 Second Avenue (7th Street) • (212) 674-4040
Great Eastern European fare including blintzes, pieroges, goulash, and a daily selection of hearty soups. It's a dive, but it's also a New York institution.

SARGE'S DELI
548 Third Avenue (36th and 37th Streets) • (212) 679-0442
This all night Jewish style deli serves up great big Corned-beef and Pastrami sandwiches all night. Don't miss out on the super thick milkshakes.

YAFFA CAFE
97 St. Marks Place (Avenue A and 1st Avenue) • (212) 674-9302
This kitschy, cheap, East Village late night retro haunt serves up eclectic food with middle-eastern and Asian influences. The good news is there are lots of vegetarian eats and a great garden in the back.

SUPERMARKETS

FOOD EMPORIUM • Locations Throughout the City
Open twenty-four hours weekdays; until 12:00 A.M. on Saturday and Sunday.

TRANSLATOR

ALL-LANGUAGE SERVICES INC.
545 Fifth Avenue (at 45th Street) • (212) 986-1688
Round-the-clock translations.

ESSENTIAL NEW YORK MEDIA

LOCAL TELEVISION CHANNELS
Channel 2 WCBS
Channel 21 WLIW - PBS
Channel 4 WNBC
Channel 25 WNYE - PBS
Channel 5 WNYW - FOX
Channel 31 WPXN-PAX TV
Channel 7 WABC
Channel 41 WXTV
Channel 9 WWOR - UPN
Channel 47 WNJU
Channel 11 WPIX - WB
Channel 55 WLNY
Channel 13 WNET - PBS
Channel 63 WMBC
Channel 68 WHSE

NEW YORK CITY RADIO STATIONS

AM Stations

WABC	770	Talk/News
WMCA	570	Religion/Talk
WADO	1280	Spanish Language
WMTR	1250	Pop Standards
WALK	1370	Adult Contemporary
WNSW	1430	Big Band/Nostalgia
WBBR	1130	News
WNYC	820	News/Talk
WCBS	880	News
WNYG	1440	Spanish Language
WEVD	1050	News/Talk
WOR	710	Talk/News
WFAN	660	Sports
WPAT	930	Contemporary
WFAS	1230	Westchester News
WQEW	1560	Children's Programming
WGBB	1240	News/Talk
WRHD	1570	Rock
WGSM	740	Country
WRIV	1390	Big Band/Nostalgia
WHLI	1100	Oldies
WVNJ	1160	Big Band/Nostalgia
WICC	600	Adult Contemporary
WVOX	1460	Talk/Nostalgia
WINS	1010	News
WWDJ	970	Christian Music
WJWR	620	Sports
WWRL	1600	Gospel/Talk
WKDM	1380	Spanish Language
WWRU	1660	Spanish Language
WLIB	1190	Talk/Caribbean
WWRV	1330	Ethnic/Religious
WLIM	1580	Big Bands/Talk

WZRC	1480	Rock
WLUX	540	Nostalgia

FM Stations

WALK	97.5	Adult Contemporary
WKTU	103.5	Pop and Disco
WAXQ	104.3	Classic Rock
WLIE	102.5	Mainstream Country
WBAB	102.3	Rock
WLIR	92.7	Progressive Rock
WBAI	99.5	Varied
WLNG	92.1	Oldies/Top 40
WBAZ	101.7	Light Contemporary
WLTW	106.7	Light Contemporary
WBGO	88.3	Jazz
WLVA	96.1	Adult Contemporary
WBIX	105.1	Adult Contemporary
WMJC	94.3	Country
WBLI	106.1	Adult Contemporary
WNEW	102.7	Talk
WBLS	107.5	Urban Contemporary
WNWK	105.9	Multi-ethnic
WCBS	101.1	Oldies
WNYC	93.9	Classical
WCWP	88.1	C.W. Post Campus
WNYE	91.5	Community Services
WDHA	105.5	Rock
WPAT	93.1	Spanish Romance
WEBE	107.9	Adult Contemporary
WPLJ	95.5	Top 40
WEHM	96.7	Adult Rock
WPLR	99.1	Comedy/Rock
WEZN	99.9	Adult Contemporary
WPSC	88.7	Top 40
WFAS	103.9	Adult Contemporary
WQCD	101.9	Contemporary Jazz

WFDU	89.1	Fairleigh Dickinson
WQHT	97.1	Top 40/Urban
WFMU	91.1	Varied
WQXR	96.3	Classical
WFUV	90.7	Fordham University
WRCN	103.9	Rock
WHCR	90.3	C.C.N.Y.
WRHU	88.7	Hofstra University
WHFM	95.3	Rock
WRKS	98.7	Urban Contemporary
WHPC	90.3	Nassau Comm. College
WRTN	93.5	Big Band/Nostalgia
WHTZ	100.3	Top 40
WSKQ	97.9	Spanish Romance
WHUD	100.7	Light Contemporary
WSOU	89.5	Seton Hall University
WJUX	103.1	Oldies/Adult Contemporary
WUSB	90.1	Stony Brook University
WKCR	89.9	Columbia University
WXRK	92.3	Alternative Rock
WKHL	96.7	Oldies
WWXY	107.1	Country
WKJY	98.3	Adult Contemporary

THRIVING
DAY-TO-DAY

THE TOP TEN SIGNS THAT YOU HAVE BECOME AN INTREPID NEW YORKER:

1. You say "The City" and expect everyone to know this means Manhattan.
2. You secretly envy cabbies for their driving skills.
3. Your favorite movie has DeNiro in it.
4. You can get into a three hour argument about how to get from Columbus Circle to Battery Park at 3:30 PM on a Friday, but you can't find Oklahoma on a map.
5. The Subway should never be called anything fancy like The Metro.
6. You think that $7.00 to cross a bridge is a fair price.
7. The most frequently used part of your car is the horn.
8. You see nothing odd about the pace of an auctioneer's speaking.
9. You pay much more for your monthly parking space than most people in the U.S. pay for rent.
10. You have 27 different menus next to your phone.

PERCEPTIONS VS. REALITIES

New Yorkers make a sport of complaining about what they have to put up with every day. The fact that blaring horns, jack hammers and gridlock are a perpetual state of mind; that it's wise to take a folding chair and rations when waiting on line to renew your driver's license; that it would be nothing short of a miracle to encounter a salesperson who actually values your patronage; that you can unselfconsciously strike up a conversation with a stranger, without being eyed as a potential stalker; that you can find a plumber who brings the right tools the first time and doesn't leave a mess. Fact is, many New Yorkers don't get consumed by these problems because they have figured out that obstacles created by a mega-metropolis can be minimized, if not completely circumvented. These are the New Yorkers who don't let New York City control them. Try it their way and watch coping turn into thriving.

> ONE INTREPID NEW YORKER LIVES IN A BUILDING IN WHICH ALL 30 TENANTS KNOW EACH OTHER. WE BABYSIT FOR EACH OTHER, WATER EACH OTHER'S PLANTS AND FEED PETS, EXCHANGE HAND-ME-DOWNS, AND ASK THE "HANDY" TENANTS FOR HELP WITH HOUSEHOLD REPAIRS.

SOLUTION: TURN "RESIDING" INTO "BELONGING" AND MAKE NEW YORK CITY REALLY FEEL LIKE HOME

If you don't yet feel as though you really belong in New York City, you haven't made the connections that make all the difference.

Plot a ten-block radius around your neighborhood, and create your own small town. New Yorkers who feel at sea in a vast, urban sprawl, haven't visualized the area they live in as their own neighborhood and community. The fact is, they have names, such as Chelsea, Carnegie Hill, Gramercy Park, and the West Village, and each one has their own "Main Street". Each neighborhood has its own merchants who can accommodate all your basic needs - the town pastor and rabbi, the librarian who will call you when your favorite book comes in, the local public school, the neighborhood's fire house, your community affairs police officer who will help you make your streets safer, a block association that wants you to volunteer, a community board that will help you improve your quality of life, even a neighborhood newspaper dedicated to what's happening in your neck of the woods.

Plot your neighborhood boundaries, and create small-town relationships with the neighbors, merchants and city workers within, and the image of urban sprawl will transform into a village of neighbors who protect, depend on and watch out for one another.

Get to know thy neighbor. Nothing is more comforting than knowing that your neighbors are looking out for you. And it's so easy to break the ice. Invite them over for a drink; strike up a conversation in the elevator; offer to water their plants or pick up their mail when they go away — You get the picture. Before you know it, you'll be borrowing sugar, offering to babysit, receiving packages for each other, and not thinking twice about borrowing ten dollars until tomorrow.

Participate in your neighborhood block association or community board. Every neighborhood has one. If you want to feel connected to your "village", volunteer a little bit of your time. This is where you will find the neighbors, local merchants and city workers who are looking for the same small-town spirit as you, and offering their time to maintain it. It's also a great networking center for finding babysitters, new friends, reputable local handymen, potential business contacts, and so much more.

WHEN YOU LIVE IN A BUILDING WITHOUT A DOORMAN, YOU MIGHT TRY INTRODUCING YOURSELF TO THE DOORMAN OF ANOTHER BUILDING IN YOUR BLOCK . FOR A YEARLY GOOD WILL FEE, MANY OF THEM ARE HAPPY TO ACCEPT DELIVERIES FOR YOU WHEN YOU ARE NOT HOME.

THE INTREPID NEW YORKER HAS BEEN KNOWN TO ARRIVE HOME IN A CAB ONLY TO FIND OUT THEY HAD NO CASH. WE FELT COMPLETELY COMFORTABLE ABOUT ASKING ONE OF OUR LOCAL MERCHANTS TO LOAN US THE TAXI FARE. IF YOU DON'T YET FEEL COMFORTABLE ENOUGH TO DO THE SAME, YOU STILL HAVE SOME RELATIONSHIP-BUILDING TO DO.

SOLUTION:
TURN BIG-CITY INDIFFERENCE INTO SMALL TOWN "SERVICE WITH A SMILE"

Cultivating loyal relationships with your local service providers is the only way of ensuring excellent service in a city big enough for surly attitudes and incompetence to survive. Treat the good service people in your neighborhood like extended family; the same way you would if you did live in a small town. They really will return the gesture, and give you their best cuts of meat, deliver after hours for you, lend you emergency taxi money and that's not all:

IT'S STILL POSSIBLE IN THE ERA OF BIG BANK MERGERS, ATM'S, AND VOICE MAIL, TO GET PRIVATE BANKING -STYLE CARE. WHEN OPENING AN ACCOUNT, NEVER WALK IN OFF THE STREET. CALL AND MAKE AN APPOINTMENT WITH A BANK OFFICER. IF YOU CAN GET A REFERRAL, EVEN BETTER. THAT OFFICER, FROM THAT POINT ON, WILL BE YOUR DIRECT LIASION AND ADVOCATE FOR ALL YOUR NEEDS.

ONE INTREPID NEW YORKER IS TERRIBLE AT ARRANGING FLOWERS. SO INSTEAD, SHE TAKES HER VASES TO HER FLORIST, AND HE DOES THE ARRANGING, AT NO EXTRA CHARGE.

Your mailman will:

- look out for special packages and letters you are expecting
- bring you stamps if you ask him
- mail letters for you

Your doorman or building superintendent will:

- hold packages for you
- spot parking spaces or watch your car
- let you use the phone in the lobby for local calls
- tip you off to apartments coming available
- help you with chores on their day off
- turn you onto the good handymen
- look out for your kids if they are "home alone"
- walk your dog

Your garage manager will:

- park your car in an easy-to-access space
- help with small maintenance problems
- drive your car to be fixed when you can't
- bargain with you for lower rates if you don't use your car every day
- help you get city resident parking tax rebates

Your green grocer and butcher will:

- tell you when special produce is in
- make sure you are getting the very freshest of what they have
- let you in on special, upcoming sales
- give you quarters for the laundry
- let you pay later if you are short on cash

In general, your neighborhood merchants will:

- bend the rules for you
- deliver after hours, on their way home

- give your request priority handling
- special-order items for you
- turn you on to other good service-providers in the area
- provide a safe haven if you need it
- possibly even barter with you.
  (We once helped our florist find an apartment in exchange for a month's worth of fresh flowers).

SOLUTION:
SCOUT OUT THE QUALITY SERVICES IN YOUR NEIGHBORHOOD

Anyone can put up a shingle in NYC with claims of quality service, and they do...by the 1000s. The choices in your own little neighborhood alone can make your head spin. But you can separate the wheat from the chaff by following simple guidelines:

Get referrals: We may get to sound like a broken record on this, but referrals are the best way to go. Ask neighbors, friends and other local services in the area for their recommendations.

Educate yourself: You need to know at least the basics about what to expect from a service provider. The way to do the homework is by calling the well known, high-quality service providers in the city, (the ones most of us can't afford), and ask them what you should expect from the local merchant you are considering. You can also contact the Department of Consumer Affairs; they may have pamphlets and advisories on the subject you are researching. Here are some examples:

Dry Cleaners

Can they steam delicate clothes?
Pressing is the #1 procedure that ages clothes because it wears down the fibers.

How often do they distill their solvents?
Clothes are dry-cleaned with them and the more often the solvents are distilled, the

THE VERY TOP DRY CLEANERS CLEAN ONLY TWENTY SHIRTS AN HOUR. THEY DO THE COLLARS AND CUFFS BY HAND. THEN THEY PUT THE SHIRTS IN PLASTIC CONTAINERS OVERNIGHT SO THAT THEY ARE PERFECTLY MOIST FOR PRESSING. THIS TYPE OF SERVICE WILL RUN YOU $7 A SHIRT. BY CONTRAST, YOUR AVERAGE LOCAL DRY CLEANER WILL USE HUGE COMMERCIAL MACHINES THAT CLEAN ONE HUNDRED SHIRTS PER HOUR, AND PRESSING MACHINES THAT HAVE A TENDENCY TO PINCH COLLARS AND CUFFS. THIS SERVICE WILL RUN YOU ABOUT $1.50 A SHIRT. AN IN BETWEEN OPTION IS TO HIRE A LAUNDRESS AT $10 AN HOUR WHO COMES TO YOUR HOME AND CLEANS THREE SHIRTS PER HOUR FOR A TOTAL OF $3.50 A SHIRT.

brighter and cleaner your clothes come back. The top dry cleaners distill their solvents three times a week.

Do they clean delicate fabrics (silks and sequins) with fluorocarbon solvents? They should.

Do they use light starch on shirts? Starch cuts a shirt's life in half.

Do they cover delicate buttons and belt buckles before cleaning? You also want them to remove shoulder pads and clean belts separately from the garment. Make sure you tell them about specific concerns before handing them your clothing.

Photo Store

Is their processing equipment state-of-the-art? Photos processed with out-of-date equipment will not be clear and the color will be off.

Is the photography equipment and work station white glove clean? If it is not, negatives may become dusty or scratched, and these defects will show up on the photos.

Do they change the processing chemicals regularly? Old chemicals will produce color photos that will fade over time.

Is the service quick? Sometimes you will pay more for fast service, but if you want the photos quickly, it may be worth it.

Is the paper processed on high quality paper such as Kodak or Fuji? It should be.

What extra features does the photo store offer, like restoration of old photographs and reprinting of old prints?

Give a service a trial test:

Give your local shoe repair, dry cleaner, auto mechanic and photo store a test. Ask them about the service they provide and how they charge; if they are defensive and less than forthcoming, move on.

Comparison shop:

Get at least three estimates on the cost of the same repair, and find out if they all provide the same level of service.

When it comes to fine and treasured items, it's penny-wise and pound-foolish not to spend what it takes to have them properly maintained. Put them into the hands of the most experienced and reputable service providers. New York has the very finest in craftsmen and repair experts.

THE INTREPID PAGES OF...
ESSENTIAL
SERVICE PROVIDERS

You won't be able to find all the essential services you need within a ten-block radius; therefore, we are including our list of services that have been given the Intrepid New Yorker "Seal of Approval."

$ = inexpensive   **P** = pickup*   * Pick up and delivery is available
$$ = moderate   **D** = delivery*   throughout most of Manhattan
$$$ = expensive   unless otherwise indicated.

We suggest:

APPLIANCE STORE

GRINGER & SONS • 29 First Avenue (at 2nd Street) (212) 475-0600 • $$$ • D

At Gringer you can find restaurant-quality appliances for gourmets, the latest quiet dishwashers, and front-loading water-saving washing machines. They will install the appliances and, for an additional fee, cart away your old ones.

BOOKSTORES

BARNES & NOBLE • Locations Throughout NYC • $

All the best-sellers mentioned on *The New York Times* list are discounted, as are all hard-cover books. They also have tables of other discounted books such as art, literature, cooking, etc. This chain is noted for carrying a large selection of textbooks at their store at 18th Street and Fifth Avenue, and they take back secondhand books for credit. Most locations have Starbucks cafés, and also sell music and software.

BORDERS BOOKS & MUSIC
5 World Trade Center (corner of Church and Vesey Streets) (212) 839-8049 • $

461 Park Avenue (at 57th Street) • (212) 980-6785 • $

You can spend a whole day here browsing through three floors of books and music, and when you tire, you can enjoy lunch at their café. Like Barnes & Noble, Borders discounts books on *The New York Times* bestsellers list, as well as all hard-cover books. They also feature lectures and book signings by best-selling authors and have children's' storytelling and sing-a-longs.

GOTHAM BOOK MART • 41 West 47th Street • (212) 719-4448 • $

"Wise men fish here" reads the sign over the entrance. Good selection of literature with very helpful salespeople.

SKYLINE BOOKS & RECORDS
13 West 18th Street • (212) 675-4773 • $

The staff at Skyline will gladly hunt down those rare, hard-to-find books, including those that have gone out-of-print.

THE STRAND • 828 Broadway (at 12th Street) • (212) 473-1452
95 Fulton Street (between William and Gold Streets)
(212) 732-6070 • $

A great source for buying secondhand books. It is also a wonderful place in which to browse.

COIN COUNTERS

Coming to more neighborhood stores including Food Emporiums.

A & P SUPERMARKET
10 Union Square (at 14th Street) • (212) 353-3840

A simple process in which you feed your coins into a machine, get a receipt that you give to customer service, and receive bills in return. They take 7¢ on the dollar, but that sure beats the time-consuming task of separating your coins and rolling them up in wrappers when you give them to a bank.

DRUGSTORES

It is a good idea to get to know your local drugstore. You want to establish a relationship for those rush deliveries and special concerns. Try to open a house charge account and give them a little business each month. They tend to be on the pricey side so you don't want to do your everyday and bulk shopping there.

CVS/pharmacy • Locations Throughout the City • $

DUANE READE DRUGSTORES
Locations Throughout the City • $ • D

Some locations are open 24-hours.

METRO DRUG STORES
13 East 8th Street • (212) 982-7325 • $ • D
1299 Second Avenue (68th Street) • (212) 772-0104 • $ • D

The 68th Street location is open twenty-four hours, including the pharmacy.

KAMWO HERB AND TEA COMPANY
211 Grand Street • (212) 966-6370 • $$ • D

A Chinese pharmacy which offers customers alternative medicine.

The medicine is usually in the form of dried herbs, plant-life or animal parts that is boiled as tea or soup and drunk.

PATHMARK DRUGS • Locations Throughout the City • $

RICKY PHARMACY • 718 Broadway (Waverly Place & Washington Place) • (212) 979-5232 • $ • limited delivery

They have an excellent selection of family-sized items. They discount Tiffany perfume and they often have discontinued lines of products that you'd given up looking for.

RITE AID PHARMACIES • Locations Throughout the City (800) RITE-AID • $ • limited delivery

Some locations are open 24-hours.

VALUE DRUGS
630 Third Avenue (at 41st Street) • (212) 682-3191 • $ • D
1221 Avenue of the Americas (48th and 49th Streets)
(212) 575-0047 • $ • limited delivery

ZITOMER DEPARTMENT STORE INC. • 969 Madison Avenue (75th and 76th Streets) • (212) 737-5561 • $$$• D

This is not your average drug store. Zitomer's carries everything — from high-end clothing, toys, electronics, jewelry, and cosmetics — to the latest European skin products. They also have a complete pharmacy for all your medical needs. Even if you don't need something, you'll have a fun time browsing through the store.

DRY CLEANERS

There must be as many dry cleaners in New York as there are Chinese restaurants. How do you find a good one? A lot of people complain about their local cleaner, but truthfully, if you are diligent about what you tell your dry cleaner or laundry to do, you should get good service. (See the section above for dry-cleaning tips.) The following cleaners stand out in the crowd. Since they are on the more expensive side, you may opt to clean only your special occasion and treasured items at these places.

JEEVES
39 East 65th Street
(212) 570-9130 • $$$ • P/D

Whites tend to stay white. Shirts can be laundered, tears repaired, and stains almost always come out.

JOHN HARRISON
Pick-up and Delivery only: Plant in LIC
(212) 744-6155 • $$ • P/D

Very good. Monthly billing and winter storage available.

MADAME PAULETTE DRY CLEANERS
1255 Second Avenue (at 66th Street)
(212) 838-6827
160 Columbus Avenue (67th Street
[in the Reebok Sports Club])
(212) 501-1408 • $$$ • P/D

Wedding gowns grace the window of Madame Paulette's—they specialize in cleaning and preserving them. They also clean special-occasion garments, and leather, suede, and silk items.

MEURICE GARMENT CARE • 31
University Place (8th & 9th Streets) •
(212) 475-2778 • $$$ • P/D

Bring your designer clothing and special occasion garments to Meurice. They treat your fine garments with care.

PERRY PROCESS CLEANERS • 1402 Lexington (92nd & 93rd Streets) • (212) 628-8300 • $$ • P/D

Excellent stain treaters. They clean a variety of difficult fabrics, such as suede and leather. Monthly billing and winter storage available.

TIECRAFTERS
252 West 29th Street • (212) 629-5800 • $$ • P/D

Cleans and repairs all ties. Can alter any tie to match the styles of the day. A real find, especially with what ties cost these days.

WINDSOR • (718) 294-2400 • $$$ • P/D only

You can usually call for a same day pickup. They do an excellent job on whites and hard-to-clean delicate fabrics.

GLOVE CLEANER

GLOVE MASTERS • 808 East 139th Street, Bronx, NY 10454 (718) 585-3615 • $$ • D

They clean gloves of all different fabrics, including suede and leather. Send your gloves to Glove Masters with a check for $10.25 for a short pair, $20.75 for gloves over the elbow. Make sure you include your name, address, and telephone number. You will get your gloves back in two weeks.

HAT CLEANERS

PETER & IRVING • 36 West 38th Street • (212) 730-4369 • $

With over thirty years under his belt at Peter & Irving, Horace Weeks is a true artisan at cleaning and restoring hats. He will work with any kind of hat that comes his way, from cowboy to top hat. All work is done in the shop.

LEATHER CLEANER

LEATHERCRAFT PROCESS
31 University Place (8th & 9th Streets)• (212) 564-8980
245 East 57th Street • (212) 564-8980 • $$ • D

LeatherCraft Process uses either of these locations as a drop-off point for customers to bring their leather garments. The drop-off point is actually inside Meurice Garment Care. They will send your item to the LeatherCraft facility in New Jersey where they clean, redye, and soften leather. You will be sent a bill in the mail. After you send in payment, your goods will be cleaned and shipped back to you. This process takes about three weeks.

EXTERMINATOR

ACME EXTERMINATING • 460 Ninth Avenue (35th and 36th Streets) • (212) 594-9230 • $$

Unfortunately New York is full of rodents and bugs and you must take necessary precautions. We have found Acme to be responsible and timely. There is no magic secret; just constant upkeep.

TERMINIX • (718) 945-0922 • $$

You can set up an appointment with a Terminix inspector for a free home inspection and estimate. Prices and the frequency of extermination will vary depending on your problem. If you have a severe roach problem, your home would need to be exterminated once a month. This monthly service would cost about $520 for the year. Terminix uses low odor chemicals or a Max Force gel which is a repellent that is put into cracks.

FLORISTS

The type of flower arrangement you like is as personal as the type of art that appeals to you. Don't get bullied into going to "name" florists. Others can do just as well given some input from you.

BLUE WATER FLOWERS • 265 Lafayette (Prince & Spring) (212) 226-0587 • D • $$

At Blue Water, you can order arrangements by the stem. Your order will be delivered in a clear glass ginger jar.

DIMITRI'S GARDEN LTD. • 1992 Second Avenue (102nd & 103rd Streets) • (212) 831-2810 • $ • D

Dimitri's Garden is the place to buy all types of plants. You can find exotic plants here, small and large varieties, even trees. They can also create one-of-a-kind table arrangements. If you wish to give a plant as a gift, they will deliver anywhere in Manhattan. Talk to George. He is knowledgeable and friendly.

FELLAN FLORIST • 1040 Third Avenue (61st & 62nd Streets) (212) 288-7848 • $$$ • D

Fellan Florist can design the most spectacular, over-the-top floral arrangements. They make exquisite floral centerpieces for parties and special occasions. They are especially skilled at translating your ideas into reality.

THE FLOWER DISTRICT • Sixth Avenue from 26th Street to 29th Street • $ • Some D

We suggest you walk the area looking and pricing. The entire area specializes in plants and flowers, both real and dried. What the stores lack in personal service you get back in serious discounts.

IRENE HAYES, WADLEY, SMYTHE 1 Rockefeller Plaza (at 49th Street) • (212) 247-0051 • $$$ • D

This florist has been around forever. Their experience shows in their stunning, creative arrangements, using the finest, freshest flowers available.

MATTHEW DAVID FLOWERS 301 West 18th Street (212) 627-2086 • D • $$

There is a $200 minimum order required to purchase flowers at Matthew David. They provide spectacular arrangements for restaurants, parties, weddings, and corporate spaces.

SANDRA'S FLORISTS 100 East 96th Street (212) 987-4844 • $$ • D

Marco is very creative, and has an ability to supply clients with exactly what they really ask for. Call your order in the day before. They are as good at making a $25 arrangement as they are at landscaping your terrace.

SPRING STREET GARDEN 186 ½ Spring Street • (212) 966-2015 • $$ • D

They are quite accommodating and have a good eye for what will last.

STONEKELLY 328 Columbus Avenue (75th & 76th Streets) (212) 875-0500 • D • $$

The florists here have a good sense of color and will work with your color schemes. They deliver throughout Manhattan with a minimum order of $50.

GOURMET FOOD STORES

Everyone knows about the following food stores, and for good reason. They are the best.

AGATA & VALENTINA
1505 First Avenue (at 79th Street) • (212) 452-0690 • $$$ • D

A diverse selection of fruits and vegetables, cheese, bread, meats, fish oils, pasta, juices and prepared foods. Their prepared dinner foods are great and the prices are reasonable. Their baked goods and specialty coffee drinks are worth the calories.

BALDUCCI'S
424 Sixth Avenue (at 9th Street)
(212) 673-2600 • $$$ • D

An old Village favorite offering fresh pro-duce, cheese, cold cuts, and prepared foods.

BARNEY GREENGRASS
541 Amsterdam Avenue (86th & 87th Streets)
(212) 724-4707 • $$$ • D

All kinds of smoked fish. A real New York tradition!

CITARELLA FINE FOODS
2135 Broadway (75th Street)
(212) 874-0383 • $$ • D
1313 Third Avenue (75th Street) • (212) 874-0383 • $$ • D

Offers a delicious variety of fresh fish, meat, prepared foods, breads, pasta, and pasta sauce. The East Side location carries a large assortment of produce.

DEAN & DELUCA
560 Broadway (at Prince Street) • (212) 226-6800 • $$$ • D

Incredible choice of exotic fruits and vegetables, cheeses, breads, pasta, and much, much more.

ELI'S MANHATTAN WAREHOUSE
1411 Third Avenue (80th Street) • (212) 717-8100 • $$ • D

The latest and greatest of Eli Zabar's amazing food stores. A beauti-ful shop offering similar selections to the Vinegar Factory.

FAIRWAY
2127 Broadway (74th & 75th Streets) • (212) 595-1888 • $
2328 Twelfth Avenue (132nd & 133rd Streets on the Hudson River) • (212) 234-3883 • $ • D

Prices are as low as we have seen for high-quality cheese, cold cuts, salads, smoked fish, and produce. The 132nd Street location has items available in bulk.

IF YOU WISH TO LEARN THE ART OF FLOWER ARRANGING, CONSIDER TAKING A COURSE AT PARSON'S SCHOOL OF DESIGN. THE TWELVE-WEEK CLASSES ENABLE YOU TO COMPLETE AN ARRANGEMENT NEARLY EVERY WEEK. CALL (212) 229-5690 FOR MORE INFORMATION.

GARDEN OF EDEN
314 Third Avenue (23rd and 24th Streets) • (212) 228-4681 • $
162 W. 23rd Street (6th and 7th Avenues) • (212) 675-6300 • $

An incredible selection of prepared foods. Also available are fresh produce, cheese and more.

GOURMET GARAGE
117 7th Avenue • 699-5980 • $ • D
453 Broome Street (off Mercer) • (212) 941-5850 • $ • D
301 East 64th Street • (212) 535-5880 • $ • D

A no-frills style store that offers quality food at low prices. They carry a great selection of produce, some of which is organic, fresh pasta, cheese, and prepared foods.

GRACE'S MARKETPLACE • 1237 Third Avenue (71st & 72nd Street) (212) 737-0600 • $$$ • D

The freshest of the fresh can be found at Grace's. Everything, from produce to pastries, is replenished each day.

THE VINEGAR FACTORY
431 East 91st Street • (212) 987-0885 • $$ • D

Come here to fulfill all your gourmet needs. The Vinegar Factory offers a fish market, butcher, flower shop, over 500 different types of cheese, fresh produce and prepared foods. Sandwiches are prepared on Eli's delicious home-baked bread. Brunch is served on the weekend.

WHOLE FOODS IN SOHO
117 Prince Street • (212) 982-1000 • $$ • D

The largest health food store in the city; includes the widest selection of organic produce.

ZABAR'S
2245 Broadway (82nd & 83rd Streets) • (212) 787-2000 • $$ • D

This place makes New York great.

HARDWARE STORES

You can repair more than you think on your own and spend less money in the process if you know where to buy the right parts and tools. These two stores will guide you so that making a mistake is nearly impossible. They are also a great source for everything from halogen bulbs to odd-shaped sponges.

GRACIOUS HOME
1220 Third Avenue (70th and 71st Streets) • (212) 517-6300
1992 Broadway (67th Street) • (212) 231-7800 • $$$ • D

Overall, the best, most helpful well-stocked hardware/supply store in Manhattan. If they don't carry the item, they will try and get it for you. And the best part is, if you have a major credit card, you can just phone in your order. You don't even have to go.

SIMON'S HARDWARE & BATH • 421 Third Avenue (29th and 30th Streets) • (212) 532-9220 • $$ • D

Simon's has a very large bath hardware selection. They sell everything from tile, marble, and stone, to medicine cabinets, tubs, sinks, jacuzzis, etc.

LAUNDRIES

Depending upon how concerned you are with perfection, your local laundry should be able to satisfy most of your needs. For those antique linens and fine sheets, expect to pay more for no-worry cleaning.

LINENS LIMITED LAUNDRY • By mail: 240 North Milwaukee Street, Milwaukee, Wisconsin 53202 • (800) 637-6334 • $$

We know many people who ship their fine linens to be cleaned here. They pay attention to all the details.

SERGIO • (718) 562-4788 • $$

Sergio is a find. He can arrange to come to your home one day a week and do all your laundry, including your shirts.

LIQUOR STORES

Shop around for liquor. Prices and services vary a great deal all over the City. If you know exactly what you want, and don't need a lot of information and attention, there are great discount places to take advantage of.

ASTOR WINE & SPIRITS
12 Astor Place (near Broadway)
(212) 674-7500 • $$ • D

A true emporium taking up a wide corner swath in Greenwich Village. A well-run operation with a knowledgeable staff and very good sales that motivate customers to use the ubiquitous shopping carts. They are good at judging how many bottles you will need for a party and they are usually willing to take back unopened bottles.

BEACON WINES & SPIRITS
2120 Broadway (74th Street)
(212) 877-0028 • limited delivery • $

A West side favorite offering a good selection of wines at fair prices.

A CONVENIENT AND FUN WAY TO SAMPLE SOME OF THE BEST MICRO-BREWED BEER IS TO JOIN THE DIRECT MERCHANT BEER ACROSS AMERICA CLUB (800) 854-2337. EACH YEAR THE CLUB CHOOSES 24 OF THE MOST POPULAR BEER MICRO-BREWED THROUGHOUT THE COUNTRY. AS A MEMBER, YOU WOULD RECEIVE TWO SIX PACKS OF TWO DIFFERENT BEERS EACH MONTH, FOR A TOTAL OF 24 DIFFERENT BEERS FOR THE YEAR. THESE BEERS ARE DIFFICULT TO FIND LOCALLY. INCLUDED WITH YOUR SHIPMENT IS A HISTORY OF THE BEER, FOOD RECIPES TO COMPLEMENT THE BEER, AND A QUARTERLY MAGAZINE. THE COST IS $24.95 PER MONTH INCLUDING TAX, SHIPPING, AND HANDLING.

BEST CELLARS
1291 Lexington Avenue
(86th & 87th Streets)
(212) 426-4200 • $ • D

This wine store carries wines from all over the world priced at $10 and under. They offer free delivery if you order wine by the case (12 bottles), otherwise there is a $5 delivery charge.

GARNET WINES & LIQUORS
929 Lexington Avenue
(68th & 69th Streets)
(212) 772-3211 • $ • D

Their very reasonable prices make up for a slight lack of personal service. If you know what you want, and you don't want to spend much, this is the place.

K & D WINES & SPIRITS
1366 Madison Avenue
(95th & 96th Streets)
(212) 289-1818 • $ • D

This family-owned and -operated business is the largest wine shop on Madison Avenue. They have an extensive selection of both national and international wines. Phone orders are handled with the same concern and knowledge as in-person purchases.

MORRELL & CO. WINE & SPIRITS MERCHANTS
1 Rockefeller Plaza • (212) 688-9370 • $$ • D

An upscale store that stocks national and international types of wine and liquor. They publish a catalog a couple of times a year which highlights special vintages and sales.

SHERRY-LEHMANN
679 Madison Avenue • (61st & 62nd Streets)
(212) 838-7500 • $$ • D

Getting a bottle from Sherry-Lehmann is like getting a gift from Tiffany. The name is sure to impress. In order to make choosing a wine easier, they have an impressive catalog which showcases on-sale wines and currently featured wines.

67 WINE & SPIRITS INC.
179 Columbus Avenue (68th Street)
(212) 724-6767 • D • $

A well-established Lincoln Center area wine shop with a great look, helpful staff and fair prices.

NEWSSTANDS

New York has it all when it comes to news and information in any language

DEPENDABLE NEWS SERVICE
360 West 52nd Street
(212) 586-5552 • $

The only store where you can find back issues of your favorite American dailies and weeklies.

EASTERN NEWSSTAND
Met-Life Building
200 Park Avenue (at 45th Street)
(212) 687-1198• $

The largest and most comprehensive newsstand in the city is located here. If they don't have it, you can bet they can get it, providing it's current.

HOTALINGS • 142 West 42nd Street • (212) 840-1868 • $$

The indispensable store to locate almost every out-of-town domestic and foreign-language newspaper and periodical—for a markup. Be sure to phone ahead as supplies are limited and deliveries lag by a day or more of publication date. For a small fee, they will reserve for you.

UNIVERSAL NEWS
977 Eighth Avenue (57th and 58th Streets) • (212) 459-0932 • $

A newsstand with space. You can even read your favorite glossy at a café table.

NOTIONS STORES

Remember life before fancy specialty stores when a hanger was just a hanger and not a piece of art? Believe it or not, you can still buy a plain old hanger.

GREENBERG & HAMMER
24 West 57th Street • (212) 586-6270 • $

A small Midtown store. Great for all your basic sewing supplies. High rents have forced most of these notions stores out of business. Thank goodness this one still exists.

PATERSON SILKS
90 Delancey Street • (212) 929-7861
156-158 East 86th Street • (212) 722-4098
151 West 72nd Street • (212) 874-9510 • $

A discount fabric store that also carries notion supplies like threads, pins, buttons, and zippers.

P & S FABRICS
355 Broadway (Franklin & Leonard Streets) • (212) 226-1534 • $

P & S is another discount fabric shop that stocks basic notion items.

TENDER BUTTONS • 143 East 62nd Street • (212) 758-7004 • $

Imagine a store that spends twenty minutes helping you pick out a 60-cent button. It has the most extensive selection of buttons in the city, not to mention a wonderful collection of cuff links.

PHOTO SHOPS

One-hour photo developing is the greatest for instant gratification, but you do pay more for it, and you won't necessarily have the best pictures. New York has some of the most experienced film labs in the world. For important pictures it can be worth it to use them. And you won't always pay more.

ALKIT PRO CAMERA
222 Park Avenue South (at 18th Street)
(212) 674-1515 • $$$ • D

In addition to selling cameras and equipment, they also do in-house film processing. They can do simple jobs, as well as more technical ones. The quality is top-notch. They will messenger your job to you for a fee.

CLICKS ONE HOUR PHOTO
49 West 23rd Street • (212) 645-1971 • $$

A one-hour shop that turns out clean, clear photos with good color. Professional quality is guaranteed. They will re-do your photos if you are dissatisfied for any reason.

DUGGAL COLOR PROJECTS INC.
3 West 20th Street • (212) 242-7000
560 Broadway (Prince & Spring Streets)
(212) 941-7000 • $$$ • D

Duggal is a professional lab that specializes in high-quality color and black and white film processing and digital scanning. For a fee, they will deliver your job to you.

MODERNAGE CUSTOM COLOR LABS
649 Lexington Avenue (54th & 55th Streets) • (212) 752-3993
1150 Avenue of the Americas (44th & 45th Streets)
(212) 997-1800
9-11 Maiden Lane • (212) 227-4767 • $$$ • D

Specializes in contact sheets and enlargements. They develop on the premises and expertly reproduce old photographs. Bring any photo that requires special attention here. ModernAge will messenger your finished product to you for a fee.

MYSTIC COLOR LAB
By mail: P.O. Box 144 Mason's Island Road, Mystic, CT 06355
(800) 367-6061 • $ • D

A mail-order photo house. They send you the prepaid postage security mail pouch and all you do is slip your film in the bag with a check. It takes about a week to get your photos back. A great service, especially for those of us who never get around to taking the film in in the first place. And it doesn't cost extra for the luxury.

PROPRINT • Locations Throughout the City • $$

Some locations have a one-hour turnaround time. They do a good job on no-frills film processing.

SEAMSTRESS/TAILOR

Always a challenge to find someone you like but always a necessity. Any of these people can help you maintain your wardrobe and do good alterations. For additional names and numbers of people who make and repair clothes, see the last chapter entitled "HOW TO OPERATE LIKE A VIP ON A POOR MAN'S BUDGET."

ABE'S TAILOR SHOP
1013 Sixth Avenue (37th and 38th Streets) • (212) 921-1193 • $

Joseph D'Attoma has been sewing for over forty years. His experience is evident in his meticulous alterations of men's and women's clothing. He does the fittings himself and all hems are hand-sewn.

CLAUDIA BRUCE • 140 East 28th Street • (212) 685-2810 • $$

Specializes in difficult alterations as well as the everyday hems and loose buttons. By appointment only.

EUROPA • 328 East 66th Street • (212) 249-8716 • $$

Aaron is one of the nicest, most attentive shopkeepers in the city. He is an expert in both men's and women's alterations.

SEW CHIC • 32 W. 46th Street • (212) 840-1439 • $$

From basic alterations to custom designs for children, women and men.

SOPHIA • 440 East 75th Street • (212) 744-8239 • $

She has a good feeling for how a garment should fit, and if she has the time, she is great at making duvet covers, skirts for your bed, etc.

SHOE REPAIR SHOPS

New York is a walking city so shoes tend to wear down fast. When you have spent megabucks for new shoes, you want to repair your favorites rather than replace them. A good cobbler can make them last years longer. It is worth it to pay a little more.

ANDRADE BOOT AND SHOE REPAIR
379 Amsterdam (78th-79th Streets)
(212) 787-0465 • $$

First-class service - you will never need to buy a new pair.

EVELYN & SAM • 400 East 83rd Street • (212) 628-7618 • $$

The best in the city for dying shoes and bags. They also do expert work on cleaning bags and briefcases.

JAMES SHOE REPAIR
1415 Lexington Avenue (92nd & 93rd Streets)
(212) 722-0041 • $$

Nick Pecchia never forgets a pair of shoes or the person who brought them in. He does give you a ticket but that is only for your peace of mind. He repairs all shoes, belts, and bags. An artisan from way back, he can restore nearly any pair of shoes to its original condition. And the turnaround time is fast.

JIM'S SHOE REPAIR • 50 East 59th Street • (212) 355-8259 • $$

A great repair place that is centrally located. A wonderful shop to get a shine while you watch the parade of people go in and out.

Shoe Service Plus • 15 West 55th Street • (212) 262-4823 • $$

The best place to repair those stilettos.

T.O. DEY • 9 East 38th Street • (212) 683-6300 • $$

Custom shoemaking as well as all types of repair work.

VIDEO RENTALS

What's great about these six stores and one online service is that all except two pick up and deliver, a wonderful luxury if you're sick in bed or if you just don't want to face the sleet and cold.

BLOCKBUSTER VIDEO • Locations Throughout the City • $$

Membership is free with a major credit card. Largest selection of current and noncurrent releases for rent and for sale. Abundant copies of each video so you have a good chance of getting what you want.

EVERGREEN VIDEO
37 Carmine (Bleeker and Bedford) • (212) 691-7362 • $$

A video store known for carrying a large selection of American movie classics as well as an extensive collection of foreign films. Membership is free with a major credit card.

FLIKS VIDEO TO GO
175 West 72nd Street • (212) 721-0500 • $$ • P/D

You can simply become a free member with a major credit card, or you can take advantage of the many prepaid plans that entitle you to free pick up and delivery services, free rentals, and priority video reservations, among other perks. Deliveries from 59th to 80th Street on the West side.

KIM'S VIDEO AND MUSIC
6 St. Marks Place • (212) 505-0311
350 Blecker Street (212) 675-8996 • $$

A hugh selection of videos can be bought or rented. The sales staff, made up of young independent film junkies, pride themselves on their unusual selections.

VIDEO ROOM
1487 Third Avenue (at 84th Street) • (212) 879-5333 • $$ • P/D

If you take out an $89 yearly membership you will receive free pick-up and delivery service as well as one free video a month. Free membership with a major credit card is also available for walk-in service. Locations covered: from 59th to 96th Streets, East Side to West Side.

VIDEO STOP INC.
367 Third Avenue (between 26th and 27th Streets)
(212) 685-6199 • $$ • P/D

Free membership with a major credit card, or a $79 Super Club

VAL-PAK IS A FREE PACKET OF COUPONS THAT CAN BE USED AT LOCAL RESTAURANTS, STORES AND SERVICES FOR DISCOUNTS. THE INTREPID NEW YORKER SUGGESTS YOU CALL THEM TO SEE IF THEY COVER YOUR AREA.
212-772-0136.

membership, which includes 12 free rentals, free pickup and delivery, video reservations, and, rent three videos, get one free. Locations covered: from Houston to 49th Streets, East River to Eighth Avenue.

WWW.KOZMO.COM • $$ • P/D

An online video rental service that offers a list of thousands of available films, along with reviews, staff recommendations, and links to other films arranged by categories. Can deliver your movie within an hour or less of your order. Video rental fees are similar to those of traditional video stores.

SOLUTIONS:
BUILD PLAYTIME INTO YOUR LIFE BY CUTTING MEGAMETROP-OLIS-SIZE CHORES IN HALF

New Yorkers never have enough "down time", and it's a serious quality-of-life issue for us. We work very long hours, are actively involved in community and cultural endeavors, and raise children. We also spend a lot of time doing chores; without cars or one-stop shopping super-stores and malls, we spend about five

YOU CAN ORDER A COMPLETE DESCRIPTION OF WHAT ALL THE OVERNIGHT DELIVERY SERVICES OFFER AND COST BY CALLING THE BETTER BUSINESS BUREAU AT 212-533-7500 AND ASKING FOR THE BBB ADVISORY ON CHOOSING AN OVERNIGHT DELIVERY SERVICE.

hours a week, 260 hours a year, getting errands done. That's a ten day vacation lost to tasks we don't like to do! We always feel deprived of free time, especially for taking advantage of this city's world-class pursuits. The Intrepid New Yorker has gotten errand-time down to a system, and cut it in half. How? By figuring what resources provide the shortcuts.

NEW YORK CITY DELIVERS! EVERYTHING! AND USUALLY FOR FREE.

No savvy New Yorker would buy or repair anything if they had to pick it up or take it in themselves. If you can't "call for it," then it isn't worth having, and local merchants figured out long ago that free pick-up and delivery services was the way to a New Yorker's wallet. So if you are carting your own groceries, liquor, flowers, hardware, take-out food, prescriptions, and dry cleaning, you are probably tripling your errand time. And for you overachievers, you can use your office as a pick-up and delivery center.

TAKE ADVANTAGE OF PERSONAL CARE SERVICES THAT MAKE HOUSE CALLS.

Add up the amount of time it takes just getting from appointment to appointment. The tailor, seamstress, laundress, manicurist, haircut-ter, exercise instructor - will all come to you. And you don't have to go "high end" to find them. We have found all sorts of quality peo-ple willing to make house calls. If you do end up spending a little more, you may decide that the quality-of-life improvement is well worth it. Here's how to find them:

• Word of mouth through colleagues

• Ask the service people you already patronize if they are interested

• Call the professional and vocational schools in New York and inquire about hiring their teachers or their star graduate students. This route can save you a bundle.

DO YOUR MAILING FROM HOME OR THE OFFICE.

There are so many competitive mailing services that the prices for priority service keep coming down. And they'll come to your door with wrapping materials, then pack it and mail it. And all for a few extra dollars. And in NYC our famous bike-wielding messengers will deliver a package across town for half what it would take in a round trip taxi.

SHOP ONCE A MONTH AND AT HALF PRICE FOR ALL YOUR HOME AND FOOD STAPLES.

New York City does not have suburban-style one-stop shopping supermarkets, and the ones we do have are cramped, dusty and not very enticing. So we shop for food the way Europeans do — by picking up fresh meat and produce from exotic, mouthwatering, gourmet markets. It's a pricey way to shop, but we wouldn't trade this urban perk for anything. And many of us balance the budget by purchasing our household staples from wholesalers. And most will open their doors to consumers who are willing to buy in bulk:

- beverages - from beer to seltzer
- dairy products
- meats for the freezer
- dry goods such as paper towels, napkins, light bulbs, batteries, etc.
- stationery supplies
- cleansers, detergents, drugstore items

Here's how you find them: You can find wholesalers who will sell to the consumer by looking through the Business-to-Business Yellow Pages (we'll tell you where to get one in this chapter.) You look under "meat" or "stationery" for example, and call them to find out how much you have to buy to make it worth their while, and whether they deliver. If their minimum is too high, you can always go in on it with a friend or neighbor.

If they don't deliver, here's how you pick up the order: Plan one day a month to do all your essential shopping. Place your orders in advance so they are ready when you get there. If you have a car in the city, go with a friend who can wait in the car while you pick up. If you don't have a car, we find it really pays to hire a car service, which you can do for as little as $18 an hour. The money and hours saved by shopping once a month at wholesale prices makes the car service well worth it.

The Intrepid Pages of
House-Call
Personal Care Services

You'll be surprised by how many different types of professionals will make house calls beyond the ones we've listed below.

$ = inexpensive
$$ = moderate
$$$ = expensive

COOKS

Wouldn't it be nice to come home to a home-cooked meal? You can find a cook who will come to your home for no more or less than it would cost to eat out. One way to do it inexpensively is to contact professional cooking schools (see page oo), or call:

AMANDA CUSHMAN • (212) 749-2110 • $$

Amanda's culinary skills range from French and Italian cooking techniques, to spa, vegetarian, and low-fat dishes. She has expertise in and prefers to cater cocktail and dinner parties, and can also help in the selection of staff, flowers, rentals, and entertainment.

DINE BY DESIGN
325 Houston Street • (212) 253-6408 • $$

They will plan menus and create personally designed healthy meals delivered to your home.

THE DINNER GUY • (718) 222-8654 • $

Mark has a gourmet food background and has taken to feeding discerning New Yorkers in their home. His same-day order and delivery allows you to choose from a changing menu. Prix Fix dinner is $23.00 - minimum order $20.00.

JANIE FEINSTEIN • (212) 759-5029 • $

Janie can either cater a big party, drop off dinner, or come to your home to prepare a well-rounded delicious meal.

WARREN KATZ • (732) 727-0434 • $$

Warren has fourteen years of cooking experience as hotel chef, restaurant chef, caterer, and instructor. He can come to your home to prepare meals, or you can take advantage of his private gourmet cooking class parties the next time you want to dazzle your guests. Some popular classes include: "Sushi and Maki Making" and

"Southern Sunday Brunch." Warren also offers in-home cheese and dessert making lessons.

HEALTHY TAKEOUT

If you are unable to hire a cook, you may want to explore healthy takeout as the next best option. There is a multitude of takeout facilities that cater to people with dietary restrictions and nutrition concerns. The following is a sampling:

GOURMET THE NATURAL WAY
306 Rumsey Road (Yonkers)
(888) 834-6880 • $$

This four-year-old company serves up organic and vegetarian dishes. They change their menu every week and offer five dinner selections, three lunch entrées, and dessert. They will also cater to your individualized nutrition needs. There is a minimum of $38 for three dinners which include soup and salad, and a $7.50 delivery charge to Manhattan.

HEALTHY HOME COOKING
(888) 567-7510 • $$

An organic, vegetarian, and kosher service which was formed six years ago, Healthy Home Cooking draws on a variety of ethnic cuisines and seasonal vegetables to create their tasty and nutritious dishes. There is a minimum of $38.88 for three dinners, each with a sixteen-ounce soup and sourdough bread, as well as a one-time $49 membership fee paid with your second order. Delivery charge to Manhattan, Brooklyn, and Queens is $6.50.

HERBAN KITCHEN • 290 Hudson Street • (212) 627-2257 • $$

Herban Kitchen, an organic restaurant that offers both vegetarian and non-vegetarian dishes, will deliver home-cooked meals to your door. You can order as many meals at a time as you want (you can freeze them). They offer an early evening and late evening delivery service. Delivery is free within a fifteen-block radius, $5 anywhere else in Manhattan up to 96th Street.

EXERCISE

If you don't exercise because you can't ever seem to make it to the gym, then have the trainer come to you, at home or at the office. It does cost more, but it can be a worthwhile extra expense in terms of time saved and really getting committed to being in shape once and for all.

ABC
(ATHLETIC BODIES FOR CHILDREN...OF ALL AGES)
(212) 642-5969 • $$

Lisa-Michelle Ciancio teaches a program of personal training to children, adults, and families. She instructs kids (of all ages) how to inline skate, swim, ski, and bicycle (training wheels to two-wheels). She also teaches gymnastics and aerobics. Lisa-Michelle has been working with children for 14 years, and is very enthusiastic and positive in her approach to help a child achieve proficiency in a sport and to have a healthy body. Instruction is $50 an hour and a ten session package is $350. She will travel with families on ski or swim vacations as an instructor.

BRENDA DIBARI • (917) 749-7959

Brenda works with people of all capabilities from tri-athletes to beginners. Her pleasant and encouraging manner will get you in shape very quickly.

CLASSIC BODIES • (212) 737-8440 • $$

Classic Bodies can arrange private, at-home instruction. They offer various techniques: stretch, weight training, calisthenics, yoga, and aerobics. It will cost approximately $60 an hour.

ENERGETICS UNLIMITED
(212) 879-1566 • $$

Bonita Porte owns this very personalized training company, which has been keeping New Yorkers in shape and good health for 20 years. Bonita has the unique ability to match your needs with exactly the right trainer. Energetics rates are $65 per one-hour session. They have recently added Energetic Seniors,® specializing in mature adults, 50+. Bonita also offers Energetic Juniors,® designed for children and teens from 8-18 years old, starting at $60 per session.

IF YOU DO DECIDE TO CHALLENGE YOUR BODY OUTSIDE YOUR HOME OR OFFICE, CHECK OUT THREE MEGA FITNESS/SPORTS COMPLEXES WHICH HAVE REVOLUTIONIZED FITNESS IN NEW YORK CITY. ASPHALT GREEN, SITUATED ON 5.5 ACRES OVERLOOKING THE EAST RIVER ON THE UPPER EAST SIDE, OFFERS A 50-METER OLYMPIC POOL, AN ASTROTURF ATHLETIC FIELD, GYMNASIUMS, AND RUNNING TRACKS. FOR MORE INFORMATION, CALL (212) 369-8890.

THE CHELSEA PIERS SPORTS & ENTERTAINMENT COMPLEX IS A 30-ACRE WATERFRONT SPORTS VILLAGE LOCATED ALONG THE HUDSON RIVER WHICH FEATURES A GOLF CLUB, ROLLER AND ICE SKATING RINKS, MARITIME CENTER, AND FIELDHOUSE, COMPLETE WITH A ROCK CLIMBING WALL. CALL (212) 336-6666 FOR MORE INFORMATION.

THE REEBOK SPORTS CLUB ON THE UPPER WEST SIDE IS A 140,000 SQUARE FOOT, SIX FLOOR FACILITY WHICH OFFERS ITS MEMBERS A SWIMMING POOL, BASKETBALL COURT, BOXING CLASSES, AND A ROCK CLIMBING WALL IN AN ATTRACTIVE, EXCLUSIVE SETTING. THEY CAN BE REACHED AT (212) 362-6800.

IF YOU'RE SERIOUS ABOUT HOME FITNESS, YOU MAY WANT TO CONSIDER PURCHASING GYM EQUIPMENT FOR YOUR HOME. THE GYM SOURCE OFFERS A LARGE SELECTION OF EQUIPMENT AND HELPFUL SALESPEOPLE. THEY ALSO PROVIDE EQUIPMENT RENTAL. FOR MORE INFORMATION, CALL (212) 688-4222, OR VISIT THEIR STORE AT 40 EAST 52ND STREET.

GYM IN A BAG? PEX, INC., A PERSONAL TRAINING FACILITY, HAS CREATED "GYM IN A BAG," A COMPACT AND PORTABLE KIT OF EXERCISE ACCESSORIES, VIDEO, AND INSTRUCTIONAL WORKOUT CARDS THAT MAKES IT POSSIBLE TO EXERCISE EFFECTIVELY WITHOUT MACHINERY, EVEN IN TIGHT QUARTERS. FOR MORE INFORMATION, CALL PEX AT (212) 254-1915.

LIVINGSTON MILLER
(212) 662-4814 • $$-$$$

He has been helping people to feel better with a steady regime of exercise for over fifteen years. He can teach aerobics, stretching, weights, as well as therapeutic techniques.

METHOD FITNESS
(212) 876-3434 • $$

David Guzman founded his company to cater to baby boomers who want to exercise at home and avoid crowded gyms. Although a large portion of his clients are over 40, he can design programs for people under 40 as well. One of David's personal trainers (he currently has over 40 trainers) will come to your home, office, or apartment building gym. After an evaluation, a trainer will design an individualized fitness program that stresses nutrition and diet, cardiovascular exercise, and strength and muscle training. They can also set up an inexpensive home gym. The first one-hour consultation is free. Then you would need to purchase a minimum of 12 one-hour sessions. The cost runs between $58 to $68 for each session.

TERRY KING • (718) 788-0437 • $$$

Terry designs home gym systems and acts as a personal trainer as well.

FIREWOOD & ICE DELIVERY

Why go out in the cold when delivery can be made right to your door.

AA ARMATO WOOD & ICE
(212) 737-1742 • $$

There is a 3-5 bundle minimum depending on where you live. Bundles cost $8 each and consist of 10-12 split logs. They offer same day delivery.

PAUL BUNYON FIREWOOD
(718) 892-0891 • $$

Firewood orders are taken every day from 8:00 A.M. to 10:00 P.M. They deliver on Tuesday and Saturday in Manhattan. Payment by cash or check is accepted.

MAKEUP ARTISTS & HAIRDRESSERS

It is just as easy to get someone to come to your home to cut your hair or apply your makeup as it is to go to a salon. Ask at your own favorite places or consider ours.

BARBARA CAMP • (212) 828-5969 • $$

Barbara will come to your home and make you look like royalty. She will teach you how to apply your own makeup. A onetime visit from her could change your look forever.

JIM INDERATO • (212) 684-5062 • $-$$

Jim is an agent for some of the top hair and makeup people in New York. All you need to do is call Jim and tell him what you need and how much you want to spend. He is great at matching your needs with his list of professionals.

KRISTEN BARRY • (212) 685-8049 • $$$

Kristen has experience as a hair stylist for celebrities. Although you will pay for her expertise, she will gladly come to your home to fulfill your hairdressing needs, including cut, styling, and color.

LORI KLEIN • (212) 996-9390 • $$

You can arrange for a onetime makeup lesson, special occasion makeup applications, or even get a group of friends together for a class.

TINA • (212) 369-9102 • $$

Tina has worked for some of the most prestigious hair salons in New York. She enjoys doing haircuts for people in their homes.

MASSAGE

ELIZABETH WILLOUGHBY • (212) 226-1240 • $$

Elizabeth specializes in foot reflexology, a holistic approach to preventative medicinal healthcare.

LARRY WEINBERG • (516) 829-3643 • $$

Larry will even come to your hotel room. He is an expert in both Swedish and Amma massage. And if he still feels tension, he doesn't stop when the hour is up.

THE SWEDISH INSTITUTE • (212) 924-5900 • $$

If you call Dolores on Tuesday, Wednesday, or Thursday, she will arrange for a licensed massage therapist to come to your home or office. She will match your needs with the right therapist. It costs $55 to $75 an hour.

TOM STOCKER • (212) 802-4744 • $$

Tom specializes in Swedish and Shiatsu massage, as well as reflexology. Trained at the Swedish Institute, Tom has been making clients feel relaxed for 17 years.

SEAMSTRESS

ANNE KYRIAZIS • (201) 843-6544 • $$

Anne is the ultimate in men's and women's alterations. She can work with any type of fabric.

DEBORAH ANDERKO • (212) 289-2988 • $$$

Deborah offers a full range of professional alterations for ladies and men. She specializes in custom bridal and wedding party wear. Custom dressmaking by way of duplicating those favorite items in your closet is a valuable service to her clients. Fabric shopping services, swatching, and home visits are available at an additional fee.

The Intrepid Pages of
Delivery-Only Services

DIAL-A-DINNER • (212) 779-1222 • $$$

This service offers home delivery from Manhattan's finest restaurants, including The Palm, La Côte Basque, and China Grill. There is a 20 percent fee over the cost of the meal. Your dinner will be delivered to your door by a tuxedoed staff person, and they guarantee the meal will be piping hot. Call for a catalog of menus.

THE MILKMAN • (212) 279-6455 • $

Why not enjoy the convenience of having your milk and other beverages delivered right to your door (or at least to your lobby). The Milkman will deliver milk, orange juice, soda, iced tea, and other beverages. The prices are not much more than what the supermarket charges, and already include a delivery fee. There is no fee to set up an account.

NYC SHOP • (888) NYC-SHOP • $$

NYC Shop offers customers the convenience of supermarket shopping over the phone. You place your order by phone or fax and your items will be delivered free the next day. You can order items in small quantities or in bulk. They have a catalog of all their products and carry all the popular brands. Payment is accepted in the form of a check or Visa/MasterCard.

URBAN ORGANIC • (718) 499-4321 • $$

Urban Organic delivers fruits and vegetables to your home once a week. Boxes come in three sizes, 1-2 people, $27; 2-4 people, $37; and family, $52. Each box consists of between 16 and 20 fruits and vegetables, and will always include carrots, potatoes, a leafy green salad vegetable, apples, bananas, oranges, and grapefruits. The other items will vary depending on what is fresh and available. They also have a line of organic groceries and dairy products that they can deliver with your produce order.

WWW.BN.COM

You can order books online and have them delivered right to your home. Barnes & Noble is an online bookstore with over 2.5 million titles at a 40 percent savings. The web site features book reviews, recommendations, bestseller lists, author interviews, and so much more. You can even read the first chapter of a book you are interested in purchasing. They also sell music, computer games, gifts and toys, and now feature an online auction.

AMAZON.COM • www.amazon.com

Much like Barnes & Noble, Amazon.com offers books and much more.

ETOYS.COM • www.etoys.com
TOYSMART.COM • www.toysmart.com

These sites are great for finding children's toys, games, books and music. Your favorite toy store also probably has an online site by now.

URBANFETCH.COM • www.urbanfetch.com

This site is perfect for busy New Yorkers. They deliver a variety of items and are continually updating their service.

KOZMO.COM • www.kozmo.com

Another great site for busy New Yorkers. Delivery guaranteed within one hour. Videos, magazines, candy and much more.

The Intrepid Pages of

Doing Your Mailing from Home

$ = inexpensive
$$ = moderate
$$$ = expensive

OVERNIGHT, SECOND-DAY, & REGULAR MAIL SERVICES

FEDERAL EXPRESS
(800) 463-3339 • $$$
8:00 A.M-8:30 P.M.

Fed Ex will pick up within one hour of calling and provide you with some packing materials. Pickups only in the afternoon till 8:30 P.M.

UNITED PARCEL SERVICE
(800) 742-5877 • $$
7:00 A.M.-7:00 P.M.

UPS has a second-day delivery service that is less expensive than the next-day delivery offered by other companies. There is a pickup fee of $5 in addition to the shipping charge.

> YOU CAN SAVE YOURSELF A TRIP TO THE POST OFFICE AND ORDER STAMPS BY MAIL. CALL THE STAMP FULFILLMENT SERVICES OF THE US POST OFFICE AT (800) 782-6724 AND HAVE YOUR MAJOR CREDIT CARD HANDY.

UNITED STATES POSTAL SERVICE
(212) 330-2542 • $ • 8:30 A.M.-6:00 P.M.

Express mail on demand pick-up service is available for up to seventy-pound packages. Their last pickup is at 6:00 P.M. and you must call at least one hour before.

OTHER MAILING SERVICES

MAIL BOXES ETC. • Locations Throughout the City • $$$

They can take care of most of your mailing and packing needs but there is no pickup and delivery. It is the alternative to going to the post office to mail a package.

MOBILE MESSENGER • (212) 751-7765 • $$

If you need to get a letter or package messengered around the City, Mobile is the company to call. They will pick up and deliver C.O.D. if you do not have an account.

NJ SHIPPERS • (973) 844-1947 • $$$

This company ships valuable items nationally and internationally. They specialize in the shipment of antiques, art, and furniture, and will crate the items if necessary. NJ Shippers will pick up the items from your home. Speak with Ismael Colon or Marianne Stella.

RSA SHIPPING • (800) 221-9370 • $$

Most overnight companies and even the post office have weight limitations. RSA can ship very large packages. All items must be pre-packed but they do pick up and deliver.

THUNDERBALL • (212) 675-1700 • $

An efficient messenger service with a polite and intelligent staff. The service is very good and the prices are inexpensive. They accept cash, personal check, and credit cards.

WALSH MESSENGER • (516) 746-4348 • $$

An efficient messenger service that can transport both small and large packages. You can set up an account with them or pay by cash. They do not accept personal checks or credit cards.

The Intrepid Pages of
Where to Find Wholesale (or close to it) Staples

$ = inexpensive   **D** = deliver
$$ = moderate
$$$ = expensive

Buying food in New York is a treat because you can truly find any herb, spice, noodle, etc. that you desire; however, you often pay the price for such specialty items. We attempt to cut your staples bill in half so that you have more left over for those fun foods that make shopping and cooking so exciting.

BEVERAGE WHOLESALERS

Why pay top dollars for sodas, beer, and mixers when you don't have to? And many places deliver.

B & E QUALITY BEVERAGE
511 West 23rd Street • (212) 243-6812 • $ • D

GRILL BEVERAGE BARN
350 West Street (Houston Street & the West Side Highway)
(212) 463-7171 • $ • D

NY BEVERAGE WHOLESALERS
428 East 91st Street • (212) 831-4000 • $ • D

FOOD STORES & SOURCES

CHELSEA MARKET
75 Ninth Avenue (15th & 16th Streets)

Chelsea Market is a huge wholesale and retail marketplace which houses high-end suppliers of a wide range of foods, everything from milk to cookies. Some samplings include, but are not limited to:

AMY'S BREAD • Chelsea Market (75 Ninth Ave.)
(212) 462-4338 • $

Amy's offers daily-special loaves at 40 to 50 percent off, and regular items are about 35 percent off retail. Cash only.

MANHATTAN FRUIT EXCHANGE • Chelsea Market
(212) 989-2444 • $

At Manhattan Fruit, there is no minimum purchase required—you can buy one banana or 100 cases at the same rate. Cash only.

NIGHT BAGEL • Chelsea Market
(888) 729-8800

Owned by Ruthy (it's next door to Ruthy's Cheesecake), Night Bagel offers about twenty varieties of bagels, all baked here 24 hours a day. Wholesale and retail prices are the same. Cash only.

RONNYBROOK FARM DAIRY
Chelsea Market • (212) 741-6455 • $

Ronnybrook stocks dairy products from the family farm in Ancramdale, New York. Case lots here are at least 30 percent cheaper here than in gourmet stores. Cash only.

RUTHY'S CHEESECAKE & RUGELACH BAKERY
Chelsea Market • (212) 463-8800 • $

You can find old-fashioned rugelach and twenty-five different fla-vored cheesecakes at Ruthy's. Cash, checks, and major credit cards are accepted.

CIAO BELLA GELATO COMPANY
262 Mott Street (between Prince & Houston)
(212) 226-7668 • $

Here you can purchase gelato and sorbet in bulk. The minimum for delivery is three large tubs or five small ones. Cash and checks are accepted.

FAIRWAY
2328 Twelfth Avenue
(132nd & 133rd Streets on the Hudson River)
(212) 234-3883 • $ • D

Prices are as low as we have seen for high-quality cheese, cold cuts, salads, smoked fish, and produce.

JUST FOOD • (212) 674-8124 • $

Community Supported Agriculture is an innovative program designed to connect farmers with New Yorkers. It gives interested parties an opportunity to buy shares in a grass-roots cooperative of consumers and farmers. The shares, which you would purchase at the start of the growing season, help support the farmers. In exchange, you would receive a supply of fresh produce each week from June until early December. The produce, most of which is organic, is delivered to cen-tral locations for pickup by members. The general fee is $300 for the season which should feed two people each week. General information is available from Just Food, a liaison for the New York groups.

MAZUR & JAFFE • 25-27 Peck Slip • (212) 962-6420

Come early in the morning to this fish store, located a block north of the Fulton Fish Market. There is a minimum quantity of about 5 pounds of fish. Prices are 30 percent less than retail. If you pay a little more, they will clean and fillet your fish. Cash only.

METROPOLITAN AGRI
412 Greenwich Street • (212) 431-3504 • $

Metro Agri is the wholesale arm of the Gourmet Garage. At this busy Tribeca warehouse, you buy by the case, from a selection of about 500 fruits, vegetables, mushrooms, and herbs. Prices are about 30 to 40 percent off retail. If you're placing an order over $100, call in advance and they will have it ready for pick up. Cash only.

MY BROTHER'S FARM • (212) 615-6733 • $ • D

They offer year-round delivery of locally grown organic vegetables and fruit The selection changes each week, bread from Sullivan Street Bakery, cheese, and a recipe from one of the restaurants My Brother's Farm supplies. The length of the delivery plan varies; the 24-week plan is $25 a week. It's probably a good idea to share the food with a neighbor as the package is plentiful.

PATRICIAN WAREHOUSE
58-66 57th Streets, Queens • (718) 417-4650 • $

An importer and distributor of high-quality Italian fare sells discounted sausage, pasta, canned peppers and other Italian goods in their Queens warehouse. Although the warehouse may be out of the way, the low prices may be well worth the effort.

GREENMARKETS

On the next two pages is a list of locations and yearly schedules of the greenmarkets throughout the City. There is no cheaper or fresher way to buy your produce, baked goods, cheeses, flowers, lobsters, and many other wonderful foodstuffs. All items are sold directly to you with no middleman, so no markup. You can't be sure exactly which items are being sold that day, so be flexible with your grocery list.

LA MARQUETA
East 115th Street and Park Avenue • (212) 534-4900

A year-round marketplace which houses two buildings—one, an open-air market with flea and farmer's markets; the other an indoor building with "mom and pop" vendors selling wares like fabric, confectionery, and music. There are also Creole and Latin restaurants in the indoor market. The marketplace hours are 7 A.M. to 7 P.M, Monday through Saturday.

GREENMARKET SCHEDULE

MARKET	DAYS	DATES
MANHATTAN		
Bowling Green (Broadway & Battery Place)	Thursdays	Year-round
World Trade Center (Church & Fulton Streets)	Tuesdays Thursdays	June-November Year-round
City Hall (Chambers & Centre Streets)	Tuesdays, Fridays	Year-round
P.S. 234 (Greenwich & Chambers Streets)	Saturdays	April-December
Federal Plaza (Broadway & Thomas Street)	Fridays	Year-round
Harrison Street (Greenwich & Harrison Streets)	Wednesdays	April-December
Lafayette Street (Lafayette & Spring Streets)	Thursdays	July 10-November
Tompkins Square (Seventh Street & Avenue A)	Sundays	June-December
St. Marks Church (East 10th Street & Second Avenue)	Tuesdays	June-November
Abingdon Square (West 12th Street & Eighth Avenue)	Saturdays	June-December
Union Square (East 17th Street & Broadway)	Mondays, Wednesdays, Fridays, Saturdays	Year-round
Sheffield Plaza (West 57th Street & Ninth Avenue)	Wednesdays, Saturdays	Year-round
Verdi Square (72nd Street & Broadway)	Saturdays	June 14-November
I.S. 44 (West 77th Street & Columbus Avenue)	Sundays	Year-round
West 97th Street (Between Amsterdam & Columbus Avenues)	Fridays	June-December
Minisink Town House (West 143rd Street and Lenox Avenue)	Tuesdays	July 15-October
West 175th Street (at Broadway)	Thursdays	June-December

GREENMARKET SCHEDULE

MARKET	DAYS	DATES
BRONX		
Lincoln Hospital (East 149th Street & Park Avenue)	Tuesdays, Fridays	July 11-October
Poe Park (East 192nd Street & Grand Concourse)	Tuesdays	July 15-November
BROOKLYN		
Williamsburg (Broadway & Havemeyer Street)	Thursdays	July 10-October
Albee Square (Fulton Street & DeKalb Avenue)	Wednesdays	July 9-October
Grand Army Plaza (at entrance to Prospect Park)	Saturdays	Year-round
Windsor Terrace (Prospect Park West & 16th Street)	Wednesdays	July 9-November
QUEENS		
Jamaica Farmer's Market (90-140 160th Street, north of Jamaica Avenue)	Wednesdays, Fridays, Saturdays	Mid-April-mid November
STATEN ISLAND		
St. George Borough Hall Municipal Parking Lot (St. Mark's & Hyatt Streets)	Saturdays	June 14-November

THE INTREPID NEW YORKER BUYS MEAT WHOLESALE. EVERY MONTH WE BUY ABOUT TEN POUNDS OF CHICKEN, TWELVE LAMB CHOPS, TEN POUNDS OF CHOPPED MEAT, AND TWELVE STEAKS. WE CALL OUR WHOLESALE MAN TO TELL HIM WHAT WE WANT AND HOW WE WANT IT CUT. HE WRAPS THE MEAT IN FREEZER PAPER IN THE PORTIONS WE REQUEST AND THEN DELIVERS IT TO OUR DOOR. THE BILL IS LESS THAN HALF WHAT WE WOULD PAY IN A SUPERMARKET AND IT'S FREEZER-READY! AND WE ARE ALWAYS AMAZED TO FIND THAT IT ACTUALLY FITS IN OUR TINY NYC FREEZER COMPARTMENT.

WE TELL OUR CLIENTS WHO DON'T WANT TO SHOP WHOLESALE THAT THEY CAN AT LEAST DO ONCE-A-MONTH SHOPPING AT THEIR LOCAL SUPERMARKET. YOU CAN BUY THEIR CHEAPER, GENERIC LABELS IN BULK, AND TAKE ADVANTAGE OF ONGOING SALES. AND OF COURSE, ALL SUPERMARKETS DELIVER.

MEAT WHOLESALERS

Your freezer can hold much more than you think so don't be frightened by the minimum requirements.

DIAMOND MEAT PACKERS
37 Ninth Avenue (13th and 14th Streets)
(212) 727-2067 • $

Diamond buys wholesale in the meatpacking district and breaks up those vast quantities for resale, but still charges much less than a retailer. Steak, lamb, and pork are sold by the pound at very reasonable prices. Cash and checks are accepted.

14TH STREET FOOD DEPOT
147-20 94th Avenue (between Suthin Boulevard and 148th Street)
(212) 366-6668 • $

You can get most of your wholesale meat here, but they also sell eggs, cheeses in bulk, vats of olive oil, nuts, butter, and other staples. You purchase in large quantities and save bundles.

PASTRIES

LET THEM EAT CAKE
193 Columbia Street, Brooklyn
(212) 989-4970 • $ • D

They bake for many of the gourmet food stores throughout the City and they will also sell to you at wholesale prices. They also cater.

STATIONERY SUPPLIES

STAPLES
Locations Throughout the City
(800) 333-3330 for delivery in NYC • $

Every item you could possibly want for the home or office. There's a $10 delivery charge for orders under $50.

YOU CAN CUT DOWN THE AMOUNT OF TIME YOU ARE FORCED TO WAIT FOR ALL TYPES OF HOME SERVICING, REPAIRS AND INSTALLATION BY AT LEAST HALF:

An annoying fact of life in NYC is the insulting amount of time you are forced to wait for home servicing for phone and cable as well as repairs, pickups and deliveries. These service providers are notoriously indifferent to consumer relations, although they seem to be trying a little harder these days. New York City dispatchers will tell you there's no way to give you a specific time of arrival, that you have a choice of waiting from 8am to 1pm or 1pm-6pm – take it or leave it. Don't be surprised if, by the end of the day, they are a "no-show" due to overscheduling and job delays. It's infuriating. Well, you don't have to take it:

YOU CAN GET THE FIRST APPOINTMENT OF THE DAY FROM THE UTILITY COMPANIES:

You have to bypass the dispatcher and ask to speak to a supervisor. If you are told the supervisor is unavailable, insist on speaking to someone who is a decision maker, even if you have to go all the way to the top. We have found that the executive secretaries to the president can be very helpful. When you get a decision-maker on the phone, tell him politely that you can't afford to take five hours off from your job, and that you must have a more specific time of arrival, such as the first or last appointment of the day. The chances are very good that you are going to get a runaround in the beginning, but don't give up; you will prevail. Make sure you keep a list of the names and titles of people you have talked to. It's the only way to turn anonymous voices into accountable, customer service representatives. And they tend to be much more cooperative when they know you have their names.

HERE'S HOW YOU GET AN APPOINTMENT TIME NAILED DOWN WITH OTHER HOME SERVICE PROVIDERS SUCH AS APPLIANCE REPAIRMEN AND FURNITURE DELIVERYMEN.

The dispatchers may not set their appointment schedules until the night before, so you can't set it up in advance. However, most delivery people carry beepers or have cell phones nowadays. So, you can ask them to call you at your office when they are one or two stops away from your home and meet them there when they arrive. Don't let the dispatcher tell you there is no way to reach the guys on the truck. It's just not true.

THE BEST APPOINTMENT OF THE DAY TO REQUEST IS THE FIRST. YOU CAN'T GET STOOD UP DUE TO JOB DELAYS.

IF YOU LIVE IN A DOORMAN BUILDING, MAKE SURE YOU KNOW THE HOURS THE BUILDING ALLOWS SERVICE PROVIDERS TO MAKE CALLS.

BEWARE OF THE "PHONE SLAMMING" PHENOMENON WHEREBY LONG DISTANCE CARRIERS CAN ACTUALLY SWITCH YOUR LONG DISTANCE SERVICE OVER TO THEIR COMPANY WITHOUT YOUR PERMISSION. YOU CAN PREVENT "PHONE SLAMMING" BY CALLING YOUR LOCAL PHONE COMPANY AND TELLING THEM TO PUT A FREEZE ON YOUR ACCOUNT, GIVING YOU SOLE AUTHORITY TO CHANGE YOUR LONG DISTANCE CARRIER.

MAKE SURE THAT ONCE YOU'VE GOTTEN THE APPOINTMENT THAT YOU ARE GETTING THE RIGHT MAN AND TOOLS FOR THE JOB:

The Intrepid New Yorker has learned the hard way. We've gone through hoops to get the first appointment of the day, only to get the wrong man or the wrong tools for the job. Be very specific about the type of repair or installation you need. And don't expect dispatchers to ask you all the right questions. Spell it out for them.

Here are some names and phone numbers you may need to keep in your back pocket if you aren't getting any satisfaction from your basic home services.

THE INTREPID PAGES OF

UTILITY COMPANIES

CABLE TELEVISION

RCN of New York
Chairman and Chief Executive Officer—
Mr. David McCourt
Secretary—Ms. Blair Turner
President—Mr. Mark Haverkate
Secretary—Ms. Brid Grant
(609) 734-3700

Time Warner Cable
President—Mr. Barry Rosenblum
Assistant to the President—
Ms. Dorothy Leonard
General Manager—Mr. Howard Szarfarc
Executive Secretary—Ms. Hilda Caban
(212) 598-7200

ELECTRIC

Con Edison
President—Mr. Eugene McGrath
Secretary—Ms. Melba Hernandez
(212) 460-4982

TELEPHONE

AT&T
President—Mr. John Walter
Assistant to the President—
Ms. Rosanne Kennedy
(908) 221-2000

Bell Atlantic
Chairman and Chief Executive Officer—
Mr. Ray Smith
Secretary—Ms. Terry Dougherty
(212) 395-2552

NEW YORK CITY AND THE BOROUGHS ARE RUNNING OUT OF PHONE NUMBERS. FORTUNATELY, TO MAKE IT EASIER FOR RESIDENTS, YOU WILL BE ABLE TO KEEP YOUR CURRENT AREA CODE, 212 OR 718. ONLY PEOPLE WHO REQUIRE NEW PHONE NUMBERS MAY POSSIBLY BE GIVEN A NEW AREA CODE, 646 FOR MANHATTAN RESIDENTS, AND 347 FOR 718 AREA CODE USERS. THE NEW AREA CODE CHANGE WILL HAVE NO GEOGRAPHIC BIAS. YOU WILL RECEIVE THE NEW AREA CODE DEPENDING ON THE PARTICULAR AREA CODE WHICH IS AVAILABLE AT THE GIVEN TIME THAT YOU NEED A NEW NUMBER. IT IS ALSO POSSIBLE THAT YOU WILL AGAIN RECEIVE A 212 OR 718 AREA CODE.

WHEN WE GET STUCK TRYING TO PROGRAM THE VCR, OR MAKING THE COMPUTER DO NEW TRICKS, WE DON'T WASTE TIME DENYING WE CAN'T UNDERSTAND THE MANUALS. WE CALL IN THE HIGH-TECH KIDS FROM NEARBY SCHOOLS, WHO GIVE US GREAT EXPERTISE AND DON'T CHARGE THE EXORBITANT RATES PROFESSIONALS CHARGE.

TECHNOLOGY OF THE FUTURE? A TREND IS BEGINNING TO TAKE SHAPE AT A FEW LUXURY BUILDINGS IN THE CITY. DUAL STAR COMMUNICATIONS HAS EQUIPPED THESE BUILDINGS WITH HIGH-TECHNOLOGY OPTIONS. EACH APARTMENT IS WIRED FOR UP TO 12 TELEPHONE LINES, INCLUDING A T-1 LINE FOR ULTRA-FAST MODEM SPEED. DUAL STAR IS ALSO A LOCAL PHONE SERVICE AND CABLE OPTION, BUT ONLY TO THE RESIDENTS OF THESE NEW LUXURY BUILDINGS. AS FOR MOST MANHATTAN RESIDENTS WHOSE BUILDING IS NOT EQUIPPED WITH DUAL STAR TECHNOLOGY, BELL ATLANTIC IS DOING ITS PART TO KEEP UP WITH THE COMPETITION. THEY HAVE RECENTLY INSTITUTED A SERVICE TO UPGRADE MODEM LINES AND MORE TECHNOLOGY BREAKTHROUGHS ARE IN THE MAKING.

MCI

Chairman—Mr. Bert Roberts, Jr.
Assistant to the Chairman—
Ms. Pamela Montrose
Chief Executive Officer—Mr. Gerald Taylor
Assistant to the Chief Executive Officer—
Ms. Linda Payne
(202) 887-2171

RCN of New York

Chairman and Chief Executive Officer—
Mr. David McCourt
Secretary—Ms. Blair Turner
President—Mr. Mark Haverkate
Secretary—Ms. Brid Grant
(609) 734-3700

Sprint

President—Mr. Ron Le May
Assistant to the President—
Ms. Monica Lundgren
(913) 624-6000

Laissez Faire Markets

COMPETITION IN THE MARKET-PLACE HAS BEGUN TO OPEN NEW DOORS FOR MANHATTAN RESIDENTS. IT USED TO BE THAT CONSUMERS HAD LIMITED TELEPHONE, CABLE, AND ELECTRIC SERVICE OPTIONS. NOW COMPETITION IS ALLOWING CONSUMERS TO CHOOSE FROM A RANGE OF COMPANIES AND STILL RECEIVE QUALITY SERVICE, BUT AT MUCH MORE FAIR PRICES.

ONE SUCH COMPANY THAT HAS OPENED NEW CHANNELS FOR CONSUMERS IS RCN. RCN IS A COMMUNICATIONS COMPANY IN COMPETITION WITH BELL ATLANTIC, TIME WARNER CABLE, AT&T, MCI, AND SPRINT. RCN PROVIDES LOCAL AND LONG DISTANCE SERVICE, AS WELL AS CABLE TV SERVICE. RCN CLAIMS TO OFFER ALL OF THE SERVICES THAT THESE COMPANIES PROVIDE, AT LESS EXPENSIVE PRICES. RCN CAN BE REACHED AT (800) 891-7770.

IT USED TO BE THAT CON EDISON HAD A MEGA-MONOPOLY FOR ELECTRIC SERVICE IN MAN-HATTAN. NOW THROUGH RETAIL CHOICE, CONSUMERS CAN CHOOSE A DIFFERENT SUPPLIER OF ELECTRICITY, AND STILL HAVE CON EDISON DELIVER IT. THESE RETAIL CHOICE COMPANIES OFFER CUSTOMERS AS MUCH AS A 20 PERCENT ELECTRIC SAVINGS.

COMPETITION IS VERY PREVALENT AMONG LONG DISTANCE PHONE COMPANIES, WITH NEW COMPANIES AND SERVICES BEING OFFERED EVERY DAY. EVEN INTERNET PROVIDERS SUCH AS AMERICA ONLINE NOW OFFER INEXPENSIVE LONG DISTANCE SERVICE. YOU NEED TO SHOP AROUND TO FIND THE BEST DEAL. ALWAYS READ THE FINE PRINT. WHAT SOUNDS LIKE A GOOD DEAL MAY ACTUALLY REQUIRE YOU TO CALL ONLY ON SUNDAYS OR TO STAY ON THE PHONE FOR TWENTY MINUTES TO RECEIVE A DISCOUNT. SOME COMPANIES ALSO CHARGE MONTHLY FEES. MANY COMPANIES ARE WILLING TO MATCH OR BEAT THE COMPETITIONS' PRICES. DON'T BE AFRAID TO HAGGLE.

SOMETIMES WE JUST CAN'T DO IT ALL, AND EVEN IF WE COULD, IT ISN'T WORTH THE LOSS OF QUALITY TIME. WHEN THE INTREPID NEW YORKER IS MAXED OUT ON PROJECTS AND CHORES, WE HIRE "ERRAND RUNNERS".

When we really need some help we go straight to the dozens of colleges and universities in New York City, and post a request for a college student with their temporary employment offices. It's a wonderful way to get smart, responsible young people to help out when it's all gotten to be too much.

The Intrepid Pages of
Errand Runners & Personal Service Companies

LOCAL COLLEGES & UNIVERSITIES

APEX TECHNICAL SCHOOL • Placement Office • (212) 645-3300

They specialize in automotive, air conditioning repair and welding. Fax your job description to Ms. Walker at (212) 645-6985. You can work out the fee with the student.

BARNARD COLLEGE • Career Services Office • (212) 854-2033

Mail your job description to Office of Career Development, Barnard College, 11 Milbank, 3009 Broadway, New York, NY 10027-6598, or fax it to (212) 854-2188, Attention: Office of Career Development. It will be posted and the fee is set between you and the student.

BARUCH COLLEGE
Office of Career Development • (212) 802-6710

Fax a job description, including the job requirements and compensation to (212) 802-6714.

COLUMBIA UNIVERSITY
Student Employment Office • (212) 854-2391

They will post the job description on their board. There is no set fee. You will negotiate that with the student you hire.

FORDHAM UNIVERSITY
Career Planning and Placement • (212) 636-6280

You can fax a job request to (212) 636-7048. Include a job description, hours needed, and compensation.

GLOBE INSTITUTE OF TECHNOLOGY
Student Services • (212) 349-4330

Job requirements should be faxed to (212) 227-5920.

HUNTER COLLEGE
Career Development Office • (212) 772-4850

You can fax a brief job description with the skills needed to (212) 772-5438, Attn: Laura Pickett. The pay rate can be worked out between you and the student.

KATHERINE GIBBS SECRETARIAL SCHOOL • (212) 973-4940

Ask for Julia Slick. She will post the job. The fee is set by you and the student.

NEW YORK UNIVERSITY
Student Employment Office • (212) 998-4757

You can fax a job description to (212) 995-4197. You should include a job title, rate of compensation (set by you), skills needed, time needed, as well as your phone and fax. You can also list a job description on-line at www.nyu.edu/careerservices.

PERSONAL SERVICE COMPANIES

CROSS IT OFF YOUR LIST • (212) 725-0122

Linda Rothschild runs this organization/concierge services business for the home and the office. Linda's concierge services run the gamut of helping people to move, to running errands, shopping, waiting in line, and bill paying.

INDIVIDUAL SOLUTIONS • (917) 954-0936

Whatever the task "consider it done," says Shana Ehrlich who has done everything from planning romantic getaway weekends to over-seeing contractors. Individual Solutions will organize your life, or just your closet; return all your unwanted Tiffanys; plan a fabulous dinner party; find the perfect gift for the niece or nephew you don't know so well; do your grocery shopping; create filing and organizational systems for your home or office (clutter control), or help find the perfect piece of art for the empty space on your wall.

PAPERCHASERS • (212) 721-4991

President Barbara Fredericks Fields and her staff can help you take care of chores that always go by the wayside. They can coordinate a move, respond to mail, pay bills, schedule appointments, and shop.

SAVED BY THE BELL • (212) 874-5457

Susan Bell has been making people's lives easier since 1981. She specializes in special events planning as well as personal services. Susan and her associates will help with a move, assist in the renovation of your home, gift shop, and take care of your holiday cards. She can also plan weddings, parties, and bar/bat mitzvahs.

SOLUTION:
GETTING IN AND OUT AND AROUND NEW YORK CITY WITHOUT "ROAD RAGE".

It's not easy. Our old, tired infrastructure will never catch up with our 7 million plus population that swells daily with commuters, service providers and shoppers. If you traveled from one end of Manhattan to the other without traffic or lights, it would take you as little as ten minutes. With 9 to 5 traffic, an hour or more! Congestion is a quality of life issue amongst New Yorkers. We are always devising ways to make the commute more bearable. Some of us even set it up so that we don't ever have to leave our own neighborhoods! Bottom line — you can walk it, bike it, bus, subway, or cab it, even drive it. Your commute can take you five minutes or forty-five minutes. The solution is to make certain you pick the least stressful approach for your sense of well being.

FIGURE OUT HOW YOU WANT TO COMMUTE BEFORE YOU PICK YOUR NEIGHBORHOOD:

20 blocks equals about a mile. If you want to be able to walk to work from home, then you should choose the neighborhoods that are within a half a mile to a mile radius. If you don't mind the subway, but you don't want to have to walk five or ten minutes to get to the nearest station, find an apartment within a block or two of it. Here are all your options:

New York is a walking city: Manhattan is actually much smaller in scale than it appears. It "sprawls" vertically, not horizontally. Lengthwise, tip to tip, is about 12 miles, widthwise, about 1½. That you can walk it is one of the most appealing aspects of life here. Many New Yorkers have never owned a car. Everything you could possibly ever want or need is within walking reach, or a subway stop or two. Some of us are most comfortable staying within the boundaries of our own neighborhood. Many of us enjoy and use every neighborhood and are familiar with all of NYC's nooks and crannies. Within two–five miles you can traverse such neighborhoods as the Upper West Side, Times Square, The Village, Soho, Lower East Side, Little Italy, and Chinatown. What's endlessly fascinating is the fact that these neighborhoods are so ethnically and aesthetically diverse that you could swear you've crossed the border into another land.

By subway: It is hard to convince newcomers that our subway system is actually one of the best in the world. But much of the negative press is old news. Most of our subways are graffiti-free and air conditioned, and many stations have been renovated and are much better policed. You will see that Wall Street commuters, families, CEOs, evening theatre goers, students, and blue collar workers – all use the subway because it is undeniably the most accessible, efficient and inexpensive way to get to and from any part of Manhattan and its boroughs. And no matter where you are, or where you have to go, there is a subway stop within a few blocks, and during peak hours, local and express trains arrive at a given station every two or three minutes. A new computerized "metro card" has all but replaced tokens. You can purchase as many rides on a card as you want. You can transfer with it free of charge when changing to a bus or another subway, within two hours. In terms of safety, use common sense. Peak hours are much safer than late-night hours when you may be the only one standing on a subway platform. Travel the subways only during those hours that are well within your comfort zone. In terms of commute, it's almost impossible to spend more than 20 minutes on a subway if you live and work in Manhattan, unless you have to change trains to get across town as well as "downtown". If you want to keep your commute to under twenty minutes, consider a neighborhood that is on the same subway line as your workplace. If you don't mind thirty to forty minutes door-to-door, then you can live anywhere.

By bus: Some people just hate going underground, so they take the bus. It costs the same as a subway. There are bus stops on almost every other corner, going both North and South and East and West. The accessibility and the price can't be beat; the problem is efficiency. There is so much traffic in New York that buses, during peak hours, can be slowed to a crawl. There's also a snag in the system that has been getting nothing more than lip service for years; buses tend to stack up together, so four will come in a row and then none for another ten or fifteen minutes. It is maddening. But if you have a short commute, it can be a relaxing way to travel.

Ferries: They are back! The concept of ferrying people to work has made a comeback here in New York. And if you are on one of their commuting routes, it can be a wonderful way to start and end your day.

Yellow Cabs: They are expensive. A one mile drive will set you back about $4.00 including tip. But they are a way of life in the big apple. They are very convenient and just a simple hail away...

unless, of course, you are trying to hail a cab when everybody else is...when it's raining, during rush hour, at theatre time...in other words, when you really, really need one! But we know how to increase your odds:

DON'T STAND PASSIVELY AMONGST ALL THE OTHER PEOPLE LOOKING FOR CABS, HOPING ONE WILL STOP FOR YOU. THE IDEA IS TO GET OUT IN FRONT OF THE PACK BY WALKING AGGRESSIVELY TOWARD THE CABS YOU SEE COMING YOUR WAY.

During early morning rush hour, taxis are dropping commuters off in the midtown and downtown areas, and returning uptown empty. So look for them on the uptown avenues. The reverse is true at evening rush hour.

When the whole world seems to be looking for cabs, the best bet is to head toward the outermost avenues in

Manhattan, away from the hordes.

Gravitate toward areas where taxis are most likely to drop off passengers:

- On the Upper East Side, early morning taxis are dropping passengers at all the Park Avenue doctor's offices and private schools.
- If you live in the East 50s and 60s, cabbies change shifts in Queens and come back over the 59th Street bridge looking for fares.
- If you live near a large hotel, or the bus and train stations, you will find them.
- If you are near the theatre district at curtain time, you'll find them.

Car services: New Yorkers in the know use car services. Many of them aren't more expensive than a cab, and depending on what you are using them for – such as a trip to the airport – it can actually be less. The beauty is that they are more luxurious than our yellow cabs, you can reserve them in advance, and they offer door-to-door service. They really pay off on bad-weather days and at those times you can't afford to be late. Just make sure you shop for a reputable one, and check each company's cost schedules. Referrals are the way to go. If you work for a company in NYC, they are sure to have an account with at least one of them. If not, open your own. You can put all fares on a credit card if you wish.

Renting cars: That's what we "carless" New Yorkers do when we want to get out of the city. And it's not a bad deal. Even if you rented a car every weekend of the year, you would still be paying considerably less than what it would cost on car payments, gas, and garages. Having said that, most rental car companies in New York City charge exorbitant rates, make customers feel second rate, and take the naive "for a ride". So there's a few smart consumer guidelines to follow:

Compare rates. They vary widely in the business and change regularly for daily,

> YOU DON'T ALWAYS HAVE TO FIGHT FOR A CAB, YOU CAN SHARE ONE. DON'T BE SHY ABOUT ASKING. IT DOESN'T COST EXTRA TO MAKE TWO STOPS AND YOU CAN SPLIT THE FARE.

> THE INTREPID NEW YORKER RENTS CARS FROM THE NEAREST AIRPORT, BECAUSE THE PRICES ARE ALMOST HALF THOSE IN MANHATTAN. IT PAYS IN EVERY WAY, BECAUSE YOU CAN RETURN THE CAR TO ONE OF THEIR MANHATTAN GARAGES. SO IT'S ONE $15 - 20 CAB FARE, AND IT WON'T TAKE YOU MORE THAN FIFTEEN MINUTES TO A HALF AN HOUR TO GET THERE, DEPENDING ON WHERE YOU LIVE.

THE INTREPID NEW YORKER HIGHLY RECOMMENDS THAT YOU JOIN AN AUTOMOBILE CLUB LIKE "AAA" IF YOU DRIVE OFTEN. FOR A NOMINAL YEARLY FEE OF $55 FOR THE FIRST YEAR, $45 A YEAR THEREAFTER, AND $20 EACH ADDITIONAL PERSON, YOU CAN GET FREE BENEFITS, SUCH AS GUARANTEED EMERGENCY ROAD SERVICE, FREE TOWING TO AN AAA SERVICE STATION, DISCOUNT CAR RENTALS, TRIP PLANNING, ETC. MEMBERSHIP CAN AFFORD YOU THE PROTECTION YOU WOULDN'T BE ABLE TO GET FROM A LOCAL, INDEPENDENT RENTAL AGENCY. THEIR NUMBER IS 212-757-2000.

MANHATTAN RESIDENTS WHO REGISTER THEIR CARS IN MANHATTAN SHOULD TAKE ADVANTAGE OF THE CITY TAX REBATE. INSTEAD OF PAYING AN 18¼ PERCENT PARKING TAX, YOU PAY ONLY 10¼ PERCENT. CALL THE NEW YORK CITY DEPARTMENT OF FINANCE AT (718) 935-6694 TO OBTAIN AN APPLICATION.

weekend and weekly rentals. There can also be widespread discrepancies between rate information provided by your local branch, and what you are quoted when you call their national 800 number. Compare them.

Calling well in advance may get you a discounted fare. Always ask what discount packages are being offered and when.

Special promotions might actually make a longer rental, cheaper. For example: A 5-day rental may be more expensive than the seven-day promotional package they are offering.

There are hidden charges such as insurance fees, empty gas tank penalties, and young driver surcharges. Make sure you know about them.

There are local, independent outfits that will rent to you for much less, but consumer beware. Find out first if any complaints have been filed against them at the Better Business Bureau. Make sure they guarantee your reservation. Always take down the name of the person you talked to. Find out if they provide emergency road service. Find out exactly what's in your contract's fine print.

Inspect the car before leaving the lot and make sure everything is in order.

You do have rights! New York General Business Law Section 391-l prohibits rental car agencies from requiring a credit card. You can pay by cash up front, and leave a deposit. When you call to reserve a car, you must tell them you will be paying by cash. They will do a background check before approval, which takes as much as two weeks. Law Section 391-g provides that rental car firms may not refuse to rent to anyone eighteen years of age or older if insurance is available. If you are unjustly denied, file a complaint with the BBB.

New York City Consumer Protection Regulation 501 requires that rental car firms that take reservations make available either the car reserved or a similar car within one half hour of the reserved time, either at the reserved location or at another location to which the consumer is transported without charge. If they tell you they are out of cars, demand to talk to the manager immediately, let them know you know the law, and demand immediate satisfaction.

HAVING YOUR OWN CAR IN NEW YORK CITY:

Plain and simple, it's one of New York's biggest headaches. Traffic is just one major obstacle. Parking spaces are the other. Parking tickets are the third. New Yorkers who are bound and determined to have their own cars in the city either grin and bear the time consuming task of looking for parking spaces that won't get them ticketed or towed, or they set aside x-number of hours and dollars at the end of the month for arguing and paying traffic tickets at the ticket bureau. Those who can, throw enormous amounts of money to keep their cars in garages that cost almost as much as your car payment. Because of our traffic problem, the city does a great job of discouraging people from driving their own cars by blanketing the city with meter maids, traffic cops, more "no parking" signs than trees, and patrols of sheriff's tow trucks. No matter how you slice it, car owners pay a hefty price. Here's the best advice we can give on a raw deal:

Parking garages: In general, they will run you anywhere from $190 - $500 a month. Of course, the more convenient you want it to be - like underneath your building – the more expensive. If you only use your car on weekends, try negotiating a lesser rate with your garage. The general rule of thumb, however, is that the garages

SOME SAVVY NEW YORKERS HAVE FIGURED OUT THAT IT PAYS TO DRIVE THEIR CARS TO WORK AND PARK THEM IN THEIR COMPANY'S GARAGE. NO ALTERNATE SIDE OF THE STREET WORRIES, NO PUBLIC TRANSPORTATION HASSLES, AND YOUR COMPANY PAYS FOR THE GARAGE.

NEW YORK CITY HAS "ALTERNATE SIDE OF THE STREET" PARKING RULES SO THAT STREET-CLEANING TRUCKS CAN CLEAN. THEY ARE ENFORCED ON ALL STREETS WITH SIGNS THAT TELL YOU WHICH DAYS AND HOURS YOU CAN PARK THERE. THERE ARE CERTAIN EXCEPTIONS SUCH AS HOLIDAYS AND SNOW DAYS. CHECK THE CITY PARKING CALENDAR IN THIS BOOK FOR VERIFICATION OF THOSE DATES.

THE DEPARTMENT OF TRANSPORTATION HAS A HOTLINE THAT YOU CAN CALL FOR UP-TO-THE-MINUTE STREET CLEANING/ ALTERNATE SIDE OF THE STREET RULES. THE NUMBER IS (212) 225-5368.

located on the fringes of Manhattan, such as near the piers on both rivers, will cost you considerably less. The trade-off is you'll have to take public transportation to get there. Another option, for those who won't be using a car that often, is to find a garage in one of our other boroughs such as Queens, or across the river in New Jersey. You can park for as little as $70.

Parking garages licensed by the Department of Consumer Affairs are required to have liability insurance of at least $100,000 personal insurance for a single person and $300,000 personal injury for two or more and $25,000 property loss and damage. This does not include items stolen from your car such as golf clubs or a tape deck. The parking facility must also post a sign, as close as possible to the entrance, which states their name, address, license number, capacity, and business hours. Another sign must show their rate schedule.

Finding parking spaces on city streets: Parking spaces are scarce, and once you do find one, you have to look at all the signs posted to make sure you are not in a "no parking between 8am - 11am" zone, a "no standing" zone, an "only commercial vehicle" zone, an "only Tuesday and Thursday" zone, or a "don't even think about it ever!" zone. And those are just to name a few. And if you read the sign wrong, your car will get towed and locked up somewhere on the "dark side" of town, where sob stories just amuse the city jailers who've heard it all a million times before. You can get your car back, if you post bail, which will run you about $150, plus $15 a day for storage. You can increase your chances of finding regular parking spaces near your home if you:

- pay close attention to parking patterns and try to time your arrival to someone else's departure. You might be able to exchange regular parking spaces with local merchants who come and go at certain times.

- start a parking association with neighbors to share each other's spaces. You can inquire by dropping off flyers in the buildings in your area.

- slip your doorman, or the doorman down the street, a good will fee to spot regular parking spaces for you.

- get to know the city's parking rules and suspensions. If you aren't a typical 9 to 5er you may be mercifully out of sync with all the regulations.

ACCESS THE PARKING PAL WEB SITE AT WWW.PARKINGPAL.COM FOR ALL THE CURRENT PARKING INFORMATION YOU CAN POSSIBLY USE.

ON-LINE USERS CAN ACCESS EDMUND'S AUTOMOBILE BUYER'S GUIDE AT WWW.EDMUNDS.COM. THIS SERVICE PROVIDES A MULTITUDE OF INFORMATION ON NEW AND USED CARS, INCLUDING CAR RATINGS, PRICING, LOCAL CAR DEALERS, AND WAYS TO PURCHASE AND LEASE A CAR.

CONSUMER REPORTS HAS THREE 800 NUMBERS NO CAR BUYER SHOULD BE WITHOUT.

New Car Price Service: 1-800-933-5555 tells you what the dealer paid for the car (invoice price) vs. sticker price, invoice and sticker prices for all options and packages, current rebates, factory-to-dealer incentives, and holdbacks. Plus how to negotiate. Savings to the consumer averages $1300. (The first report costs $12 and each additional vehicle report is $10.)

Consumer Reports Used Car Price Service: 1-900-446-0500.

Costs $1.75 a minute. Offers local prices, dealer purchase price, trade-in price, private sale price (which the "books" don't cover).

Also provides information on model reliability, and prices for (1988-1998).

Consumer Reports Auto Insurance Price Service: 1-800-807-8050. Provides print-out with price list of up to 25 of the least expensive policies for the drivers and vehicles in your household.

Also, survey ratings scores, auto insurance guide and money-saving tips. (There is a fee of $12 for the first report, and $8 for each additional report).

The Intrepid Pages of
Getting Around New York

BUS SERVICE

LIBERTY LINES EXPRESS, INC. • (718) 652-8400

Liberty offers a clean and comfortable express bus service between Upper Manhattan and Midtown. For $3 (they accept coins, dollar bills, New York City transit tokens, and the Metro Card), you can travel from one of several stops on Fifth Avenue and the Upper East Side to Midtown. They also offer free connection to the Wall Street X-Change buses during weekday rush hour. Travel time from 79th Street and Fifth Avenue, to 48th Street and Fifth Avenue, is only 7 minutes. The same service is offered from Midtown to Upper Manhattan with bus stops located on Madison Avenue.

CAR RENTALS

AAMCAR
506 West 181st Street • (212) 927-7000
315 West 96th Street • (212) 222-8500

For inexpensive car rentals call AAMCAR. For $42.95 including insurance and 100 free miles, you can rent a compact car for one day. For $49.95, including insurance and 200 free miles, you can rent a compact car overnight. And for $199.95, including insurance and approximately 600 free miles, you can rent a compact car for a three-day weekend. Larger cars are available for more.

CAR SERVICE

A yellow cab from 96th Street and Park Avenue to Wall Street can cost up to $20 with tip, and much more in a traffic jam. There are many times when hiring a car can be more economical, convenient, and comfortable. Here's how they compare:

BELL TAXI • (212) 206-1700

Open twenty-four hours, seven days a week, they accept credit cards and cash. Their cars are very nice—always a Lincoln Town Car or Cadillac—and drivers wear suits. Some cars have mobile phones. To hire a car for an extended period, there is a two-hour minimum, at $30 per hour, with no charge for stops. To go to just one destination—from 96th Street and Park Avenue to Wall Street—is $19. Gratuities are expected. This company is reliable and reservations are accepted.

SABRA • (212) 777-7171

Sabra is open twenty-four hours, seven days a week. They accept cash and credit cards. They offer regular-sized sedans at $18 per hour, with a two-hour minimum. There is no charge per stop. Drivers wear street clothes. You can also request a Lincoln Town Car at $35 per hour with a three-hour minimum and no extra charge for stops. Drivers wear suits. Some of the Lincoln's have mobile phones. The cost to drive from 96th Street and Park Avenue to Wall Street is $15. They accept reservations and gratuities.

TEL AVIV
(212) 777-7777 • (212) 505-0555

They are open twenty-four hours, seven days a week and accept both credit cards and cash. Their cars are plain four-door family · cars and the drivers wear suits. To hire a car for an extended period of time, there is a two-hour minimum in Manhattan, with no charge for stops. The rate is $20 an hour. For a little extra, you can hire a Lincoln Town Car, for $25 per hour. To go to just one destination— from 96th Street and Park Avenue to Wall Street—is $16. Gratuities are expected. A reliable company that accepts reservations.

CHAUFFEURS

If you have your own car, why not?

CHAUFFEURS UNLIMITED • (212) 362-5354

They are open twenty-four hours, seven days a week, and usually need a day's notice. Their chauffeurs cannot begin a job after 8:00 P.M. The charge is $19 per hour, three hours minimum, with a 15 percent gratuity expected. The chauffeur drives under your insurance claim and wears a full uniform. Cash, check, and credit cards are accepted.

PARKING GARAGES

For the least expensive within Manhattan, always look on the outer avenues, near and along the rivers, and the extreme north and south ends of the island. Outdoor garages are less expensive than indoor ones, but weather conditions should be considered.

EDISON Properties
Locations Throughout the City

They offer long-term parking and some are open twenty-four hours, seven days a week. Depending on the garage location and how often you use your car, the rate can be as low as $195 per month, including tax, with some indoor locations.

FOR THE ULTIMATE "NEW YORK CITY" TRANSPORT, HIRE AN OLD FASHIONED CHECKERED CAB. THEY'RE REAL HARD TO COME BY, BUT NEW FAMILY (212) 749-7777 STILL HAS ONE IN THEIR FLEET.

GARAGE MANAGEMENT CORPORATION
Locations Throughout the City • (212) 888-7400

Some locations are open twenty-four hours. You can find an indoor parking lot for a monthly fee of $169 plus tax, and a $3 exit fee each time you use your car. This is a good price if you don't use your car every day. Overnight parking can be as low as $10 plus tax. The garages are clean, the staff is courteous, and very importantly, they take good care of your car.

RAPID PARK • (212) 866-1000

Rapid Park offers a special rate for people who only garage their car in the evening, seven days a week. If you use the garage from after 4:00 P.M. until 9:00 A.M. at their 33rd Street and 1st Avenue location, the monthly price is $99 plus tax. This may be a good alternative for people who use their car during the day.

SOLUTION: CUTTING THROUGH MEGA-CITY BUREAUCRACY

Red tape exists in big cities. We can't escape it. From social security and passports to driver's licenses and jury duty, we have to deal with it. New York has perhaps the worst reputation for bureaucratic boondoggles, but the city is trying to improve on its service to consumers. If you are intrepid, you can cut through a lot of it.

You can get better service from government bureaucrats by following some basic rules:

- Avoid the main government agency headquarters and find out where their smaller branches are around the city. The lines are much smaller and the government employees tend to be more helpful because they are working in a less stressful atmosphere.

- If the main headquarters is a more convenient location for you, be sure you get to the agency fifteen minutes to a half hour before the doors open, so you minimize the wait time and you get employees who are still in a good mood!

- When you have to call these agencies, do it as early in the morning as possible, before they are inundated with calls and you are put permanently on hold. Again, employees tend to be much more accommodating with the first calls of the day, not the last.

- Be polite to these employees. No matter how you slice it, they are underpaid for the very thankless job of dealing day in and day out with hostile customers who don't want to be there in the first place.

JURY DUTY

The rule is you can get one official deferment (which you can mail in), before you have to serve. After the initial exemption, the next time you are called, you must appear in person if you wish to

> WE TELL OUR CLIENTS THAT IF YOU CAN'T GET THROUGH BY PHONE TO A LOCAL GOVERNMENT OFFICE, CALL THE MAIN HEADQUARTERS IN WASHINGTON D.C. WE HAVE FOUND THESE OFFICES MORE ACCESSIBLE. WE ALSO RECOMMEND TAKING ADVANTAGE OF EARLIER TIME ZONES AROUND THE COUNTRY. IF THE OFFICES ARE CLOSED IN NEW YORK, CALL THE ONE IN CHICAGO, LOS ANGELES, ETC.

request another deferment. If you have a job that you can't afford to leave, you can push the system some and just keep sending letters, until they start insisting you appear. The address in Manhattan is 60 Centre Street, Room 139. The hours are 8am - 5pm.

The only people who are exempt are those with disabilities and catastrophic illnesses. Attorneys, nurses, doctors, psychologists, judges, law enforcers, politicians, felons, people over seventy years old, mothers who stay at home with their children, and the self-employed are no longer automatically exempt. For further information call 212-374-3810.

BIRTH CERTIFICATE - FOR MORE INFORMATION, CALL 212-788-4500

If you go in person, you can walk out with your certificate. You can obtain a birth certificate for you or your child by going to the Health Department, 125 Worth Street, Room 133, between 9am and 4:30pm. You need a driver's license or another photo I.D. from your job. The cost - $15.

If you have no I.D. with you, you can get it mailed out to you or your parents the same day. What they will need is the full name on the birth certificate, date of birth, mother's maiden name, father's name, hospital or borough where the birth occurred, and the reason for the request.

If anyone other than yourself or your child is obtaining the certificate for you, that person has to bring a signed authorization and his own proof of I.D. as well as an original photo I.D. of you.

If you want to do it all by mail, send the same information, and a check for $15, to the Department of Health, Vital Records, 125 Worth Street, NY, NY 10013, in a self-addressed, stamped envelope. It takes about six weeks. You can put it on a credit card for an extra $5.

MOTOR VEHICLE BUREAU - FOR MORE INFORMATION CALL 212-645-5550

If you are getting a **car registration, plates and license for the first time,** you must go in person to 141-155 Worth Street between 8:30am and 4:00pm. You will fill out form MV82. You have to have one proof of ownership, proof of New York State insurance, and sales tax clearance. You also need your birth certificate and proof of signature. There will be a $5 fee for the title, $5.50 for the plates, a $15 surcharge and a variable fee based on the weight of your car. If you are just **renewing your registration,** all you need is proof of signature and your renewal card.

To renew a license, bring your current license, a proof of signature (such as credit card), plus proof of your current address (such as a utility or credit card statement). The fee is $28.00. The form you will fill out there is called a MV44.

New residents have thirty days to apply for a license and register their cars. You can pick up or get sent a license application and auto registration form. A valid out-of-state license exempts you from a road test and a written test. You must, however, take a vision test and get a photo taken. You can't make an appointment by phone.

If your license has lapsed, or you are applying for your first, you have to go through a series of steps. First you have to apply for a driver's permit by passing a twenty question written test, taking a vision test, and getting a photo taken. You will pay no more than $44.25. The written tests are given from 8:30am to 3:00pm. You must then complete a five-hour course at a licensed driving school. Finally, you take the road test. Sometimes it can take a while to get an appointment in the city. It can be easier to take the road test in the suburbs outside the city.

If you are a foreigner: A foreigner can drive up to a year in the U.S. using his home country's license and an international driver's permit that they must receive before coming to the US, as long as he/she has a passport and visa. In theory, a foreigner becoming a resident has only 30 days before he has to apply for a U.S. driver's permit. But it doesn't seem to be a rule that is strictly enforced. It then takes two - three months to complete the requirements. For information about the process and documents you need to produce call:

> YOU MAY WANT TO RENEW YOUR DRIVER'S LICENSE AND/OR REGISTRATION AT THE DEPARTMENT OF MOTOR VEHICLE OFFICE AT 300 WEST 34TH STREET. THE SERVICE IS QUICK BECAUSE THEY ONLY DO RENEWALS THERE.

Motor Vehicle Bureau in New York State 212-645-5550

Motor Vehicle Bureau in Connecticut 203-840-1993

Motor Vehicle Bureau in New Jersey 609-292-6500

YOU CAN MAKE TRAFFIC COMPLAINTS BY CALLING THE DEPARTMENT OF TRANSPORTATION HOTLINE AT CALL DOT.

IF YOU FIND YOUR CAR HOOKED TO A POLICE TOW TRUCK (ANYWHERE IN MANHATTAN), THE OPERATOR IS REQUIRED TO RELEASE IT (UNLESS YOU HAVE THREE OR MORE UNPAID PARKING TICKETS).
BUT YOU WILL HAVE TO PAY A "FIELD RELEASE PENALTY" OF $75 AS WELL AS THE PARKING TICKET.

IF YOU HAVE BEEN TOWED AND STILL HAVE OUTSTANDING PARKING TICKETS, YOU'LL BE TURNED AWAY AT THE CAR POUND.
GO FIRST TO THE PARKING VIOLATIONS BUREAU AND PAY UP. IF YOU HAVE GOTTEN TOWED BELOW 96TH STREET, YOUR CAR IS PROBABLY AT PIER 76, LOCATED AT WEST 38TH STREET AND 12TH AVE.

TRAFFIC TICKETS AND TOWING

If your car is at a meter that has expired, it'll cost you $55.

If you are parked on the wrong side in a no parking street cleaning zone-$55

If you are within fifteen feet of a fire hydrant, double parked, or parked in a no parking or no standing zone, $55

Fines are calculated on a thirty-day cycle. If a fine is not paid within thirty days, you will receive a $10 penalty; sixty days, $20 penalty, and so on. Once the fine is overdue by 120 days, it goes into judgment, and interest and additional penalties are accrued.

If you encounter a traffic cop in the middle of writing out the ticket, there's no point in trying to talk him out of it because he can get suspended for an incomplete ticket.

Call the Parking Violations Bureau at 212-477-4430 to find out how to pay the fine.

If you think your car has been towed, call 212-TOW-AWAY. If it has, you go direct to the pound with the car's registration and insurance card and your driver's license. Have either $150 in cash, traveler's checks, a certified check, or a money order. You can also use the Discover card or a NYCE bank card as long as the card is in your name. It will cost you $150 plus $15 a day for storage. The hours at the pound are Monday through Friday, 7am - 11pm. 7am - 7pm on Saturdays. Closed Sundays.

If you have three or more unpaid traffic tickets totaling at least $150, you will be considered a "scofflaw", and your vehicle will be towed by the Sheriff or Marshall's office.

MARRIAGE LICENSE - FOR MORE INFORMATION CALL 212-669-2400

With the proper documents, you can get a marriage license the same day. The marriage license bureau in Manhattan is at 1 Centre Street, and all the other boroughs have one. Their hours are 8:30am to 4:30pm.

You must marry within sixty days of obtaining your license. And it is only usable in New York State.

You need to bring proof of age and identification – either a passport, driver's license, birth certificate, military I.D., or school or work I.D.

You do not need to get a blood test or physical exam.

Any prior marriages must be listed along with termination dates, where the marriage was ended, and who the defendant was in the divorce.

The fee is $30 - payable in a money order only, made out to the City Clerk of New York.

SOCIAL SECURITY CARD - FOR MORE INFORMATION CALL 800-772-1213

If you need to apply for a new card, you can do it by mail or in person. Either way it takes two to three weeks. You can call the above number to find the office closest to you.

If you lose your card, you can get a replacement by mail or in person with the following documents: originals of two forms of I.D. such as a library card, a health insurance card, a club card, etc.

If you are applying for your child, you need to send originals of the child's birth certificate, another record of his birth such as his footprints, his hospital bracelet, a

OTHER AREAS WHERE YOUR CAR MAY BE IMPOUNDED:
MANHATTAN:
PIER 76 -WEST 38TH STREET AND 12TH AVENUE, 212-971-0770;
WASHINGTON HTS:
WEST 203RD ST. & 9TH AVE., 212-569-9099;
QUEENS:
56TH RD. & LAUREL HILL BLVD., 718-786-7123;
COLLEGE POINT BLVD. (129-05 31ST AVENUE), 718-445-0100;
BROOKLYN:
FT. GREEN - BROOKLYN NAVY YARD - SAND & NAVY STS. - 718-694-0698;
BRONX:
MOTT HAVEN - 745 EAST 141ST (SUTHIN BLVD. & BRUCKNER BLVD.), 718-694-0698.

IF YOU ENTREPRENEURS WITH COMMERCIAL VEHICLES ARE SICK OF EITHER PAYING OR CONTESTING ONE MORE PARKING TICKET, CALL THE TICKET FIGHTERS. FOR A SMALL FEE THEY WILL DO IT FOR YOU. (212) 666-6514. EVEN IF YOUR VEHICLE ISN'T COMMERCIAL, THEY MIGHT BE WILLING TO OFFER A LITTLE ADVICE ON HOW TO HANDLE YOUR PARTICULAR PROBLEM.

pediatrician's bill, a document with your child's name and address on it, and some I.D. of your own like a driver's license, canceled check, utility bill, or voter's card. There is no fee for this and of course, they will return your documents. You can also apply in person as long as you bring these documents with you.

When choosing a convenient social security office, try to avoid the big headquarters. The smaller chapters get you in and out faster.

If you are a foreigner: You must get a social security card when you arrive in the U.S. for the purpose of paying U.S. taxes. Call 1-800-772-1213 to find the nearest office to you. You must go in person and bring the following documents - birth certificate, passport, Visa, and all INS papers. It usually takes two to three weeks to receive your card in the mail.

> A QUICK WALK ACROSS THE BROOKLYN BRIDGE WILL TAKE YOU TO THE BROOKLYN BRANCH OF THE NEW YORK STATE LICENSE BUREAU, LOCATED AT 210 JORALEMON STREET, (212) 417-5747.
> THIS LOCATION IS MUCH QUICKER AND LESS CROWDED THAN THE MANHATTAN BUREAU.

PASSPORT

You can get a new passport at 376 Hudson Street (West Houston and King Street), between 7:30am and 3pm, by appointment only. Their number is (212) 206-3500.

If you are getting your first passport, you must go in person, bring proof of U.S. citizenship, such as your certified birth certificate, and one photo I.D. like a driver's license, employment card, school I.D., military card, plus two passport photos that you have had taken at any number of passport photo stores around the city. The fee is $65 for a ten-year passport; $40 for people under 18 years old for a five-year passport.

If you are renewing your passport, someone else can do it for you as long as that person brings two passport photos and your old passport. The fee is $55. You can also do it by mail if you have had your passport for at least 12 years and were 18 or older at the time of issuance. You need to fill out form DSP-82 and mail that along with two passport photos, your old passport and a check for $55. It'll take about three weeks.

If you have to get a passport immediately, bring your airline tickets as proof. You will pay a $30 expediting fee to receive your passport within three business days.

Try to avoid the passport office at holiday time. The line starts to form an hour before the doors open.

You can avoid the lines at the passport office completely by applying for one at your local post office or at a local Clerks of the State Supreme Court office. If it's your first, take all the necessary documentation with you, including your two passport photos and fill out the appropriate form DSP-11. The post office or clerks of the court will send it on to the passport office.

The following post offices and Clerks of the State Supreme Court are equipped to process your passport application:

POST OFFICES*

General Post Office, 8th Avenue and 33rd Street, (212) 967-8585

Ansonia Station, 40 West 66th Street, (212) 765-2469

Church Street Station, 90 Church Street (corner of Vesey Street), (212) 330-5349

Cooper Station, 93 Fourth Avenue (corner of 11th Street),
(212) 254-1389

Franklin D. Roosevelt Station, 909 Third Avenue (between 54th and 55th Streets), (212) 330-5598

Manhattanville Station, 365 West 125th Street, (212) 662-1901

* Ask the General Post Office for post offices in the boroughs.

CLERKS OF THE STATE SUPREME COURT

Court House, 60 Centre Street, Room 160, NYC 10007, (212) 374-0615

Kings County Supreme Court, 360 Adams Street, Brooklyn, New York 11201, (718) 643-8076

County Building, 851 Grand Concourse, Bronx, New York 10451, (718) 590-7541

YOU CAN CALL THE NATIONAL PASSPORT INFORMATION CENTER TO OBTAIN THE STATUS OF YOUR PASSPORT AND FOR GENERAL INFORMATION. THEIR TWENTY-FOUR HOUR AUTOMATED SERVICE NUMBER IS 900-225-5674. IT'S 35¢ PER MINUTE OR $1.05 PER MINUTE FOR OPERATOR ASSISTANCE, 8AM TO 8PM, MONDAY THROUGH FRIDAY. YOU CAN ALSO CALL 888-362-8668 TO SPEAK WITH AN ADVISOR, FOR A FLAT FEE OF $4.95 CHARGED TO A MAJOR CREDIT CARD.

YOU CAN HIRE "PASSPORT PLUS" TO HANDLE THE WHOLE PASSPORT PROCESS FOR YOU. JUST CALL THEM AT 800-903-2842 IF YOU ARE CALLING FROM OUT OF TOWN OR LOCALLY AT 212-759-5540. THEY WILL CHARGE YOU $50 IF YOU NEED YOUR PASSPORT WITHIN A WEEK; $65 FOR TWO-DAY SERVICE; $100 FOR ONE-DAY SERVICE; $150 THE SAME DAY. IF YOU ARE GETTING YOUR FIRST PASSPORT, YOU WILL HAVE TO SHOW UP YOURSELF, BUT "PASSPORT PLUS" GUARANTEES NO MORE THAN A 20 MINUTE WAIT.

RED TAPE CUTTERS (212) 406-9898 CAN TAKE CARE OF YOUR RED TAPE WORRIES. THEY CAN HELP YOU WITH JUST ABOUT ANY SERVICE—RENEW A PASSPORT, GET A SOCIAL SECURITY CARD OR BIRTH CERTIFICATE, REGISTER A CAR, PAY PARKING FINES, EVEN RETRIEVE YOUR CAR FROM THE POUND. YOU WILL PAY A CONSIDERABLE FEE FOR THESE SERVICES, BUT IF YOU WANT TO SAVE TIME AND A LOT OF STRESS, IT MAY BE A WORTHWHILE WAY TO SPEND YOUR MONEY.

Intrepid Pages of
Indoor &
Outdoor Oases

SOLUTIONS:
TO ESCAPING BIG CITY STRESS
BY STEALING A FEW QUIET, MEDITATIVE MINUTES,
WHENEVER...WHEREVER.

Nobody needs a "meditative moment" more than a stressed-out, fast talking, fast walking, wheeling, dealing New Yorker. Mercifully, there are places throughout the city to duck into, free of charge, for a few minutes of calm. It's not exactly an ashram. We call them urban oases. They remind you about the importance of deep breathing and quiet reflection.

INDOOR OASES

AT&T • 550 Madison Avenue
(at 56th Street)
Chemcourt • 277 Park Avenue (44th and 45th Streets)
Citicorp Center • Lexington Avenue (53rd and 54th Streets)
Equitable Center • 787 Seventh Avenue (52nd and 53rd Streets)
Ford Foundation • 320 East 43rd Street
The Frick Museum Reflecting Pool • 1 East 70th Street
The Galleria • 115 East 57th Street
IBM • 590 Madison Avenue (at 57th Street)
New York Public Library • 476 Fifth Avenue (42nd Street)
Olympic Tower • 641 Fifth Avenue (51st and 52nd Streets)
Park Avenue Plaza • 55 East 52nd Street
Poets House • 72 Spring Street (between Crosby and Lafayette Streets)
Trump Tower • 725 Fifth Avenue (57th Street)
World Financial Center • West Street

OUTDOOR OASES

Cloisters • Fort Tryon Park
The Conservatory Gardens • Fifth Avenue (at 105th Street)
Greenacre Park • 51st Street (between Second and Third Avenues)
Flower Garden at West 91st Street • Riverside Park (at 91st Street)
Jefferson Library Rose Garden • 425 Sixth Avenue (at 10th Street)

WE USE MANY OF NEW YORK'S URBAN OASES TO CONDUCT BUSINESS MEETINGS. THEY ARE FREE, TRANQUIL, AND MANY HAVE TABLES TO SIT AT AND SELF-HELP FOOD SERVICE.

BUY THE QUIET MACHINE, AN ANTI-NOISE POLLUTION DEVICE TO DROWN OUT THE CITY NOISE FROM FIRST & COMPANY, P.O. BOX 916, DEPT. G, FOREST HILLS, NEW YORK 11375.

OR, RUN THE FAN ON YOUR AIR CONDITIONER.

John Finley Walk at Carl Schurz Park • 84th to 89th Streets & East End Avenue

The McGraw-Hill Waterfalls • 48th Street (between Sixth and Seventh Avenues)

Metropolitan Museum of Art Roof Garden • Fifth Avenue (at 82nd Street)

Paley Park • 53rd Street (between Fifth and Madison Avenues)

Rockefeller Center • Fifth Avenue (at 50th Street)

United Nations Garden • First Avenue (at 45th Street)

MISCELLANEOUS OASES

Churches and Synagogues Locations Throughout the City

Lenox Hill Relaxation Booth • 434-2980

The Society Library at 79th St. between Madison & Park Avenues
$135 family membership, $90 for students.

Old fashioned, self-help library in beautiful old brownstone. (You don't need to be a member to use their in-library resources. You just can't take anything out.)

ASSERTIVENESS TRAINING FOR BIG CITY LIVING

PERCEPTION VS. REALITY:

There is nothing like a trip out of town to rekindle resentments about why we New Yorkers have to put up with big-city attitudes and lousy service, when just beyond our borders, service providers are hospitable, courteous and aiming to please.

The Intrepid New Yorker believes that at least 70% of the problem is that we get what we ask for. If we resign ourselves to lousy service, it's a self-fulfilling prophesy. NYC has more services and products to offer than any other city in the world. And much of it is good to world class. If you feel victimized, you aren't doing your homework, or demanding what is already your right. Many New Yorkers have gone numb to the fact that we as consumers have all sorts of legal rights and protections. Our tax dollars pay for a Consumer Affairs Department to guarantee those protections, and the Better Business Bureau reminds us that excellent service *is* our right. If we reclaim that posture, there will be satisfied consumers in every borough. And once you get into the habit, you will feel positively reborn!

WHAT CAN HAPPEN IF NEW YORKERS BEHAVE LIKE VICTIMS, NOT CONSUMER ACTIVISTS:

l. "Sorry, we told you up front that store credit, not refund, is our policy"

I recently bought two suits at an upscale designer boutique on Madison Avenue. I had to sign a paper stating that I understood I could not get a credit card refund, only store credit. I discovered upon getting home that there were a few defects in one of the suit jackets and slacks. I went to the sales lady who had helped me and told her I thought I had a valid reason to have my credit card refunded for that item. She said sorry, you know the store policy.

2. "Your reasons for the late video rental return aren't my problem, lady"

I rented a children's video. It got lost and forgotten amongst my child's toys and didn't get returned for six days. We told the manager of our video store about our mistake; his only comment was 'sorry, not my problem, you owe $18 in late charges.' I struggled for a compromise and offered to buy the tape outright for $20, which is what it would have cost brand new. We'd both come out with something. He didn't see my point of view.

3. "Only half my dining room set got delivered"

I ordered a dining room set. At the start, I was told it would take 12 weeks to deliver. I could have lived with that if, when the time came, they delivered the complete set. Upon arrival, however, two chairs were missing.

4. "My rent-a-car fiasco"

A family rented a car for a five-day vacation in the wilderness. They didn't realize until they were hours away from the garage that there was a terrible odor in the car that didn't go away even with all the windows down. And when the windows were up, the smell was truly awful. The problem was that the vacation spot was 100s of miles from the nearest rental company."

5. "But you promised my fabric would arrive today!"

An interior decorator had promised her client that the curtains she had ordered from Paris would arrive on time to be hung for an important dinner party. On delivery day a sales clerk called to say that they had not made it into the last shipment, and that all they could guarantee is that the curtains would arrive in the next shipment, five days later and post party.

6. "A customer service rep misquoted an airfare in my favor, and the airline refused to honor the low fare"

I was taking my family along on a business trip to England, so I started shopping for airfares. After getting quote after quote that was way over budget, I finally got a customer representative at one airline who quoted me a very low fare. I couldn't believe my good fortune. Several travel agents I talked to said the fare seemed too good to be true. In double checking it through a supervisor at the airline, I was told I had heard it wrong and would have to pay the real fare, which was much higher.

7. "The airplane was delayed three hours and I had two exhausted toddlers on my hands"

I was flying home with my kids to New York City from Louisiana, with a stop in Nashville. Our plane to Nashville was delayed causing us to miss our connecting flight. I went up to the flight director to see what could be done. They had nothing to offer me except the next flight out, leaving in three hours.

DON'T DESPAIR. HAPPY ENDINGS TO THESE STORIES CAN BE FOUND, BUT ONLY AFTER READING THE FOLLOWING 4 PRINCIPLES

SOLUTION:
THE FOUR GUIDING PRINCIPLES THAT WILL GUARANTEE EXCELLENT SERVICE

PRINCIPLE #1:

Getting good service starts with being an informed consumer: The more knowledge you have about your rights, the more of an activist you will become and the greater your consumer satisfaction.

PRINCIPLE #2:

It's up to you, not service providers, to come up with creative problem-solving ideas. Unfortunately, most service providers have not been trained in customer relations or problem-solving. They haven't heard the old axiom, "the customer is always right". And the people behind the counter are not programmed to bend policies and come up with solutions to your problems. So, you have to teach them, and come up with ideas for them.

> "SINCE 'CONSUMER COPS' CAN'T BE EVERYWHERE IN THIS TIME OF BUDGET AUSTERITY, IT'S ESSENTIAL TO EMPOWER AND EDUCATE CONSUMERS TO DEFEND THEMSELVES IN THE MARKETPLACE. ONLY WHEN EACH CONSUMER FEELS LIKE HE OR SHE IS CONSUMER AFFAIRS COMMISSIONER WILL PREDATORY BUSINESSES BE MOTIVATED TO COMPLY WITH THE LAW AND DO THE RIGHT THING".
>
> — MARK GREEN, FORMER COMMISSIONER OF THE NEW YORK CITY DEPARTMENT OF CONSUMER AFFAIRS

PRINCIPLE #3:

You will only attract bees with honey. If you don't treat service providers the way you would want to be treated, all the knowledge and problem-solving skills you have acquired will get you nowhere fast. You may have every justifiable reason in the world to get nasty, but it will just make the person behind the counter dig their heels in even deeper. No matter what has transpired, make them feel competent and important, and appeal to their human side. It can turn a diffident no into a willing yes.

Abraham Lincoln agrees with us:

"It is an old and true maxim that a drop of honey catches more flies than a gallon of gall. So with men. If you would win a man to your cause, first convince him that you are his sincere friend...On the contrary, assume to dictate to his judgement, or to command his action, or to mark him as one to be shunned and despised, and he will retreat within himself, close all the avenues to his head and his heart".

PRINCIPLE # 4:

Speak up for yourself and act confident even if you don't feel it.
The greatest obstacle to getting exactly the service you want is your own lack of conviction that it is your right. Take a front-row posture. Become a consumer activist. Just make sure you are "speaking up" to a decision-maker who has the authority to bend the rules.

THOSE HAPPY ENDINGS WE PROMISED YOU WHEN YOU APPLY ALL 4 PRINCIPLES

1a. Solution to "sorry, no refund...store policy":

"I asked to speak to the store manager. I politely explained that an expensive, Madison Avenue boutique should not be selling defective clothing in the first place. Second, under the circumstances, I would like a refund. The manager apologized profusely and not only gave me a refund on my suit, but offered to make some sizing adjustments on a second jacket and pair of slacks I bought, for free."

2a. Solution to the late video rental:

"I wondered if there was some way to get through to the manager of the video store, and make him see the situation from a customer's perspective. I pulled him aside quietly in order not to make a scene, and tried to appeal to his human side by introducing myself by name, asking his name and offering my hand in greeting. I explained that up until this point I had been a loyal customer, that I don't make a habit of turning in videos late, that it was a costly error on my part...couldn't we come up with a compromise, and a reason for me to guarantee him continued patronage...He saw my point, and allowed me to purchase the video, and our relationship changed from indifferent to friendly from that moment on".

3a. Solution to the delivery of half a dining room set:

"The Intrepid New Yorker told me that I have rights to exercise regarding furniture delivery. The Consumer Affairs Department advises not to accept partial delivery. (If you accept partial delivery, the only recourse you have is to give them thirty more days to deliver the rest, or just get that portion of the money back). If you don't accept partial delivery, and if the missing pieces do not arrive within

30 days hence, you have the option to cancel the order and get a full refund. So I made the delivery men put the furniture back on the truck. And I also convinced the furniture company that it was a reasonable request to loan me a dining room set until my set arrived".

4a. Solution to rent-a-car fiasco:

As soon as the family got to their vacation spot, they called the rental office to complain. Their immediate reaction was, bring the car back. The family tried, nicely, to tell them that a day of vacation would be lost making the exchange. They had no suggestions, so the family presented them with two — the option to either send someone up to make the exchange, or a full refund for the car when it was returned at the end of the vacation. When the rental company balked, the family told them they'd simply put the charge on hold with American Express while the bill was disputed. They acquiesced, and the family got their refund. That family learned a lesson: never start out in a rental before checking that everything in it is in perfect working order.

5a. Solution to the delayed curtains from Paris:

In this age of overnight deliveries, the interior decorator suggested to the store manager that, with a little extra effort, the curtains could be shipped overnight, at the store's expense. The manager was not thrilled, but he did comply, and the curtains were up for the dinner party.

6a. Solution to the misquoted airfare:

"I told the manager that I had, in fact, heard the customer rep correctly. The reason I was so sure of myself was because I had taken the time to write down her name, direct telephone number and all the other information that she had given me, which clearly, I couldn't have dreamed up. Due to my diligence, the manager called this customer rep for verification, and had to concede to me that I had been quoted that figure. As a result, the airline was forced to give me the tickets at that low price. The motto...write everything down and keep records!

7a. Solution to airport delays and two exhausted toddlers:

We told the flight director that we knew the delay was due to bad weather and not the fault of the airline, but that under the circumstances, we were requesting an upgrade to first class, so that the family could at least spread out to get some sleep. The flight director took pity on us and gave us the upgrade, along with passes into the first class airport lounge to get some food and rest. Let's face it, he would never have volunteered it. It really pays to ask.

DCA TRAVEL ADVISORY: YOU MAY BE PAYING HUNDREDS OF DOLLARS MORE FOR YOUR SUMMER VACATION IF YOU RELY ON AIRFARES QUOTED BY ONLY ONE TRAVEL AGENT, ACCORDING TO A SURVEY CONDUCTED BY THE DCA. THE "LOWEST" ROUND-TRIP FARES FOR FLIGHTS TO NINE DESTINATIONS QUOTED TO THE DEPARTMENT BY FORTY-NINE TRAVEL AGENTS VARIED BY AS MUCH AS 115 PERCENT. THE MAIN REASON IS SIMPLE: SOME TRAVEL AGENTS ARE LAZY, NEGLIGENT, OR POORLY TRAINED. IT CAN TAKE UP TO HALF AN HOUR TO DO A COMPLETE SEARCH FOR THE LOWEST FARES TO SOME DESTINATIONS. GOOD AGENTS ARE CREATIVE AND RESOURCEFUL AND WILL KNOW ABOUT SPECIAL DEALS AND RULES NOT PROVIDED ON THEIR COMPUTERS, AND WILL EXPLORE EVERY CHANNEL OPEN TO THEM.

SOLUTIONS: FOLLOWING PRINCIPLE # 1: BECOMING AN INFORMED CONSUMER

It's simple. The more informed you are, and the more aware you are of your rights, the less chance you have of being taken advantage of. There are organizations in New York that have been set up for the sole purpose of informing and protecting you! And it will cost you nothing, or next to nothing, to use them.

THE DEPARTMENT OF CONSUMER AFFAIRS ("DCA")

This government agency was created for you and is paid for by your tax dollars - all to enforce the Consumer Protection Law forbidding "deceptive or unconscionable trade practices in the sale, lease, rental or loan of any consumer goods or services or in the collection of consumer debt". This agency is one-stop assistance for the consumer. So use it! Here's how:

Business and Service provider inquiries: By calling the DCA at 212-487-4444, employees will advise you as to whether a business has a record of previous complaints or violations on file. They will not, however, recommend a particular business or product.

Information: The DCA helps consumers prevent problems before they arise. The Public Affairs staff produces a continuous flow of consumer advisory pamphlets, booklets, and fact sheets free of charge. By calling the agency's Interactive Voice Response number - 212-487-4444 - you can receive a faxed list of publications, or you can send a self-addressed, stamped envelope to The Department of Consumer Affairs, Free Tips, 42 Broadway, NY, NY 10004. They also provide a tape library service called Tel-Consumer/Tel-Law that enables consumers to call in at 212-487-3938 and listen to over 100 tapes on important legal and consumer issues like "Credit Bureaus-Somebody Is Talking About You,

"Buying a Used Car," "Your Rights in the Supermarket", etc. Information can also be accessed on their web site at www.ci.nyc.ny.us/consumers.

Investigation and Mediation of Your Complaint: If you need help resolving a complaint, you can contact the DCA complaint line at 212-487-4444 from 9:30 a.m. -4:30 p.m. Advisors will answer questions or give referrals over the phone concerning situations as diverse as destruction of a video store's rental tape to cancellation of tours booked through travel agents. If mediation is required, your advisor will explain the process.

Licensing of Businesses: In order to further protect consumers, the DCA has the authority to license and regulate fifty-five different types of businesses, thereby requiring them to meet certain specifications of integrity, honesty, fair practices and safety. You can call the DCA to find out which businesses are required to be licensed, or request their brochure called "Do I Need A Consumer Affairs License", which lists them.

BETTER BUSINESS BUREAU ("BBB")

The BBB is a nationwide, private, non-profit corporation funded by the responsible business community. It offers membership to companies that meet their own high standards of business practice and ethics. It also offers a refuge to consumers giving them information they need to protect themselves against faulty and dishonest practices and a place to take their complaints and get help in resolving their disputes. For general inquiries about how to use the BBB, call 212-533-6200, or check their web site at www.newyork.bbb.org.

ELECTRONICS STORES MUST DISCLOSE IF THEY ARE CHARGING MORE THAN THE MANUFACTURER'S SUGGESTED RETAIL PRICE (MSRP), BUT MANY DON'T. MANY STORES MISLABEL PRICE TAGS ON DISPLAYS. YOU CAN CHECK THE MSRP BEFORE ENTERING THE STORE BY CALLING THE MANUFACTURER'S 800#.

UNDER NEW YORK STATE LAW, BUSINESSES WHICH SELL HOME FURNISHINGS, OR MAJOR APPLIANCES, ARE REQUIRED TO LIST THE DELIVERY DATE OR RANGE OF DATES IN WRITING ON THEIR CONTRACT. THIS MUST BE DONE ON THE CUSTOMER'S COPY AT THE TIME THE ORDER IS TAKEN. (THIS LAW DOES NOT COVER CUSTOM-MADE GOODS.) THE BUSINESS MUST DELIVER THE MERCHANDISE BY THE LATEST DELIVERY DATE, OR THE CONSUMER MAY: 1. CANCEL THE CONTRACT AND OBTAIN A FULL REFUND WITHIN TWO WEEKS OF THE COMPANY'S RECEIPT OF THEIR REQUEST; 2. NEGOTIATE A NEW DELIVERY DATE; 3. CANCEL THE CONTRACT AND OBTAIN CREDIT FOR THE DEPOSIT; 4. SELECT NEW FURNITURE OR APPLIANCES. THIS DOES NOT APPLY IF THE DELIVERY DELAY WAS CAUSED BY A STRIKE, ACT OF GOD, OR BY THE CONSUMER.

THE BETTER BUSINESS BUREAU

Reliability Ratings: The BBB gives companies reliability ratings that you the consumer can use to make an informed choice about whether to do business with that company. You can call the BBB at 900-CALL-BBB and, for 95c per minute, get information about a company. You can also send your request in writing to: The Better Business Bureau, 257 Park Avenue South, New York, NY 10010.

Consumer Advisories: The BBB offers advisories for consumers on topics such as getting refunds, delivery rights, mail order, credit cards, home improvement, new-and-used-car lemon law, etc. Call 212-533-6200 to order a printed copy.

Mediation/Arbitration: The BBB is not a law enforcement agency like the DCA, which means it cannot take legal action against a company or close it down. But it can mediate or arbitrate a customer's complaint. If you have a complaint, they will give you a case number and send you forms requesting information that you will read, fill out, and send back. Your mediator will then contact the company on your behalf and try to work out a settlement between you and the company in question. (You can also file a complaint on line at www.newyork.bbb.org.)

NYC DEPARTMENT OF CONSUMER AFFAIRS

CONSUMER GUIDES

- Fifty Plus Diner's Guide
- Protecting Your Privacy
- Protect Yourself From On-line Scams
- Guide to Small Claims Court
- Summary of NYC Consumer Protection Law Rules
- Avoiding Cellular Phone Fraud
- Visitors Consumer Tips (Available in English, Spanish, Italian, Chinese, Japanese, Arabic, French, and German.)
- Rights and Duties of Divorce Clients
- Beware of Immigration Services Fraud! (Available in English, Spanish, Chinese, Haitian-Creole, Arabic, French and Russian in PDF Format)
- Administrative Hearing Guide
- Fashionably Aware: The Consumer Guide to Modeling and Talent Agencies

AUTOS

- Auto Rentals
- Guide to Auto Repairs
- Guide to Used Car Purchases

HOME & HEALTH

- The High Cost of Dying- Rising Prices and Consumer Deception in the Funeral Industry
- When A Loved One Dies, A Guide to Help You Through Immediate Concerns
- Avoiding The Wedding Bell Blues: A Consumer Guide to Planning Your Wedding
- Consumer Guide to Home Improvement
- Don't Make a Move Without It: The Consumer Guide to Moving & Storage Services
- Glossary of Managed Care Terms
- The Resource Guide to Breast Cancer Services
- 1999 Prescription and Over-the-Counter Drug Survey
- 1999 Prescription and Over-the-Counter Drug Survey for Seniors

PERSONAL FINANCES

- Do-It-Yourself Guide to Fixing Your Credit Report
- Consumer Guide to Tax Preparation Services
- The Basics About "Lifeline" Basic Banking
- Losing Face: A Consumer Guide to Identity Theft
- Computers From A to Z: A Beginner's Guide to Buying a Computer
- Control Cramming! Study Your Phone Bill!

QUICK FACTS

- Shopping by Mail or Phone
- Refund Policies
- Debt Collection
- Generic Drugs

THE BBB PROVIDES AN ANNUALLY UPDATED LIST OF HUNDREDS OF BUSINESSES AND SERVICES IN THE NEW YORK AREA THAT HAVE VOLUNTEERED TO BECOME "MEMBERS IN GOOD STANDING" OF THE AGENCY. THE BBB SCREENS ITS MEMBERS CAREFULLY; THEY HAVE TO HAVE BEEN IN BUSINESS ONE YEAR, HAVE A SATISFACTORY RECORD WITH THE BBB, AND AGREE TO UPHOLD BBB'S STANDARDS - ETHICAL SELLING PRACTICES, PROMPT RESPONSE TO CONSUMER COMPLAINTS, AND TRUTHFUL ADVERTISING.

BBB CAR RENTAL ADVISORY: ADVERTISED RATES ARE NOT ALWAYS THE PRICE YOU WILL PAY. SOME FIRMS REQUIRE RENTERS TO PAY AN ADDITIONAL AMOUNT FOR FUEL, ADDITIONAL DRIVER INSURANCE, OR AN AIRPORT FEE. THE BBB MAINTAINS THAT THE ADVERTISED PRICE SHOULD BE THE PRICE CONSUMERS CAN EXPECT TO PAY. REQUIRED FEES SHOULD BE DISCLOSED IN PRINT. NOT ALL FIRMS COMPLY WITH THESE STANDARDS SO ALWAYS INQUIRE ABOUT ADDITIONAL FEES.

DCA AUTO REPAIR ADVISORY: DON'T AUTHORIZE ANY WORK UNLESS YOU UNDERSTAND EXACTLY WHAT YOU ARE SIGNING. ALWAYS READ THE SMALL PRINT. NO WORK MAY LEGALLY BE DONE WITHOUT YOUR PERMISSION. GET AN ITEMIZED BILL. CHECK IT AGAINST ANY ESTIMATE OR AUTHORIZATION FORMS SO THAT YOU ARE CERTAIN THAT YOU HAVE BEEN CHARGED ONLY FOR WORK YOU WANTED TO HAVE COMPLETED. IF YOU THINK YOU HAVE BEEN OVERCHARGED FOR PARTS, YOU MAY WANT TO ASK TO SEE THE SUPPLIER'S PARTS PRICE LIST, WHICH GIVES RETAIL AND WHOLESALE PRICES.

THERE IS A HIGHLY RECOMMENDABLE BOOK YOU CAN PURCHASE IN NEW YORK BOOK STORES CALLED: "GET-A-GRIP NEW YORK: HOW TO COMPLAIN EFFECTIVELY AND GET SATISFACTION" WRITTEN BY RAYMOND ALVIN

THE CONSUMER RESOURCE HANDBOOK

This invaluable book, published by the U.S. Office of Consumer Affairs, offers over 100 pages of general advice for the consumer on topics ranging from home financing to insurance scams. It also includes lists of nationwide organizations that can help you address problems and resolve complaints. Those lists include:

- Consumer assistance directory of consumer organizations
- Corporate consumer contacts
- State, county and city government consumer protection offices
- Trade Associations and other dispute resolution programs

You can send away for it to:

Consumer Resource Handbook
Consumer Information Center
Pueblo, Colorado 81009
719-948-3334

- or call their bulletin board system at 202-208-7679
- or locate their web site at www.pueblo.gsa.gov
- You can also send away for their *Consumer Information Catalog* of more than 200 consumer advisory publications.

CONSUMER REPORTS MAGAZINE

This monthly magazine, offering the latest consumer reports on every conceivable product from cars to toasters, can be bought off the newsstand, subscribed to, or back issues on particular products can be ordered for a small fee, by calling 914-378-2740. You can also find them at your local library or on line at www.consumerreports.org. There is an online subscription fee of $19 annually if you already have a magazine subscription; $24 if you do not.

USE THE INTREPID NEW YORKER "PREVENTATIVE CHECKLIST" TO AVOID FRAUD OR NEGLIGENCE

- Read about the product or service you are about to purchase.
- Compare stores, services offered, product brands, and prices.
- Is the service required to be licensed? Call the DCA at 212-487-4444 to find out.
- Call the BBB to make sure the company is reliable.
- Know your rights up front. Get the advisories you need to educate yourself first.
- What are the store's policies regarding returns, refunds, warranties, etc.
- Read the fine print on all contracts and receipts.
- Make sure that everything you agreed to, such as delivery fees and servicing costs, is in writing.
- Ask if there are any hidden charges.
- Put big purchase items on a credit card. If you have a problem, you can withhold payment until your credit card company completes an investigation.

> "EMPHASIZING CUSTOMER SATISFACTION IS ECONOMICAL BECAUSE IT COSTS FIVE TIMES MORE TO WIN NEW CUSTOMERS THAN TO KEEP EXISTING ONES COMING BACK."
>
> —BETTER BUSINESS BUREAU

DEPARTMENT OF CONSUMER AFFAIRS COMMISSIONER, JULES POLONETSKY'S, FIVE STEPS TO RESOLVE CONSUMER DISPUTES

1. RETURN TO THE STORE and explain your problem to the salesperson, manager, or owner of the business. Unless an agreement between the consumer and the business owner specifically states how consumer problems can be resolved (exchange, repair, refund, cancellation), you should also explain how you would like to have the complaint resolved. Call the DCA's Tel Consumer/Tel-Law tape library at 212-487-3938 and listen to Tape #103 for suggestions on how to make an effective complaint.

2. PUT THE TERMS OF THE RESOLUTION IN WRITING, and send it back to the business representative via certified mail, return receipt requested.

3. If the business representative does not agree to resolve the complaint, **IMMEDIATELY PUT THE DETAILS OF YOUR COMPLAINT IN WRITING AND SEND IT TO THE PRESIDENT OR OWNER** of the business via certified mail, return receipt requested. Keeps copies for your own records. The letter should include such details as the date of the transaction, the problem, and how you would like the problem resolved.

4. Still no satisfaction? **CONTACT THE DCA COMPLAINTS HOTLINE AT 212-487-4444.** Be patient. The agency handles over 100,000 complaints and inquiries annually. Alternatively, write to the Complaints Division and briefly describe the complaint (including the business's name and address, date of the transaction, and a contact phone where you can be reached during regular business hours). Also include documentation (copies of contracts, sales slips, receipts, bills, cancelled checks, credit card statements). If Consumer Affairs can't help you, they will refer you to the agency that can.

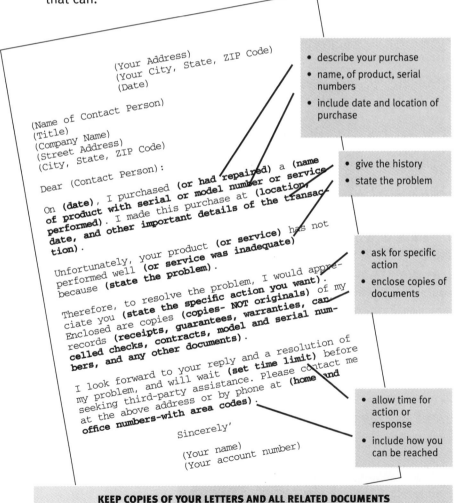

(Your Address)
(Your City, State, ZIP Code)
(Date)

(Name of Contact Person)
(Title)
(Company Name)
(Street Address)
(City, State, ZIP Code)

Dear (Contact Person):

On (date), I purchased (or had repaired) a (name of product with serial or model number or service performed). I made this purchase at (location, date, and other important details of the transaction).

- describe your purchase
- name, of product, serial numbers
- include date and location of purchase

Unfortunately, your product (or service) has not performed well (or service was inadequate) because (state the problem).

- give the history
- state the problem

Therefore, to resolve the problem, I would appreciate you (state the specific action you want). Enclosed are copies (copies- NOT originals) of my records (receipts, guarantees, warranties, cancelled checks, contracts, model and serial numbers, and any other documents).

- ask for specific action
- enclose copies of documents

I look forward to your reply and a resolution of my problem, and will wait (set time limit) before seeking third-party assistance. Please contact me at the above address or by phone at (home and office numbers—with area codes).

Sincerely'

(Your name)
(Your account number)

- allow time for action or response
- include how you can be reached

KEEP COPIES OF YOUR LETTERS AND ALL RELATED DOCUMENTS

SOLUTION:
USE YOUR COMMUNITY RESOURCES TO TURN YOUR NEIGHBORHOOD INTO A SANCTUARY

Your local New York City government is only as good as the standards set by its citizens. It takes citizen participation to maintain a community in which you are contented to live. Municipal services are already overtaxed, so you can't expect them to plan for all your needs. The good news, however, is that your tax dollars don't just get swallowed up into a black hole. Some are earmarked for your neighborhood's local Community Board, which operates at your service. This board holds regularly scheduled public meetings to hear your grievances, and then they take them up with the appropriate city officials for consideration. If you want to have a say about how your tax dollars are being spent in your community, this is the resource.

A GROUP OF MOTHERS IN CHELSEA FILED A COMPLAINT WITH THEIR COMMUNITY BOARD THAT THE NEIGHBORHOOD PLAYGROUND THEY SHARED WAS OFTEN VANDALIZED AND USED FOR DRUG TRANSACTIONS AFTER DARK. BECAUSE OF THE SWIFT AND COLLECTIVE ACTION OF BOTH THE MOTHERS AND THE BOARD, WITHIN SIX MONTHS, THE PLAYGROUND WAS EXPANDED, CLEANED UP, AND LOCKED NIGHTLY TO KEEP LOITERERS OUT.

HOW A COMMUNITY BOARD WORKS

There are fifty-nine community boards throughout New York's boroughs. Each has up to fifty non-salaried members, some appointed by the borough president, and some nominated by city council members in the district. Board members are selected from among active citizens from each community. Their job is to monitor the quality of service-providers in the district, consider zoning and land use proposals, recommend budget priorities, and function as your community information and complaint center.

IF YOU ARE NEW TO THE NEIGHBORHOOD, THE BEST WAY TO GET TO KNOW WHAT'S GOING ON IN YOUR COMMUNITY IS TO GO TO ONE OF THE REGULARLY SCHEDULED COMMUNITY BOARD MEETINGS HELD NEAR BY.

The community board's District Manager is your direct contact. District Managers function as ombudsmen, information sources, community organizers, mediators and municipal managers. They are, above all, public servants with the most direct ties to your local community.

Board meetings are held monthly to address items of concern to the community. Board meetings are open to the public, and the

COMMUNITY BOARDS ARE THE MOST GRASSROOTS LEVEL OF MUNICIPAL GOVERNMENT, SERVING AS A LINK BETWEEN RESIDENTS OF THE DISTRICT AND CITY AGENCIES. THE BOARD OFFICE HANDLES DOZENS OF COMPLAINTS EVERY MONTH RANGING IN SUBJECT FROM GARBAGE COLLECTION, TO NOISY BARS, TO BROKEN STREETLIGHTS — ANYTHING RELATED TO THE DELIVERY OF CITY SERVICES. OUR COMMITTEES HOLD PUBLIC HEARINGS EVERY MONTH ON ISSUES SUCH AS TRAFFIC AND TRANSPORTATION, RECONSTRUCTION PROJECTS IN PARKS, SIDEWALK CAFÉS, LIQUOR LICENSES, CHANGES TO LANDMARK BUILDINGS AND ZONING CHANGES. MOST BOARDS HAVE MAILING LISTS AND SEND OUT A MONTHLY CALENDAR. ALL MEETINGS ARE OPEN TO THE PUBLIC. BY GETTING INVOLVED, YOU'LL NOT ONLY LEARN ABOUT A VARIETY OF LOCAL ISSUES, BUT YOU'LL ALSO BECOME AN ADVOCATE FOR YOUR COMMUNITY.

—DENISE WOODIN, FORMER DISTRICT MANAGER, COMMUNITY BOARD NUMBER 8

public must be allowed to speak and express opinions during a portion of the meeting. However, only board members may vote. Board committees then implement what has been acted on at the meetings. Board actions and decisions are basically advisory.

You can apply to become a member of your community board. The number to call in Manhattan for an application is 212-669-8300.

The Intrepid Pages of
Community Board Take-Action Numbers & Mediation Centers

COMMUNITY BOARD # 1

Mr. Paul Goldstein
49-51 Chambers Street

(Canal Street—western border to Hudson River; eastern border to Baxter Street)
(212) 442-5050

COMMUNITY BOARD # 2

Mr. Arthur Strickler
3 Washington Square Village
(14th Street to Canal Street, the Bowery to Hudson River)
(212) 979-2272

COMMUNITY BOARD # 3

Ms. Martha Danziger
59 East 4th Street
(East River to the Bowery, 14th Street to the Brooklyn Bridge)
(212) 533-5300

COMMUNITY BOARD # 4

Mr. William Kelley
330 West 42nd Street
(14th Street to 26th Street from Avenue of the Americas to Hudson River, and 27th Street to 59th Street from Eighth Avenue to Hudson River)
(212) 736-4536

COMMUNITY BOARD # 5

Ms. Kathy Kinsella
450 Seventh Avenue (at 34th Street)
(14th Street to 59th Street, Lexington to Eighth Avenues)
(212) 465-0907

COMMUNITY BOARD # 6

Ms. Carol Pieper
330 East 26th Street

(14th Street to 59th Street, Lexington Avenue to East River)
(212) 679-0907

COMMUNITY BOARD # 7

Ms. Penny Ryan
250 West 87th Street
(59th Street to 110th Street, Hudson River to Central Park West)
(212) 362-4008

COMMUNITY BOARD # 8

Ms. Victoria Caramanle
505 Park Avenue, 6th Floor
(59th Street to 96th Street, Fifth Avenue to East River, and
Roosevelt Island)
(212) 758-4340

COMMUNITY BOARD # 9

Mr. Lawrence McClean
565 West 125th Street
(110th Street to 155th Street, Hudson River to Edgecomb Avenue)
(212) 864-6200

COMMUNITY BOARD # 10

Mr. Richard Harley
215 West 125th Street
(110th Street to 155th Street, west side of Fifth Avenue and east
side of St. Nicholas Avenue)
(212) 749-3105

COMMUNITY BOARD # 11

Ms. Jannette Irizarry
55 East 115th Street
(North 96th Street to East 142nd Street)
(FDR Drive to east Fifth Avenue)
(212) 831-8929

COMMUNITY BOARD # 12

Ms. Gregoria Feliciana
711 West 168th Street
(North side of West 155th Street to 220th Street)
(Harlem River to the Hudson River)
(212) 568-8500

MEDIATION CENTERS

There are Mediation Centers in all five boroughs that will help resolve issues, free of charge, that might otherwise go to civil or criminal court...everything from quality of life issues, such as excessive noise and restaurant odors, to common interpersonal disputes. Lawyers, teachers and police officers volunteer their time as trained mediators to resolve problems, and get agreements put in writing and signed. Resolutions take about a week although more time may be required depending on the complexity of the problem.

Manhattan Mediation Center - 212-577-1740

346 Broadway, Suite 400W
NY, NY 10013

Brooklyn Mediation Center - 718-834-6671

210 Joralemon St, Room 618
Brooklyn, NY 11201

**Bronx Institute for Mediation & Conflict Resolution
718-585-1190**

384 East 149th Street, Suite 330
Bronx, NY 10455

Queens Mediation Network - 718-523-6868

89-64 163rd St.
Jamaica, NY 11432

Staten Island Community Dispute Center - 718-720-9410

42 Richmond Terrace, 4th Floor
Staten Island, NY 10301

The Intrepid Pages of
"Quality of Life" Take-Action Numbers

BANKING PROBLEMS

Comptroller of the Currency, Northeastern district

For banking problems with national banks.
212-819-9860

Federal Reserve Board's Division of Consumer and Community Affairs

For banking problems with Federal Reserve-member banks.
202-452-3693

Federal Trade Commission

For violations of credit card solicitation regulation.
877-382-4357

New York State Banking Department

Complaints with New York State-chartered banks.
800-522-3330

COMMUNITY ACTION NUMBERS

Mayor's Action Center

Receives calls about your problems and complaints on all City issues, including the environment, housing, and social service programs.

212-788-7585

Public Advocate (watchdog office) - Mark Green

Acts as go-between for New York City residents and city agencies.

212-669-7250

Quality of Life Hotline

Quality of life complaints like noise and pollution can be reported to the representatives at this hotline, who will forward the information to the appropriate authority.

888-677-LIFE

MARK GREEN, PUBLIC ADVOCATE, HAS HIS OWN WEB SITE. AT **WWW.PUBADVOCATE.NYC.GOV/~ADVOCATE/ADVOTEXT.HTML** YOU CAN FIND OUT HOW TO BEST RESOLVE YOUR CONSUMER PROBLEMS. THE WEB SITE WILL ALSO PROVIDE YOU WITH THE NAMES AND PHONE NUMBERS OF THE APPROPRIATE CITY AGENCIES AND COMMISSIONERS.

LEGAL REFERRAL SERVICES, SPONSORED BY THE ASSOCIATION OF THE BAR OF THE CITY OF NEW YORK AND THE NEW YORK COUNTY LAWYERS' ASSOCIATION, WILL SET UP APPOINTMENTS FOR A FREE HALF HOUR LEGAL CLINIC. ISSUES COVERED INCLUDE GENERAL CONSUMER LAW, BANKRUPTCY, LANDLORD/ TENANT ISSUES, EMPLOYMENT LAW, AND FAMILY/ MATRIMONIAL LAW. PRIVATE LEGAL CONSULTATIONS ARE ALSO AVAILABLE AT $25 FOR THE FIRST HALF HOUR. IN SOME CASES, FREE PRIVATE LEGAL CONSULTATIONS CAN BE ARRANGED. CONTACT LEGAL REFERRAL SERVICES AT (212) 626-7373.

THE NEW YORK BAR ASSOCIATION PROVIDES A FREE LAW CLINIC ON MONDAYS FROM 5:30 - 7:30PM AT THE ASSOCIATION'S HEADQUARTERS AT 36 WEST 44TH ST, ROOM 310. THEY WILL ANSWER YOUR QUESTIONS ON ALL SORTS OF LEGAL MATTERS, AND WHEN NECESSARY, REFER YOU TO A PRIVATE ATTORNEY WHO CAN PROVIDE A PRIVATE CONSULTATION FOR $25 AND UP.

MOVING COMPANY COMPLAINTS
Department of Transportation
718-482-4816

NOISE
Department of Environmental Protection
A Help line for environmental noise issues, including construction activity and commercial music from bars and nightclubs.
718-DEP-HELP
F.A.N.N.Y (Friends Against Noisy New York)
A quarterly newsletter concerning all aspects of noise.
212-229-0202
State Liquor Authority/Patron disturbances
A Help line for people disturbed by companies in violation of the State Liquor License Law.
212-417-4069

PUBLIC TRANSPORTATION COMPLAINTS
MTA Customer Service
718-330-3322
Bus Customer Service
718-927-7499

"TAKE IT UP WITH THE LAW"
NY Bar Association Referral Line
212-626-7373
Small Claims Court
212-374-5776

TELEPHONE AND MAIL HARASSMENT

Annoyance Call Bureau

Provides assistance if you are the recipient of harassing phone calls, excessive hang ups, or relentless telemarketers.

212-890-6200

Direct Marketing Association - Mail and Telephone Preference Service

They can take your name off national mailing lists.

212-768-7277

Private Citizens

An organization that tells you how to fight back against junk callers and junk mailers.

800-CUT-JUNK

WEB SITES FOR THE SAVVY CONSUMER

Better Business Bureau • www.bbb.org

Consumer World • www.consumerworld.org

Consumer World is a public service, non-commercial site which has gathered over 1800 of the most useful consumer resources over the internet.

Federal Trade Commission • www.ftc.gov

The FTC enforces a variety of federal antitrust and consumer protection laws.

National Fraud Information Center • www.fraud.org

NFIC: a non-profit consumer organization to fight the growing menace of telemarketing and internet fraud.

Public Eye • www.thepubliceye.com

Monitoring internet merchants for reliability and customer satisfaction.

TenantNet • www.tenant.net

The online resource guide for residential tenants in NYC and New York state.

U.S. Consumer Gateway • www.consumer.gov

Your online link to Federal consumer information.

U.S. Securities and Exchange Commission • www.sec.gov

FEELING SAFE & SECURE

PERCEPTION VS. REALITY

Everybody has heard the news. The streets of New York have never been safer. Crime has been reduced by a stunning 40% within the last few years. And yet, unsettling headlines persist. From our perspective – a lifelong familiarity with NYC, we have always felt comfortably safe. But that genuine feeling of security comes from an intimate knowledge of our city, the constant use of plain old common sense, as well as crime prevention resources that are available to all of us.

And just as important...feeling safe and secure is about staying within our individual "comfort zones".

PSYCHOLOGICAL COMFORT ZONES:

Your psychological outlook about safety is just as important to your well-being as the crime-prevention guidelines you practice. What feels perfectly comfortable to someone else may not be comfortable to you. No matter how many people tell you how safe they feel in a building with no doorman or on a subway after 10PM, you may not. Never compromise on the level of security you need to feel safe in this city. Stay true to your own comfort zone, and it will make all the difference in the quality of your life in New York. This rule applies not only to the building you live in, but the neighborhood you call home, the places you jog, and the way you commute to work.

COMMON SENSE:

Common sense is what you already know instinctively to be true. Most crimes happen to people who aren't listening to their own good judgment, do not have their antennae up and are not paying attention to what's going on around them at that moment. If you find yourself in a situation that doesn't feel right to you, it probably isn't.

SOLUTION:
OUR NY POLICE PROVIDE SAFETY THROUGH "DO'S AND DON'T'S" PAMPHLETS

THE POLICE DEPARTMENT PUBLISHES PAMPHLETS OF BASIC SAFETY TIPS:

You can obtain them from your local precinct or by writing to the Crime Prevention Division at 34-1/2 East 12th Street, New York, NY 10003, (212) 614-6741. There are free brochures on:

- Safeguarding men
- Safeguarding women
- Safety tips for the older person
- Crime prevention for children
- Safety tips for runners
- Safeguarding your auto
- Robbery prevention for small businesses and stores
- Burglary prevention for your business
- Safeguarding your apartment

A SUMMARY OF IMPORTANT SAFETY PRECAUTIONS ON THE STREET:

- Minimize the amount of money and credit cards you carry daily or divide your money between pockets and bags.
- Don't keep your wallet in the rear trouser pocket but in an inside jacket pocket or in a side trouser pocket with a handkerchief over it or keep your wallet sideways in your pocket.
- Carry your bag close to your body, tucked in the bend of your elbow. Don't carry a bag in such a casual way that it turns you into a potential target.
- Be particularly alert in crowds.
- Park your car in a well lighted area not only to deter personal attack but to reduce the chance for auto theft.
- Avoid streets not well lit or traveled, especially at night. If you can't avoid them, have a taxi drop you off at the door and ask the driver to wait until you are safely inside.
- Take an inventory of stores and buildings in your neighborhood that can offer refuge.
- If you think someone may be following you, go to the nearest refuge immediately.

A SUMMARY OF SAFETY PRECAUTIONS FOR RUNNERS:

- Don't ever run alone in a deserted area or at night. Run in well trafficked areas if you are running alone or run with a designated partner or group. There are many jogging, blading and bike clubs you can join.

- If you must run at night, wear light-reflecting or light-colored clothing.

- Be totally familiar with your route. Know the locations of phones, call boxes, police stations, fire houses, hospitals and 24-hour businesses.

- Listen to your instincts and vary your route if you sense you are getting into potential danger.

- Run against traffic whenever possible.

- Be aware of who is around you at all times.

- Don't acknowledge or respond to verbal harassment.

- Carry a whistle or bicycle airhorn to summon emergency assistance.

- Don't wear jewelry.

- Avoid wearing headphones. Tune into your surroundings, not out.

- Always carry some form of personal I.D.

THE NEW YORK CITY POLICE DEPARTMENT OFFERS FREE SECURITY SURVEYS FOR YOUR HOME, OFFICE, OR BUSINESS. CRIME PREVENTION LECTURE PROGRAMS CAN ALSO BE ARRANGED FOR YOUR BUSINESS OR NEIGHBORHOOD CIVIC ORGANIZATION. JUST CALL OR WRITE:

COMMANDING OFFICER, CRIME PREVENTION DIVISION, 34-1/2 EAST 12TH STREET, NEW YORK, NY 10003, (212) 614-6741.

A SUMMARY OF SAFETY PRECAUTIONS FOR CHILDREN:

- Make sure you know your full name, address and telephone number and how to dial 911.

- Be sure to lock doors and windows when you are home alone.

- Never open the door to anyone you are not expecting.

- If someone calls asking for your parent or guardian, tell them they can't come to the phone and take a message.

- Don't speak to strangers in a public restroom, and don't loiter.

- Don't wear anything that shows your name.

- Always tell an adult where you are going, with whom you will be, and when you will return.

- Familiarize yourself with your neighborhood. Look for places you can go for refuge.

- Don't take shortcuts through deserted areas! Walk and play in open areas where you can see and be seen by other people.

THE NEW YORK CITY POLICE DEPARTMENT ALSO OFFERS CRIME PREVENTION DECALS FOR YOUR HOME AND AUTO AS A VISUAL DETERRENT TO A POTENTIAL BURGLAR. ANOTHER PROGRAM CALLED OPERATION IDENTIFICATION INVOLVES ETCHING YOUR SOCIAL SECURITY NUMBER INTO YOUR PERSONAL BELONGINGS SHOULD YOUR HOME BE BURGLARIZED. CALL YOUR LOCAL PRECINCT FOR MORE INFORMATION ON THESE PROGRAMS.

A SUMMARY OF SAFETY PRECAUTIONS THAT WILL PROTECT YOU AT HOME:

- Have your key ready before you get to the front door.
- Make sure your entrance way is well lit.
- Don't be polite and hold the lobby door open for a stranger who has been waiting.
- Don't buzz someone in unless you know them.
- If a stranger asks to use your phone for an emergency, don't let him in. Offer to make the call for him.
- If you arrive home and find your door open, do not go inside. Call the police from a phone booth or neighbor's house.
- Don't get on an elevator with a stranger if your own good judgment tells you not to. To avoid embarrassment say something like, "oh, I forgot my mail".

A SUMMARY OF STEPS TO TAKE TO SECURE YOUR APARTMENT:
Doors

- Check your door and door frame. Do they need to be repaired or replaced?
- All exterior doors should be either metal or solid core wood. (1-3/4 inches thick)
- Glass or thin wood panels, in or near the door, can be protected by installing polycarbonate glazing and securing with one-way screws.

Locks

- Use a dead-bolt lock with a one-inch throw bolt or a heavy-duty drop-bolt lock.
- Install a highly pick resistant and drill resistant cylinder.
- Protect the cylinder with a guard plate.
- Add a "j" bar to the door frame to prevent crowbarring the lock.
- Any additional locks should be installed 18 to 24 inches above or

below the doorknob. Consider children, the elderly and/or disabled before installing a lock too high.

- Do not use a double-cylinder lock, which is a lock that has a key on both sides. They are prohibited in multiple dwellings and can be deadly if a fire should break out.

Windows

- All accessible windows in an apartment need securing. That includes any that are within twelve feet of ground level, a building projection, a fire escape, and windows near a public hall or route. These should be secured in the open and closed position. In fact, the only absolute security available for windows with easy access is from installation of window gates.

- Skylights should be examined for access and secured if necessary.

- Windows below the roof edge may be vulnerable and should be secured using a lock as well as the pinning method.

- If you have air conditioners, check to see if they are accessible. They may require gates too.

Alarm Systems

- They are very effective as a deterrent. Epic Security Company says that nine out of ten robbers will head for a home that doesn't have one.

- There are many different types to choose from depending on your needs, so consult a security expert before deciding.

- Many security experts recommend an alarm that not only goes off at home but also at a central command station. The command station in turn calls you and the police.

- Most commercial operations buy "hard-wired", not wireless, systems due to better reliability.

> THE BEST WAY TO SECURE YOUR FIRE ESCAPE WINDOW OR ANY FIRST FLOOR WINDOW IS WITH A GATE THAT HAS BEEN APPROVED BY THE NEW YORK CITY BOARD OF STANDARDS AND APPEALS. THIS GATE IS COMMONLY KNOWN AS A "FERRY" OR "SAFETY" GATE, AND IS OPERATED BY A LATCH AND NOT A PADLOCK OR COMBINATION LOCK. THE PROTECTION AFFORDED BY THIS GATE IS ONLY AS GOOD AS THE QUALITY OF ITS INSTALLATION. THE SCREWS USED FOR INSTALLATION OF THE GATE SHOULD BE LONG ENOUGH SO THAT THEY ANCHOR THE GATE TO THE INTERIOR WALL STUD, OR THE WINDOW FRAME.
>
> — NEW YORK CITY POLICE DEPARTMENT, CRIME PREVENTION SECTION

SOLUTION:
A SAFE NEIGHBORHOOD IS CREATED BY LOCAL CITIZEN INVOLVEMENT

The best way to explain what we mean is by recounting a true story about one small Manhattan community. A young advertising executive was killed making a late-night phone call from a phone booth outside his building in the West Village. It shocked the family-oriented, tranquil neighborhood to its core; its residents had had quality-of-life problems for some time, but had never made a group commitment to do something about them. Existing block associations got together to discuss what had to be done and presented a plan to their local community board and precinct. Together they implemented the following:

> SAFETY IS ALWAYS AN ISSUE. CITIZEN ACTION IN CONJUNCTION WITH THE POLICE DEPARTMENT WORKS. A GOOD EXAMPLE OF THAT IS THE WORK THAT THE ROAD RUNNER'S CLUB HAS DONE. THEY CREATED, WITH THE HELP OF THE POLICE DEPARTMENT, THE RUNNERS SAFETY PATROL. THEY ACT AS ADDITIONAL SETS OF EYES AND EARS TO ENSURE SAFETY FOR THOSE ENJOYING THE PARKS. RECENTLY, WITH THE SAME GOAL IN MIND, THE CENTRAL PARK SKATE PATROL WAS FORMED. CITIZEN ACTION IS AT THE CORE OF ALL SAFE NEIGHBORHOODS.

- **Block patrols:** Volunteers from each block association took turns patrolling the streets at night, acting as "eyes and ears" for the local precinct.

- **Patrol vans:** The block associations got neighbors to contribute a small, monthly donation to pay for private security vans to patrol each block association's area between 8pm to 6am.

- **More police officers:** They petitioned for and got police officers added to their precinct.

Here's what one officer from the Sixth Precinct had to say about this civilian effort:

"I've been in the police force for ten years and I have never seen anything like it. This precinct has spent years trying to clean up certain areas of the Village. Since the citizens got involved, everything has changed. It can't be done without the community; and when cops see something being done, they work harder themselves-it gives them incentive. I'll give you just one example:

In the months since the community started getting involved, robberies decreased by fifty percent."

— Mike Singer, Community Affairs Officer, Sixth Precinct

BLOCK AND NEIGHBORHOOD ASSOCIATIONS ARE THE KEY TO ELEVATING QUALITY-OF-LIFE STANDARDS IN YOUR NEIGHBORHOOD.

- They have the collective muscle to make your community much safer.
- It is an official and organized forum in which neighborhood residents can address the problems in their area on an ongoing basis.
- As a collective and credible voice it can be a powerful tool for getting issues resolved when taking them before local politicians, community boards, and precincts.
- Block associations have accomplished everything from getting trees planted to closing crack houses. Use yours to plan and implement the right strategy with your local police precinct.

> "WHEN THE CITIZENS OF THE CITY GET INVOLVED IN FIXING UP AND IMPROVING THEIR NEIGHBORHOODS, THE MOST AMAZING THINGS ARE POSSIBLE, FISCAL CRISIS OR NO FISCAL CRISIS"
>
> — MICHAEL CLARK, PRESIDENT, CITIZENS COMMITTEE FOR NEW YORK CITY

How to set up a block association:

The first step toward setting up an effective block association is to call the non-profit Citizens Committee for New York City (founded by Jacob Javits) at 212-989-0909. It supports volunteer grass-roots action to improve the quality of life in City neighborhoods. It offers small grants, training publications, and technical assistance to more than 10,000 neighborhood, tenant and youth associations in the five boroughs. They will help you form new groups and strengthen existing ones and will send you a free kit called "Tools and Tactics for Neighborhood Organizing". For setting up your association the Citizens Committee for New York City recommends following the procedures outlined on the next page.

SOLUTION:
PLAN A NEIGHBORHOOD STRATEGY TO COMBAT CRIME:

No two crime problems are the same. One neighborhood might require a block patrol, another just a security patrol officer. The following experts can help you create the most effective plan for your area:

The "Anti-Crime Center" of the Citizens Committee for New York:

This center offers hands-on assistance in fighting drug-related crime by providing in-depth training and technical assistance to

MORE AND MORE
NEIGHBORHOODS AND
APARTMENT BUILDINGS ARE
HIRING PRIVATE SECURITY
GUARDS AND PATROL VANS TO
HELP KEEP THEIR AREA SAFE
AND TO ENSURE THAT
RESIDENTS FEEL SECURE,
DAY OR NIGHT...
IF A BUILDING OR A BLOCK
SHARES THE COST, THE
CONTRIBUTION PER PERSON
CAN BE AS LITTLE AS A
FEW DOLLARS A MONTH.

YOU PAY TAXES IN YOUR
NEIGHBORHOOD TOO!
MAKE YOURSELF KNOWN TO
YOUR COMMUNITY LEADERS
AND ELECTED OFFICIALS.
DON'T ASK...DEMAND THAT
YOUR RIGHTS IN YOUR
COMMUNITY ARE MET. AND
DON'T GIVE UP.
CITIZEN ACTION WORKS!

— REGGAE FITZGERALD,
VETERAN COMMUNITY
ACTIVIST

neighborhood associations, and by facilitating joint strategy planning between police and communities.

OFFICERS WITHIN YOUR LOCAL PRECINCT ARE THERE TO HELP:

Community Affairs Officer: Every precinct has one. He/she is your liaison. No question or problem is considered too small. If you have a block association, he will gladly attend your meetings. There is also a precinct council meeting monthly in which the community is invited to voice their concerns to the community affairs and commanding officers.

Community Patrol Officer: Your foot patrol officer who works with residents to resolve problems that may lie at the root of crime in a neighborhood.

Crime Prevention Officer: His/her job is to help the community make their streets, buildings, and apartments safer. If you request it, they will look at your street, your building, even your apartment, free of charge and advise you as to what steps to take to make them safe.

Organizing Your Neighborhood

l. Define the issues. Some neighborhood groups are organized to bring residents together to resolve a multitude of concerns. Some are formed to deal with a specific crisis. Define the issues and get the history on each issue by talking to your local community board, police precinct and community newspapers.

2. Research the community. What size area do you want to organize? One building? One block? Several blocks? Who are the likeliest people to join the organization? What groups are going to be the most concerned about the issues? Home owners? Parents? Local merchants? Find out what resources your community has - active local merchants and corporations, city council representative, community board - and solicit their involvement.

3. Build a core group. Recruit a handful of people to help launch the organization. Find candidates by talking to neighbors to find out who's most committed to improving the neighborhood. Leaders of churches, community centers, etc. should know some interested people. The core group will be the temporary steering committee until the general membership meeting is held. The core group should hold an organizing drive, the most common being a block party or a block "clean-up", to get the organization off the ground. Make sure you alert your community board and local precinct that you plan to hold one, and invite them to attend.

4. Hold the first of regularly scheduled general meetings: Print flyers about when and where the first general meeting is being held and post them in lobbies, grocery stores, church, temple and school bulletin boards. At the meeting, clarify the issues and goals and the first steps the group will take. A good "agenda" should include:

- Introductions.
- Picking a steering committee and determining what their responsibilities will be until by-laws can be developed and elections can be held.
- Agreeing on a name for the organization.
- An opportunity for attendees to voice opinions.
- Prioritizing the issues to be tackled and making assignments. If the issues are complicated, ask someone to head a committee on each issue.

5. Hold regular monthly meetings. Make sure you have an agenda for every meeting with clear goals and job assignments. Minutes should be taken and issues voted on.

6. Publish a newsletter. It's a great way to spread the word about your organization's activities and get other people involved.

7. How to keep your block association alive.

- Go after only those people who have a real investment in the community.
- Make sure you always have a monthly meeting with a clear agenda.
- Have at least one representative go to all the community board and police precinct council meetings that occur regularly to stay abreast of what is happening.
- Make sure your local community, government and business leaders get a copy of your newsletter.

The Intrepid Pages of
Police Precincts & Their Community Affairs Officers

PRECINCT 1 • 16 Ericsson Place • (212) 334-0611

Boundaries—South Ferry to West Houston Street,
Broadway to West Worth Street
CAO—Officer Stiles

PRECINCT 5 • 19 Elizabeth Street • (212) 334-0711

Boundaries—Allen Street to Broadway,
East Houston to Brooklyn Bridge
CAO—Detective Yat

PRECINCT 6 • 233 West 10th Street • (212) 741-4811

Boundaries—West Houston to Broadway,
South Side of 14th Street to West Side Highway
CAO—Officer Singer; Officer Haley

PRECINCT 7 • 19-1/2 Pitt Street • (212) 477-7311

Boundaries—Water Street to Allen Street,
East Houston to South Street
CAO—Officer Torres; Officer Itzkin

PRECINCT 9 • 321 East 5th Street • (212) 477-7811

Boundaries—East Houston to East 14th Street,
Broadway to East River
CAO—Officer Hernandez

PRECINCT 10 • 230 West 20th Street • (212) 741-8211

Boundaries—14th Street to 29th Street,
Seventh Avenue to Hudson Street; 29th Street to 43rd Street,
West of Ninth Avenue to Hudson River
CAO—Officer Cusicek; Officer Galasso

PRECINCT 13 • 230 East 21st Street • (212) 477-7411

Boundaries—14th Street to 29th Street,
East River to Seventh Avenue
CAO—Detective Hughes

MIDTOWN SOUTH PRECINCT • 357 West 35th Street (212) 239-9811

Boundaries—29th Street to 45th Street,
Lexington Avenue to Ninth Avenue
CAO—Officer Kelley; Officer Hennessey

PRECINCT 17 • 167 East 51st Street • (212) 826-3211

Boundaries—30th Street to 59th Street,
East River to Lexington Avenue;
34th Street to 40th Street, East River to Madison Avenue
CAO—Officer Boqucki

MIDTOWN NORTH PRECINCT • 306 West 54th Street (212) 767-8400

Boundaries—West of Lexington Avenue to Hudson River,
South of 60th Street to 45th Street
CAO—Detective Burns; Officer Giaco; Officer O'Connor

PRECINCT 19 • 153 East 67th Street • (212) 452-0600

Boundaries—59th Street to 96th Street,
Fifth Avenue to East River
CAO—Officer Petrillo

PRECINCT 20 • 120 West 82nd Street • (212) 580-6411

Boundaries—59th Street to 86th Street,
Riverside Park to Central Park West
CAO—Officer Vassallo

CENTRAL PARK PRECINCT • 86th Street and Transverse Road (212) 570-4820

Boundaries—Entire Park
CAO—Officer Sieffert

PRECINCT 23 • 164 East 102nd Street • (212) 860-6411

Boundaries—96th Street to 115th Street,
Fifth Avenue to East River
CAO—Officer Marquez; Officer Padilla

PRECINCT 24 • 151 West 100th Street • (212) 678-1811

Boundaries—86th Street to 110th Street,
Riverside Park to Central Park West
CAO—Officer Bonet

PRECINCT 25 • 120 East 119th Street • (212) 860-6511

Boundaries—Fifth Avenue East to Water Street,
115th Street to 142nd Street
CAO—Officer Patterson; Officer Flores

PRECINCT 26 • 520 West 126th Street • (212) 678-1311

Boundaries—110th Street to 133rd Street,
Henry Hudson River to west side of Amsterdam Avenue;
110th Street to 141st Street, east side of Amsterdam Avenue to
west side of Morningside Avenue
CAO—Officer Stanley

PRECINCT 28 • 2271 Eighth Avenue • (212) 678-1611

Boundaries—110th Street to 127th Street,
Morningside Avenue to Fifth Avenue
CAO—Officer Harper; Officer Flowers

PRECINCT 30 • 451 West 151st Street • (212) 690-8811

Boundaries—133rd Street to 155th Street,
Riverside Drive to Bradhurst Avenue
CAO—Officer Rijo

PRECINCT 32 • 250 West 135th Street • (212) 690-6311

Boundaries—127th Street to 159th Street,
Lenox Avenue to St. Nicholas Avenue
CAO—Officer Jennings; Officer Sebastian

PRECINCT 34 • 4295 Broadway (at 183rd Street) • (212) 927-9711

Boundaries—179th Street to 220th Street, River to River
CAO—Officer Hughes

The Intrepid Pages of
Security Sources

ALARM SECURITY SYSTEMS

All of the companies below give free estimates.

ATLAS ALARM • 99 East 34th Street • (212) 879-7000

They have the capability to design a system that works for your needs. Systems run anywhere from $600 and up. A central station is signaled when the alarm goes off and then they call the police. There is a monthly fee of $40 associated with this service.

SANDS SECURITY ALARM SYSTEMS, INC.
1601 Bronxdale Avenue, Bronx • (718) 409-9046

The sales representatives here said that unfortunately people come to them to have a system installed after they have been robbed. Depending on the amount of security one needs, a system can cost $600 and up.

WELLS FARGO PONY EXPRESS
31 Jerusalem Avenue, Hempstead • (800) 842-7669

Wells Fargo works differently than the other alarm companies listed. Here you enter into a five-year contract whereby you do not pay for the installation of the system or the system itself. There is only a $21.95 monthly central monitoring fee. The security system is yours after the five years is up. You have the option to sign a contract which is less than a five-year commitment, but then you need to pay $100 or $200 up front, depending on the length of the contract, plus a $21.95 monthly monitoring fee for the term of the contract.

AUTOMOBILE GLASS REPLACERS

Owning a car in New York City gives you a lot of freedom. However, the reality is that a window will probably be broken during a break-in at some point. If that happens, call your insurance agent. Usually you are covered if you repair it through their source. If not, call:

LIBERTY GLASS • 544 West 48th Street • (212) 265-3052

Open from 8:00 A.M. to 5:00 P.M. Monday through Friday.

MR. GLASS INC. • 441 West 16th Street • (212) 989-5550

Open from 8:00 A.M. to 5:00 P.M. Monday through Friday.

LOCKSMITHS

ABBEY LOCKSMITHS
1558 Second Avenue (at 81st Street) • (212) 535-2289

They are available twenty-four hours and service all of Manhattan. You can make an appointment in advance; we suggest the first appointment of the day. They can work on car locks as well. For emergency calls they accept cash only; during the day they accept checks and major credit cards.

VILLAGE LOCKSMITHS • 350 Bleecker Street • (212) 362-7000

This company runs only a road service business with no storefront. This is a twenty-four-hour service. They pride themselves on being at any location within one hour. They can handle car and safe locks. Cash and major credit cards accepted.

NEIGHBORHOOD CRIME STATISTICS, ON-LINE

ONLINE DATA SERVICES
8554 Katy Freeway, Suite 321, Houston, TX • (713) 365-9811

How would you like to know about the safety of a neighborhood before you buy or rent an apartment? For a fee of about $20 per one-page report, Online Data Services can provide you with statistical details regarding various categories of crime, including assault, rape, and robbery in a given area, then rate the information on a scale of A to F. If you do not subscribe to an online service, the company will mail or fax you a report.

SAFES

Safe store owners say that in today's society, a safe is good insurance. Many banks are claiming no responsibility for break-ins to their safe deposit boxes and of course you are a target when you leave a bank with your valuables.

AMERICAN SECURITY SYSTEMS INC.
18 West 23rd Street • (212) 533-0801

They sell a large number of safes and do installations.

EMPIRE SAFE • 433 Canal Street (at Varick) • (212) 226-2255

A family-owned business operating since 1904. They not only sell new safes, but are happy to try and repair the old. They have some other protection devices as well. If possible, they recommend safes that are bolted to the floor. If you live in a house, they suggest you purchase a safe that can be hidden in the floor.

SECURITY PATROL COMPANIES

Remember, check with your local precinct to determine what security patrols you are considering and what measures are legal and appropriate.

EPIC SECURITY
2067 Broadway (71st and 72nd Streets) • (212) 580-3434

They have unarmed guards for $9.95 per hour, and radio motor patrol vehicles at $15.90 per hour. They operate twenty-four hours a day. Their private city-wide radio system operates within their own fleet of radio motor-patrol vehicles, so they can respond with as many guards as is needed in any situation.

GUARDIAN ANGELS • (212) 967-0808

If your neighborhood is experiencing ongoing crime or harassment problems, you should call the Angels and put in a request for a group to come and patrol your territory. There are only 100 Angels in New York City and they must fulfill requests according to priority. In a short period of time, the Angels can make an enormous impact on a neighborhood in distress. However, they cannot do it without the support and involvement of the community.

VGI • 420 East 149th Street • (718) 665-1515

They have unarmed guards at $12 per hour and armed guards at $16 per hour. They can arrange for vehicles to patrol.

SHOPPING NEW YORK THE STREET SMART WAY

PERCEPTIONS VS. REALITY

New York City is the #1 shopping mecca in the world. It is the port from which all merchandise flows. The designers, manufacturers, wholesalers, discounters, and the retailers all operate here, and you can buy directly from all of them. That means that you can shop "til you drop", but it also means buyer beware. If you don't make it a priority to become a pro-active consumer, you can get badly taken, either by merchants who lie in wait for naive shoppers or by your own lack of shopping savvy. Learn to shop smart and you can have it all, and at the right price.

SOLUTION:
THERE ARE TWO RULES
TO TURNING A RAW DEAL INTO A REAL DEAL:

1. Become an expert consumer: Because New York City is a global shopping hub, our city government has provided critical tools to inform and protect its consumers. As discussed in Assertiveness Training, the Consumer Affairs Department and the Better Business Bureau were created to make sure consumers know their rights and how to exercise them. You can request their free pamphlets on everything from purchasing credit cards to not getting taken by an auto mechanic, to your rights regarding furniture delivery, and dozens more. Consumer Reports Magazine is also a gold-mine for the latest product evaluations, and The Intrepid New Yorker wouldn't dream of buying a high ticket item without first reading their most recent report. You can find current issues at your local library, if you don't want to subscribe to their magazine or their website.

2. Determine which shopping method best suits your needs and disposition. You may see yourself as the bargain hunter, but stop and consider whether this shopping method is the "real deal" for you. Successful bargain hunting requires sleuthing, research and expertise. It's pretty much "self-serve", and your problem to figure out how to get your purchase delivered, installed and serviced. In addition, products usually come without warranties and guarantees. The real deal may be in the convenience and peace of mind that comes with full service, retail shopping, that offers all kinds of guarantees and free servicing. And bargain-hunter wannabees, beware! Sometimes it might actually cost you less to pay full retail and far more than you bargained for, for the bargain.

SHOPPING TERMS YOU SHOULD KNOW:

Buying from a full-service retailer: Prices at the retail level have been marked up several times already, by the manufacturer and the wholesaler. Depending on what the market will bear, the markup can be 100 - 1,000% up from what it cost to make the product.

Buying from a discount-retailer ("off-price"): These are typically large retail chains that can offer 20 - 25% off the full retail price, due to the sheer volume of inventory they sell.

Buying from a wholesaler: At this level, you are buying from the dealer or "middleman" who buys directly from the manufacturer and then sells to the retailer. When you buy from the wholesaler, it's double or more what it cost to actually make the product, but at least half what it costs at the retail level.

Buying from the manufacturer: When you buy from the manufacturer, you are buying at "cost". The "cost" price is what it actually costs to make the product, with no additional markups.

SOLUTION:
WHAT SHOPPING FULL RETAIL IS ALL ABOUT

When you shop retail, you are buying a product at the highest price, but you should expect a lot of extra service for that price. Make sure you know exactly what the store promises in terms of returns, guarantees, installations and servicing before making a purchase.

The two primary reasons to consider shopping retail:

1. the store stands behind its product and its customers
2. it's the least time-consuming, most service-oriented type of shopping

The type of perks that come with retail shopping:

- **Shopping comfort** in nicely appointed, consumer-friendly stores

- **A complete line of products,** in different styles, models and sizes

- **The newest, latest and greatest, first**

- **The ability to special-order products, quickly**

- **A knowledgeable sales staff and personalized service**

- **Guarantees and warranties,** and sometimes for a lifetime!

- **All types of servicing, including** delivery, installation and repair, and sometimes at no extra charge!

- **Perks and pampering!** It can be a luxurious experience, complete with your own in-house personal shopper, phone privileges, lunch on the house, on-the-spot alterations, and trial purchases

Retail clothes typically go on sale about 60 days after the clothes arrive in the store.

That means clothes are sometimes discounted before the season even begins. Here's when they arrive in stores...you can do the rest of the math:

- Spring clothes begin to arrive mid-December.

- Summer clothes begin to arrive in March.

- Fall clothes begin to arrive mid-July.

- Winter clothes begin to arrive mid-August.

- Holiday/cruise wear begins to arrive mid-November and December.

LOYALTY TO A SALES LADY AT A PARTICULAR DESIGNER BOUTIQUE HAS ITS REWARDS! ONE SALES LADY WE KNOW PUTS ASIDE INVENTORY FOR A FAVORITE CUSTOMER, WAITS UNTIL SALE TIME, AND THEN OFFERS IT TO HER AT THE DISCOUNTED PRICE. ESTABLISHING STRONG RELATIONSHIPS BETWEEN A CUSTOMER AND A STORE MEANS EVERYTHING IN TERMS OF THE LEVEL OF SERVICE YOU CAN EXPECT.

A WONDERFUL OLD-FASHIONED SHOPPING TRADITION WORTH EXPERIENCING IS COMPLIMENTARY COFFEE SERVICE ON FINE CHINA, AND THE SINGING OF THE NATIONAL ANTHEM WITH THE EMPLOYEES OF LORD AND TAYLOR DEPARTMENT STORE, BEFORE THE DOORS OFFICIALLY OPEN AT 10:00 AM.

A few tips for retail shoppers:

Most department stores have permanent clearance centers outside Manhattan. The majority of them carry home furnishings and a few carry clothes. You can save anywhere from 30 to 70%. Most of them are open seven days a week.

SOME VERY FRUGAL BUYERS WAIT TO BUY THEIR CLOTHES AT THE END OF THE SEASON AND WEAR THEM THE FOLLOWING YEAR. THOSE SHOPPERS ARE DIEHARD BARGAIN HUNTERS WHO DON'T MIND THE HIT-OR-MISS QUALITY OF THE HUNT.

If you are shopping for an expensive brand item, it pays to ask when that brand item goes on sale. One of our clients discovered that her own wedding china went on sale every year in August in stores across the country. So her family and friends were able to buy it for her months before the wedding and save 40%.

If you buy an item at the retail price and that item goes on sale shortly thereafter, you can bring the item back to get the full discount. In addition, if you see the same item at a cheaper price elsewhere, the store may be willing to match the price.

SALES OFTEN START ONE OR MORE DAYS BEFORE THE ADVERTISED DATE, SO YOU CAN BEAT THE CROWDS AND GET THE PICK OF THE LITTER. WHEN YOU HEAR ABOUT AN UPCOMING SALE, CALL AHEAD AND ASK.

It's prudent to put big ticket items on a credit card. If there is a billing or product problem, you can withhold payment until an investigation is completed. Billing errors for which merchants are responsible include charges for items you did not order or never received; items delivered to the wrong address, in the wrong quantity, or so much later than promised that the bill arrived before the item; items that turned out to be different than what you ordered.

"Before making a purchase, compare the terms of warranties. Who offers the warranty? How long is it, and what is its start and end date. What is covered? Which parts? Which types of problems? Will the warranty pay 100 percent of the repair costs? Will it pay for parts, but not labor? Will it pay for shipping or for a loaner? Are regular inspections or maintenance required? Do you have to ship the product out of state for repairs? Always keep sales receipts and warranties." – *Consumer Resource Handbook,* U.S. Office of Consumer Affairs

Merchants must give refunds on unused, undamaged goods within twenty days of purchase unless they post an easy-to-read sign that tells you about their refund policy. Signs must be posted in any of the following four locations: 1. attached to the cash register or wherever sales are completed; 2. in a place visible to the consumer from the cash register; 3. at each store entrance; 4. on a tag attached to the item. – Department of Consumer Affairs

Refund policies differ, depending on the type of store: Small, specialty boutiques will offer a store credit, but almost never a refund. Large department stores are much more likely to offer full refunds; and the high-end chains such as Eddie Bauer and The Gap are likely to offer lifetime guarantees as well as full refund policies.

15 YEARS AGO, EDDIE BAUER SOLD US AN AIR MATTRESS WITH A LIFETIME GUARANTEE. WHEN IT RIPPED THIS YEAR, WE RETURNED IT AND RECEIVED A FULL REFUND AT TODAY'S PRICES, NO QUESTIONS ASKED! IN ANOTHER INSTANCE, WE RETURNED A WINTER JACKET TO PATAGONIA BECAUSE AFTER TWO YEARS, THE OUTER SHELL STARTED TO FLAKE. PATAGONIA SENT US A BRAND NEW ONE, FEDERAL EXPRESS.

DEPARTMENT STORE CLEARANCE CENTERS

All of the following stores accept major credit cards and personal checks.

BARNEYS • 660 Madison Avenue • (212) 593-7800

The Barneys warehouse sale runs twice a year—once in February and again the last two weeks in August, ending on Labor Day. It opens at 8:00 A.M. People begin to line up very early because it's a chance to buy goods up to 40 percent off the retail price.

BLOOMINGDALE'S
155 Glen Cove Avenue, Carle Place, LI • (516) 877-5120

They sell mostly furniture, rugs, and bedding. They're open Monday through Friday, 10:00 A.M. to 9:30 P.M., Saturday, 10:00 A.M. to 6:00 P.M., and Sunday, noon to 5:00 P.M.

FORTUNOFF
750 Zeckendorf Boulevard, Westbury, LI • (516) 832-9000

They sell outdoor and indoor furniture, as well as home furnishings and jewelry. Open Monday through Saturday, 10:00 A.M. to 9:30 P.M., and Sunday, 11:00 A.M. to 6:00 P.M.

LORD & TAYLOR
3601 Hempstead Turnpike, Levittown, LI • (516) 731-5031
839-16 New York Avenue, Huntington, LI • (516) 673-0009

They sell clothing for children and adults. The Levittown store is open Monday through Friday, 10:00 A.M. to 9:00 P.M., Saturday, 10:00 A.M. to 6:00 P.M., and Sunday, 12:00 P.M. to 6:00 P.M. The Huntington store hours are Monday and Tuesday, 9:00 A.M. to 6:00 P.M., Wednesday through Friday, 9:00 A.M. to 9:00 P.M., Saturday, 10:00 A.M. to 6:00 P.M., and Sunday, noon to 6:00 P.M.

MACY'S • 155 Glen Cove Road, Carle Place, LI • (516) 746-1490

Furniture, electronics, bedding, and rugs are sold here. Open from 10:00 A.M. to 9:00 P.M. Monday through Friday, Saturday from 9:30 A.M. to 6:00 P.M., and Sunday from 11:00 A.M. to 5:00 P.M.

NEIMAN MARCUS
1634 Franklin Mills Circle, Philadelphia • (215) 637-5900

At Neiman Marcus' clearance center you can find discounted clothing, shoes, housewares, accessories, and jewelry. The store hours are Monday through Saturday, 10:00 A.M. to 9:30 P.M., and Sunday, 11:00 A.M. to 6:00 P.M.

OFF-FIFTH • 1504 Old Country Road, LI • (516) 228-2165

Off-Fifth stores are also located in Paramus, NJ, Clinton, CT, and Riverhead, NY. Off-Fifth is Saks Fifth Avenue's outlet center. Here you can find clothing, shoes, towels, and linens. The store's hours are Monday through Saturday, 10:00 A.M. to 9:30 P.M., and Sunday from 11:00 A.M. to 6:00 P.M.

THE PROS AND CONS OF SHOPPING DISCOUNT ("OFF PRICE" RETAIL)

Discounters such as Sears, Toys R Us, and K Mart have been shopping mall staples for suburbanites and country folk for decades. What's new is that discount superstores of all varieties have finally taken permanent hold in New York City. And it has changed the way New Yorkers shop dramatically. You don't ever have to shop retail if you don't want to, but there are pros and cons to discount shopping:

The pros:
- The savings are routinely 20-25% off the full retail price.
- You get the same warranties and guarantees (at the well-established chains).
- They will often match the lower price you saw at a competitor's store.

The cons:
- You won't find the more unique brands.
- The environment can often be frenetic.
- The service is pretty much "self-serve."
- Items are more likely to be "out of stock" and have to be special-ordered.
- Sizes, styles and models can be limited.
- They commonly don't offer cash refunds, just store credit.

EVEN THE BETTER DISCOUNT CHAINS RARELY OFFER FULL-SERVICE PERKS. THEY PROBABLY WON'T DELIVER, WRAP, SHIP, INSTALL OR REPAIR, AND CERTAINLY NOT FOR FREE. SO FACTOR THOSE COSTS INTO THE PURCHASE PRICE. SHOP AROUND FIRST. YOU MIGHT FIND THAT THE PRODUCT YOU WANT IS ON SALE AT A FULL-SERVICE RETAIL ESTABLISHMENT, AND THAT THEY DON'T CHARGE FOR DELIVERY AND INSTALLATION. ANOTHER EXAMPLE OF WHEN RETAIL SHOPPING IS THE REAL DEAL.

DON'T GET TRAPPED BY FALSE "GOING OUT OF BUSINESS" SALES. SOME SHOPS ADVERTISE THEM IN ORDER TO LURE CUSTOMERS; SOME ADS AND SIGNS SAY "LOST OUR LEASE" OR "EVERYTHING MUST GO". ONCE LURED IN, CUSTOMERS MAY DISCOVER THAT MERCHANDISE "ON SALE" COSTS MORE THAN THE SAME MERCHANDISE AT THE REGULAR PRICE IN OTHER STORES. ASK OTHER STORES IN THE NEIGHBORHOOD HOW LONG THE SIGN HAS BEEN UP OR CALL THE BBB.
- BETTER BUSINESS BUREAU

SOLUTION: BARGAIN BASEMENT SHOPPING: IT'S TRUTH AND CONSEQUENCES

FACTORY OUTLETS

Factory outlets are big business around the NYC tri-state area. There are three or four "outlet towns" within 1-1/2 hours of the city. You'll find Coach, Donna Karan, Ralph Lauren, Ann Taylor, Gucci and many more. When we think of outlets, we traditionally think excess designer inventory deeply discounted to up to 40% off the retail price. That concept has been altered dramatically over the years, primarily because the small, off-the-beaten-track outlet store has largely been replaced by national outlet chains located in "outlet malls". There is no way that designers could stock all their outlets with excess inventory; it has become a huge secondary business for them, and that means the rules of the game have changed at many of these outposts, so buyer beware:

- It is now widely known within the industry that designers, more often than not, create separate lines of inventory just for their outlets.

- Designer merchandise made solely for outlets (or "direct-to-outlet") are usually made with inferior materials.

- Sales at large outlet chains are now more typically around 10% and sometimes you may actually fare better hitting the sales at retail establishments.

- Authentic excess-inventory outposts still exist, but they are the exception and they typically belong to designers who own only one or two.

The pros of factory outlet chains:

- They are more shopper-friendly than many discounters, the merchandise is well laid out, and the stores operate more like full-service retail stores in terms of convenience and sales help.

- Designer-owned outlets have more inventory than a sample sale or off-price store because they function more and more as secondary outlets for additional lines of inventory.

- They usually take credit cards and have good refund policies.

The cons:

- You have to travel a distance to access them.

- Impulse buying is a real risk unless you plan ahead regarding which designers you want to hit and how much you plan to spend.

- It's more hit or miss in terms of finding the sizes and styles you want.

- There's a good chance you are buying an inferior line of merchandise that has never been in a retail store.

BEFORE PURCHASING AT FULL PRICE RETAIL, THE INTREPID NEW YORKER OFTEN CALLS THE OUTLET TO COMPARE PRICES. MANY OUTLETS WILL TAKE A CREDIT CARD OVER THE PHONE AND SHIP, THEREBY ELIMINATING THE NEED TO TRAVEL. ALWAYS WORTH A SHOT.

KEEP IN MIND WHY YOU ARE SHOPPING FOR THAT PARTICULAR DESIGNER. IT MIGHT NOT MATTER TO YOU IF THE MERCHANDISE IS BEING MADE JUST FOR THE OUTLET BECAUSE IT STILL HAS THE DESIGNER LABEL.

THE INTREPID PAGES OF
FACTORY OUTLETS

SECAUCUS OUTLET • Secaucus, New Jersey

Although Secaucus is the closest outlet center to New York City, we find it a bit depressing and certainly hard to navigate. They do have many well-known brand names, but we found much of the merchandise to be tattered and old.

THE CHELSEA GROUP OUTLETS

Our pick for outlet shopping are the outlets owned and operated by The Chelsea Group. The merchandise we saw in these outlets appeared to be in tip-top shape. They make an effort to design their centers for convenience. There are benches for resting, restaurants to dine at, walkways that are easy to manipulate with strollers, and a peaceful ambiance. The Chelsea Group manages the entire operation, setting strict guidelines that all of their stores must follow. At both of the locations below you will find some of the latest designers' apparel, brand-name sportswear, coats, furs, shoes, intimate apparel, accessories, fine china, crystal and silver, home furnishings and house wares, jewelry, gifts, luggage, and leather goods. They both have brochures detailing all their shops and can be reached by bus from the Port Authority. Call either of the following outlets for directions and brochures:

LIBERTY VILLAGE
Flemington, New Jersey • (908) 782-8550

Fifty-five miles from New York City.

WOODBURY COMMON
Central Valley, New York • (914) 928-7467

Fifty-five miles from New York City.

FRANKLIN MILLS
Philadelphia, Pennsylvania • (800) 336-MALL

This Outlet Center, housing over 200 stores, is located less than two hours from Manhattan. Shops include popular names—Neiman Marcus, Saks Fifth Avenue, Burlington Coat Factory, Filene's Basement, Bed Bath & Beyond, the Gap, Donna Karan, Bally, Guess, Brookstone, Remington, and the list goes on and on. Savings are as much as 60 percent off retail prices. Buses run to and from the Port Authority on Saturday and Sunday.

TANGER OUTLET MALL
Riverhead, Long Island, New York
(516) 369-2732

This center which offers over 160 stores, is less than 1¹/₂ hours from Manhattan. You can find many upscale stores including Barneys, Saks, Brooks Brothers, Donna Karan, J Crew and Kenneth Cole. You will also find outlets like the Gap and Banana Republic. The mall offers two food courts as well as a complimentary trolley that transports you between areas.

FACTORY OUTLETS
IN NEW YORK CITY

ABC CARPET & HOME
1055 Bronx River Avenue
(718) 842-8770

If you not already familiar with ABC you must make a trip to the outlet. Great prices on so much of their terrific merchandise including furniture, linens, and rugs.

PORTICO BED & BATH
233 10th Avenue
(212) 807-8807

Why not get a bargain on some of their luxurious merchandise.

SAMPLE SALES

This is a form of bargain hunting that is unique to New York, because the city is the home base of most fashion designers and their showrooms. Designers have to clear out leftover inventory to make way for their new lines of furniture, glassware, rugs, clothes, accessories, etc. Predominant sale months are November, December, April and May, but they take place all year long.

The pros:

• Prices range from cost to wholesale - up to 70% off.

The cons:

• It's leftover inventory, so there's much less to choose from.

> OUTLET MERCHANDISE THAT COMES FROM A RETAIL STORE HAS ITS PRICE TAG PRINTED ON BOTH SIDES. IF THE PRICE TAG IS PRINTED ON ONLY ONE SIDE, IT HAS COME DIRECTLY FROM THE MANUFACTURER.

> CHAIN STORES MAY SELL THEIR PRODUCTS AT DIFFERENT PRICE POINTS DEPENDING ON THE ECONOMIC PROFILE OF THE AREA IN WHICH THEY ARE LOCATED. IT CAN PAY TO FIND OUT WHICH STORES OFFER THE BIGGEST BANG FOR YOUR BUCK, EVEN WHEN INCLUDING SHIPPING AND HANDLING COSTS.

- You will be digging for merchandise in a chaotic, cluttered atmosphere.
- You will have to try on clothes behind a clothing rack, if they let you try them on at all.
- You have to pay cash.
- People get carried away with impulse purchases, turning a real deal into a raw one.

Tips for sample sale shoppers:

- In anticipation of a sample sale, check out the designer's line in the retail stores and make a list of items you want including their model and style #s. If it's clothes, try them on for fit. Examine the merchandise for quality. Make sure that the item at the sale matches the retail item in quality, style and fabric.

Publications that give you the when, what and where of upcoming sales:

Fashion Update

Quarterly listing up to 150 sales. Subscription price $65 a year.

1274 49th Street, Suite 209
Brooklyn, NY 11219
718-377-8873

The S & B Report

Monthly, listing every major designer showroom sale from jewelry to furniture. Subscription price $59 a year. A black belt subscription costs $124 and includes weekly sales updates.

56 1/2 Queen Street
Charleston, SC 29401
877-579-0222
www.lazarshopping.com

New York Magazine

Weekly magazine - newsstand. Has a terrific "sales and bargain" page.

The New York Times-Sunday Style Section

Newsstand. The style section features ads for current sales.

**SHOPPING
NYC'S WHOLESALE DISTRICTS:**

Because New York City is a national wholesale hub, there are multi-block wholesale districts in Manhattan in which certain kinds of products are clustered. There's the perfume district, lighting district, textile and linens district, plants district, fashion accessories district, beverages district and so on. These wholesalers operate out of hole-in-the-wall-style storefronts, warehouses, or office buildings, and many have signs that say they sell only to the trade. But, more and more are opening their doors to consumers, and if you are willing to purchase "in bulk", you can gain access just about anywhere. It is rough and tumble, no-frills shopping at its funkiest, but the savings are tremendous.

Tips for wholesale shopper wannabees:

- **Don't be intimidated to call or walk into a wholesale establishment.** The worst they can say is no, they won't sell to you, but more times than not, they will say yes.

- **The best enticement to a wholesaler is the phrase "bulk purchase".** If you are willing to purchase in quantity, you'll have no problem buying wholesale. Your options are to go in on it with friends, or buy in quantity on your own in anticipation of upcoming birthdays, holidays and special events.

- **You can find wholesalers by walking the districts or looking them up in the Business To Business Yellow Pages.** You'll find everything from Ralph Lauren bath sheets and clothing accessories, to fine china, beverages and the finest cuts of meats.

PRIVATE SALES THROUGH SOIFFER/HASKIN (718) 747-1656

TO GET INVITED TO PRIVATE SALES OF DESIGNER CLOTHING, SHOES AND ACCESSORIES, GET ON THEIR MAILING LIST.

MERCHANTS MAY NOT ADD A SURCHARGE TO THE REGULAR COST OF GOODS OR SERVICES IF CONSUMERS PURCHASE WITH A CREDIT CARD; HOWEVER, THEY CAN OFFER A DISCOUNT FOR CASH TRANSACTIONS.

- BETTER BUSINESS BUREAU

WHOLESALE SHOPPING AT TRADE SHOWS:

Another venue for wholesalers. Manhattan holds enormous trade show conventions every year. Hundreds of exhibitors from all over the tri-state area and the country set up booths to display their wears to the retail trade. They include shows devoted to gifts, linens, toys, accessories, gourmet food, stationery and so on. Although they are considered off-limits to consumers, there are legitimate ways to shop them and purchase at wholesale prices.

- **Your business card is the ticket into trade shows:** If your business relates to personal service, you have a good chance of getting in the door. Present your business card at the door.

- **Ask the exhibitors if they are willing to sell individual samples that day.** They are especially likely to say yes on the last day of the convention to avoid return shipping costs.

- **Pick a particular convention to do your gift purchasing for the year.** It's a great way to get birthday, "special event" and holiday gifts purchased for family, friends, and business associates. Tell the exhibitor you would like to place an order, and ask about minimum order requirements, which can vary a great deal.

You can find out when trade shows are being held by calling the New York City Visitor's Bureau at (212) 397-8222, the Jacob Javits Convention Center at (212) 216-2000.

THE INTREPID PAGES OF
WHOLESALE DISTRICTS

WHOLESALE PLANTS:
Sixth Avenue from 24th to 28th Streets

Plants, trees, flowers—real, dried, or fake. It's here and all at wholesale prices. The service isn't great and you may want to re-pot the plant once you get it home, but the bargains can't be beat. We recently came home with $75 worth of goods that would have cost us $150 uptown. Throw in the cab fare there and back, and it was still well worth it. If you can't get it all in a cab, they will deliver for a small fee. Just make sure you get a receipt and hold onto it until you get your delivery.

WHOLESALE MILLINERY SUPPLIES:
Upper 30's between Fifth Avenue and Avenue of the Americas

This is mostly a wholesale district for hat supplies, but you may be able to find some great deals on hats.

WHOLESALE PHOTO EQUIPMENT AND SUPPLIES:
14th to 23rd Streets, Third to Fifth Avenues

Buy, fix, and stock your camera here. You will find specialty dealers as well as used-equipment stores. Shop around and hold out for the best deal.

WHOLESALE LINGERIE:
Between Delancey and Hester Streets, from Essex to Allen

Here you will find nearly a dozen shops with discounted bathrobes, nightgowns, and hosiery.

WHOLESALE AUTO EVERYTHING:
Queens Boulevard from 51st Avenue to 72nd Street in Elmhurst

Dozens of body shops, supply and accessory stores, some ordinary, some that specialize in everything from rims to tinted windows.

ANTIQUES AND FURNITURE RESTORATION:
Atlantic Avenue in Brooklyn Heights;
Bruckner Boulevard between 132nd and 138th Streets
in the Port Morris section of the Bronx

It's worth a trip to Atlantic Avenue in Brooklyn to browse through the abundant antique shops. Comb through Bruckner Boulevard in the Bronx for special deals and restoration expertise that is far superior to many more expensive places in the city.

WHOLESALE LIGHTING:

Third Avenue from 7th Street to Houston, Bowery from Houston to Chinatown's Chatham Square

This is a mini-lighting town with serious wholesale bargains. Dozens of lighting stores line the streets. Most have a large selection of inventory, are nicely laid out, and are shopper friendly.

WHOLESALE RESTAURANT SUPPLIES:

Third Avenue two blocks above Houston Street, and Bowery several blocks below Houston

These wholesale stores sell commercial-grade kitchen appliances, ovens, sinks, bar stools, chairs, butcher block tables, glassware, china—you name it—to restaurants, diners, and delis. They will also sell to the consumer with no minimums. It's an experience not unlike rummaging through a garage sale, so don't expect the red carpet treatment, but you can find extraordinary buys.

WHOLESALE CLOTHING

A wholesale clothing district exists, but it is not open to the public, period! You can gain access but only through the professional services of a personal shopper (see the VIP chapter).

WHOLESALE GIFTS, TOYS, AND ACCESSORIES

Buyers come in to place their orders with the dozens of showrooms that are housed within the following:

The Gift Building
225 Fifth Avenue

The Toy Building
200 Fifth Avenue

The Accessories Building
320 Fifth Avenue
330 Fifth Avenue
389 Fifth Avenue
393 Fifth Avenue
417 Fifth Avenue

Theoretically, they are closed to the public because they only sell in bulk and only to stores. But if you need to buy certain items in bulk, let's say a dozen of a particular belt to give as Christmas presents, or half a dozen bracelets as bridesmaids gifts, they might be willing to sell to you. It's up to the discretion of an individual showroom.

Your savings will be considerable. It is absolutely worth a try. Nothing ventured, nothing gained.

Another way to get in and not have to purchase in bulk is by hiring a personal shopper who by profession is permitted access to these "to the trade only" showrooms. Just be aware that personal shoppers have agreements with a specific group of showrooms; they can't access all of them.

SHOPPING NYC'S FLEA MARKETS AND THRIFT STORES:

We have them all over the city, and as you can well imagine, they provide some of the most interesting and eclectic treasure hunting in the country. In fact, some of our flea markets are famous, and attract consumers and antique dealers from all over the tri-state area. And sometimes the deals are truly amazing. Our advice on how to shop them...Just have a blast, and try not to get addicted!

A few tips for the flea market shopper:

l. The best time to go is at the crack of dawn - when the dealers get there for the best picks.

2. The other best time to go is at the end of the day - slim pickings maybe, but the best prices because the vendors don't want to cart unsold inventory home. They are very negotiable at this time of day.

3. You can get a leg up on flea market happenings by going on line; www.ci.nyc.ny.us/html/cau/html/events.html.

SHOPPING BY PHONE:

• Shop national/international boutique chains for the best deal. Example:

a. **Baccarat Crystal:** If the dollar is

A MULTIBILLION DOLLAR INDUSTRY HAS EMERGED AROUND "GRAY MARKET" GOODS. THEY ARE NOT COUNTERFEITS BUT "PARALLEL IMPORTS", WHICH ARE NOT MADE FOR U.S. CONSUMPTION, BUT MAY BEAR A VALID U.S. TRADEMARK WITHOUT THE U.S. TRADEMARK HOLDER'S CONSENT. THE GOODS (WHICH ARE PRIMARILY ELECTRONICS) FIND THEIR WAY INTO LOCAL STORES WHERE THEY COMPETE WITH DOMESTIC VERSIONS. THEY ARE USUALLY LESS EXPENSIVE, BUT CAN COME WITHOUT U.S. WARRANTIES, AREN'T ELIGIBLE FOR MANUFACTURERS' REBATES, AND THEIR INSTRUCTIONS ARE WRITTEN IN A FOREIGN LANGUAGE. IN NEW YORK STATE, ANY RETAILER OFFERING THESE GOODS MUST POST A VISIBLE SIGN LISTING THEIR LIMITATIONS. IF A MERCHANT VIOLATES THIS LAW, THE BUYER HAS UP TO TWENTY DAYS AFTER THE PURCHASE TO REQUEST A REFUND.

- BETTER BUSINESS BUREAU

IF YOU CALL (212) 675-3535, THE PEOPLE WHO MANAGE THE TOY BUILDING WILL TELL YOU WHEN CERTAIN SHOWROOMS ARE HAVING SAMPLE SALES AND WHEN THEY WILL BE OPEN TO THE PUBLIC. THEY OFTEN OCCUR DURING THE HOLIDAY SEASON AND BEFORE AND AFTER THE BIG TOY FAIR CONVENTIONS IN NEW YORK CITY.

KURT S. ADLER, INC., "SANTA'S WORLD", WHICH IS THE LARGEST WHOLESALER OF CHRISTMAS ORNAMENTS IN THE WORLD, OPENS ITS DOORS TO THE PUBLIC THE MONDAY BEFORE THANKSGIVING UNTIL THE WEEK BEFORE CHRISTMAS TO UNLOAD THEIR INVENTORY. THEY HAVE OVER 20,000 ORNAMENTS, TREES, GARLANDS, NATIVITY SCENES, AND LIGHTS, AND THEY CONTINUALLY REPLENISH THEIR STOCK. THEY ACCEPT CASH ONLY AND ARE LOCATED AT 1107 BROADWAY (AT 25TH STREET), (212) 924-0900.

strong in Paris, call the Paris store and get the item shipped from there. You will have to pay shipping and duty but the savings are still substantial.

b. Frette Sheets: Recently we priced them in NY at $300. In their Los Angeles store they were on sale for $170.

- Wholesale by Mail catalogs and books: There are more and more of them available to consumers. Example:

a. Wholesale by Mail Catalog (by Lowell Miller): 600 pages of wholesalers who will sell to the consumer through the mail with saving of up to 70%. You can purchase this book at any major bookstore.

b. Shop-by-Mail Report: Published twice a year by the same people who put out the **S & B Report,** the **Shop-by-Mail Report** lists over 250 manufacturers and stores that offer shopping by mail. By knowing the manufacturer's name, style, and product numbers, it is possible to order merchandise at 40 to 70 percent savings. You can call the **S & B Report** at (877) 579-0222.

THE INTREPID PAGES OF
GOOD DISCOUNT SHOPPING

ANTIQUES
CHELSEA ANTIQUES BUILDING
110 West 25th Street • (212) 929-0909

The Chelsea Antiques Building offers twelve floors and more than 100 shops that cater to just about every taste. You can find considerable savings at the consignment area on the main floor.

BOOKS
BARNES & NOBLE
600 Fifth Avenue (at 48th Street)
(212) 765-0592

Other locations throughout the City. They discount all the best-sellers by 30 percent, and all hard-cover books by 10 percent.

BORDERS BOOKS & MUSIC
5 World Trade Center
(corner of Church and Vesey Streets)
(212) 839-8049
461 Park Avenue (at 57th Street)
(212) 980-6785

Also discount the best-sellers and hard-cover books.

CLOTHING, CHILDREN'S
AIDA'S & JIMI'S MERCHANDISING
41 West 28th Street • (212) 689-2145

Girls' clothing from three months to size 16, boys' to size seven. They offer some name brands. Call ahead to see what kind of a selection they have, and to make sure it's in the size you need.

CONWAY
225 West 34th Street • (212) 967-7390

Each of the nine locations have children's departments, but the largest and most fully stocked is this one. Although it has lackluster looks, it is neatly organized and the brands which are usually discounted, such as Sahara Club, French Toast, and Rachel's Kids, are reduced even more here. Infants' socks and burping diapers are also a great, inexpensive find.

DAFFY'S
335 Madison Avenue (at 44th Street)
(212) 557-4422
1311 Broadway (at 34th Street)
(212) 736-4477
111 Fifth Avenue (at 18th Street)
(212) 529-4477
135 East 57th Street • (212) 376-4477

For designer and European imports of girls' dresses (on a hit-or-miss basis) try Daffy's.

KIDSTOWN
10 East 14th Street • (212) 243-1301

Most of the major kids' labels at 20 to 40 percent off list price are sold here. You can find Keds knock-offs for $2.99, leggings for $4.99, cotton and rayon dresses that rarely top $10, and inexpensively priced Fruit of the Loom boxers and briefs.

LITTLE FOLKS
123 East 23rd Street • (212) 982-9669

Here you can find popular children's brands like Carters, Flapdoodles, Absorba, and OshKosh at 20 percent off retail prices. They carry sizes from newborn to size 14 for boys and girls.

OLD NAVY CLOTHING CO.
610 Avenue of the Americas (at 18th Street) • (212) 645-0663

Old Navy carries a large assortment of children's basics, including jeans, sweatshirts, t-shirts, turtlenecks, socks, and pajamas at very reasonable prices, in sizes from infant to size 16 for girls and boys.

RICHIE'S CHILDREN'S SHOES
183 Avenue B (11th and 12th Streets) • (212) 228-5442

A family-run business whose emphasis is on quality and knowledge and, most of all, fair prices. They won't attempt to oversell you and they believe that most kids need only one pair of shoes.

CLOTHING, MEN'S

DAFFY'S • 111 Fifth Avenue (at 18th Street) • (212) 529-4477
1311 Broadway (at 34th Street) • (212) 736-4477
335 Madison Avenue (at 44th Street) • (212) 557-4422
135 East 57th Street • (212) 376-4477

Daffy's is a good bet for men's designer sportswear. Here you can find Calvin Klein, Ferre, Giorgio Armani, and others at good discount prices in a well-laid-out manner.

DOLLAR BILLS
32 East 42nd Street • (212) 867-0212

This is the place to go if you are in search of European designer clothing at fair prices. Be prepared to spend some time looking through the racks but if you do, you should find Armani, Ferre, and Byblos, just to mention a few.

EISENBERG & EISENBERG
85 Fifth Avenue (at 16th Street)
(212) 627-1290

Large selection of designer tuxedos for sale and for rent.

GILCREST CLOTHES, INC.
900 Broadway (19th and 20th Streets)
(212) 254-8933

Since 1931, the staff at Gilcrest has enforced the Old World tradition of serving and pleasing the customer. In addition to providing uncompromising service, they also offer a large selection of better designer European and domestic men's suits, like Valentino and Ungaro. Prices range from $269 to $799. You can also purchase or rent formal-wear here. Free expert tailoring is available at the store.

FOR THE PRICE OF A LOCAL CALL YOU CAN FIND OUT SALES AND SPECIAL PROMOTIONS THAT ARE GOING ON AROUND THE CITY. INSIDER SHOPPING'S EASY TO NAVIGATE VOICEMAIL SYSTEM PROVIDES SALES INFORMATION ON WOMEN'S, MEN'S, AND CHILDREN'S APPAREL AND ACCESSORIES, TOYS, SPORTING GOODS, AND GIFTS. LISTINGS ARE UPDATED ON A WEEKLY BASIS. 212 55-SALES YOU CAN ALSO ACCESS THEIR WEBSITE AT WW.INSHOP.COM.

GORSART
9 Murray Street (Broadway and Church Streets)
(212) 962-0024

Founded in 1921, Gorsart says that their biggest competitors are the full-retail midtown men's shops selling the same merchandise but at 35 percent higher prices. At Gorsart you can choose from over 5,000 first-quality suits in all sizes.

LOEHMANN'S INC.
101 Seventh Avenue (16th and 17th Streets) • (212) 352-0856

A large store filled to capacity with men's and women's clothing and accessories. Men can find shirts, ties, slacks, some suits, and casual-wear at incredible prices.

L.S. MEN'S CLOTHING • 19 West 44th Street • (212) 575-0933

L.S. stocks some of the best and most well known domestic designer labels for more than 40 percent off retail and they are usually the current styles. We have seen Ralph Lauren and Hickey Freeman at low prices.

THE SMART SHOPPER'S GUIDE
TO THE BEST BUYS FOR KIDS

WRITTEN AND RESEARCHED
BY SUE ROBINSON,
THIS COMPREHENSIVE GUIDE
TELLS YOU WHERE TO FIND
DESIGNER CLOTHING,
TOYS, FURNITURE,
AND MORE AT BARGAIN
PRICES. THE BOOK IS SOLD AT
MAJOR BOOKSTORES.
IT OFFERS HELPFUL,
UP-TO-DATE DISCOUNT TIPS,
INCLUDING LISTINGS OF
SAMPLE SALES.

MOE GINSBURG
162 Fifth Avenue (21st Street)
(212) 982-5254

Throughout this six-floor, 60,000 square feet store you will see just about anything a man could want—over 50,000 suits, outerwear, shoes, sportswear, formal wear, undergarments, and accessories. The price range for suits, some of which are 100 percent wool, are $230-$460. The eighth floor houses the outlet where items are discounted even more than on the other floors. The store has a great selection, is well-laid-out, and has tailors on-staff.

OLD NAVY CLOTHING CO.
610 Avenue of the Americas
(at 18th Street) • (212) 645-0663

Great buys on men's casual-wear, including jeans, khakis, sweaters, sweatshirts, and underwear.

PAN AM MEN'S CLOTHING
50 Orchard Street • (212) 925-7032

Pan Am offers a generous collection of men's suits, overcoats, sports jackets and slacks. 80 percent of the merchandise is from Italian designers; the rest are mostly domestic labels. Suits range from $200 to $450.

SYMS
400 Park Avenue (at 54th Street) • (212) 317-8200
42 Trinity Place • (212) 797-1199

An excellent, varied selection of men's suits, overcoats, and casual-wear.

T.J. MAXX
620 Avenue of the Americas (18th and 19th Streets)
(212) 229-0875

Savings galore on men's designer casual-wear, outerwear, and accessories. Ties, dress socks, and casual button down shirts can be found here at very inexpensive prices. Items are all on one level, in areas that are close to each other, so it's easy to find what you want.

CLOTHING, WOMEN'S
AARON'S
627 Fifth Avenue, Brooklyn • (718) 768-5400

It is a little hard to get to, but it is worth the trip. Tahari and Anne Klein II are just two of the top designers that abound in this well-laid-out shop. Their prices are 25 percent to one third lower than department and specialty stores. The clothes are all grouped by designer so you don't have to weed through piles of clothes searching out your favorite label.

BEST OF SCOTLAND
581 Fifth Avenue (47th and 48th Streets) • (212) 644-0415

Here you will find the lowest prices on fine cashmere in the City. They carry a wide variety of scarves, shawls, gloves, sweaters, and blankets. The sweaters sell from $185 and up, but remember, cashmere from Scotland is the best.

BLUE DUCK SHEARLINGS
463 Seventh Avenue, Suite 702 (at 35th Street)
(212) 268-3122

Blue Duck manufactures and sells gorgeous Shearling coats at almost-wholesale prices. You can purchase a coat right off the rack or have one custom-made to your specifications. Since the factory is located right in Manhattan, a custom-made coat can be manufactured in a short period of time. It's best to call ahead to meet with owner Barry Novick.

THE CARLISLE COLLECTION
16 East 52nd Street • (212) 751-6490 • By Appointment Only

The Carlisle Collection is a bridge line (priced between high-end and designer) of tailored clothing which is sold directly to the customer, and therefore, not available in stores. You can either go to an independent contractor's home to purchase merchandise, or buy items directly from the showroom. The clothes consist of classic tailored separates—jackets, blouses, skirts, and slacks—manufactured with European fabrics, and designed to mix and match. A ladies jacket sells for about $500; a suit, for $1,000. You can also purchase belts, costume jewelry, and scarves.

DAFFY'S
335 Madison Avenue (at 44th Street) • (212) 557-4422
1311 Broadway (at 34th Street) • (212) 736-4477
111 Fifth Avenue (at 18th Street) • (212) 529-4477
135 East 57th Street • (212) 376-4477

All the major designers of women's fashions can be spotted here at one time or another. The store is appealing and well laid out. You don't feel like you are shopping in a bargain basement even though the prices are quite low.

DESIGNER'S PROMISE
93 Nassau Street • (212) 513-1532

You can find excellent savings at Designer's Promise. Current designer career and sportswear is restocked twice a week.

DOLLAR BILLS
32 East 42nd Street • (212) 867-0212

At Dollar Bills, women can find good buys on fashionable European designer clothing at low prices. Very well known names can be found here, but remember, you must be prepared to spend some time sifting through the merchandise. We have spotted Armani, Ungaro, Fendi—need we say more?

FILENE'S BASEMENT
620 Avenue of the Americas (18th and 19th Streets)
(212) 620-3100
2222 Broadway (at 79th Street) • (212) 873-8000

Very affordable prices on designer women's career and sportswear. Swimsuits are a fraction of what they sell for in the department stores.

JANAK
200 West 70th Street, Suite 12C • (212) 787-0278
By Appointment Only

Janak is a small showroom filled with current designer women's-wear at 40 to 70 percent off retail prices. You will find women's business suits, dresses, smart casual-wear, sweaters, and lingerie. Sizes and colors can be ordered if they are not available in the store.

LA CRASIA GLOVES
304 Fifth Avenue (at 31st Street) • (212) 594-2223

La Crasia is the place to go for all types of gloves. They manufacture and discount leather, fabric, even wedding gloves.

LEA'S DESIGNER FASHION
119 Orchard Street • (212) 677-2043

Eugene Gluck's family are pioneers in the discount designer business. His store overflows with European designer merchandise, at one-third off retail prices, in sizes 4 to 16.

LOEHMANN'S INC.
101 Seventh Avenue (16th and 17th Streets) • (212) 352-0856

The premier discounter offers floors of women's merchandise, including suits, sportswear, evening-wear, coats, dresses, accessories, jewelry, and intimate apparel. You can find real steals here, but be prepared to sort through the racks.

T.J. MAXX
620 Avenue of the Americas (18th and 19th Streets)
(212) 229-0875

It's hard not to buy something here—the prices are that good, and everything is on one level so it's easy to find what you want. T.J. Maxx offers women's designer casual and dress-wear, intimate apparel, outerwear, and accessories at drop dead prices. We spotted many domestic designer labels—Jones New York, Donna Karan, Calvin Klein, Liz Claiborne, among many others.

COSMETICS AND PERFUME

COSMETICS PLUS
Locations Throughout the City

The most comprehensive discount perfume and cosmetics store in New York City. Their merchandise is fresh, which is important for cosmetics.

17th STREET BETWEEN BROADWAY AND FIFTH AVENUE

This is the perfume store mecca of New York City. Just walk and price the bottles. Be sure to check that the merchandise is fresh.

ELECTRONICS

B&H PHOTO
420 9th Avenue • (212) 444-5040

B&H is gigantic and very easy to maneuver around. The store sells all items related to photography including sound systems. Great prices, great service. Closed on all Jewish holidays.

J & R MUSIC & COMPUTER WORLD
23 Park Row (Beekman and Ann Streets) • (212) 238-9000

A huge selection of cellular phones, cameras, audio and video equipment, and computers.

P.C. RICHARD
120 14th Street (at Union Square) • (212) 979-2600
205 East 86th Street (2nd & 3rd Avenues) • (212) 289-1700

Competitive rates on computers, TVs, VCRs, stereo equipment, fax machines, copiers, and other electronic equipment. The staff is especially helpful and informative.

WHEN PURCHASING ELECTRONICS AT A DISCOUNTER ALWAYS TRY TO BARGAIN. USUALLY THE SALESPERSON HAS SOME FLEXABILTY IN THE PRICE OR AT LEAST MAY BE ABLE TO GIVE YOU SOME ADDITIONAL MERCHANDISE AT NO COST. USUALLY THE SUPERVISOR WILL GIVE THE SALESPERSON THE ROOM TO NEGOTIATE.

VICMARR STEREO AND TV
88 Delancey Street
(Orchard and Ludlow Streets)
(212) 505-0380

This is a first-rate discount shop that is run by a friendly well-informed gentleman, Mel Cohen. He keeps his prices low and his sales staff does not give you a hard sell. He is well stocked with telephones, stereo equipment, microwaves, and more.

INNOVATIVE AUDIO
150 East 58th Street • (212) 634-4444

This is a real find when you are looking for stereo equipment. Not only is Elliot Fishkin one of the nicest, most accommo-dating people, he is also one of the most knowledgeable. His prices can be negotiated and he does know exactly what system you need and will never try to oversell to you.

Although this shop is not really discount, it is next to impossible to find full-service electronic stores in the City. Their expertise and quality of service make it an easy way to shop and sometimes that is the bargain.

GENERAL STORE
BRADLEES
40 East 14th Street • (212) 673-5814

Inexpensive finds on household items, clothes, appliances, toi-letries, toys, and infant accessories.

CENTURY 21
22 Cortland Street (Broadway and Church Street)
(212) 227-9092

A discount designer department store selling everything from cloth-ing for men, women, and kids to general household appliances. You can find some great inexpensive gifts. We call it the "Thrifty Man's Bloomingdale's."

K-MART
1 Penn Plaza (at 34th Street)
(212) 760-1188
770 Broadway (8th Street and Astor)
(212) 673-1540

This renowned discount store has finally made its way to the City.

Come here for just about anything—inexpensive toys, appliances, clothing basics, house wares, and cosmetics.

ODD-JOB TRADING
149 West 32nd Street • (212) 564-7370
66 West 48th Street • (212) 575-0477
10 Cortland Street (Broadway & Church Street) • (212) 571-0959
465 Lexington Avenue (45th and 46th Streets) • (212) 949-7401
390 Fifth Avenue • (35th and 36th Streets) • (212) 239-3336

The merchandise changes daily and is similar in all stores. They have household items, toys, clothing, accessories, and more. They buy closeouts from manufacturers and sell them for about 75 percent of what they are sold for in other stores.

GIFTS

CERAMICA GIFT GALLERY
1009 Sixth Avenue (37th and 38th Streets) • (212) 354-9216

Silver, china, and crystal at discounted prices, even Baccarat. All you need to do is call and tell them what you want and they will ship it. Friendly and timely service.

MICHAEL C. FINA • 545 Fifth Avenue • (212) 557-2500

It is very hard to get anyone at this store on the phone due to the incredible volume of business that they do. However, they have a great selection of china, crystal, silver, pewter, and good baby gifts. They do have a mail-order business, which might be the way to go.

NEWMANS • 39-23 Bell Boulevard, Bayside • (718) 229-0358

Discounts from 15 percent to 50 percent off the major silver, china, and crystal manufacturers' retail prices. They will take phone orders, or you can visit their store. They will ship anywhere. Newmans accepts MasterCard, Visa and Discover. Ron is very friendly, helpful, and good about following-up on an order.

HANDBAGS & ACCESSORIES

FINE & KLEIN HANDBAGS
119 Orchard Street • (212) 674-6720

Fine & Klein has been in the discount designer handbag business for 52 years. They offer value and selection in handbags—a bag for every purpose, every time of day, and every fabric. You can also find good deals on wallets, attaché cases, and accessories.

SUAREZ NEW YORK
450 Park Avenue (56th and 57th Streets) • (212) 753-3758

All Suarez' merchandise is high quality, elegant, and imported from

Europe. They discount expensive designer handbags and accessories, such as wallets, scarves, belts, and shoes.

HOSIERY AND UNDERGARMENTS

UNDERWEAR PLAZA
1421 62nd Street, Brooklyn • (718) 232-6804

Dior, Eve Stillman, Calvin Klein, Vassarette, Bali, and Natori all can be found in this discount shop. Lingerie, slippers, and undergarments at low, low prices. It's worth the trip, and remember, with prices this good, buy in bulk.

Women are always in need of stockings. Here are three places that are happy to sell to you in bulk quantities with the best possible price:

L'EGGS BRANDS
By mail:
1 Hanes Place Catalog, P.O. Box 5000, Rural Hall, NC 27098
(800) 300-2600

NATIONAL WHOLESALE COMPANY
By mail: 400 National Boulevard, Lexington, NC 27292
(910) 248-5904

NO NONSENSE LEGWEAR
By mail:
300 Dougherty, P.O. Box 26095, Greensboro, NC 27420-6095
(800) 677-5995

Ask for Carol Burke.

LINENS

BED BATH & BEYOND
620 Avenue of the Americas (18th and 19th Streets)
(212) 255-3550

A large selection of kitchen, bed, bath, and general home items at discounted prices. They carry popular bedding brands, such as Laura Ashley, Sheridan, Wamsutta, and Royal Sateen.

GRAND STREET ON THE LOWER EAST SIDE

This street is lined with shops. While browsing you should be comparing prices. Don't be afraid to bargain!

HARRIS LEVY IMPORTERS
278 Grand Street (Eldridge and Forsythe Streets)
(212) 226-3102

One of the more "upscale" linen and bath shops located on the Lower East Side. Their emphasis is on quality merchandise and their prices are less than uptown. All major brand names including down comforters.

Large department stores have fairly good "white sales" where you can get good deals. So check their prices before going discount shopping. In particular:

BLOOMINGDALE'S
1000 Third Avenue (at 59th Street) • (212) 705-2000

MACY'S • 151 West 34th Street • (212) 695-4400

PAPER GOODS

GEMINI PAPER GOODS
449 Third Street, Brooklyn • (718) 768-5568

For paper napkins, matchbooks, place cards, ribbons, envelopes, and all other party accessories (all can be monogrammed) at excellent prices. Just give them a call and they will be happy to fill any order by mail.

PLANTS

HOME DEPOT
131-35 Avery Avenue (Queens) • (718) 358-9600
112-20 Rockaway Blvd. (Queens) • (718) 641-5500

These two locations have a large selection of house plants in their own nurseries, at a fraction of what they cost in Manhattan.

RECORDS, TAPES, AND CD'S

HMV RECORDS
1280 Lexington Avenue (86th and 87th Streets)
(212) 348-0800
2081 Broadway (at 72nd Street) • (212) 721-5900

HMV is the largest music store in the city, with over 40,000 square feet of space. Their sales staff is more than accommodating in guiding you through this well-laid-out store. They encourage questions and will even play the album that you want to hear. Due to its size and volume of sales they keep their prices low compared to other music stores in the city.

TOWER RECORDS
692 Broadway (at 4th Street) • (212) 505-1500
1961 Broadway (at 66th Street) • (212) 799-2500

Tower Records was the first to open a massive music store in New York City. They sell a complete range of music and try to be as helpful as possible. Their large size allows them to offer quite good prices.

VIRGIN MEGASTORE
1540 Broadway (45th & 46th Street) (212) 921-1020
52 East 14th street (at Union Square)• (212) 598-4666

These stores sell records, books, laser disks, CD ROMs, video games, and much more.

SHOES FOR MEN AND WOMEN

AMS SHOES OF MANHATTAN
1690 Second Avenue (at 87th Street) • (212) 426-6600

Discounts on all major brands of women's shoes.

STATESMAN SHOE • 6 East 46th Street • (212) 867-0450

This store is mostly for men. They stock sizes 5AA through 15EEE and are accommodating in trying to get you your size. Bass, Rockport, Nunn Bush, Stacy Adams, Bostonian, and Florsheim.

ORCHARD STREET

This is New York City's original shoe bazaar. It is hit or miss but women in particular will have over ten stores to choose from.

SPORTING GEAR

MODELL'S SPORTING GOODS • Locations Throughout the City

You can find a large selection of sporting equipment and apparel at Model's. Their athletic shoe prices are especially inexpensive. They will match or beat the competition's prices.

THE SPORTS AUTHORITY
401 Seventh Avenue (at 33rd Street)
(212) 563-7195
845 Third Avenue (at 51st Street)
(212) 355-9725
57 West 57th Street • (212) 355-6430

A well-stocked store filled with a variety of sporting equipment at reasonable prices. In addition to selling such items as tennis racquets, golf clubs, bicycles, and all the related accouterments, they also offer athletic footwear and apparel.

TOYS

All the following stores sell toys way below the full retail toy stores in New York City. Some major brand-name items sell for 50 percent less than other stores. Unless you are looking for a specific European or a unique toy, you should always check at these stores first.

KAY-BEE TOY INC
901 Avenue of the Americas
(32nd and 33rd Streets)
(212) 629-5386
2411 Broadway (89th Street)
(212) 595-4389

TOYS "R" US
1293 Broadway (at 33rd Street)
(212) 594-8697
24-32 Union Square East
(15th and 16th Streets)
(212) 674-8697

WATCHES

YAEGER WATCH CORPORATION
578 Fifth Avenue (at 47th Street)
(212) 819-0088

All major American and European designer watches are sold here at 33 to 40 percent off retail. You might have to wait a few weeks till they can get your watch in, but your savings can be thousands of dollars. Of course, they come with all the original guarantees and warranties.

YOU CAN ORDER JUST ABOUT ANYTHING ON THE WEB. WE HAVE ALL HEARD OF THE GIANTS LIKE AMAZON.COM FOR BOOKS, E-BAY FOR COLLECTABLES AND PRICELINE.COM FOR AIRFARES. BUT IT STILL CAN FEEL CONFUSING AND A BIT LIKE SHOPPING IN A BOTTOMLESS PIT. UNLESS YOU HAVE A FAVORITE E-COMMERCE OR STORE SITE, YOU CAN SPEND HOURS HUNTING FOR THE BEST BARGAIN, WHETHER LOOKING FOR ELECTRONICS OR TRIPS, NOT KNOWING IF OR WHEN YOU HAVE COVERED ALL THE POSSIBILITIES. IN ADDITION, THE CONSUMER-FRIENDLY TECHNOLOGY ISN'T QUITE THERE YET, IN TERMS OF SHOPPING EASE. THE CONCEPT THAT YOU CAN SHOP FOR VIRTUALLY ANYTHING WITHOUT LEAVING YOUR HOME IS INTRIGUING AND CAN BE A TIME-SAVER, BUT YOU HAVE TO ENJOY THE PIONEERING ASPECT OF FEELING YOUR WAY THROUGH THE INTERNET.

LEISURE
NEW YORK STYLE

SOLUTION:

If we have accomplished our goal, you now know how to live more efficiently and frugally, and how to access the city and your community effectively. Presto: You should now have more time and money to spend during your leisure hours. No matter what your passion — sports, pursuing a hobby, volunteering, or simply seeking entertainment — there is no better city to find opportunities and experts in your area of interest. This chapter will tell you where to find them.

THE INTREPID PAGES OF

HOBBY CLUBS, SCHOOLS, AND FUN ORGANIZATIONS RUN BY THE PROS

No matter what your passion or hobby, no matter what your level of ability or the amount of time that you have to spend, you can be part of the doing and learning that abounds in New York City, and you can do it in the company of pros.

ACTING

HB STUDIO • 120 Bank Street • (212) 675-2370

HB offers over 200 different classes to choose from including movement, singing, acting, play writing, speech, and more. They are open seven days a week from 9:30 A.M. to 8:45 P.M. on the weekdays and 10:00 A.M. to 4:00 P.M. on the weekends. The price depends on the particular package that you choose.

NEW YORK FOUNDATION FOR THE ARTS
155 Avenue of the Americas (Spring Street) • (212) 366-6900

Newsletters, grant information, a job-listing bulletin board, and more can be obtained from this not-for-profit agency that was created to help arts organizations and artists in all disciplines cope in New York.

ADVENTURE

ADVENTURE ON A SHOESTRING
300 West 53rd Street • (212) 265-2663

This thirty-six-year-old organization arranges several visits a week to unique places and people in New York City for its members (e.g. a chat with a handwriting analyst, a guided tour of a newspaper, a walking tour of "haunted" Greenwich Village, etc.) Membership is $40 for one year from the time you join, plus a $3 attendance fee at each event. There may be occasional additional charges for theatre and restaurant costs and one-day bus trips.

SIERRA CLUB • 2 West 47th Street • (212) 302-6826

This political action committee has been dedicated to preserving and protecting the environment for one hundred years. The Atlantic and New York City Chapter Outing Committees lead hikes, ski trips, backpacking, river touring, bike trips, and City walks every weekend. The cost of these outings is minimal to members.

Membership fee is $35 per year and entitles you to the monthly magazine and seasonal newsletter. There is an additional fee for the national and international outings schedule.

ARCHITECTURE

THE ARCHITECTURAL LEAGUE
457 Madison Avenue (50th and 51st Streets) • (212) 753-1722

The membership fee runs $50 per year for those thirty-five and under and $85 for those over thirty-five. You will be invited to more than thirty-five different events throughout the year, all relating to architecture issues, problems, and history. You will receive a poster for each season's programs, discounts on certain books, and more.

ART

THE ARTS STUDENTS LEAGUE OF NEW YORK
215 West 57th Street • (212) 247-4510

They are open seven days a week and offer classes in painting, drawing, sculpture, and graphics. For $150 a month, you can take classes five days a week for three and a half hours a day. For $75 a month, you can take two classes a week, and for $48 a month you can take one evening class a week.

NEW YORK STUDIO SCHOOL
8 West 8th Street • (212) 673-6466

At this school, students take life-drawing and painting classes, offered both in the evenings and on weekends and as part of a full-time, three-year program.

THE 92nd St Y • 1395 Lexington Avenue • (212) 415-5562

They offer a wide range of painting, drawing, sculpture, ceramics, jewlery & metalsmithing, and even bookbinding classes. Do not despair if you are a novice, all levels of expertise are addressed. www.92ndsty.org

ASTRONOMY

AMATEUR ASTRONOMERS ASSOCIATION
1010 Park Avenue • (212) 535-2922

This organization boasts over four hundred active star-gazing members in the metropolitan area. Membership entitles you to lecture programs at the Museum of Natural History, evening get-togethers to discuss advanced theories, and of course, actual gazing events. You can access their web site at www.aaa.org.

BILLIARDS

THE BILLIARD CLUB • 220 West 19th Street • (212) 206-POOL

They have a total of thirty-three pool tables. Open seven days a week, the fee ranges from $7 per table per hour during the day and $12 per table per hour after 7:00 P.M.

BIRDWATCHING

NEW YORK CITY AUDUBON SOCIETY
71 West 23rd Street • (212) 691-7483

There are always weekend outings to local New York City bird habitats as well as occasional weekend trips. You can attend lectures and films throughout the year. Membership is $20 and there is a separate fee for the outings.

BRIDGE

BEVERLY BRIDGE CLUB
150 Central Park South (at 59th Street) • (212) 246-5989

Open daily from 9:00 A.M. to 10:00 P.M. The admission fee in the evening is $11 and $4 for dinner. The admission fee is also $11 during the day and lunch is included. They offer classes for all levels of play, including beginners for $25 per class.

BUSINESS AS A PASSION

AMERICAN WOMEN'S ECONOMIC DEVELOPMENT CORPORATION
71 Vanderbilt Avenue (45th and 46th Streets) • (212) 692-9100

AWED was designed to help only women who want to start their own business or who have their own business. For $55 per year they will send you their monthly calendar of events and for an extra fee they will counsel you on any aspect of your business.

NEW YORK BUSINESS FORUMS
605 Madison Avenue (58th Street) • (212) 832-6984

Founded in 1984, NYBF was created to stimulate interaction among business founders and managers, and representatives of major corporations. They hold monthly breakfast meetings. The fee for most is $85, which includes the meal.

COOKING

JAMES BEARD FOUNDATION
167 West 12th Street • (212) 675-4984

Become a member of this famous culinary center and have the opportunity to dine with great chefs from all over the world who come here to prepare and share their gastronomic delights.

KAREN LEE • 142 West End Avenue • (212) 787-2227

Karen Lee has been a nationally recognized author, teacher, and caterer for the past twenty-six years. Her classes fall into four main categories: East/West cooking (blending of Eastern and Western cooking techniques and ingredients); vegetarian cooking; Italian;

and classic Chinese. Karen's recipes contain high-flavor, low-fat ingredients, organic vegetables, and grains. New classes form every four to six weeks, September through May, and are offered both in the morning and the evening. All the classes offer active, hands-on participation.

NEW YORKERS LOVE TO EAT!!
TWO GREAT
RESTAURANT/FOOD
RESOURCES THAT EVERY
NEW YORKER MUST HAVE ARE
THE ZAGAT GUIDE
(A VERITABLE RESTAURANT
BIBLE)
AND NEW YORK EATS
BY ED LEVINE
(A DESCRIPTIVE FOOD
SOURCE GUIDE.)

LAUREN GROVEMAN'S KITCHEN
By appointment
(914) 834-1372

Lauren's goal is to teach people to create food that not only looks, smells, and tastes wonderful but that inspires the people who eat it to want to do it themselves. All her recipes are original and there is nothing she cannot prepare; she is considered to be one of the up-and-coming chefs in the country. She has classes for all levels of ability.

PETER KUMP'S
NEW YORK COOKING SCHOOL
50 West 23rd Street • (212) 410-4601

The New York Cooking School is a small school dedicated to teaching cooking as a fine art in the tradition of European cooking schools. In addition to gaining a thorough background in French techniques, students also study cuisines from a variety of other countries. This is a place for those who are serious about good food and cooking, whether for a restaurant, catering operation, take-out shop, or personal enjoyment. Classes are offered during the day, evening, and weekends.

DANCE

ABIZAID ARTS • 107 Grand Street • (212) 941-8480

Classes are offered for all different types of dance, including ballet, salsa, and Brazilian, to name a few. The cost runs about $11 per session. Class cards, which entitle you to discounts, are available.

ARTHUR MURRAY DANCE STUDIO
677 Fifth Avenue (between 53rd and 54th Streets)
(212) 935-7787

Anyone interested in ballroom or freestyle dancing should make an appointment for a half-hour consultation. They have the capability to tailor a program to fit your need in either group or private lessons. There are eight teachers on staff.

NEW YORK SWING SOCIETY • (212) 696-9737

The membership fee is $35 per year and entitles you to discounts to their dances. Dances are held at Irving Place, 17 Irving Place (at 15th Street). The doors open at 7:00 P.M. and the band plays from 8:00 P.M. to 12:00 A.M. They also offer a free lesson with admission once a month. Additional dance instruction is available for a fee.

ROSELAND BALLROOM • 239 West 52nd Street • (212) 247-0200

Roseland is open for ballroom dancing on Sundays, from 2:30 P.M. to 11:00 P.M. They offer a deejay and a live orchestra for $11.

FILM

ANTHOLOGY FILM ARCHIVES
32 Second Avenue (at 2nd Street) • (212) 505-5181

Here they feature independent and avant-garde films, sometimes with a question and answer period led by the director. There are different levels of membership. The minimum membership fee is $50 a year and the screenings are $5. Certain events are only offered to members and some are free.

ANGELIKA FILM CENTER • Houston & Mercer • (212) 995-2000

One of the few remaining quirky theaters offering an amazing selection of foreign and independent films. The ornate foyer is half the fun.

FILM FORUM • 209 West Houston • (212) 787-8110

Almost thirty years old, this theater has become a legend for showing some of the best US and foreign independent films.

FOREIGN CULTURES

ALLIANCE FRANÇAISE • 22 East 60th Street • (212) 355-6100

For the basic membership fee of $65 a year, you can attend most events for free, such as lectures, readings, and films, and have full use of their library. Members also receive discounts to dance performances and theatre events. You do not have to be fluent in French to partake, but you obviously must have some understanding or at least a strong desire to learn.

THE ASIA SOCIETY
725 Park Avenue (at 70th Street) • (212) 288-6400

For $100 a year, you will receive a newsletter three times a year that announces all the upcoming cultural activities and events. Your membership entitles you to free admission to gallery exhibits and discounted tickets for films, performances, and lectures. Every year they pick a different country to focus on. They are a wonderful resource for any questions you may have concerning this part of the world.

THE ENGLISH-SPEAKING UNION
16 East 69th Street • (212) 879-6800

This is a not-for-profit educational and cultural organization that is dedicated to strengthening friendship among English-speaking people. A $90 per year membership entitles you to access their library, lectures, films, and their daily tea hour to which you may bring non-members.

FIERI • 25 West 43rd Street • (212) 413-5703

This is an Italian cultural organization that meets once a month to discuss educational topics, hold lectures, or partake in a cultural event. They also have other events throughout the year. Membership is $40 per year.

GOETHE INSTITUTE
1014 Fifth Avenue (at 82nd Street) • (212) 439-8700

There is no fee to belong to this German cultural organization; just put your name on their mailing list. They will send you information about their movies, lectures, and exhibitions. They also have an extensive lending library for you to use.

ITALIAN CULTURAL INSTITUTE
686 Park Avenue (68th and 69th Streets) • (212) 879-4242

This is a government organization that will put you on their mailing list and notify you about film, art, and music events as well as lectures on all aspects of Italian culture. Some events are free of charge and held at museums, concert halls, and theatres throughout New York.

THE JAPAN SOCIETY • 333 East 47th Street • (212) 832-1155

The basic membership fee is $55 for the year. This entitles you to a monthly newsletter filled with articles, upcoming programs, and activities, a calendar of events published once a month, and discounts on films, performing arts events, language classes, exhibits, and Japan Society publications. An understanding of Japanese is not necessary to enjoy yourself here.

GLASS-BLOWING

URBAN GLASS
57 Rockwell Place
(between Dekalb and Fulton Streets), Brooklyn
(718) 625-3685

This is the only glass-blowing institute in New York City. You can either make an appointment to blow your own glass ($20 to $45 per hour with some supplies and tools provided), or you can attend a weekend workshop, an eight-week course, or a twelve-week course. Courses range from beginner through advanced and range between $300 and $650, including materials.

HORTICULTURE

HORTICULTURE SOCIETY OF NEW YORK
128 West 58th Street • (212) 757-0915

This is a place where you can pursue garden design, flower arranging, vegetable growing, the art of bonsai, and overall plant nurturing. The basic membership fee is $35 and includes a discount on courses, access to the "plant hotline" on Tuesday and Thursday, from 3:00 P.M. to 4:00 P.M., discounts on purchasing plants at their shop, a newsletter telling you about upcoming events, and more.

PHOTOGRAPHY

INTERNATIONAL CENTER FOR PHOTOGRAPHY
1130 Fifth Avenue • (212) 860-1777
1133 Sixth Avenue • (212) 768-4682

Both a school and a museum. The school and darkroom space is located in the uptown location.

MY OWN COLOR LAB • 18 West 27th Street • (212) 696-4107

They rent darkrooms for developing color film only. All rooms come completely equipped. The rate is $9.99 per hour.

PHOTOGRAPHICS UNLIMITED
17 West 17th Street • (212) 255-9678

You can develop black and white film here. The cost is $8.50 per hour with a minimum of two hours. The rooms come fully equipped except for film developer and paper. You need to reserve two days in advance.

POETRY AND LITERATURE

THE NEW YORK OPEN CENTER
83 Spring Street • (212) 219-2527

The center offers wonderful live storytelling throughout the year for a nominal fee. Call to receive their catalogue.

THE NEW YORK PUBLIC LIBRARY PUBLIC EDUCATION PROGRAM
Fifth Avenue at 42nd Street
(212) 930-0855

The library offers a series of lectures by distinguished lecturers in the evening at $10 per ticket. Call for a brochure of upcoming topics and speakers.

92ND STREET Y
1395 Lexington Avenue (at 92nd Street) (212) 427-6000

This is one of New York City's meccas for all kinds of cultural events, lectures, and classes with the world's best-known authors and experts from every field. A small fee is charged for each event; call for a catalogue.

FEW THINGS IN MANHATTAN ARE FREE... THE PUBLIC LIBRARY SYSTEM IS SOMETHING THAT IS. WITH OVER SIXTEEN MILLION BOOKS IN ITS FOUR RESEARCH AND 85 BRANCH LOCATIONS, THE NEW YORK PUBLIC LIBRARY IS ONE OF THE LARGEST AND MOST COMPLETE LIBRARY SYSTEMS IN THE WORLD. ANYONE WHO LIVES, WORKS, OR ATTENDS SCHOOL IN NEW YORK STATE, INCLUDING A CHILD WHO CAN WRITE HIS/HER OWN NAME, CAN OBTAIN A FREE BORROWER'S CARD. CARDS MAY BE APPLIED FOR AT ANY BRANCH.

POETRY SOCIETY OF AMERICA
15 Gramercy Park South
(212) 254-9628

This society was founded in 1910 and its mission is to completely support the working poet. You can attend seminars, tributes, and readings. Call for a calendar that is published twice a year.

SHAKESPEARE AND COMPANY BOOKSELLERS
939 Lexington Avenue (68th Street)
(212) 570-0201
716 Broadway (Washington Place)
(212) 529-1330

You can learn about their readings by visiting the bookshop. The downtown location sometimes advertises readings in *The Village Voice*.

THE WEST SIDE YMCA
5 West 63rd Street • (212) 787-6557

This Y sponsors a tremendous amount of readings by fiction writers, nonfiction writers, and poets. Call to be placed on their mailing list. A small fee is required for each event.

POLITICS
LOCAL ASSEMBLY AND COUNCIL PERSON

Call your local political officials to find out where the nearest political organizational club is located. They should be able to tell you about clubs of all affiliations.

ROCK CLIMBING

59TH STREET RECREATION CENTER
533 West 59th Street • (212) 397-3157

This center has an artificial climbing wall.

EXTRA VERTICAL CLIMBING CENTER (THE ATRIUM)
61 West 62nd Street • (212) 586-5382

With over 30,000 square feet of climbing wall space, this 50 foot vertical wall offers a variety of climbs for the amateur to the expert. Day passes available.

MANHATTAN PLAZA HEALTH CLUB
482 West 43rd Street • (212) 563-7001

Though smaller than other walls in New York, Manhattan Plaza offers a very challenging terrain. Adult day passes are available.

THE SPORTS CENTER AT CHELSEA PIERS
23rd Street and the Hudson River • (212) 336-6083

One of the best indoor climbing walls in the country is located here, with an incline of textured fiberglass 46 feet high and 100 feet long. Routes range from beginner to overhanging lead climbs on "the roof" that will challenge experts.

SINGING

BRANDY'S PIANO BAR • 235 East 84th Street • (212) 650-1944

Every night is open mike night at Brandy's from 9:30 P.M. to 4:00 A.M. The accompanist will play any standard, but if there is a particular arrangement you like, bring your own music.

DON'T TELL MAMA CABARET & NIGHTCLUB
343 West 46th Street • (212) 757-0788

Ming Phan owns this club, which features an open mike night every night from 10:00 P.M. until 3:00 A.M.

DUPLEX CABARET • 61 Christopher Street • (212) 255-5438

Open mike at the downstairs bar begins at 9:00 P.M. every night. Don't be surprised if your waiter or bartender performs.

NEW YORK CHORAL SOCIETY
881 Seventh Avenue • (212) 247-3878

During the summer anyone may join the summer sing. It is held at CAMI Hall, 165 West 57th Street. Tickets to participate cost $8, payable at the door. Call to be put on their mailing list.

SOMMELIER

INTERNATIONAL WINE CENTER • (212) 627-7170

Call to put your name on their mailing list. They offer wine tasting events throughout the year to which members attend at a discount.

TASTERS GUILD INTERNATIONAL
230 West 79th Street • (212) 799-6311

This is an international organization that holds twenty to thirty events each year consisting of wine and food dinners and tastings for everyone from the novice to the connoisseur. The Gramercy Park Hotel is the headquarters for the wine tastings and the dinners are held at different restaurants throughout the City. Local membership is $20 and entitles you to discounts at events. National membership is $35 and includes eight issues of Wine and Spirits magazine, three issues of the Tasters Guild Journal, and discounts at wine shops and wineries throughout the country, as well as discounts to their events. Non-members are also welcome to the events, but they will have to pay more to attend.

THE WINE WORKSHOP
160 West 72nd Street, 2nd Floor • (212) 875-0222

You can become a true wine connoisseur if you attend workshops through this organization. They host a multitude of classes over the course of the year, including "Essentials of Wine," "Viva Italia!," "Tour De France," and many more. Most of the classes are held at The Culinary Loft at 515 Broadway. Call Jana Kravitz for more information.

STAND-UP COMEDY

BOSTON COMEDY CLUB • 82 West 3rd Street • (212) 477-1000

You can attend New Talent Night on Monday nights at 9:00 P.M. You must bring six paying customers the first time you perform; four people from then on. There is an $8 cover charge and a two-drink minimum. For more information, call the host, David J., at (212) 254-5424.

IMPROVISATION
433 West 34th Street • (212) 279-3446

Four times a year the owner of this club, Silver Sanders Friedman, holds auditions for their Monday night showcases.

STAND-UP NEW YORK • 236 West 78th Street • (212) 595-0850

Every night of the week (except Saturday) at 7:00 P.M., anyone can stand up at the microphone and perform eight minutes of material, as long as they bring three paying customers. The cover ranges from $5 to $12 and a two-item minimum is required.

TABLE GAMES

BACKGAMMON CLUB
136 West 72nd Street • (212) 787-4629

Open seven days a week from 2:00 P.M. to 9:00 P.M., this small space offers the backgammon player a chance to play for either a monetary profit or loss. You will be charged $4 an hour per person.

MANHATTAN CHESS CLUB
353 West 46th Street • (212) 333-5888

Open daily from 11:00 A.M. to 11:00 P.M., they offer lectures, seminars, and open exhibition matches. The yearly membership fee is $330 for males and $150 for females. Non-members can also attend the club at $5 a visit (the first visit is free).

THE VILLAGE CHESS SHOP
230 Thompson Street (3rd Street)
(212) 475-9580

They have fourteen tables set up for chess play from noon to midnight seven days a week. The cost is $1 per hour. All levels of play are welcome.

TRAVEL

JOSEPH VOS
AT VALERIE WILSON TRAVEL
475 Park Avenue South
(between 32nd and 33rd Streets)
(212) 592-1311

A full-service travel agency that can fulfill any conceivable request and ones you never thought of.

NOW VOYAGER • (212) 431-1616

A cheap way to travel is by becoming a courier, but you usually give up your luggage space. There are many restrictions and rules to follow, but it sure is an inexpensive way to go.

WIMCO
P.O. Box 1461, Newport, RI 02840
(800) 932-3222

This company can help you find a villa or house to rent in the Caribbean and Europe. They will provide you with a destination piece or catalogue that contains descriptive information on where you wish to travel.

EVEN IF YOU DON'T HAVE A CAR, YOU CAN TAKE DAY TRIPS OUT OF THE CITY. METRO NORTH OFFERS ONE-DAY GETAWAYS THAT DEPART FROM GRAND CENTRAL STATION DURING THE SPRING, SUMMER AND EARLY FALL. THE PLANNED EXCURSIONS FEATURE DESTINATIONS SUCH AS MYSTIC SEAPORT AND OTHER ATTRACTIONS IN CONNECTICUT, ANTIQUING AND TOURING WINERIES IN NEW YORK STATE, AND TOURING MANSIONS IN THE HUSDON RIVER VALLEY. CALL (212) 532-4900 FOR FURTHER INFORMATION AND A BROCHURE. THE LONG ISLAND RAILROAD OFFERS DAY TRIPS DURING THE SUMMER TO LONG ISLAND BEACHES, FIRE ISLAND, THE HAMPTONS, AND OTHER LONG ISLAND POINTS OF INTEREST. CALL (718) 217-5477 IN THE SPRING FOR INFORMATION AND A BROCHURE.

YOU CAN PURSUE A PASSION BY TAKING A WALKING TOUR OF NEW YORK. THE 92ND STREET Y OFFERS A VARIETY OF TOURS, INLUDING "NEW YORK SPORTS SCENES," "A CHOCOLATE LOVER'S GUIDE TO NEW YORK," AND "NEW YORK REFLECTIONS: THE CITY'S GLORIOUS GLASS WALLS AND WINDOWS." CALL (212) 415-5628 FOR A COPY OF THEIR CATALOGUE.

WHEN TRYING TO FIND THE LOWEST AIR FARE TO A PARTICULAR DESTINATION, IT IS BEST TO CHECK WITH SEVERAL TRAVEL AGENTS. A GOOD AGENT WILL NOT SIMPLY RELY ON INFORMATION PROVIDED ON THE COMPUTER, BUT WILL ALSO KNOW ABOUT SPECIAL DEALS AND WILL PLACE EXTRA PHONE CALLS TO GET THE BEST DEALS. IN ADDITION, CHECK WITH THE TRAVEL AGENT AFTER THE TICKET HAS BEEN PURCHASED TO DETERMINE WHETHER THE FARE HAS BEEN REDUCED. EVEN IF YOU HAVE TO PAY A MINIMAL PENALTY FOR A TICKET CHANGE, THE DIFFERENCE MAY BE WORTH IT. DO NOT HESITATE TO LOOK ON THE INTERNET FOR CHEAP FARES. IF YOU HAVE A FLEXABLE TRAVEL SCHEDULE YOU MAY BE ABLE TO SECURE A GOOD DEAL.

TRAVEL NEWSLETTERS
THE DISCERNING TRAVELER (800) 673-7834

This newsletter offers practical, easy-to-use guides to destinations from Maine to Florida and Eastern Canada. A one-year subscription includes six issues, one of which is a romantic hideaway issue, and costs $50. The authors have also published several guide books.

FAMILY TRAVEL FORUM • (212) 665-6124

This newsletter features articles about travelling with children, to locations such as resort destinations and cities around the world. They offer both a printed and an online newsletter. A comprehensive subscription is $48 per year, and allows you to access restricted areas on the website, which is www.familytravelforum.com.

PASSPORT • (800) 542-6670

This monthly newsletter covers a broad view of travel throughout the world, with a strong emphasis on Europe. The cost is $75 a year.

WEBSITES
For tickets

www.priceline.com, www.thetrip.com and www.cheaptickets.com.

For Travel Information

www.frommers.com and www.fodors.com

THE INTREPID PAGES OF
THE Y's

There are Y's throughout the City that have wonderful fitness facilities. The atmosphere is relaxed and the emphasis is on having fun and getting in shape. If you are looking for a game of basketball or racquetball, a running mate, or simply a friendly face, you will most likely find it at the Y. This is the small-town answer to the problem of working out in the Big Apple, and it sure can be a refreshing change from many of the trendy health clubs in the City. The Y's often offer special programs for children, teenagers, and the elderly.

MCBURNEY YMCA • 215 West 23rd Street • (212) 741-9210

Membership Rates:
Men and Women—$134 initiation fee; $59 per month

Facilities:
Stairmaster, treadmills, Universal equipment, indoor pool, indoor track, paddle ball courts, basketball, sauna, steam and massage.

92nd STREET Y
1395 Lexington Avenue (at 92nd Street) • (212) 427-6000

Membership Rates:
Men's full membership—$995

Women's full membership—$895

They offer limited-hour memberships for less money.

Facilities:
Indoor pool, two gyms, volleyball, racquetball, basketball, track, aerobics and exercise classes, yoga, steam, sauna, massage, two whirlpools, towel and laundry service.

VANDERBILT YMCA • 224 East 47th Street • (212) 756-9600

Membership Rates:
Men and Women—$804

Facilities:
Two pools (one for lap, one for lessons), Nautilus, free weights,

Karate, yoga, Stairmaster, Lifecycles, NordicTrack, aerobic and exercise classes, steam, sauna and massage.

WESTSIDE YMCA • 5 West 63rd Street • (212) 787-4400

Membership Rates:
Men and Women—$708

Facilities:
Silex, Nautilus, Stairmaster, bikes, free weights, aerobics classes, two pools, indoor track, handball, squash, racquetball, sauna, steam and massage.

YWCA • 610 Lexington Avenue (53rd Street) • (212) 755-4500

Membership Rates:
Men and Women—$395 plus $60 Y membership

Facilities:
Fitness room, pool, weight rooms, Stairmaster, bikes, treadmills, indoor track, steam and sauna.

THE INTREPID PAGES OF
CITY-FUNDED RECREATION CENTERS

The City-funded recreation centers are clean, organized, and inexpensive. Membership costs are the same at each one and entitle you to free use of all the centers.

ALFRED E. SMITH RECREATION CENTER
80 Catherine Street • (212) 285-0300

Membership Fee:

Free	12 years old and under
$10	13-17 years old
$25	18-54 years old
$10	55 years old and up

Facilities:
Nautilus, cardiovascular equipment, indoor and outdoor basketball courts, and badminton.

ASSER LEVY RECREATION CENTER
FDR Drive at 23rd Street • (212) 447-2020

Membership Fee:
Same as above

Facilities:
Aerobics, weights, machines, Universal equipment, rowing machines, indoor and outdoor pools.

CARMINE RECREATION CENTER
1 Clarkson Street • (212) 242-5228

Membership Fee:
Same as above

Facilities:
One indoor and one outdoor pool, two weight rooms, aerobics, volleyball, and two indoor basketball courts.

EAST 54TH STREET
348 East 54th Street • (212) 397-3154

Membership Fee:
Same as above

Facilities:
Indoor pool, Nautilus equipment, free weights, cardiovascular

FOR EXERCISE AND BEAUTIFUL VIEWS, VISIT THE 28-ACRE RIVERBANK STATE PARK, WHICH OVERLOOKS THE HUSDON. FACILITIES INCLUDE INDOOR AND OUTDOOR POOLS, RUNNING TRACK, GYM AND WEIGHT ROOM, ATHLETIC FIELDS FOR GROUPS, AND PLAY AREAS FOR CHILDREN. THERE IS A SMALL REGISTRATION FEE AND A NOMINAL FEE FOR SOME ACTIVITIES. FOR FURTHER INFORMATION, CALL (212) 694-3600. THE PARK IS LOCATED AT 679 RIVERSIDE DRIVE AT WEST 145TH STREET.

machines, ballet, yoga, karate and aerobics classes, running track, and an indoor basketball court.

HAMILTON FISH RECREATION CENTER
128 Pitt Street • (212) 387-7688

Membership Fee:
Same as above

Facilities:
Adult and children swimming pools, handball and basketball courts, weight room with free weights, weight training machines, billiards, and ping pong.

WEST 59TH STREET
533 West 59th Street • (212) 397-3159

Membership Fee:
Same as above

Facilities:
Free weights, cardiovascular equipment, indoor pool, and an indoor basketball court.

THE INTREPID PAGES OF

SPORTS ON YOUR OWN OR WITH A LEAGUE

You may not realize it, but you do not need to leave the City to find a softball game, shoot hoops with friends, take a dip on a hot summer day, go horseback riding, take a hike, practice archery, or even play eighteen holes of golf. New York is a city of parks in which you can do all of the above and more if you just know where to go. There are 28,074 acres of green space in New York City, including 854 playgrounds, 15 miles of beach, hundreds of tennis courts, 7,000 acres of natural areas, 20 major recreation centers, 13 golf courses, and more. In Manhattan alone, there are 2,628 acres of park land...that's 17 percent of Manhattan.

The first call you need to make is to the New York City Parks and Recreation press office: (212) 360-8141, or try the City Parks Foundation at (212) 360-1399. Ask them to send you a copy of the Green Pages. This is a sixty-page booklet that lists all the facilities and programs the Department of Parks and Recreation offers with phone numbers, addresses, and facts, from cricket fields to carousels. It's free and you should not be without it.

> THE CHELSEA PIERS SPORTS & ENTERTAINMENT COMPLEX CAN FULFILL EVERY SPORTS ENTHUSIAST'S DREAM. THIS THIRTY-ACRE WATERFRONT SPORTS VILLAGE, LOCATED ALONG THE HUDSON RIVER, FEATURES A GOLF CLUB, ROLLER AND ICE SKATING RINKS, MARITIME CENTER, AND FIELD HOUSE, COMPLETE WITH A ROCK CLIMBING WALL. CALL (212) 336-6666 FOR MORE INFORMATION.

Now that you know that New York City is not lacking in any recreational facility, we want you to understand that there are hundreds of teams and organizations to join. Whether you are an aspiring or retiring hockey player, baseball enthusiast, or tennis buff, no matter your sport or your level of skill, there is a group out there just waiting for you to join. Depending on the activity you choose, you may need a permit from the Parks Department and of course there may be a charge to join a league or group.

ARCHERY

WILLOWBROOK PARK, Staten Island • (718) 698-2186

A permit is not required and there is no charge, but you must bring your own equipment, including target. Saturday and Sunday mornings are often reserved for teams. Willowbrook Park is open from dawn to dusk.

BADMINTON

The U.S. Badminton Association

Provides information about events and clubs. Look online at www.usabadminton.org or call (719) 578-4808.

For the best selection of badminton rackets and equipment, go to Paragon, 867 Broadway (at 18th Street), (212) 255-8036.

On Your Own:

NEW YORK BADMINTON
1075 Second Avenue (at 56th Street)
(212) 752-4340

This group is open to the public and holds sessions on Friday nights and Sundays during the day. You can request a schedule of fees and playing times each season. For further information, contact Veronica at (718) 205-0987.

ALFRED E. SMITH RECREATION CENTER
80 Catherine Street • (212) 285-0300

Badminton is played on Friday evenings, from 6:00 P.M. to 10:00 P.M. You must pay the Center's yearly membership rate of $25.

Club:

BADMINTON CLUB OF THE CITY OF NEW YORK
Second Avenue at 68th Street • (212) 535-1609

This is a private club, where members play on Saturdays from 11:00 A.M. to 2:00 P.M., from October to March. You can first play as a guest, and then join for $225 per year.

BASKETBALL

On Your Own:

BASKETBALL CITY
West 23rd Street and Twelfth Avenue • (212) 234-6677

You can rent a court or participate in open playtime.

There are hundreds of outdoor basketball courts in New York City.

Rumor has it that you can find a serious game at 76th Street and Riverside Drive as well as West Fourth Street and Sixth Avenue. You can find a light game on 77th Street between Amsterdam and Columbus Avenues.

Leagues:

BASKETBALL CITY
West 23rd Street and Twelfth Avenue • (212) 234-6677

They offer both men's and women's leagues.

NEW YORK URBAN PROFESSIONALS ATHLETIC LEAGUE
200 West 72nd Street • (212) 877-3614

The director is John Bykowsky. There are four seasons and approximately 350 teams of all different abilities. Players can join as individuals or teams. Call their office for specific fee information. Games are played on weekday evenings in various high schools throughout Manhattan. The teams are made up of people in professional jobs during the day. Women are welcome.

YORKVILLE SPORTS ASSOCIATION • (212) 645-6488

Speak to Al Moralis. Teams or individuals can join. There are women's leagues as well.

BICYCLING

On Your Own:

In Central Park the drive is closed to motor vehicles at certain times. On weekends, it is closed all day. On weekdays, it is closed from 10:00 A.M. to 3:00 P.M. and 7:00 P.M. to 10:00 P.M. On holidays, it is closed from 7:00 P.M. to 6:00 A.M. You can rent bikes from Loeb Boathouse, (212) 861-4137, at $8 per hour for a three-speed, $10 per hour for a 10-speed, and $14 per hour for a two-seater. Pedal carriage rentals (for two adults and two small children) are available at 67th Street and West Drive (in front of Tavern on the Green), (212) 860-4619, at $15 per hour. Another good ride is Riverside Park promenade from West 72nd Street to 100th Street.

Clubs:

NEW YORK CYCLE CLUB
Post Office Box 20541,
Columbus Circle Station
New York, NY 10023
(212) 828-5711

The New York Cycle Club currently has over 1,400 members. They organize rides every weekend and welcome cycling enthusiasts of all different abilities. As a member, you would be entitled to a monthly newsletter that provides a schedule of upcoming rides, as well as a monthly dinner meeting. For more information on membership fees and benefits, send a self-addressed stamped envelope to the address listed above. You can also access their web site at www.nycc.org.

BOATING
CENTRAL PARK AT THE LOEB BOATHOUSE • (212) 517-4723

March through November, $10 per hour for a rowboat (and they will watch your stroller, etc.); May through October, $30 per hour for a gondola ride for up to five people.

BOCCIE
On Your Own:

In Manhattan you can find boccie courts in the following areas, to name a few: J.J. Walker Park, at Seventh Avenue South and Clarkson Street; Houston Street and Pitt Street; Washington Square Park, at Tango Court.

BOWLING
On Your Own:
AMF CHELSEA PIERS
23rd Street and West Side Highway • 212 835-2695

Open daily from 9:00 AM to 1:00 AM, weekends till 4:00AM. They have 40 lanes and all in state of the art condition.

BOWLMOR LANES
110 University Place (12th and 13th Streets) • (212) 255-8188

Open daily from 10:00 A.M., forty-four lanes.

LEISURE TIME
625 Eighth Avenue (40th and 41st Streets at Port Authority) (212) 268-6909

Open daily from 10:00 A.M., thirty lanes.

Leagues:

Call Bowlmor, Leisure Time, or AMF Chelsea Piers to find a league that fits your ability.

BOXING
BLUE VELVET BOXING CLUB
23 West 24th street • (212) 822-1960

An upscale boxing club for people who want to get in to shape, have fun and develop a skill. They will customize a membership that fits your needs.

CHURCH STREET BOXING GYM • 25 Park Place • (212) 571-1333

There is a set monthly membership fee, but training fees are negotiated between you and the various trainers on site. Church Street is also a great place to watch boxing. High-energy crowds, which have included Mike Tyson, pack the place for its periodic Friday night fights.

GLEASON'S GYM • 75 Front Street, Brooklyn • (718) 797-2872

Hours are Monday through Friday, 7:00 A.M. to 9:00 P.M.; Saturdays, 9:00 A.M. to 5:00 P.M. This is one of the best facilities. It has a 21,000-square-foot gym with three rings. They offer private lessons. Here you will find professional boxers as well as office workers by day who are boxers by night. Men and women.

CROQUET

On Your Own:

Call (212) 360-8133 to get a City permit. Cost is $30 for the season (May through November). In Manhattan, you can play croquet in Central Park, north of Sheep Meadow at 67th Street near East Drive.

Clubs:

THE NEW YORK CROQUET CLUB • (212) 369-7949

Free two-hour clinics are offered on Tuesdays at 6:00 P.M. Call to obtain membership information and a schedule of upcoming events and tournaments.

DIVING

PAN AQUA DIVING
460 West 43rd Street, just east of 10th Avenue • (212) 736-3483

The staff teaches diving courses at five pools located in area Y's and health clubs. During the summer, they offer local dive trips to Long Island, and throughout the year, they offer trips to more exotic locations including the Caribbean.

FISHING

For freshwater fishing, people who are sixteen years old or over must get a license. You can obtain one at Paragon Sporting Goods, located at 867 Broadway (at 18th Street), (212) 255-8036. Check to see if the fish are edible no matter where you catch them.

On Your Own:

Riverside Park along the Hudson River Esplanade from West 72nd Street to 84th Street and West 91st Street to 100th Street.

Lighthouse Park on the northern tip of Roosevelt Island.

For three days during the months of May, July, and October, the Battery Park City Park Corporation in conjunction with the Cornell Cooperative Extension offers free fishing lessons. They even provide the equipment. And of course the fish are then set free. Call (212) 267-9700 to find out the exact days.

FRISBEE

On Your Own:

You can pick up a freestyle game on any nice day in Central Park at Sheep Meadow. A popular spot for ultimate frisbee is at North Meadow, 97th Street and Fifth Avenue.

Leagues:

FLYING DISC ENTERPRISES • (212) 662-0391

Speak to Mark Danna.

GOLF

You can even play golf in New York City; and yes, the courses are clean, well organized, challenging, and accessible by subway. You can reserve a tee-off time at eight of the golf courses by calling (718) 225-GOLF about one and one-half weeks in advance. You can play alone or in a group of up to four. Tee times are well adhered to.

CHELSEA PIERS DRIVING RANGE
West 23rd Street and The Hudson River • (212) 336-6666

A four tier driving range open from 5:00 AM to midnight seven days a week. It accommodates about 400 people and it is heated so don't worry about the chill from the Hudson River.

GOLFPORT • Long Island City, Queens • (718) 472-4653

Golfport is a public driving range along the East River in Queens (next to Tennisport, listed below) that has ten heated and lighted stalls. The facility is open seven days a week: Monday through Friday, 10 A.M. to 8 P.M., and Saturday and Sunday, 10 A.M. to 6 P.M. The last buckets are sold one hour before closing. Lessons are available by appointment only. Buckets range in price from $5 to $15 depending on size, and there is no fee for club rentals.

RANDALLS ISLAND FAMILY GOLF CENTER • (212) 427-5689

This complex features a driving range, 2 18-hole miniture golf courses, 9 batting cages, a pro shop, and picnic tables. A pro is available for lessons. They are open year-round, seven days a week, from 8:00 A.M. to 11:00 P.M. in the summer, and 9 A.M. to 9 P.M. in the winter. They even have a shuttle that leaves from 86th Street and 3rd Avenue every hour.

HIKING

On Your Own:

In Manhattan there is a nature trail at Inwood Hill Park that is 2.2 miles long. The Urban Park Rangers also lead guided tours in Central Park. For more information, call (212) 360-1406 or (1-888) NYPARKS.

Organizations:
ATLANTIC CHAPTER OUTINGS • (212) 791-2400

The Sierra Club offers free hiking excursions. You can get specific information by visiting their web site at www.sierraclub.org/chapters/ny.

HORSEBACK RIDING
CHELSEA EQUESTRIAN CENTER • (212) 367-9090

Individual or group lessons are offered. All riding is done inside the center. They will do a total evaluation and then make recommendations

CLAREMONT RIDING ACADEMY
175 West 89th Street • (212) 724-5100

English-style riding. You can ride on your own in the park, but you must be an experienced rider. Fee: $35 per hour. They also offer group and private lessons. Hours are daily, Monday through Friday, 6:30 A.M. to 7:00 P.M.; Saturday and Sunday, 8:00 A.M. to 4:30 P.M.

OLD SALEM FARM
P.O. Box 317, North Salem, New York • (914) 669-5610

Old Salem is a full-service training and boarding facility with an exceptionally experienced staff. The Old Salem Farm trainers and students exhibit their horses in the most competitive events.

ICE HOCKEY
On Your Own:
WOLLMAN RINK
59th Street and Sixth Avenue (Central Park)
(212) 396-1010, ext. 15

Wollman offers adult pick up games on Thursday evenings. Speak with Phil, the hockey director.

Leagues:
BROOKLYN BLADES • (718) 595-2808

This women's recreational ice hockey league welcomes beginners as well as advanced players. Call to receive more information or visit their web site at www.brooklynblades.org.

LASKER RINK IN CENTRAL PARK • (212) 396-0388

A competitive league for both youth and adults.

SKY RINK AT CHELSEA PIERS
23rd Street and the Hudson River • (212) 336-6100

Sky Rink at Chelsea Piers has two indoor ice skating rinks that are open year-round. Leagues and clinics are available for youths and adults.

WOLLMAN RINK
59th Street and Sixth Avenue (Central Park)
(212) 396-1010, ext. 15

Youth leagues (no adult leagues are offered) meet three times a week at Wollman Rink. Call Phil, the hockey director, for more information.

ICE SKATING

Skates to rent and lessons are available at all the locations below.

On Your Own, Outdoor:

LASKER RINK
106th Street, South of Lenox Avenue (Central Park)
(212) 396-0388

26,000 square feet; October through March.

ROCKEFELLER PLAZA
49th-50th Streets off Fifth Avenue • (212) 332-7654

7,800 square feet; October through April.

WOLLMAN RINK
59th Street and Sixth Avenue (Central Park) • (212) 396-1010

33,000 square feet; October through March.

On Your Own, Indoor:

ICE STUDIO
1034 Lexington Avenue (73rd and 74th Streets), 2nd Floor
(212) 535-0304

40' X 60'; open year-round.

SKY RINK AT CHELSEA PIERS
23rd Street and the Hudson River • (212) 336-6100

Two indoor skating rinks are open year-round.

KITE FLYING

Central Park in the Sheep Meadow.

RACEWALKING

On Your Own:

The Central Park Reservoir is 1.58 miles long.

Clubs:

THE PARK RACE WALKERS CLUB
320 East 83rd Street, Box 18, New York, NY 10028-0013
(212) 628-1317

Speak with Stella Cashman. You don't have to be a "speed setter" or even have experience to become involved. They meet on

Tuesday and Thursday at 7:15 P.M. in Central Park. On Saturday, Sunday, and holidays, they meet at 8:00 A.M. To receive a schedule of park races, send a self-addressed stamped envelope to the above address.

ROLLER SKATING, IN-LINE SKATING

On Your Own:

THE ROLLER RINKS AT CHELSEA PIERS
23rd Street and the Hudson River
(212) 336-6200

Chelsea Piers has the only two outdoor, regulation-sized, professionally surfaced in-line and roller skating rinks in Manhattan.

WOLLMAN RINK
59th Street and Sixth Avenue
(Central Park)
(212) 396-1010

They are open May through September. Call for hours and rate information.

Schools:

LEZLY SKATE SCHOOL • (212) 777-3232

Indoor and outdoor lessons. Group and private instruction is offered for all levels of ability.

THE ROLLER RINKS AT CHELSEA PIERS
23rd Street and the Hudson River
(212) 336-6200

Call for group and private lesson hours and rates.

RUNNING

On Your Own:

Run in Central Park, especially when it is closed to traffic. (See the Bicycling section, above, for information about hours closed.) You also can use the indoor tracks in the City recreational facilities, listed above. For those who are energetic and want to run in beautiful surroundings, you can get a seasonal pass ($10) to run in

BIG CITY KITE CO. AT 1210 LEXINGTON AVENUE (82ND STREET), (212) 472-2623, HAS A GREAT SELECTION OF KITES.

WALKING SHOES ARE DIFFERENT FROM RUNNING SHOES. A GOOD PLACE TO GO IS SUPER RUNNERS, LOCATED AT 1337 LEXINGTON AVENUE (AT 89TH STREET), (212) 369-6010. THEY LET YOU WALK AROUND THE BLOCK.

A GOOD PLACE TO RENT IN-LINE SKATES IS BLADES WEST, 120 WEST 72ND STREET, (212) 787-3911. THEY ARE OPEN MONDAY THROUGH SATURDAY, 10:00 A.M. TO 8:00 P.M. AND SUNDAY UNTIL 6:00 P.M. FEES ARE $16 PER TWO HOURS OR $27 FOR A WHOLE DAY. A CREDIT CARD DEPOSIT OR $200 CASH DEPOSIT IS REQUIRED. YOU WILL NOT BE CHARGED IF THE SKATES ARE RETURNED.

the Bronx Botanical Gardens during off-hours (6:00 A.M. to 10:00 A.M.). The pass can be obtained from the security office from 9:00 A.M. to 5:00 P.M. during the week except Monday when the garden is closed to everyone. For more information, call (718) 817-8705.

Clubs:

NEW YORK ROAD RUNNERS CLUB
9 East 89th Street, New York, NY 10128 • (212) 860-4455

Club hours are Monday through Friday, 10:00 A.M. to 8:00 P.M.; Saturday until 5:00 P.M., and Sunday until 3:00 P.M. If you run at all, you should join the Road Runners. Membership dues are $30 per year for which you receive: reduced fees for Road Runners races (they hold many, including the marathon), New York Runner Magazine bi-monthly, a monthly newsletter, free running clinics, discounts at shops around New York City, and computerized annual race results of your races. They also offer free group races for members and non-members, Monday through Friday at 6:30 A.M. and 6:30 P.M., Saturday and Sunday at 10:00 A.M.

SAILING

On Your Own:

MANHATTAN SAILING SCHOOL
North Cove off Battery Park City • (212) 786-0400

This sailing school offers a variety of sailing classes. Call to receive a brochure.

THE NEW YORK SAILING SCHOOL
22 Pelham Road, New Rochelle, NY 10801 • (914) 235-6052

They have a whole fleet of boats available for rental, including Solings, Sonars, and Merit 25s. The boats range from 22 feet to 40 feet and rentals cost between $80 and $450 per day. You must be ASA certified or tested by them at a one-time cost of $25. They also offer instruction. Call or visit their web site, www.nyss.com for more information.

Clubs:

THE NEW YORK SAILING SCHOOL • 22 Pelham Road, New Rochelle, NY 10801 • (914) 235-6052

Unlimited sailing rentals are included in the $480 membership fee.

SOCCER

On Your Own:

Soccer fields in Manhattan where you may find a game:

In Central Park:

The Great Lawn, 81st to 86th Streets;
North Meadow, 97th to 104th Streets

East River Park:

East River at 6th Street and the FDR Drive (Field #9)

Dyckman Park:

Hudson River and Dyckman Street

Inwood Park:

West 207th Street and Seaman Avenue

Riverside Park:

Riverside Drive at West 104th and 108th Streets

Thomas Jefferson Park:

First Avenue and 111th Street

Leagues:

THE COSMOPOLITAN SOCCER LEAGUE • (201) 861-6606

They represent over twenty clubs of all different levels. Call them and they will suggest a club that is appropriate for your needs.

SOFTBALL

On Your Own:

To put your own game together you will need a permit in Manhattan. The office is at 16 West 61st Street, (212) 408-0209.

Leagues:

CENTRAL PARK SOFTBALL LEAGUE • (212) 877-1496

The League Commissioner is Bill McHugh. He welcomes advanced men and women players who have played softball competitively. Leagues play at Hecksher Ball Field (on the west side of the park between 62nd and 65th Streets). The season begins in April. The fee to join is $100 per person, $1,800 per team.

WOMEN ATHLETES OF NEW YORK • (212) 759-4189

Speak with Elaine Rosenberg. This is an all-women's softball league. Individuals or teams may join.

YORKVILLE SPORTS ASSOCIATION • (212) 645-6488

Speak with Al Moralis. They have more than two-hundred teams in male, female, and co-ed leagues. All different abilities are welcome.

SWIMMING

There are even more pools available than those already mentioned at the Ys and the City recreation centers.

On Your Own:

ASPHALT GREEN • 91st Street and York Avenue • (212) 369-8890

Asphalt Green boasts an immaculate 50-meter Olympic pool. A yearly swimming membership is $833.

LENOX HILL NEIGHBORHOOD HOUSE
331 East 70th Street • (212) 744-5022

Membership fee is $365 for the year. Pool hours are limited. (They also have a fitness room with a variety of equipment).

MARYMOUNT MANHATTAN COLLEGE
221 East 71st Street • (212) 517-0400

The charges are based on what type of swim you want, lap, recreational, etc. Times are limited.

At Public Pools:

The city has many public pools that are open from June or July until Labor Day. All public pools are free, and some offer organized lap swimming and swimming lessons. For further information, call (718) 699-4219 or call the facility directly. In Manhattan, try these public pools:

HIGHBRIDGE POOL
173rd and Amsterdam Avenue • (212) 927-2400

JACKIE ROBINSON POOL
146th Street and Bradhurst Avenue • (212) 234-9606

JOHN JAY POOL
77th Street and Cherokee Place • (212) 794-6566

LASKER POOL • 110 Street and Lenox Avenue • (212) 534-7639

MARCUS GARVEY POOL
124th Street and Fifth Avenue • (212) 410-2818

THOMAS JEFFERSON POOL
112th Street and First Avenue • (212) 860-1372

Leagues:

THE RED TIDE • (212) 439-4676

Call the hotline for information on becoming a member, as well as a schedule of upcoming workouts. This is a fairly serious group of swimmers who like to compete.

TENNIS
On Your Own:

In Manhattan there are 98 courts. Locations include Central Park, East River Park, Inwood Hill Park, Fort Washington Park, Frederick Johnson Playground, Riverside Park, and an indoor bubble at Randalls Island. A permit is needed. You can obtain one from the Arsenal at Central Park (830 Fifth Avenue at 64th Street) or call (212) 360-8133. Fees are: adults—$50; seniors—$20; under eighteen—$10.

MIDTOWN TENNIS
341 Eighth Avenue (26th and 27th Streets) • (212) 989-8572

Indoor tennis is available year-round on eight courts.

TENNISPORT • Long Island City, Queens • (718) 392-1880

This tennis club along the East River in Queens (next to Golfport, listed above) offers 16 indoor courts and 13 outdoor courts. A junior membership, for players under thirty-five, costs $1000 per year with restricted playing times. A full membership costs $3000 per year with no time restrictions. Court time fees apply to both memberships

Leagues:
U.S. TENNIS ASSOCIATION LEAGUE • (914) 696-7000

This is a recreational league for adults according to skill level, ranging from beginners to advanced players. Single-gender games as well as mixed doubles games are available. Call for membership fee information.

VOLLEYBALL
On Your Own:

NEW YORK URBAN PROFESSIONAL ATHLETIC LEAGUE
200 West 72nd Street • (212) 877-3614

Co-ed men's and women's volleyball league. There are four seasons. They play one evening a week, at various gyms throughout the City, and players are grouped by ability. Fees are $80 for an individual, and $800 for a team.

WOMEN ATHLETES OF NEW YORK • (212) 759-4189

Women only may join as individuals or as a team. Contact Elaine Rosenberg.

YORKVILLE SPORTS ASSOCIATION • (212) 645-6488

Speak with Al Moralis. Co-ed volleyball teams are organized based on ability. You can either join as an individual or a team. They play weekday evenings.

WHERE TO VOLUNTEER IN NYC

Instead of simply complaining about what is wrong with New York City, you can actually help make it right. And in doing so, we guarantee you will begin to like New York more and feel much more connected to the city in which you live and work.

TYPES OF VOLUNTEER WORK AVAILABLE

There are six general categories in which volunteers are needed. They are: culture, education, human services, recreation, public interest, and health. Within each of these categories, there are numerous places you can work and many different jobs that need to be done.

CULTURE

Some of the places you can work:

- museums
- zoos
- nursing homes
- libraries
- landmark preservation
- environmental programs

Some of the work you can do:

- serve as a docent
- build exhibits
- paint
- perform
- lead discussion groups

EDUCATION

Some of the places you can work:

- elementary schools
- youth programs
- after-school programs
- community centers
- day-care centers

Some of the work you can do:

- tutor in a variety of subjects
- set up courses
- advocate
- teach résumé writing
- be a mentor

HUMAN SERVICES

Some of the places you can work:

- veteran groups
- AIDS organizations
- friendly visiting programs
- runaway programs
- telephone hotlines

Some of the work you can do:

- be a big brother/sister
- deliver food
- plan programs
- interpret/translate
- read to the blind

RECREATION

Some of the places you can work:

- playgrounds
- settlement houses
- hobby clubs
- senior citizen centers
- parks

Some of the work you can do:

- help with animal care
- coach a team
- organize field trips
- raise funding for programs
- teach plant care

PUBLIC INTEREST

Some of the places you can work:

- government agencies

- criminal justice
- school boards
- community boards
- tax offices

Some of the jobs you can do:

- serve as a court liaison
- write press releases
- lobby for legislation
- advise small businesses
- research issues

HEALTH

Some of the places you can work:

- counseling centers
- emergency disaster programs
- infant/child development
- rehabilitation clinics
- hospice programs

Some of the work you can do:

- teach parenting
- keep records
- drive an ambulance
- entertain
- feed and visit the ill and frail

HOW TO VOLUNTEER

The process can often seem forbidding, but there are reasons why it can take a while to finally be placed and accepted by an agency. For one, the higher the skill level required by the job you want, the longer it will take to begin your work. In the extreme case it can take up to six months to begin. Often, the smaller, less glamorous or newer agencies are the ones that are most indebted to their volunteers.

There may be several steps that you need to follow to find the right volunteer job for you:

- Call for further information about an organization listed below to begin your search.
- Once you decide on the organization, you may be asked to fill out an application.

- After receiving your application, the organization may ask you to come in for an interview.
- If accepted, you may have to go through a training or orientation period.

Then you will be ready to begin.

WHERE TO LOOK FOR A VOLUNTEER JOB

BIDE-A-WEE • 410 East 38th Street • (212) 532-4986

Volunteers work with dogs and cats. They walk and socialize dogs, and feed, clean cages for, and socialize cats. Volunteers also can participate in a pet therapy program, where they take their pets to nursing homes and hospitals to visit with patients. Call for an application.

THE BRONX ZOO • (718) 220-5141

See description under Central Park Wildlife Center below.

THE CENTRAL PARK WILDLIFE CENTER • (212) 439-6500

Volunteers act as wildlife guides and education docents and assist with a variety of activities. The main purpose of the volunteer is to educate the general public and create enthusiasm for wildlife. Both the Bronx Zoo and the Central Park Wildlife Center have application procedures and interviews, and require extensive training.

THE CHILDREN'S AID SOCIETY • (212) 979-2788

The Children's Aid Society provides services to New York City's neediest children and families. Volunteer opportunities are tailored to each volunteer's interests and schedule, and range from one-day programs to longer-term commitments. Programs are diverse, and include mentoring and tutoring, fundraising, holiday events programs, Saturday outings programs, and community service days. For further information, call the volunteer hotline (listed above) or visit the website at www.childrensaidsociety.org.

LITERACY PARTNERS • 30 East 33rd Street • (212) 725-9200

This organization provides free instruction in reading and writing to adult beginning readers. Tutors participate in a training program, and commit to working with a student group twice a week for two hours each evening. Volunteers also can participate in other programs that require less time commitment. Call to get further information and an application.

THE MAYOR'S VOLUNTARY ACTION CENTER
49- 51 Chambers Street • (212) 788-7550

Contact Carol Friedland, Deputy Director. The MVAC has been in existence for thirty-five years and is the largest clearinghouse for volunteers in the City of New York. They deal with over 2,000 different agencies in both the public and not-for-profit sector that offer nearly 3,000 different jobs. You need to make an appointment to go in for an interview. The good thing about the MVAC is the depth of their knowledge and the amount of agencies that deal with them. The bad thing is that it can take up to a month for them to meet with you.

NEW YORK CARES • 116 East 16th Street • (212) 228-5000

New York Cares was founded in 1986 to assist and organize people who wanted to volunteer, but who were being discouraged by the long waiting time and the lack of any group activities. New York Cares organizes young working adults in hands-on projects with the fifty-plus not-for-profit agencies with which it is affiliated. For the most part, the volunteers work in team projects that address many of the City's most pressing social and environmental problems. They are well-known for their annual coat drive and projects to clean up City schools.

NEW YORK CITY HUMAN RESOURCES ADMINISTRATION, OFFICE OF VOLUNTEER SERVICES • (212) 331-3431

Volunteers participate in the Office's programs to benefit the aging, young, ill, lonely, and others in need of assistance. Activities include making home care visits, working with victims of domestic violence, and working with children. Call to schedule an appointment. The office will put your name and interests into a database and will match your interests to current programs.

THE PARTNERSHIP FOR THE HOMELESS
305 Seventh Avenue • (212) 645-3444

This is one of the country's largest service-providing agencies that deals exclusively with homelessness issues. Volunteers, and churches and synagogues, help provide shelter, transitional and permanent housing, health and mental health counseling, employment counseling, and other services. Call to get information and an application for their six specific programs.

PARTNERSHIPS FOR PARKS • (212) 360-1357

This organization, which coordinates volunteering for New York City parks, is a joint initiative between the Parks Department and the City Parks Foundation. Call the hotline at the number listed above to learn about current projects, and to get the number for the park volunteer coordinator in your neighborhood. The organization tries to cultivate local friends of parks groups, and sponsors large city-wide clean-up events in the Fall and Spring.

RETIRED SENIOR VOLUNTEER PROGRAM (R.S.V.P.)
105 East 22nd Street • (212) 614-5555

R.S.V.P. recruits seniors ages 55 and older to volunteer in various agencies and non-profit organizations. They have over 600 listings with organizations such as hospitals, museums, headstart programs, tax counseling programs, and others. Call Nikkia McDonald to get an application and set up an interview.

THE SAMARITANS • (212) 673-3000

This is the New York branch of the world's largest suicide prevention network that operates the city's 24-hour suicide prevention hotline. Volunteers must commit to a rigorous training program and volunteer schedule. Call for an application.

UNITED WAY OF NEW YORK CITY
99 Park Avenue • (212) 973-3800

The United Way provides funding to over 800 nonprofit agencies and hospitals throughout the five boroughs. The agencies fight hunger and homelessness, provide health care and services to patients with AIDS, provide care for the young and the elderly, and help people build stronger neighborhoods. Call for the Volunteers in Action Manhattan Guide that lists all the many volunteer opportunities available. You also can look online at www.uwnyc.org.

THE VOLUNTEER REFERRAL CENTER
161 Madison Avenue • (212) 745-8249

This organization is associated with over 400 not-for-profit agencies throughout New York. It takes about one week to set up an appointment and then they try to place you right away.

The following organizations are religious in their orientation; however, they all accept funding from the government and therefore service all people.

CATHOLIC CHARITIES OF NEW YORK
1011 First Avenue (55th Street) • (212) 371-1000

The Catholic Charities are connected to over one hundred different agencies that deal with the homeless, shelters, food programs, Big Brothers, and more. Sometimes they want to interview you and other times you are put into direct contact with the people for whom you want to work. Either way, the process takes about two weeks.

THE FEDERATION OF PROTESTANT WELFARE AGENCIES
281 Park Avenue South (at 22nd Street) • (212) 777-4800

Contact Peter Cavino, Program Director. This group has connections with over 265 member agencies. They separate your volunteer interests into three different programs: (1) The Traditional Program: hands-on work, i.e., soup kitchens; (2) The Skilled Program: professional people who want to use their skills, i.e., lawyers and doctors; and (3) The Board Membership Program: people who have the talent and the expertise to sit on boards of newly emerging and established agencies. They do an initial screening over the phone and then set up an appointment to see you within the week.

THE UNITED JEWISH APPEAL
FEDERATION OF JEWISH PHILANTHROPIES
130 East 59th Street • (212) 836-1883

The UJA is affiliated with over 130 agencies. After an initial conversation over the phone, they will send you an application. The application gives them a profile of your talents, time commitments, and interests. Then you will need to attend an orientation and possibly set up an interview.

THE INTREPID PAGES OF
LEISURE HOTLINES

CENTRAL PARK NUMBERS
(212) 794-6564

This number connects you to the Dairy in Central Park, which is the visitor's center. They hold a multitude of events all year long.

(212) 860-1370

This is the number for the Charles A. Dana Discovery Center. If you put your name on their mailing list, they will send you a quarterly calendar as well as special event information for the Discovery Center and Belvedere Castle.

(212) 360-8111

If you need a live person at the Parks Department . . .

(212) 360-8183 or 408-0209

This reaches the Arsenal, the office of permits for the park.

CITY-WIDE INFORMATION
(888) NY-PARKS

This number is the City of New York Parks and Recreation special events phone line. The twenty-four-hour recorded hotline tells you about the daily events taking place in all the City's parks. You can also receive a free calendar of special events by calling this number.

AN EASY WAY TO FIND OUT ABOUT EVENTS AND FUNDRAISERS THAT ARE GOING ON IN THE CITY IS TO OBTAIN A SUBSCRIPTION TO NEW YORK MASTERPLANNER. CALL (212) 832-5908 TO RECEIVE MORE INFORMATION.

(212) 484-1222

New York Convention and Visitor's Bureau.

(212) 397-8222

If you wish to receive printed information from the New York Convention and Visitor's Bureau, call this number.

NEW YORK CITY LEISURE ONLINE

You can explore what's happening in the City without leaving home. See the Tool Kit chapter for general websites.

MUSEUMS
METROPOLITAN MUSEUM OF ART

www.metmuseum.org

MUSEUM OF MODERN ART

www.moma.org

MUSEUM OF NATURAL HISTORY

www.amnh.org

MUSEUM OF TELEVISION & RADIO

www.mtr.org

MUSIC/DANCE/THEATRE

NEW YORK CITY BALLET

www.nycballet.com

NEW YORK CITY OPERA

www.metopera.org

THEATERS AND PRODUCERS

www.broadway.org

TOURIST ATTRACTIONS

OFFICIAL TOURISM SITE OF NY

www.nycvisit.com

CHINATOWN

www.chinatown-ny.com

RADIO CITY MUSIC HALL

www.radiocity.com

STATUE OF LIBERTY

www.nps.gov

TIMES SQUARE

www.times-square.org

FAMILY CONNECTIONS

RAISING CHILDREN IN THE BIG APPLE

PERCEPTIONS VS. REALITY

Raising children in New York City is so much more than imagined by suburban families who can't picture city life as a viable option for kids. The children who thrive here have parents who have made city living a lifestyle choice. These parents want to expose their kids to all aspects of the city, even if it means forfeiting a small-town environment, tree houses, and backyard barbeques. For these kids, the entire city is a "backyard" that offers unlimited opportunities and enrichment on a world-class level. And the city long ago figured out how to provide its family resources in an organized, professional and safe manner, sometimes even with door to door kid pick-up and delivery.

SOLUTIONS:
ENRICHMENT OPPORTUNITIES FOR FAMILIES

NYC HAS ALL THE SAME LEAGUES, PLAYING FIELDS AND "Ys" OFFERED IN THE SUBURBS, BUT THAT'S JUST THE FIRST LAYER OF OPPORTUNITY FOR KIDS OF ALL AGES. BEYOND THAT, THE DEGREE OF DIFFICULTY, EXPERTISE AND VARIETY IS UP TO YOU.

- On their own, parents can take full advantage of what NYC has to offer by joining family membership plans at museums, sports facilities such as Chelsea Piers and Asphalt Green, children's theatre workshops like Applause, the Art Students League, and the 92nd Street Y, to name a few.

- Through private after-school programs, kids can enroll in museum workshops, music classes, performing and fine arts classes at renowned cultural institutions, classes at any number of universities, as well as sports leagues and classes for every type of aspiring athlete...all taught by the pros.

- Public schools offer after school programs by reaching out into the community to NYC's museums, theatre repertory companies, professional sports facilities, and hobby clubs for budding chess players, scientists, karate experts and artists.

THE PARENTS LEAGUE GUIDE TO NY & ACADEMIC CALENDAR IS AN EXCELLENT COMPREHENSIVE RESOURCE WHICH LISTS HUNDREDS OF SERVICES, EVENTS, ACTIVITIES, AND OUTINGS AVAILABLE TO NEW YORK CITY AREA FAMILIES. THE GUIDE IS FREE TO MEMBERS AND $15 FOR NON-MEMBERS ($17, IF YOU NEED IT TO BE MAILED TO YOU). CALL (212) 737-7385 FOR MORE INFORMATION.

SOLUTIONS: PARENTS CAN CREATE A FAMILY-FRIENDLY ENVIRONMENT WITHIN THE CONCRETE CANYONS.

SOME OF THE WAYS:

- Choose a neighborhood loaded with recreational amenities: New York families are attracted to neighborhoods that are within walking distance to museums, multiplex movie theatres, Barnes & Noble superstores and indoor playgrounds. In addition, in the last few years, state-of-the-art indoor and outdoor recreational facilities are cropping up all over the city. Families are using them as their "country clubs", and they've got everything! - hockey rinks, track, beach volleyball, olympic-size pools, basketball courts, gymnastics, climbing walls, quiet reading areas, outdoor sun decks, restaurants, spas, even golf ranges.

- Choose schools and houses of worship that are located within your general community: This is not always possible, but it's worth aiming for. All communities, whether urban or suburban, revolve around their houses of worship, "Ys" and schools. This strategy offers an opportunity for closer parent involvement, local friendships for your kids, and an extended network of families helping each other with "car pooling", babysitting and watching out for each other's kids.

- Live in full-service buildings with common recreation areas: Because of an obvious demand, many of the newer high-rise apartment buildings have "rec rooms", in-door playrooms for babies and toddlers, roof-top decks, party rooms, even health club facilities. These common spaces create an indoor community for kids, parents and caregivers. They also make small apartment spaces feel much less confining. And some of NY's older buildings have started to fill the need by converting basement and storage space into rec rooms and health facilities.

- Live within walking distance of a major park: Our parks are our backyards. We use them for biking, rollerblading, fishing, cross-country skiing, playing in ice hockey and little leagues, after school programs, picnics, frisbee playing, and much more. If you don't live within walking distance, you are less likely to use them, so consider the importance of a nearby park before you choose your apartment.

SOLUTIONS:
PARENTS CAN GET UP TO SPEED ABOUT WHAT IS AVAILABLE FOR KIDS IN THE CITY BY TAPPING INTO RESOURCES THAT ARE DESIGNED FOR THAT PURPOSE.

KEY RESOURCES FOR PARENTS

PARENTS LEAGUE OF NEW YORK
115 East 82nd Street • (212) 737-7385

Yearly membership, $75. The most valuable and comprehensive resource for parents in NYC. The league is a nonprofit organization run by dedicated parents and the independent schools. They provide up-to-date information and free consultation on everything from education to babysitters. It has been helping parents since 1913, and is a gold mine of resources. Walk into their well-staffed, bustling office with file cabinets up to the ceiling, and see for yourself. Or call Patricia Girardi, The Parents League's extremely knowledgeable Executive Director. You can use the League to:

- Consult about schools
- Find out about summer camp opportunities
- Select toddler activities
- Look at what's available in after-school programs
- Find a babysitter, young helper or tutor
- Organize a birthday party
- Plan a family vacation

Membership includes:

- Parents League Guide to NY: discusses children's activities, babysitting services, after-school programs, party services, parent resource centers, workshops, etc.
- Parents League News: a newsletter published three or four times a year which highlights what has been going on at The Parents League.

- Parents League Review: published once a year, the Review is a book of articles of interest to parents, written by parenting experts.
- Toddler Book: lists all types of toddler programs available in New York City, what they are, and what they cost.

THE 92ND STREET Y PARENTING CENTER
1395 Lexington Avenue • (212) 415-5609
Main Y number: (212) 427-6000

The Parenting Center at the 92nd Street Y is a nurturing and educational haven for parents and their children. It offers a wide selection of programs and activities for parents and kids, newborn to five years old. Parents can participate in discussion groups and workshops that focus on children from toddler to teen. Call Fretta Reitzes, Director of the Center for Youth & Family. She has been dedicated to giving assistance, support and resources to parents for more than a decade. You can pick up the Y's seasonal catalog of events and programs in the lobby.

CITY BABY: A RESOURCE FOR NEW YORK PARENTS FROM PREGNANCY TO PRESCHOOL
CITY & COMPANY PUBLISHERS

WRITTEN BY NEW YORK CITY MOMS KELLY ASHTON AND PAMELA WEINBERG, CITY BABY IS A COMPREHENSIVE GUIDE FOR EXPECTANT AND NEW PARENTS LIVING IN THE METROPOLITAN AREA. CITY BABY HELPS PARENTS FIND A HOSPITAL, OBSTETRICIAN, PEDIATRICIAN, MATERNITY CLOTHES, BABY FURNITURE AND TOYS, NANNIES AND DAYCARE, NEW MOM CLASSES, AND MUCH MORE. THE BOOK IS AVAILABLE AT MOST MAJOR BOOKSTORES.

BANK STREET BOOKSTORE
2879 Broadway (at 112th Street)
(212) 678-1654

Owned and operated by The Bank Street College of Education, this bookstore is an excellent resource of educational books for parents, teachers and children. Parents can find information on everything from what is being taught in schools today to what to look for in a quality day care center.

BIG APPLE PARENT
36 East 12th Street • (212) 533-2277

A monthly newspaper that focuses on ages birth through ten years. A yearly subscription is $28. You can also find it free in schools, pediatricians' offices, libraries, children's stores and maternity wards at hospitals. It offers news and feature articles pertinent to New York City families and a calendar of upcoming events. You can visit their web site at www.bigapple-parents.com.

FAMILY PUBLICATIONS
37 West 72nd Street • (212) 787-3789

You can find their pamphlets free in pediatricians' and obstetricians' offices, kids' stores, schools, and major corporations. They offer a Family Entertainment Guide, Working Parents Guide, Expectant Parents Guide, Class Trip Directory, and Birthday Party Directory. You can also purchase these guides for a fee if you are unable to locate complimentary copies.

FROMMER'S: NEW YORK CITY WITH KIDS — for ages 2 - 14

Macmillan Publishers

Written by Holly Hughes, you can find this wonderful book in most New York City bookstores. Just some of the areas covered in the book:

- What to do for fun in the city with kids
- Holidays, parades, street fairs, special events
- Shopping for clothes, shoes, books and toys
- Family friendly accommodations and restaurants

NEW YORK FAMILY MAGAZINE
914-381-7474

A magazine focusing on ages birth through thirteen years. A subscription is $30 for twelve issues a year. It offers a calendar of children's events, and articles on issues pertinent to parents living in New York City. You can also obtain free copies of New York Family at pediatricians' offices, museums, children's stores, and drug stores.

PARENTGUIDE
419 Park Avenue South (28th and 29th Streets) • (212) 213-8840

A monthly newspaper with helpful parenting articles, as well as information on monthly community events for children. You can find complimentary copies of ParentGuide at pediatrician's offices and bookstores. A yearly subscription costs $19.95. You can access ParentGuide's Internet site at www.parentguidenews.com.

NEW YORK'S 50 BEST PLACES TO TAKE CHILDREN
CITY & COMPANY PUBLISHERS

AUTHOR ALLAN ISHAC HAS COMPILED A FUN GUIDE BOOK FOR PARENTS, GRANDPARENTS, TOURISTS, AND TEACHERS LOOKING FOR A GUARANTEED GOOD TIME FOR KIDS. THIS IS NOT YOUR AVERAGE GUIDE BOOK. HERE YOU WILL FIND UNUSUAL SPOTS SUCH AS A MAGIC STORE WITH FREE MAGIC SHOWS EVERY DAY, AND A KID-FRIENDLY STORE WITH BINS FULL OF 25-CENT TOYS. NEW YORK'S 50 BEST PLACES CAN BE PURCHASED AT MAJOR BOOKSTORES IN THE CITY.

PARENTING ONLINE
EQUINOX PRESS PUBLISHERS
THIS HELPFUL BOOK WRITTEN
BY MELISSA WOLF NAVIGATES
THROUGH THE SOMETIMES
CONFUSING REALM OF THE
INTERNET. HER BOOK GUIDES
PARENTS TO ALL THE
INFORMATION THEY COULD
WANT ON PARENTING, AND
ALLEVIATES SPENDING HOURS
HUNTING. MORE THAN 100
WEB ADDRESSES ARE
FEATURED AND BRIEF
EXPLANATIONS OF THE SITES
ARE INCLUDED. YOU CAN ALSO
VISIT WOLF'S WEB SITE AT
WWW.PARENTINGONLINE.COM.
PARENTING ONLINE CAN BE
PURCHASED AT MOST MAJOR
BOOKSTORES.

Child Care for New York Families

SOLUTIONS:
MAKING THE RIGHT CHILD CARE CHOICES FOR BUSY NEW YORK FAMILIES REQUIRES PRACTICAL AS WELL AS PHILOSOPHICAL CONSIDERATIONS.

There are many approaches to child care in NYC. And within each approach, there are hundreds of possible care providers. In a big city, poor quality care can hide in plain sight. Parents have to spend a good deal of time evaluating their own needs to determine which approach is best for them, and then do their homework to make sure they are getting the highest quality care for their children. There are no short cuts to this process, but on the other hand, there's no decision that's more important to get right.

Consider the following issues before choosing a type of care:

- **What is best for your child?** Age and temperament play a major role when making child care choices. Is he at an age where he would thrive in the company of peers in an environment that has plenty of stimulating activities, materials, and staff members? Or is he still so young that he will respond best to one-on-one nurturing? Some school-age children hunger for after-school activities; others fare better spending their afternoons at home.

- **There are philosophical choices to be made:** Do you prefer one person taking care of your child in a home environment? The right caregiver can provide a stimulating environment right at home, creating age-appropriate activities and play groups.

Or do you prefer group care in which your child is stimulated by other children and multiple caregivers in a busy, active environment?

• **There are practical matters to be considered:** What are your financial limitations?

Day-care centers are usually less expensive than in-home care. But—how practical is the travel time to and from the day care center you are considering? And if you have numerous home-related responsibilities, it might be more cost-effective to hire an at-home caregiver who can also do housekeeping and errands, and shuttle kids to playdates and activities.

SOLUTIONS:
TO FIND THE RIGHT AT-HOME CAREGIVER - FIRST DEFINE YOUR NEEDS.

• **Do you need a trained nanny?** Some parents, particularly dual career parents, want a professionally trained and educated caregiver. These caregivers expect to function as a "co-parent" and age-appropriate teacher to your children. Their salaries will range from $400 to $800 a week depending on the amount of training they've had.

• **Maybe you don't need a credentialed nanny, but a mature, loving babysitter who can also double as your housekeeper?** Most likely this is someone without professional training but who has had prior child care experience. In this case the goal is to get someone who is reliable, loves children, and is willing to do some housekeeping and maybe even a little cooking for the family. Salaries will range from approximately $275 - $500.

• **Does an au pair make better sense for you?** An au pair is usually an exchange student who contracts to live with a family for a certain period of time. For anywhere from $100 - $300 a week, it is contractually agreed that she provides help with light housework and helps with child care. Be aware that because au pairs are usually college age, they function more as mother's helpers, and are closely supervised by the parents. Fees for one year's placement through an au pair agency run about $3500, which includes airfare, health insurance and orientation services. If the au pair quits, agencies will typically do their best to find a replacement in the area so the parents don't get stuck with another airfare charge.

The best ways to find an at-home caregiver:

Word of mouth is, hands down, the best way to find a babysitter. Nothing beats keeping your ear to the playground, school, and the office. Put the word out to parents, and other babysitters, who always have a great network. Bulletin boards at schools, pediatrician's offices, and toddler programs can produce results. The key is to network as far and wide as you can.

Placing or looking for ads in the paper. *The Irish Echo, The New York Times* and *The Village Voice* are the best papers in which to look for a qualified nanny. If you place your own ad, make sure you state clearly what you are looking for, so that you don't get calls from inappropriate candidates. Be prepared to be inundated with calls. We recommend you let your answering machine take the messages. If you don't like the way the candidate sounds, eliminate that person from your list of callbacks.

You can go through agencies that specialize in placing baby-sitters and household help. Reputable agencies can do the screening and interviewing for you. You tell them what you are looking for, and they conduct the search, check references and choose the best candidates for you to interview. You pay a hefty commission that is usually equal to one month of your sitter's salary, with a 60-day guarantee. You may also be responsible for the nanny's airfare. If within the first month of employment you are not happy with your choice, the agency will typically send you more candidates at no extra charge. Make sure all agreements between you and the agency are included in a written and signed contract. Even the so-called "reputable" agencies are sometimes unethical in their practices, by misrepresenting their candidates, not conducting thorough background checks, or not honoring their refund or replacement policies. Make sure you understand the con-

BEFORE YOU HIRE YOUR BABYSITTER, FIND OUT EXACTLY WHAT YOUR LEGAL OBLIGATIONS ARE TO HER. WHETHER SHE IS AMERICAN OR FOREIGN BORN, THERE ARE A VARIETY OF PAYROLL TAX, INSURANCE, AND POSSIBLE IMMIGRATION ISSUES YOU NEED TO ADDRESS TO AVOID FINES AND PENALTIES. IN AN OFF-THE-BOOKS ARRANGEMENT, YOU CAN RUN INTO PROBLEMS IF THE CAREGIVER DECIDES TO FILE FOR SOCIAL SECURITY BENEFITS AT A LATER DATE. IF SHE CAN PROVE PRIOR EARNINGS, YOU COULD BE LIABLE FOR YEARS OF UNPAID TAXES AND INTEREST, PLUS FEES FOR LATE FILING. TO FIND OUT WHAT YOU NEED TO KNOW, CALL: UNEMPLOYMENT INSURANCE AT 518-457-9000; SOCIAL SECURITY AT 800-772-1213; WORKMAN'S COMPENSATION AT 718-802-6954.

PARENTS CAN CALL THE DEPARTMENT OF CONSUMER AFFAIRS AT 212-487-4444 TO DETERMINE WHETHER AN AGENCY IS LICENSED OR IF ANY COMPLAINTS HAVE BEEN FILED AGAINST THEM.

CHILD CARE, INC HAS A GREAT BOOKLET CALLED "IN-HOME CARE: FINDING AND WORKING WITH A CAREGIVER IN YOUR HOME". IT INCLUDES WORKSHEETS FOR THE PHONE AND FACE-TO-FACE INTERVIEWS, FOR CHECKING REFERENCES, AND A SAMPLE AGREEMENT. YOU CAN ORDER ONE BY CALLING 212-929-4999, OR SEND A CHECK OR MONEY ORDER FOR $5 TO CHILD CARE, INC., 275 SEVENTH AVENUE, 15TH FLOOR, NEW YORK, NY 10001. BE SURE TO INCLUDE AN ADDRESS WHERE THE BOOKLET SHOULD BE SENT.

tract, that all agreements are in writing, and that the agency is licensed and bonded in NYC.

EVER SINCE ZOE BAIRD LOST THE ATTORNEY GENERAL APPOINTMENT BECAUSE OF OFF-THE-BOOK PAYMENTS TO HER NANNY, MORE PARENTS ARE DOING IT LEGALLY.

• First you have to apply for an employer identification number (EIN) with the IRS.

• You must file quarterly tax returns, although you are only obligated to withhold social security and medicare taxes, not state or federal.

• Then there's the filing of federal and state unemployment tax information.

• You must also buy two insurance policies - workers' compensation and disability- for anyone who works in your home at least 40 hours a week.

• For state employment tax forms, as well as a pamphlet called the "Employer's Guide to Unemployment Insurance", call The New York State Department of Labor at 518-457-5718. To buy policies, call the State Insurance Fund at 212-312-9000. If you want a summary of these laws, the IRS offers the "Household Employer's Tax Guide"–publication 926. Call 800-TAX FORM for a copy. The New York State Department of Taxation and Finance prints "What You Need To Know If You Hire Domestic Help" – publication 27. Call 800-462-8100 for a copy.

The screening process is half the battle

Telephone screening comes first: Telephone screening will help you eliminate most of the unsuitable candidates. Make sure the applicant is interested in the specific duties you have in mind, and that the applicant can verify her entire employment history; if there's a gap that isn't verifiable, walk away.

- What types of child care experience have you had? What ages? For how long?
- What other types of work experience have you had?
- What do you like about working with children?
- Why are you looking for a new job?
- Does the salary meet your expectations?
- How many references can you give me?
- What is your green card status? How would you like to be paid?
- Explain your own home situation. Do you have children? Family? A support system in place?

> THE INTREPID NEW YORKER DOES A LOT OF SCREENING OF NANNIES FOR OUR CLIENTS. RULE NUMBER ONE IS NEVER EXPECT YOUR CHILD CARE GIVER TO DO SOMETHING THAT YOU ARE UNWILLING TO DO YOURSELF. THE RETENTION OF YOUR HELP IS IN DIRECT PROPORTION TO THE AMOUNT OF RESPECT THAT YOU GIVE THEM.

Check references: Call *at least* two. Listen to the person's tone of voice as well as what is actually said. Does he/she sound positive and forthcoming? Some important questions to ask:

- What are this person's strongest qualities?
- What are her shortcomings?
- How dependable and on time is she in general?
- Why is she no longer working for you?
- Would you hire her again?

Interview applicants in your home: Have a candidate come for an hour or two so you can see how she interacts with your child. See how comfortable you feel with her. Talk to her about your child-rearing philosophy - everything from how and when to discipline to what types of daily activities you think should be organized for your child. Get her opinions. Do you sense she has the interest and ability to grow with your child and help him develop? Ask specific questions:

- Tell me about your education, training, background, interests, green card status, etc.
- Are there any personal issues that might prevent you from being committed to the job for at least a year or more?
- How do you envision your role as caregiver?
- What is your preferred way of communicating with parents? What type of relationship do you hope to have with them?
- Describe your previous child care experience (hours worked, daily responsibilities).

AT LEAST TWO REFERENCE-CHECKING SERVICES ARE AVAILABLE TO BOTH NANNY AGENCIES AND PARENTS: MIND YOUR BUSINESS - 888-869-2462 AND AMERICAN INTERNATIONAL SECURITY CORPORATION - 703-691-1110. THEY CHECK CREDENTIALS, CRIMINAL AND MOTOR VEHICLE RECORDS, CREDIT AND EMPLOYMENT HISTORY, ETC.

"BEFORE HIRING A CAREGIVER FOR YOUR CHILD, YOU MUST TALK TO REFERENCES, AND ALWAYS MEET WITH YOUR CANDIDATES IN PERSON. LISTEN VERY CAREFULLY TO WHAT YOU ARE BEING ASKED. IF THE PRIMARY CONCERNS ARE, "WHEN IS MY VACATION? HOW MANY SICK DAYS DO I GET? DO I HAVE TO DO ANY CLEANING?- THAT WILL TELL YOU A LOT ABOUT THE PERSON. BUT AN INTERVIEW DOESN'T ALWAYS PAINT THE CORRECT PICTURE, SO DON'T COMMIT TO ANYBODY UNTIL YOU HAVE GIVEN THEM A ONE-TO-TWO WEEK TRIAL RUN. A GOOD AGENCY WILL LET YOU DO THAT BEFORE REQUESTING THEIR FEE."

- FRANCES STEWART, OWNER, FRANCES STEWART AGENCY

- What do you see as your strengths? Weaknesses?

- My child is X years old. What do you think is important to plan in an average day for him? How would you stimulate him and help him to develop?

- How do you feel about structure in a child's life (regular meals, play dates, activities, naps, etc.)?

- How do you feel about discipline? How would you handle upsets? If my child cries when I leave for work, how would you handle it? What would you do if my child were suddenly missing? What would you do if my child were scalded?

- Do you have training to perform the Heimlich maneuver and CPR? How would you handle an emergency?

Define the relationship you want with your babysitter right from the start:

Nothing will make this relationship deteriorate faster than a lack of clarity about all job requirements and expectations. Mutual respect, trust, and total candor are essential, if this most important relationship is to thrive. Agree on all aspects of the job description - everything from degree of childrearing authority to housekeeping duties. Create an atmosphere that is open to regular communication about your child as well as job-related issues and problems. Make sure there's no confusion about hours, ability to be flexible, overtime pay, sick days, and vacation and paid holidays.

Have her start a few days before you return to work so you can observe if:

- She responds to your child with affection, warmth and good humor

- She handles your child's upsets in a loving, calming and supportive manner

- She complements your childrearing methods
- She enjoys talking to you about your child's development and little accomplishments
- She encourages curiosity and confidence by helping your child learn to explore and experiment
- She creates age-appropriate daily activities
- She appears to feel good about herself and the work she's doing
- Your child appears comfortable and happy around her

If you need part-time baby-sitters you can call any number of baby-sitting agencies who can provide them, even at the eleventh hour.

If you go through an agency, today's rates start at about $10 an hour for a minimum of four hours. The goal is to have three or four regulars that you like and trust. For much less money and no minimum you can call any local university employment office for student baby-sitters. (Barnard has a well-known service). Or if you are a member of the Parents League, you can get their list of babysitters who live in your area. Beth Israel School of Nursing will post your request if you call 212-614-6110. Many pediatricians will let you post a notice as well. If your children are school age and you really don't need help until late afternoon, consider sharing a babysitter with another parent who needs one in the morning hours or find a student who has afternoons free.

CHILD DEVELOPMENT EXPERT, AMY HATKOFF, OFFERS TRAINING WORKSHOPS FOR CAREGIVERS IN NYC CALLED "NANNYWISE", WHICH OFFERS CLASSES ON CHILD DEVELOPMENT, SELF-ESTEEM, AGE-APPROPRIATE LEARNING, POSITIVE DISCIPLINE AND RESPONSES TO EVERYDAY SITUATIONS. MOMS AND DADS CAN ALSO SIGN UP FOR A SERIES OF CLASSES CALLED "PARENTWISE". TO FIND OUT ABOUT CLASS SCHEDULES AND LOCATIONS, CALL 212-534-5623.

IT IS POSSIBLE TO FIND A CAREGIVER BY NETWORKING IN YOUR OWN BUILDING. MORE THAN LIKELY YOU MIGHT FIND A TEENAGER OR ELDERLY PERSON LOOKING FOR SOME EXTRA MONEY AND COMPANIONSHIP.

SOLUTIONS:
FOR SOME PARENTS,
QUALITY "GROUP DAY CARE" IS THE ANSWER.

Group day care has had its share of bad press, but high quality care in small family-operated centers or large group centers is available, and for many parents, it works better for them than at-home care.

THE AGENCY FOR CHILD DEVELOPMENT (ACD) ADMINISTERS ALL PUBLICLY FUNDED DAY CARE IN NEW YORK CITY. FOR PARENTS WHO NEED FINANCIAL ASSISTANCE FOR DAY CARE, THE INFORMATION AND REFERRAL UNIT OF ACD CAN GIVE YOU INFORMATION ABOUT YOUR ELIGIBILITY AND PUBLICLY FUNDED DAY CARE. CALL 718-FOR-KIDS.

Family Day Care

Family day care is the oldest form of day care in this country. Your child will spend the day with a small group of children in the home of a provider who lives in your community. These homes must meet certification regulations of the New York City Health Code. No day care home can provide care to more than two children less than two years of age or to more than six children total. Many parents choose this type of care because it provides daily stimulation and socialization, while at the same time remaining small, nurturing and homey. Typically, a family care provider can be more flexible about hours and days of operation, as well as schedules and daily activities. Due to less overhead costs, it can also be less expensive...averaging about $250 a week. The downside is that providers typically have less training in child development, and the program may be far less structured in terms of learning and use of materials.

Family day care homes are organized: Family Day-Care Networks, the local link to family centers, are found in most communities. They help supervise and monitor the centers, and they are happy to assist parents in finding programs. If no network exists where you live, organizations like Child Care, Inc, can help you.

Group Day Care/Early Childhood Programs

Centers caring for seven or more children under the age of six must have a license issued by the NYC Department of Health. That license is renewed every one or two years and must be prominently displayed. They must comply with specific requirements for facilities, health, safety, staffing and education programs. Parents who prefer this environment are looking for qualified educators, daily enriching activities for kids and a more school-like atmosphere. Here's what you need to know about group care.

- **The cost averages about $350 a week**

- **Day care facilities in NYC average about 55 kids in each.** They can have as few as eight kids or as many as three hundred. Every center is run by an educational director. All teachers must be certified. Teacher/child ratios must be regulated. For children ages 2 — 12 months, the ratio is 4 to 1. For groups 12 months - 2 years and 2 - 3 years, the ratio is 5 to 1.

- **Centers can be called day care, nursery, child care, preschool, or prekindergarten.** Child care is often thought of as "custodial" and nursery school as "educational". Not so. Many nursery schools have "extended" hours, and many child care centers have educational programs. The main difference is sponsorship - they might be private, nonprofit, or for-profit; they could be group care chains, schools, or religious institutions.

- **Large centers can have a downside:** these large centers may provide less-focused attention for your child. You as a parent have to establish relationships with more than one caregiver in order to stay on top of your child's well-being and development. There is less flexibility in hours, structure and program structure.

- **There are organizations dedicated to the task of identifying quality group care.** The organizations listed below will give you referrals, (not recommendations), as well as comprehensive guidelines to help you assess the quality of a program and the type of care that will best suit your needs.

- **There are "minimum standards" set by the NYC Health Code for licensing centers.** The New York City Department of Health, Bureau of Day Care, regulates the care of children up to six years of age in group and family centers in order to protect their health, safety, and well-being. The following organizations can give you referrals, and free pamphlets with quality-assessment procedures:

Child Care, Inc. 212-929-4999

This is a not-for-profit membership organization that not only helps parents find quality, affordable child care, but also provides training and support services to those who work with young children, and serves as an information clearinghouse on important child care issues. Trained counselors will help you find the right type of child care program from over 9,000 licensed programs including infant/toddler centers, family day-care networks, Head Start centers, early childhood programs, after-school centers, and summer day camps.

Day Care Council of New York, Inc. 212-213-2423

Functions much the way Child Care Inc. does. They too will help you review your options for care and provide you with guidelines for choosing a quality program. The agency has knowledgeable counselors with whom you can talk. If your particular issue does not have an easy answer, the counselors will put their heads together with the director of the program to come up with the appropriate solution for your needs.

"THERE ARE MANY DIFFERENT CHILD CARE OPTIONS FOR PARENTS. ONE OPTION IS NOT NECESSARILY BETTER THAN ANOTHER. AND EVERY OPTION HAS ITS BENEFITS. MOST IMPORTANTLY, PARENTS NEED TO FEEL SECURE AND COMFORTABLE WITH THEIR CHOICE. AND THEIR CHOICE MUST MEET THEIR FAMILY'S EMOTIONAL, FINANCIAL AND LOGISTICAL NEEDS. YOU MUST NOT LET YOURSELF FEEL THREATENED OR INSECURE BY ANOTHER PARENT WHO SAYS, 'I WOULD ONLY WANT MY CHILD TO....'

- FRETTA REITZES, DIRECTOR OF THE CENTER FOR YOUTH AND FAMILY AT THE 92ND STREET Y

The Bureau of Day Care, The New York City Department of Health 212-676-2444

This is the licensing agency for child care services (public and private) operating within New York City. It also offers consultation, education, information, and technical assistance to individual groups, organizations, and networks involved in child care. The agency has an intimate knowledge about each center because they have to monitor them regularly to determine their eligibility for retaining their licenses and certificates. The Intrepid New Yorker encountered two high-level staff members there who made us feel extremely secure about the professionals behind the day-care licensing system. They really know their stuff. Contact Virginia Lee, Training Coordinator, Bureau of Day Care; or Harriet Yarmolinsky, Director, Group Family Day Care.

There are also professionally agreed upon standards and industry-wide statements on what constitutes "maximum standards" for quality care. *The National Association for the Education of Young Children* can also help parents zero in on quality care. In addition to the minimum standards required, the NAEYC has created a strict accrediting system for "maximum standards" for which day care programs can volunteer to be evaluated. It is based on years of study and research. Because it is voluntary, if a center has not been accredited, it doesn't mean it is not good. You can write for a list of accredited programs. You can also write for brochures, checklists and catalogues the NAEYC provides to determine quality care based on their "maximum standards". Send a self addressed, stamped envelope to:

NAEYC
National Association for the Education of Young Children
1509 16th Street NW
Washington, D.C. 20036
424-2460, ext. 633

Some of this information can also be accessed at NAEYC's web site, www.naeyc.org.

Some of the most important issues on the checklist:

- Make sure the center is properly licensed and certified.

- Find out about education, experience and leadership skills of the caregivers and their own ongoing educational development plans.

- Look at the interaction between caregivers and kids — this may be the most important determinant of quality.

- Analyze the program for age-appropriate activities, materials and equipment, structure of meals, naps, excursions and play, and proper stimulation planned for intellectual, emotional and social development.

- Determine how open they are to parent involvement.

- Look at the morale and treatment of the staff.

- Examine the space allocated per child and the atmosphere of that space.

THE NAEYC RECOMMENDS THAT THE ADULT/CHILD RATIO FOR TWO YEAR OLDS SHOULD BE ONE TO FOUR OR ONE TO SIX WITH NO MORE THAN TWELVE CHILDREN IN THE GROUP. FOR THREE AND FOUR YEAR OLDS, ONE TO EIGHT OR ONE TO TEN, WITH NO MORE THAN TWENTY CHILDREN IN THE GROUP. THEY ALSO RECOMMEND THAT THERE BE THIRTY-FIVE SQUARE FEET OF INDOOR PLAY SPACE PER CHILD. PARENTS WORRY ABOUT THE EFFECT OF LEAVING YOUNG CHILDREN FOR LONG DAYS IN GROUP CARE AND THE INSTITUTIONALIZED FEELING OF THE CARE. THE SOLUTION TO THIS PROBLEM, THE NAEYC SAYS, IS DIVIDING SPACES INTO SOFT AND COZY INTEREST CENTERS SO CHILDREN CAN BE ALONE OR IN SMALL GROUPS. A GOOD PROGRAM SHOULD FEEL LESS LIKE A SCHOOL AND MORE LIKE A BUSY FAMILY.

THE INTREPID PAGES OF
NYC CHILD CARE/ HOUSEKEEPING SERVICES

CHILD CARE/HOUSEKEEPING AGENCIES

AVALON NURSES REGISTRY
162 West 56th Street • (212) 245-0250

Avalon has been in business for over fifty years. We find them efficient and reliable, and as long as you explain your needs they will
try hard to match you up. Their hours are 8:30 A.M. to 6:00 P.M.

Baby Nurse:	One child: $130 per twenty-four-hour day (fee included); $13 per hour, eight hours minimum; $3 car fare Twins: $200 per twenty-four-hour day (fee included); $20 per hour, eight hours minimum; $3 car fare Triplets: $300 per twenty-four-hour day (fee included); $30 per hour, eight hours minimum; $3 car fare
Baby-sitter: Speak to Geri	$10 per hour (4 hours minimum); $3 car fare up to 8:00 P.M.; $8 after 8:00 P.M.; $15 after midnight $2 per extra hour, per child.

DOMESTICALLY YOURS AGENCY INC.
535 Fifth Avenue (44th and 45th Streets) • (212) 986-1900

Paul Rifkin knows the ins and outs of the placement business and
has been running his company since 1986. Paul works very hard to
make sure that there is a good match between the needs of a care-
giver/housekeeper and a client. All of the people whom Paul
employs must have local, checkable references. These references
are validated by the person's occupation and where they reside.
Domestically Yours is open from 9:00 A.M. to 4:00 P.M.

Baby Nurse: Speak to Racquel	$100-$150 per twenty-four-hour day; fee is 20 percent of what the nurse earns
	Twins: add $50 to the nurse's salary for multiple births
Child Care	$350 and up per week; fee: 10 percent of the nanny's annual salary; one-week trial period; two months guarantee

FOX AGENCY • 30 East 60th Street • (212) 753-2686

John Battaglia is a pleasure to talk with and works hard to serve his clients' needs. This family-run agency has been in existence since 1936. Fox's hours are 8:30 A.M. to 4:00 P.M. They do have an answering machine which they check on a regular basis.

Baby Nurse:	$150 per twenty-four-hour day; $12 per hour, 4 hours minimum; fee: 10 percent of wages earned
Child Care:	$350 and up per week; fee: 6 weeks salary, thirty-day trial period
Baby-sitter:	$12-$15 per hour (4 hours minimum); fee: 10 percent of wages earned

FRANCES STEWART AGENCY
1220 Lexington Avenue (82nd and 83rd Streets)
(212) 439-9222

Frances has had her own agency for over ten years. She is quite responsive to your needs and will go the extra mile to be sure that you are happy. Office hours are 9:00 A.M. to 4:00 P.M. After that leave a message on her machine and she will return your call.

Baby Nurse:	One child: $150 per twenty-four-hour day (fee included); $18 per hour, 8 hours minimum Twins: $225 per day (fee included) Triplets: $275 per day (fee included)
Child Care:	$350 and up per week; fee: 5 weeks salary, thirty-day trial period
Baby-sitter:	$13 per hour (4 hours minimum), two months or younger $12 per hour (4 hours minimum), two months or older $1 per extra hour, per child

PAVILLION AGENCY INC. • 15 East 40th Street • (212) 889-6609

A reputable company which has been around for 37 years. Pavillion only employs nannies who have a minimum of two years experience working with one family. They will also only hire people who reside locally. In addition to employing child care workers, Pavillion also hires housekeepers, cooks, drivers, and butlers. Cliff Greenhouse, who runs this family business, is especially knowledgeable and responsive to the needs of his clients. Pavillion's hours are 9:00 A.M. to 5:00 P.M.

Baby Nurse: Speak to Seth Greenberg	$150-$200 per twenty-four-hour day; fee is 30 percent of what the nurse earns
Child Care: Speak to Cliff Greenhouse	$400 and up per week (after taxes); fee: six weeks salary; thirty-day trial period
Baby-sitter: Speak with Holly Rucki	$10-$15 per hour; fee: thirty percent of what baby-sitter earns (fee is minimum of $30)

NEW YORK STATE DEPARTMENT OF LABOR, HOUSEHOLD DIVISION
Mrs. Cruz • (212) 621-0719

They accept job orders for housekeepers for private households in Manhattan. Applicants must have been employed for six months during the last year and have a current reference that is checked by the agency. Make sure you get two more references from a candidate you are interested in. Best of all, there is no fee to the Department of Labor. You would pay the housekeeper directly, in cash, at a salary of at least $7 per hour, plus car fare, for a minimum of four hours. We have hired people in this manner and the system works.

RESOURCES
109-21 72nd Road, Forest Hills, NY • (718) 575-0992

Resources has been in existence since 1987. Manuel owns this agency that places child-care workers from the Phillipines.. Manuel and Emmelda try very hard to make the right placement.

Baby Nurse:	$120-150 per twenty-four-hour day; fee: varies depending on length of employment and the clients' needs
Child Care:	$350 and up per week; fee: three weeks salary, half due on placement, remainder at end of first month; three month guarantee
Baby-sitter:	$10 per hour

AU PAIRS/NANNIES/SITTERS

AU PAIR IN AMERICA
(203) 869-9090
Contact: Shana Petersen

The American Institute for Foreign Study Scholarship Foundation developed this program to promote exchanges between International youth and American families. "Au pairs are welcomed as full-fledged family members." Au pairs are between the ages of eighteen and twenty-six. They make a one-year commitment. They require private room and board. Au pairs work no more than forty-five hours per week spread over five and a half days, and duties include child care and light housekeeping which relates to the child. The salary is $140 per week for pocket money (51 weeks). The au pair is also entitled to two weeks paid vacation. Au Pair in America requires a $300 application fee, as well as a $4,500 program fee, payable one month before arrival. In addition, "The host family includes the au pair on family outings and some special events and vacations and helps the au pair enroll in educational and/or cultural enrichment courses that are offered by the local adult community education program. The host family is responsible for up to $500 in tuition fees per year." A community counselor will reside in your community to maintain contact with you and your au pair throughout the year-long exchange.

BEACON HILL NANNIES, INC.
Newton, Massachusetts • (800) 736-3880 Contact: Beverly

Beacon Hill can provide au pairs eighteen and over, and nannies twenty-one and over. All are U.S. citizens or have a green card.

Au Pairs: Require their own room, and medical coverage. They will work about a forty-five-hour work week. Their duties include child care and light housekeeping, not acting as the family housekeeper. Au Pairs earn generally $350 to $500 per week. The fee is $1,700, plus $125 for a criminal record check, with up to two replacements during the year.

Nannies: College-educated with Early Childhood or Child Development courses. They receive about $400 to $600 per week. The placement fee is $3,350 plus a $375 application fee, which includes a videotaped interview of all the candidates. The fee also includes up to two replacements during the year.

Beacon Hill has a payroll system where you pay the agency and then they pay the nanny every two weeks. There is a $150 per month administrative fee for this service, but they will then reduce the placement fee.

MORAINE PARK TECHNICAL COLLEGE
Fond du Lac, Wisconsin • (920) 924-3205

This school offers a serious one or two-year program that encompasses all areas of child care. The graduates see themselves as professionals in the field of child care. There is no placement fee because it is a community college. The placement office does an excellent job in working with their graduates to be sure that they not only have a job but one that is appropriate for them. Their grad-

> "WHEN YOU EMPLOY A CAREGIVER OR HOUSEKEEPER, IT IS SO IMPORTANT TO ASSUME NOTHING AND COMMUNICATE EVERYTHING. DEVOTE THE TIME TO TRULY COMMUNICATE WITH THE PERSON YOU EMPLOY SO THAT YOU BOTH UNDERSTAND WHAT IS EXPECTED OF EACH OTHER. ONLY IN THIS WAY WILL YOU BOTH BE SATISFIED."
>
> PAUL RIFKIN, OWNER, DOMESTICALLY YOURS AGENCY, INC.

uates usually get paid between $350 to $650 per week. Speak with Susan Drieger, who will send you an information package and all the necessary paperwork, including course descriptions, which describe the training the students receive.

PINCH SITTERS • (212) 260-6005

This is a temporary agency for baby-sitting services that has been in business for 13 years. You can book a sitter in advance or at the last minute, depending upon availability. The fee is $12 per hour, including the placement fee, with a minimum of 4 hours.

SULLIVAN COUNTY COMMUNITY COLLEGE (914) 434-5750, ext. 316

Graduates who complete the Early Childhood program receive a two-year associate degree. Call Arlene Gordon, the director of the Early Childhood program. Her office would be happy to post your request. Because this is a community college, there is no fee for placement. The job fee is negotiated between you and the applicant.

DAY CARE

BASIC TRUST • (212) 222-6602

This is a child-care center that takes children ages 3 months to 4 years. The hours are 8:00 A.M. to 5:45 P.M. The cost is $18,564 per year, from September through mid-August, for five days a week.

INNOVATIVE LEARNING CENTER • (212) 523-7461

This is a child-care center/preschool that takes children ages 2 months to 5 years. The hours are 7:00 A.M. to 6:00 P.M. The cost is $1083 per month for five days a week, and they also offer two and three day programs.

DOULAS

When a mother needs mothering, call one of these doula services. Different than a baby nurse, a doula focuses on all the needs of the new mother by offering practical assistance as well as emotional support.

IN A FAMILY WAY INC. • 124 West 79th Street • (212) 877-8112

Christine Kealy is the Director of In a Family Way which has been in business since 1991. This doula service offers minimum packages at 12 hours for $360 or 15 hours for $420. If you need additional help after the initial package, you will be billed at $28 per hour in three-hour increments by the day or week. Christine also offers workshops that discuss how to care for your baby and yourself.

MOTHER NURTURE • (718) 631-BABY

Mother Nurture usually works with about six doulas, so call early if you think you might want to go this way. There is a $25 registration fee that includes interviewing the doula in your home. Doulas earn around $19 an hour.

THE INTREPID PAGES OF

OTHER IMPORTANT PARENTING RESOURCES

BABY LIFE CLASSES

In addition to the classes listed below, many of New York's hospitals and Y's offer child safety classes.

BABY-LIFE • (201) 836-1616

One of the first baby life classes in existence, Noel Merenstein founded Baby-Life fifteen years ago. A former emergency medical technician and a certified CPR instructor, Noel's classes stress ways to prevent accidents from occurring. Participants practice CPR, mini-Heimlich maneuvers, and mouth-to-mouth resuscitation on dolls. Classes last three and a half hours, cost $58 per person, and are taught at Park East Synagogue on the Upper East Side.

SAVE-A-TOT • (212) 725-7477

This three-hour class teaches baby and child safety fundamentals—CPR, choking, drowning, poisoning, and childproofing. It is taught by a certified American Heart Association instructor and a registered nurse. The class is $50 per person, $100 per couple. You must call to make an appointment. Classes are given at Pediatric Associates, 317 East 34th Street. Pamela Brower will come to your home if you have five or more people in the class.

BABY PROOFING COMPANIES

BABY PROOFERS PLUS • (800) 880-2191

This company will come to your home for a free inspection to examine potential safety hazards. They will provide you with a written estimate that will include a fee for installation and safety products. The charge is $75 per hour plus the cost of the products. Baby proofing a two-bedroom apartment generally takes two hours to complete.

CHILD PROOFERS • (212) 366-5132

This company also will come to your home to give you a free evaluation. They offer cost-effective solutions to child-proofing your home, with the cost for a two bedroom apartment generally running between $200-400. They also will be happy to speak to mother's groups about child-proofing and safety issues.

BREAST FEEDING SPECIALIST
BEVERLY SOLOW • (212) 567-1112

Beverly is a board certified lactation specialist who offers counseling and support to breast feeding mothers. You can take a two-hour pre-natal breast feeding class for $35. After the baby is born, Beverly will meet with you for an initial one-and-a-half to two-hour visit ($165). Follow up visits are about $120.

DIAPER SERVICE
TIDY DIAPERS • (800) 732-2443

People concerned with the environment have the option to use cotton, non-disposable diapers through Tidy Diapers. By providing pre-folded cotton diapers with waterproof pin-less velcro diaper covers, Tidy Diapers makes using "old-fashioned" diapers just as easy as using disposable diapers. They provide a weekly service to exchange your soiled diapers for clean ones. Diapers are sterilized and ph-balanced when cleaned. The prices are half of what disposable diapers cost.

EXERCISE:
PRE-NATAL AND POST-PARTUM
BODY BY BABY • (212) 677-6165

Jane Kornbluh instructs women in pre-natal and post-partum exercise, both privately and in group classes, at various locations throughout the City. She also teaches Lamaze classes for first time parents, and provides refresher sessions for parents who forgot what they learned the first time.

INFANT EXERCISE & MASSAGE
DIANA SIMKIN, INC. • (212) 348-0208

Diana teaches baby massage and exercise. The classes consist of four to ten people and are held at the Rhinelander Children's Center on the Upper East Side. Your baby must be at least eight weeks old. Five sessions cost $95.

YOU ARE REQUIRED BY LAW TO INSTALL WINDOW GUARDS IN YOUR APARTMENT IF YOU HAVE CHILDREN ELEVEN YEARS OLD OR YOUNGER RESIDING IN YOUR HOME. THE GUARDS ARE A SERIES OF HORIZONTAL BARS THAT ARE INSTALLED ON THE LOWER HALF OF THE WINDOW ON THE OUTSIDE OF THE FRAME. IF YOU RESIDE IN A RENTAL BUILDING, THE LANDLORD MUST PROVIDE THE GUARDS. IF YOU LIVE IN A CO-OP, THE MANAGEMENT IS RESPONSIBLE FOR INSTALLING AND MAINTAINING THEM. DEPENDING ON YOUR PARTICULAR SITUATION, THERE MAY BE FEES ASSOCIATED WITH THE PURCHASE AND/OR INSTALLATION. CONDO OWNERS ARE INDIVIDUALLY RESPONSIBLE FOR INSTALLING GUARDS. CALL YOUR LOCAL LOCKSMITH FOR HELP IN PURCHASING AND INSTALLING THEM.

FORMING A MOTHER'S PLAYGROUP CAN BE A HUGE SANITY SAVER FOR MOMS WHO STAY AT HOME. SHARING STORIES, COMPARING NOTES, AND JUST SHOOTING THE BREEZE WHILE YOUR CHILD IS PLAYING WITH OTHER CHILDREN IS A FUN WAY FOR YOU AND YOUR CHILD TO SPEND A COUPLE OF HOURS. ONE INTREPID NEW YORKER JOINED HER PLAY GROUP WHILE PARTICIPATING IN A NEW MOTHER'S SEMINAR AT THE 92ND STREET Y. TWO YEARS LATER, THIS GROUP OF 13 MOTHERS IS STILL GOING STRONG, AND NOW HAS A FEW NEWBORN ADDITIONS. CONTACT YOUR LOCAL Y, HOSPITAL, OR YOUR PEDIATRICIAN TO LEARN HOW TO FORM OR JOIN A MOTHER'S PLAYGROUP.

POST-PARTUM COUNSELING & SUPPORT

THE RECEIVING BLANKET
(718) 499-3806

Lisa Arnone, a clinical social worker, offers counseling to women who suffer from post-partum depression. She offers group or individual therapy at her office in Brooklyn Heights. Group therapy costs $25 per visit, and you must commit to six to eight weeks. Each individual session costs $70.

THE SCOOP ON SCHOOLS

PERCEPTION VS. REALITY

The information is confounding at best. The headlines are still shouting that the public school system is broken...but there are thousands of parents who believe passionately in that system. There are 100's of public elementary, middle and high schools in NYC alone, and 32 districts with their own policies and approaches...and parents can apply to any of them. To add to choice overload, the facts are notoriously hard to access, and the sensational headlines give parents a misleading and inaccurate first impression. So what's fact, what's fiction, and what tools are you given to separate them? How do you choose, or do you even have a choice? Truth is...there are outstanding public schools on all levels and more than enough variety to accommodate any child's particular needs. In addition, there are dozens of good world renowned private schools — more than enough for every child to get a great education. We've got the facts, and the tools.

SOLUTIONS:
PUBLIC SCHOOLS:

THE TRUTH IS THAT MANY OF THE GOOD PUBLIC SCHOOLS IN NYC ARE EVERY BIT AS GOOD AS PRIVATE, AND SOME MIGHT ARGUE, BETTER!

It is true that many NYC public schools have problems associated with over crowding, bureaucratic boondoggles that keep some mediocre teachers in, some great teachers out, and budget cuts that leave classrooms with a shortage of supplies and extra curricular activities. But the silver lining is that the picture is not nearly as bleak as the headlines portray; many of NYC's schools are renowned, many more than not have successfully met the challenges, even surpassed expectations; and every year, dozens of innovative and intriguing new schools open at the grass roots level. The fact is, it's impossible to kill the spirit for educational excellence in this city, and there are reasons why:

- **NYC's public school teachers are some of the most talented in the country.** NY draws the best and the brightest from every profession, and that includes teaching. First, every public school teacher is required to have a Masters degree (within five years of starting to teach), and many come from the finest teaching colleges. Second, NYC's public school teachers' salaries are much higher than those in private school settings. Third, many teachers are second career opportunists, and are teaching by design, not by default.

- **NYC's principals are given freedom to "create" and carry out their own visions.** NYC has hundreds of examples of a principal that took the helm at a troubled school and turned it into an innovative success.

- **There is no other international city that offers more enrichment opportunities for public schools...**There is irony in the fact that because public schools don't have the money for the type of enrichment programs private schools take for granted, they reach out to the community to form alliances with world class museums, universities, cultural institutions, professional theatre, and fortune 500 businesses.

  Foundations such as Annenberg have given millions of dollars in grants to schools to improve their arts programs. Musicians from Lincoln Center along with dancers from The City Ballet work with the students to create plays, recitals etc. Some schools have a partnership with The Central Park Conservancy. The Conservancy offers scientific workshops to introduce students to the wonders of nature. The museum of Natural History offers a workshop dealing with astronomy. Not only do all these cultural institutions offer programs for students, they also do extensive staff development for the teachers so that there is continuity between what goes on in the classroom and the institutions.

- **NYC's public school children are exposed to every nationality from around the globe.** Children have a great opportunity to learn about the world through relationships with their own classmates.

- **NYC's public school parents are educational activists:** PTAs in public schools are not only well-oiled machines, they're driven by parents who want the best for their kids, and will do whatever it takes to make it happen, from volunteering their time and expertise, to raising hundreds of thousands of dollars annually to fill in the gaps in budgets and curriculum. Many of the dollars raised are used to pay for "enrichment" teachers and supplies that are not always funded by the City. Music and art teachers, instrumental programs, supplies and even books are paid for by PTA dollars. Sometimes the funds are spent for athletic programs such as track teams and field days and even lunch time enrichment activities such as a chess or math club. Many schools use PTA dollars to create after school programs.

SOLUTIONS:
ELEMENTARY & MIDDLE SCHOOLS
FOR NYC FAMILIES THERE IS CHOICE

In theory, NYC's public schools operate on the premise of parental freedom to choose the school best suited for your child. One is permitted to apply to any of the 100s of public schools in the city, even those outside your local neighborhood zone and district; however, with 32 school districts all with separate policies, admissions procedures, school philosophies as well as parents standing on line for those schools most coveted throughout the five boroughs, the process can be daunting, and it doesn't always produce the results you want.

CALL THE OFFICE OF THE CHIEF EXECUTIVE FOR COMMUNITY SCHOOL DISTRICT AFFAIRS AT 718-935-2799 TO GET A COMPLETE LIST OF ALL THE 32 SCHOOL DISTRICTS.

First, there's some academic jargon you need to know.

Traditional classrooms: The emphasis is on the basics such as reading and math. Teachers teach from the front of the class to kids sitting at desks.

Progressive classrooms: Far more the norm today, these classrooms are divided into busy "pods" – co-operative groups – of kids on the floor or at tables working on different activities and interacting at various academic paces.

Gifted and Talented Programs: These programs usually require that kids test into them and they can range from general academics to an emphasis on a particular study such as music or science. Some accept children from all over the city, others only from the neighborhood or district.

Magnet Schools: A school that is centered on a theme and then weaves that theme throughout the entire curriculum.

Homogeneous Grouping: Grouping children by ability. This approach is more typical in traditional schools.

Heterogeneous Grouping: Children at different levels of ability are mixed together.

Alternative: Multi age grouping

English as a Second Language (ESL): All students are taught in English, but take separate classes to become fluent in English. Bilingual class: teachers teach English but also help students maintain fluency in their native language. Dual-language immersion: some of the students speak English, others their native language, teachers teach both languages so that the students learn both.

Second, there is a method to this madness:

Every neighborhood has a local public school to which your child is entitled to enroll. You want to find out which one is yours. The city is divided into school districts. And each district is divided into local school zones. If you are fortunate to live in a neighborhood zone or "catchment area" with a coveted public school, all you have to do is register your child in the spring for the following year. The most important document you have to produce is proof of residence. Call your district to find out which school is "yours". Kids inside the zone get priority, kids outside the zone, second priority, kids outside the district, third priority.

If you want to access schools outside your zone: Call or visit your local district office to find out about "free choice" policy and to which schools outside your zone you can apply. Some Gifted And Talented programs require that your child take an admissions test; others may accept by lottery. Your child will require permission, called a "variance", to attend any school outside your zone, and you will either apply directly to the school or through the district office. It is important to have a backup plan, by applying to more than one school.

Information gathering: Visit your district office to get whatever brochures, information and report cards they have on the schools in their area. Not known for being very accessible when it comes to information gathering, district offices can be off-putting, but it's the right place to start. In addition to pamphlets and brochures, all schools now publish annual performance report cards, and they can be obtained through the district as well. It's important to note, however, that indicators such as reading scores can be misleading. A school that does not have the best reading scores may, regardless, be one of the most innovative and exciting schools in town.

- **The 92nd Street Y conducts an annual public school forum for parents:** Every fall, the 92nd St. Y sponsors a series of lectures on NYC's public schools as an option for parents. Call the Y at 212 427-6000 for more information.
- **Call the Parent Teacher Association** in each school you are interested in. The districts as well as the individual schools have the contact numbers for the PTA. Parents are a critical source for accurate feedback about a school.

The search strategy: In September, start contacting schools. Sign up early for the tours, as they can close out quickly. Find out what the process is; depending on the school, you might not be able to interview with the principal until the tour is concluded; to be admitted to certain programs, your child may be required to be tested. Usually the process is completed by the end of January; by February some letters of acceptance to "out-of-zone" schools, may be in the mail; by April registration, you'll know if you are on a waiting list, in, or out.

If your child is entering middle school, your school will be automatically providing you with information about schools in your district. Most districts have a wide range of school options, from schools that require an admission test to schools that offer open enrollment. There is quite a variety, so do your research. If your school has a guidance counselor make an appointment early in the fall to meet with him. The guidance counselor should have an idea of the kind of middle school that might best fit your child. If you find yourself on a waiting list, don't despair; schools have cancellations during the summer, so make sure you stay in constant touch with the head of admissions to show your enthusiasm for the school.

Meeting application deadlines: Manhattan schools typically conduct tours starting in October and request that applications be submitted in December. Once you know the deadlines, make a point of being one of the first in the door.

It is a prudent idea to find objective sources for information outside the public school system: It's important to get independent opinions outside the school system for a more objective perspective. On the following pages is a list that offers a well rounded view for schools throughout New York City:

NATIONAL TRAINING AND EVALUATION CENTER, INC.

15 West 84th Street
New York, New York 10024
(212) 877-4480

Victor Toledo owns and operates this testing center that administers the tests for admission into public schools. As a tester and consultant to the Board of Education for twenty years, he has an excellent grasp on public schools in New York City. He offers consultation to parents who want to find the right public school for their child based on the test scores and the type of programs they are interested in.

CENTER FOR EDUCATIONAL INNOVATION AND PUBLIC EDUCATION ASSOCIATION

39 West 32nd Street
New York, NY 10001
(212) 868-1640

This is one of New York City's most highly respected advocacy groups and the second oldest in the nation. It was set up to promote public education, study it, and make it better, and the bias is toward parent advocacy. The PEA is set up to answer your questions about schools.

NEW VISIONS FOR PUBLIC SCHOOLS

96 Morton Street
New York, New York 10014
(212) 645-5110

New Visions is a non-profit educational organization, which mobilizes private and public support to improve New York's public schools. The organization has also formed New Visions public schools, thirty-two of which are in existence at the present date. These schools are smaller in size and offer an alternative for those who seek a more intimate, academically rigorous, and community-based education than many public schools currently provide. Eileen Newman or Michael Webb, Senior Program Officers, can discuss the New Visions schools as well as other public schools with you in more detail. You can call the office and have them send you an information package. You can also get detailed information on New Visions, as well as links to other education and research sites on the Web, at www.newvisions.org.

PUBLICATIONS

- *THE PARENTS' GUIDE TO NEW YORK CITY'S BEST PUBLIC ELEMENTARY SCHOOLS,*

  Is written by Clara Hemphill of the Public Education Association, and published by Soho Press. Clara researched over 100 public schools, and actually viewed classes in session while gathering her information. The book is an invaluable resource for parents who wish to send their children to public schools.

> EVERY YEAR
> *THE NEW YORK TIMES*
> PUTS OUT A SPECIAL SECTION
> ON NYC'S PUBLIC SCHOOLS
> THAT INCLUDES AN
> "AT-A-GLANCE" REPORT CARD
> ON ALL SCHOOL IN THE FIVE
> BOROUGHS

- *PUBLIC MIDDLE SCHOOLS, NEW YORK CITY'S BEST*

  Is written by Clara Hemphill. A terrific guide to the best schools throughout the city from the smallest magnet programs to the larger zoned schools.

- *NEW YORK NETWORKS FOR SCHOOL RENEWAL: DIRECTORY OF PARTICIPATING SCHOOLS.*

  This directory offers a look at the many small public schools from elementary through high school participating in the NY Network for School Renewal. The Network is a five-year Annenberg Foundation Urban Challenge Initiative that seeks to improve the quality of public education and to reshape the city's school system through the expansion and nurturing of small public schools that work together in small networks to support better teaching, learning and accountability. Currently there are over 125 such schools supporting over 50,000 students. For more information contact Director Iris Morales at 212-369-1288.

THE INTREPID PAGES OF
MANHATTAN
PUBLIC SCHOOL DISTRICTS

COMMUNITY SCHOOL DISTRICT ONE
80 Montgomery Street • (212) 602-9700

Area covered: Most of the Lower East Side and East Village
Community School Board President: Ms. Elena Seliciono
Community Superintendent: Ms. Sonia Diaz Salcedo

COMMUNITY SCHOOL DISTRICT TWO
333 Seventh Avenue (at 28th Street) • (212) 330-9400

Area covered: All of Manhattan below 96th Street on the East Side
and below 59th Street on the West Side, except the part of the
Lower East Side in District One
Community School Board President: Ms. Karen Feuer
Community Superintendent: Ms. Elaine Fink

COMMUNITY SCHOOL DISTRICT THREE
300 West 96th Street • (212) 678-2800

Area covered: West Side from 59th Street to 122nd Street
Community School Board President: Ms. Ronni Wattman
Community Superintendent: Ms. Patricia A. Romandetto

COMMUNITY SCHOOL DISTRICT FOUR
319 East 117th Street • (212) 828-3501

Area covered: East 96th Street to East 128th Street
Community School Board President: Mr. John Estrella
Community Superintendent: Ms. Evelyn Castro

COMMUNITY SCHOOL DISTRICT FIVE
433 West 123rd Street • (212) 769-7500

Area covered: Most of central Harlem up to 151st Street and Adam
Clayton Powell Blvd.
Community School Board President: Ms. Sandra Rivers
Community Superintendent: Ms. Thelma Baxter

COMMUNITY SCHOOL DISTRICT SIX
4360 Broadway (185th and 187th Streets) • (212) 795-4111

Area covered: From Convent Avenue and 131st Street to 212th
Street and Broadway
Community School Board President:
Mr. Roberto Lizardo
Community Superintendent (Acting):
Mr. Brian Morrow

SOLUTIONS:
THERE ARE KEY ISSUES TO CONSIDER THAT WILL MAKE THE CHOOSING EASIER.

- **Location:** It stands to reason that if you send your kids to a school within your own neighborhood, your community connection and sense of involvement will be that much greater. Watch parents walking their kids to school every day and you'll get what we mean by the warm greetings and great camaraderie you encounter along the way.

- **Size:** There is a wide disparity in the sizes of public schools in this city...from tiny alternative schools with less than a hundred students to those with 1000s. Size has an impact on environment, so you need to make sure the particular environment meets your child's disposition and needs.

- **Teaching philosophy:** Consider what's right for your child and your values. Some Gifted and Talented Programs come with pressure, a competitive atmosphere, and a hierarchy of "haves" and "have nots". Some children fare much better in a more traditional, structured classroom, some fare better in an environment where they can explore their own interests.

- **Quality of teaching:** There is no debate here. How good are the teachers...where did they do their schooling, how experienced are they, and most importantly, how much do they inspire and excite the children in their classrooms?

SOLUTIONS:
WHAT TO LOOK
FOR WHEN YOU VISIT

Parents, don't be thrown by the security guard and institutional-green walls that greet you at the door. It in no way reflects what's going on inside.

What counts are the following:

- **The Principal sets the tone for the whole school.** What is your overall impression of the principal and the environment he/she has created for the children. Is the atmosphere happy, vital, energetic, organized, structured, respectful...is the principal a "hands-on" leader who is out of the office watching what is going on in the hallways and classrooms? Does the principal have a clear vision/philosophy for the school and is that vision being enforced in the classrooms?

> "THE CITY OF NEW YORK OFFERS A WIDE VARIETY OF AFTER SCHOOL PROGRAMS FOR CHILDREN OF MANY VARIED ABILITIES. IF PARENTS PUT IN THE TIME AND EFFORT, THEY CAN FIND SUITABLE PROGRAMS FOR THEIR CHILDREN. WITH THE CONSIDERABLE SAVINGS THEY'VE MADE BY NOT PAYING FOR PRIVATE SCHOOL, THEY WOULD BE ABLE TO OFFER THEIR CHILDREN ENRICHMENT POSSIBILITIES OUTSIDE OF SCHOOL THAT OTHER CHILDREN MIGHT NEVER GET."
>
> VICTOR TOLEDO,
> PRESIDENT,
> NATIONAL TRAINING AND
> EVALUATION CENTER, INC.

- **What's going on in the classrooms and hallways:** Classrooms and hallways that are overflowing with projects, drawings, writings and books tell you a lot about productivity, level of energy, excitement and ambition. Read the writings on the walls. Look at the quality of what you are reading. Observe the children; are they engaged? Bored? On task? Excited with their activities? Are the classrooms, libraries, etc. a place you would want to spend the day?

- **Does the school feel well-run, organized, safe?** Observe the atmosphere during class changes, lunch time and dismissal. How do the teachers put the kids on the bus? How do the kids make class changes? If your instincts tell you the environment feels well organized, supervised and safe...trust them.

- **What are the kids reading and writing:** Interesting classrooms are filled with all kinds of literature for all levels of learning and are by no means textbook driven. For instance, kids in the earliest grades of the better public schools are already writing and authoring their first books.

- **How much freedom do the teachers have to create interesting approaches to learning?** There should be a strong curriculum base on which teachers can collaborate, experiment and test individual styles of teaching. This flexibility empowers teachers and contributes to morale, motivation and passion for the enterprise. Some other important questions to ask: what kind of staff development is there for teachers? What connections does the school have with teaching universities and student teachers? What is the turnover rate of teachers?

- **What is the quality of the after school programs provided?** Find out what type of after school programs are offered. How organized is it, how many choices of activities are there and what is the caliber of the instruction. Some of the better programs include five or six choices each afternoon, from science and computer workshops to Native American Arts, theatre workshops, and Judo.

- **How ambitious is the principal's reach out into the community to secure grants and enrichment programs with other institutions and businesses?** This tells you a great deal about a principal's motivation to create and maintain high standards for school opportunities and performance.

- **How active is the PTA:** If the PTA is not a "tour de force" in the public school you're inspecting, something isn't right. You want to find out what types of fundraising events the PTA put together every year, and for what that money is earmarked. How involved are they with school based planning, curriculum and enrichment opportunities?

- **What extra curricular programs exist: What kinds of programs are available in science, art, theatre and sports?** Many public schools have to raise funds and pull in volunteers to make these non-essential classes available.

SOLUTIONS:
NYC PUBLIC HIGH SCHOOLS:

The high schools are administered by the borough office, not the district office. The Board of education is located at 110 Livingston Street, Brooklyn, New York, 11201, 718 935-2000.

The board publishes a yearly directory of the NYC Public Schools. Call 718-935-3451 to receive a copy. This booklet has a detailed description of all the high schools as well as the admissions process.

SPECIALIZED HIGH SCHOOLS

The Board of education publishes a booklet about the specialized high schools. You can receive it at your public middle school or call 718-935-3415.

ONE OF THE MAIN DIFFERENCES BETWEEN PUBLIC AND PRIVATE SCHOOLS IS THE EMPHASIS ON STAFF DEVELOPMENT. PUBLIC SCHOOLS ENCOURAGE STAFF DEVELOPMENT IN A VERY AGGRESSIVE WAY. FOR EXAMPLE IN DISTRICT 2, $2 MILLION WAS ALLOCATED AND SPENT ON STAFF DEVELOPMENT. STAFF DEVELOPMENT IS MANDATED FOR ALL TEACHERS. TEACHERS ARE GROUPED TOGETHER AND TRAINED IN A SIMILAR WAY SO THAT THEY ARE ALL DELIVERING A SIMILAR PRODUCT. THIS ENSURES THAT TEACHERS AND ADMINISTRATORS STAY ON TOP OF THE LATEST TRENDS IN EDUCATION SUCH AS TERC MATH AND BALANCED LITERACY. AS A PARENT, IN ADDITION TO LOOKING AT THE QUALITY OF STAFF DEVELOPMENT IN A PUBLIC SCHOOL, YOU SHOULD MAKE SURE THERE IS A PHILOSOPHY IN PLACE, STRONG LEADERSHIP, AND A COMMITMENT TO PARENT INVOLVEMENT IN A HOLISTIC WAY.

CARMEN FARINA, PRINCIPAL P.S. 6, MANHATTAN

PARENT INVOLVEMENT IS A CRITICAL COMPONENT TO ANY GOOD PUBLIC SCHOOL. THAT COMMITMENT CAN BE EXHIBITED IN MANY DIFFERENT WAYS FROM INDIVIDUAL FINANCIAL CONTRIBUTIONS, RAISING FUNDS FROM THE COMMUNITY AROUND THE SCHOOLS THROUGH WEEKEND FLEA AND FARMERS MARKETS, TO SPENDING TIME DOING CLERICAL WORK, TO ACTUALLY OFFERING YOUR OWN EXPERTISE TO THE PRINCIPAL. YOU NOT ONLY WILL FEEL LIKE A VALUABLE MEMBER OF THE SCHOOL COMMUNITY BUT THE MESSAGE THAT IT SENDS YOUR CHILD IS EQUALLY IMPORTANT.

THE LEVEL AND SPIRIT OF PARENT INVOLVEMENT TELLS YOU A LOT ABOUT THE QUALITY OF THE SCHOOL.

There are four specialized high schools that require an admission exam. These four schools are considered to be the most academically rigorous: Stuyvesant High School, Bronx High School of Science, Brooklyn Technical High School and Fiorello H. LaGuardia High school of Music and Art and Performing Arts. Admissions are based on test scores with the exception of LaGuardia where an audition is required. Plain and simple... The highest scores are admitted to Stuyvestant, second Bronx High school of Science, and third Brooklyn Tech.

Because admission is based on test scores it is critical that you prepare. There are a variety of test preparation classes.

Princeton Review (212) 362-6900

Geller Rosenstein Feldman (212) 864-4085

HIGH SCHOOL RESOURCES:
If your guidance counselor cannot assist you, call one of the following numbers.

Office of High School Admissions
22 East 28th Street
9th Floor
New York, New York 10016
(212) 481-7034

Supervisor of Guidance For Manhattan
122 Amsterdam Avenue
New York, New York 10023
(212) 501-1100

Supervisor of Guidance For Bronx
3000 East Tremont Avenue
New York, New York 10461
(718) 430- 6300

Supervisor of Guidance For Brooklyn
1600 Avenue L
Brooklyn, New York 11230
(718) 258-4826

Supervisor of Guidance For Brooklyn/Staten Island
715 Ocean Terrace- Building A
Staten Island, New York 10301
(718) 390-1500

Supervisor of Guidance for Queens
30-48 Linden Place
Flushing, Queens 11354
(718) 281-7500

Supervisor of Guidance for Alternative High Schools
131 Livingston Street
Brooklyn, New York 11201
(718) 935-5433

SOLUTIONS:
RESOURCES FOR KIDS WITH SPECIAL NEEDS

By law, public school children with special needs are entitled to special education. It is critical that you educate yourself to find out what your rights are, what exactly you can ask for, and how to negotiate your way through an obstacle-strewn bureaucracy. There are excellent programs out there that do a superb job of providing the special help required, and still manage to mainstream the child in regular classrooms. But you need resources to help you find your way, because the type and quality vary enormously.

SOME SPECIAL ED PROGRAMS PLACE SPECIAL ED STUDENTS INTO REGULAR CLASSROOMS IN ORDER TO OFFER CHILDREN WITH SPECIAL NEEDS A CHANCE TO STAY AND GROW WITH THEIR PEERS. SOME ARE SEPARATED INTO SPECIAL EDUCATION CLASSROOMS. AT THE VERY LEAST YOU SHOULD LOOK FOR A SCHOOL THAT BELIEVES THAT EVERY CHILD WITH SPECIAL NEEDS CAN MAKE PROGRESS, HAS YOUR CHILD'S BEST INTERESTS IN MIND, AND THAT PROUDLY AND PUBLICLY PROMOTES THEIR SPECIAL ED PROGRAM.

RESOURCES FOR CHILDREN WITH SPECIAL NEEDS
200 Park Avenue South • (212) 677-4650

A not-for-profit advocacy and referral agency: They provide resources and information on all kinds of activities including educational opportunities for children with special needs.

MANHATTAN PARENT RESOURCE CENTER
22 East 28th St • (212) 481-5584

An advocacy group that empowers parents who have children with special needs. They educate parents about the educational programs that exist for children, and also run support groups for families in need.

PARENT-TO-PARENT • 1-800-405-8818

A not-for-profit organization whose sole purpose is to create a peer environment for parent and child. Call them and they will match you and your child with another family in your similar situation.

PRIVATE SCHOOLS

Put simply, there are over 100 private schools in NYC, and most are good, and many are world class. Parents have literally unlimited choices for every age group starting with toddler programs through the twelfth grade. Take your pick of philosophies, approaches, degree of difficulty, single sex or co-ed. The downside is that they are extremely expensive with nursery schools starting in the $7,000 - $11,000 range and escalating from there! In addition, NY parents tend to get caught up in an overheated, over hyped competition over a handful of the most sought after and exclusive schools, perpetuating the myth that they are the only schools that will put the child in the running for the ivy leagues. NYC parents need to relax a little, and do more homework...they would find that there are dozens of truly fine schools that have what it takes to provide a first rate education.

SOLUTION:
INFORMATION ABOUT NYC'S PRIVATE SCHOOLS IS WELL ORGANIZED AND SIMPLE TO ACCESS. THERE ARE A FEW KEY RESOURCES THAT WILL GIVE YOU A SERIOUS HEAD START ON MATERIAL GATHERING.

EDUCATIONAL RECORDS BUREAU • 212-672-9800

Since 1969, ERB has served as the central testing agency for the Independent Schools Admissions Association of Greater New York. Children must test with ERB to gain admission into any private school. For a fee, ERB also offers a consultation service with a staff psychologist to assist parents in selecting an appropriate school.

THE PARENTS LEAGUE • 212-737-7385

Once you pay your $75 to become a member for one year, The Parents League will help you in your search. They offer a School Advisory Service for member parents who need advice about the process of applying to schools and how to access information about them. They also sell the "New York Independent Schools Directory", which is published by The Independent Schools Admission Association of Greater New York, in cooperation with The League. The League also sponsors Independent School Day in the fall at which school representatives hand out materials, answer questions and so on. You can also attend their "Forum on Admissions", at which admission directors answer parents' questions about the process.

The Manhattan Family Guide to Private Schools

By Catherine Hausman and Victoria Goldman, SoHo Press. It provides pertinent, need to know information about all the private schools. Written by parents, for parents.

Catholic Schools Directory - Office of the Superintendent of Schools Archdiocese of New York, 1011 First Ave. NY, NY 10022 371-1000 ext. 2870

They sell a comprehensive directory to all the parochial schools in New York State. The cost of the booklet is $8.00.

The Independent Educational Consultants Association

4085 Chain Bridge Road, Suite 401, Fairfax, VA 22030. 703-591-4850 or 800-808-4322. An accredited association of education consultants to private schools throughout the country. The Association has regional consultants nationwide who help students of all ages identify suitable schools, colleges and educational programs. They also sponsor regional conferences, workshops and meetings in various parts of the country throughout the year. They are happy to send a directory of NY area consultants, free of charge.

NURSERY SCHOOLS

NYC parents get overly agitated by the nursery school admissions process, and "the what-ifs" if their children don't get into the most coveted programs. Their concerns are fueled mostly by unfounded rumors and over-the-top assumptions. In order to set the record straight, we went right to the source for a realty check — The Parents League.

- **Contrary to public opinion,** there *are* enough places for every three-year-old looking for a spot in a regular nursery school.

- **Contrary to public opinion,** three-year-olds are not penalized in the admissions process if they have not previously attended a "traditional" toddler school. (Traditional means that the child is left at school for two or three hours a day for a few days a week.)

  In fact, many children under three aren't even ready for this type of program. Many educators believe that the creation of these toddler programs back in the 1970s was tied to economic need, not scholastic need.

- **Contrary to public opinion,** there are dozens more excellent nursery school programs in NYC than the handful parents have been misled to believe are "it", if you want a guaranteed place in the better schools later on. In fact, the notion that the exclusivity and popularity of the nursery school has any bearing on the future educational opportunities for your pre-k child is slightly ridiculous. We suggest you look in your own neighborhood first for a school that is convenient and an integral part of your community.

How to find a good nursery school:

- **Talk to friends and neighbors about the schools in your area:**
  Your church or synagogue may have a good nursery school. Once again, The Parents League will gladly help you in the search.

- **Child Care Inc. • 212-929-7604**
  The leading private childcare advocacy organization. Counselors can give you advice and information on hundreds of licensed programs, and for a small fee, a listing.

- **The Manhattan Directory of Private Nursery Schools, by Linda Faulhaber.**
  The definitive book on over 150 nursery programs, educational approaches, facilities, admissions procedures, hours and tuition. At any local bookstore.

- **Call the admissions office of the schools a full year prior to the attendance date and request an application form and catalogue.**
  Some nursery schools declare the cut off time for application requests, just after Labor Day. Ask about admission procedures and deadlines, tours and interviews.

What to consider when looking into nursery schools

- How far from home is it?
- Is the tuition affordable?
- What are the age qualifications?
- Do the hours meet your needs? Do you need a morning or afternoon program, extended hours or an all-day center?
- Is the teaching method appropriate? There are many choices from Montessori, Developmental, Progressive, Traditional to eclectic.

What to look for on the tour

Nancy Schulman, Director of the 92nd Street Y Nursery School gave us these tips:

- **Classrooms should be clean, spacious and well organized,** and have a wide variety of toys and materials that can be used constructively and creatively.

- **An early childhood program should have a high adult/child ratio with well-trained teachers.** There should be time for large and small group activities that are both teacher initiated and child initiated.

- **Look for a nurturing environment that is creative and child centered.** Routines and activities need to be well organized yet flexible to meet the needs of the individual child.
- **Observe how the teachers handle interactions and conflicts between children.**
- **Observe how the school views and handles separation between child and parent.**
- **Trust your instincts.** Is it a place where you and your child feel comfortable? Are the interactions between children and teachers warm, respectful, attentive, happy?

APPLICATION PROCESS TO PRIVATE & PAROCHIAL SCHOOLS

As we mentioned earlier, it would be hard to find another city anywhere in the world with as large a number and as wide a range of fine private schools. The process for applying to an ongoing school is no different from the nursery school process in terms of deadlines, tours, and interviews...except that children going into kindergarten have to be tested before entering this next stage of schooling.

How the testing process works

ISAAGNY: stands for the Independent Schools Admissions Association of Greater New York and is a membership organization of over 100 nursery and private, ongoing schools. The purpose of ISAAGNY is to standardize through testing the qualifications for leaving nursery and entering ongoing schools. It also has a standardized process that notifies parents in March about which schools have accepted their children, and then gives them a few weeks before requesting a decision. The Parents League is a volunteer off-shoot of ISAAGNY, and offers, among many other services, free consultation with parents of students at ISAAGNY schools.

ERB: stands for the Educational Records Bureau, and most ongoing schools require a test administered by them. Students in nursery schools that are members of ISAAGNY may take the test on school premises. Others are tested at ERB's offices at 220 East 42nd Street. These tests are similar to an IQ test, and include age appropriate materials and questions. These test results, in addition to a comprehensive evaluation written by the nursery school director, are forwarded to the private schools. Call 212-672-9800 to make an appointment.

Admissions notification

2, 3, 4 year olds	notification is mailed March 8	Parents reply by March 17
K & 1st grade	notification is mailed February 18	Parents reply by March 4
2nd - 12th grade	notification is at discretion of school	Parents need not reply till March 1

Issues to consider that will help you choose a school:

- Single sex or coed/religious affiliation/number of grades/size of school
- The mission statement of the school - what is its philosophy, traditions and history?
- Extended day and after school offerings (especially for working parents)
- Academic demands
- Comfort level and commonality with other parents
- The Principal. What do your instincts tell you about the leader of the school?

A REJECTION TO A SCHOOL THE FIRST YEAR MIGHT TURN INTO AN ACCEPTANCE THE NEXT YEAR. DON'T TAKE IT PERSONALLY. SCHOOLS HAVE TO CONSIDER SIBLINGS AND LEGACIES, WHO GET ADMITTED FIRST. THEY THEN HAVE TO WEIGH DIVERSITY, A BALANCE OF GIRLS VS. BOYS AS WELL AS THE PERSONALITIES AND DISPOSITIONS OF THE STUDENT BODY.

Admissions Process:

- Contact the schools after Labor Day for brochures and application forms and procedures
- Have your nursery school fill out the school report form from the admissions packet
- Fill out ERB testing forms in early October
- Attend school tours and interviews. If you really like a school, the more enthusiasm you show on a consistent basis, the higher your chance for admission.
- By early January, your schools of choice should have all completed information, including letters of reference, test scores, teacher recommendations, applications, etc. Make sure they do.
- If you are wait-listed, call your school of choice and remind them of your interest
- Call the schools you have rejected, and let them know

PAROCHIAL SCHOOLS

Catholic parochial schools cost considerably less than private schools. Many in New York City do not have the same amenities as the private schools. It is very important that you investigate your choices with the same vigor that you would for public or private schools.

THE CATHOLIC CENTER • (212) 371-1000

The Superintendent of Schools
Office of Archdiocese of New York
1011 First Avenue
New York, NY 10022

www.schoolofchoice.com
www.nycatholicschools.org

IT'S A
DOG'S LIFE...

PERCEPTION VS. REALITY

New Yorkers are some of the most passionate animal lovers in the world.

And that truth is reflected in the unusual "human/pet" relationships playing out on the streets of New York. Park Avenue ladies taking their designer-clothed toy poodles for a manicure; "alternative lifestylers" out strolling with talking parrots and iguanas perched on their shoulders; Great Danes sharing their masters' eggs benedict at a tony sidewalk cafe; exotic felines on leashes in Central Park. We've even met a beloved tarantula named Larry, and a diapered chimpanzee.

Having a pet in a standoffish city is, without a doubt, the best way to strike up conversations with strangers, make fast friends and find lovers. Walk out onto the street with a pet, and you won't get past your front door before someone comes up to pat, oooh, and aah. Take a dog out to a dog run in central park early in the morning; and don't be surprised if you find yourself chatting about kibble and kennels with the likes of Henry Kissinger or Rosie O'Donnell. Even the suspicious, the surly, and cynical are reduced to unrestrained bigheartedness around animals in this city.

Having a dog, however, in mega-city conditions (a tiny apartment and no backyard) has to be carefully considered. You have to be committed to the attention and care it takes to raise a physically and emotionally healthy pup. Those who do it with their eyes wide open are a totally devoted crowd.

SOLUTION:
RAISING A HAPPY PET IN A BIG CITY

New Yorkers are Dog Crazy:

City dogs are very high maintenance: puppies are irresistible but don't get sucked into buying a dog until you fully realize how much time you have to devote to him on a daily basis. They have to be taken out—not let out—to go to the loo and be exercised, at least three times a day. And like any human, dogs left alone for long stretches every day are going to become lonely and out of sorts. Then there's the small apartment space that you both have to share. We suggest that you babysit for a neighbor's dog for a few days to a week to get the idea. You'll know very quickly if a dog fits comfortably into your lifestyle. If you travel a good deal or keep long hours at work, think twice. No. Make that three times.

However, contrary to opinions of country folk, dogs can have a happy, safe and stimulating life in the city. Devoted owners take them everywhere - jogging, brunching, shopping and browsing. They have lots of buddies to play with daily at the many "leash-free", fenced-in dog runs in the parks. Due to the busy schedules of dog owners, doggie day care centers are an option, and they present a regular opportunity for a change of atmosphere and playdates. And strictly-enforced leash laws keep dogs away from the kinds of troubles their country cousins get into.

New Yorkers are even more cat crazy too:

Just try getting tickets to the national cat shows that come to town. New Yorkers love, love, love their cats...and will argue their merits vs. dogs any day. They don't have to go outside for any reason; in fact, most cats hate leaving the comfort of their cozy apartments. If you aren't home during the day, instead of feeling guilty, get two, so they can keep each other company. You can have all the satisfaction that dog owners get out of finding an interesting breed or a delightful disposition, and

THE BETTER BUSINESS BUREAU REPORT ON "PET GUIDELINES" STATES THAT THE PURCHASER OF A DOG OR CAT MUST BE GIVEN INFORMATION ABOUT ALL VACCINATIONS AND WORMING WHICH HAVE BEEN ADMINISTERED, AS WELL AS A RECOMMENDATION THAT THE PURCHASER SEE A VETERINARIAN FOR A FOLLOW-UP EXAMINATION. THEY SHOULD ALSO BE INFORMED THAT NYC LAW REQUIRES ALL ANIMALS TO BE LICENSED BY THE AMERICAN SOCIETY FOR PREVENTION OF CRUELTY TO ANIMALS, AND SHOULD BE GIVEN THEIR FORM. THE A.S.P.C.A. SHOULD RECEIVE A REGULAR REPORT OF ALL DOG SALES TO NYC RESIDENTS. PURCHASERS SHOULD CHECK WITH LOCAL AUTHORITIES REGARDING APPLICABLE LOCAL REGULATIONS GOVERNING LICENSING, EXERCISING, ETC.

sharing your life with a loyal, lovable companion...minus all the extra responsibilities.

New Yorkers are a diverse lot, if the pet population is any indication:

We keep all kinds of exotic pets. There have been the occasional tales about boa constrictors ending up in our sewer system, or animal rescuers finding a lion in a four-floor walk up. We advise something a little tamer and better qualified for urban living. But whether it's a python or a parrot, pet stores supply them, NYC vets know how to heal them and you can find pet sitters who actually know how to care for them.

There are plenty of animal-friendly services in NYC:

For a price, there's no shortage of expert quality caregiving for any type of pet when you need it: From at-home petsitters, animal daycare centers, and professional dog walkers, to boarding houses, vets that make house calls and the finest animal hospitals, New York City has it all...and in great supply. And because New Yorkers tend to treat their pets like children, these service providers have to offer all kinds of extra frills, pampering and TLC, in order to compete for business.

From three star hotels that welcome pups, restaurants that have menus for mutts, to leash-free park runs and pet taxis, this city is catering more and more to pet-loving patrons.

City pet laws:

There are some. Dogs have to be on a leash at all times. The one exception is the designated dog runs in the parks. "Pooper Scooper" laws demand that you clean up after your pet. Period. Fines for ignoring either of these laws can run up to $250.00.

Apartment landlords do not have to accept dogs. Many only allow dogs below a certain weight. Make sure you know the building's rules before purchasing a dog, or moving into an apartment. There is a NYC "pet waiver" law, however, that states that when a tenant has a pet in violation of their lease, the landlord has a period of three months

PET CARE EXPERT AND DIRECTOR OF "TWO DOGS & A GOAT," CHARLOTTE REED, SAYS IT IS IMPORTANT TO HAVE CURRENT PHOTOS OF YOUR PET AVAILABLE AT ALL TIMES. SHOULD HE BE LOST OR STOLEN, YOU WILL BE ABLE TO RELEASE A FLYER WITH A PICTURE OF YOUR PET.

THE BBB STATES THAT NEW PET OWNERS SHOULD BE GIVEN INFORMATION AT THE TIME OF PURCHASE ABOUT THE CARE OF THE ANIMAL. BROCHURES ON THIS SUBJECT ARE AVAILABLE FREE AT THE A.S.P.C.A., 424 EAST 92ND ST., NYC 10028.

FINDING A HOTEL ROOM FOR YOU AND YOUR PET IS NO EASY TASK. THE HIGHER END HOTELS TRY TO ACCOMMODATE.

TRY:

THE CARLYLE

THE PIERRE

THE SOHO GRAND

THE MARRIOTT MARQUIS

THE ROYALTON

within which to serve the tenant with court papers seeking removal of the pet. If the landlord does not take any action during this time period, the tenant can keep the pet for as long as he chooses to stay in the building. For more information, contact attorney Maddy Tarnofsky at 212-932-9787. She specializes in tenant/pet rights. You can also call Jeff Delott, another excellent attorney who knows pet laws, at 212-452-9738 (4 LAW PET).

There are steps to take if your pet is lost or stolen. New York City is a lucrative area for pet thieves. To avoid having your dog stolen, never let your dog off the leash, and never leave your dog tied up where you can't see him at all times. It is a good idea to become a member of one of the organizations and registry services that provide stolen or lost pet protection. Two places to call: 800-Stolen-Pet and Petfinders at 800-666-5678. If your dog is lost, contact the police precincts and the local ASPCA and give them a complete description. Because the ASPCA is open 24 hours a day, it's a likely place for the dog wardens to take him. Go in person to the ASPCA every day to see if your dog has been brought in; don't accept a "no" over the phone.

The Intrepid Pages of
Pet-Related Services

$** = inexpensive   **$$** = moderate   **$$$ = expensive

ADOPT A PET

These adoption organizations each have different requirements for adopting a pet which may include providing proof of identification and references. Call ahead to make sure you take the necessary information with you.

ASPCA • 424 East 92nd Street • (212) 876-7711

It will cost you $50 to adopt a dog or cat, but these fees include various shots, spaying and neutering costs, carrying cases, and literature.

BIDE-A-WEE HOME ASSOCIATION
410 East 38th Street • (212) 532-4455

It will cost you $30 to adopt a dog or cat over six months old and $55 to adopt a dog or cat under six months, which includes spaying/neutering fees and shots.

CENTER FOR ANIMAL CARE AND CONTROL • 326 East 110th Street (212) 722-3620

After an animal is rescued, it is brought back to the Center and given the necessary veterinary care. Adoption fees are $60 for dogs and $55 for cats which includes a veterinary exam, vaccinations, spaying/neutering, and a free follow-up exam.

> CHARLOTTE REED, PET CARE EXPERT, STATES THAT THE DECISION TO ADOPT A SHELTER PET IS AN IMPORTANT ONE. SHELTER ANIMALS, ESPECIALLY, NEED A LOT OF LOVE AND UNDERSTANDING. BUT BY ADOPTING A PET FROM A SHELTER, YOU ARE GIVING AN ANIMAL A NEW LEASE ON LIFE.

HUMANE SOCIETY • 306 East 59th Street • (212) 752-4840

Dogs cost $50 to $100; cats cost $50 or $75. The Humane Society will contribute $10 toward spaying or neutering.

EMERGENCY NUMBERS

BOBST HOSPITAL OF THE ANIMAL MEDICAL CENTER
510 East 62nd Street • (212) 838-8100

The only animal hospital in the City with a doctor on-call twenty-four-hours a day.

NATIONAL ANIMAL POISON CONTROL CENTER • (800) 548-2423

POISON CONTROL • (212) 340-4494

Some animal assistance.

VETS WHO MAKE HOUSE CALLS

WHEN CHOOSING A VET, FIND OUT WHICH HOSPITAL THE VET IS AFFILIATED WITH. IT IS IMPORTANT THAT THE HOSPITAL IS NOT TOO FAR FROM YOUR HOME AND IS OPEN TWENTY-FOUR HOURS.

What pet likes going to a vet's office? Having a vet come to your home offers your pet the security of being in a comfortable environment, and enables you, the owner, a convenient option, especially if you own more than one pet.

DR. AMY ATTAS • (212) 246-6068

Aside from x-rays and surgery, Dr. Attas can provide any service that is done at a vet's office at your home. She can examine, vaccinate, trim nails, clean ears, take blood, and even provide chemotherapy at home. A technician accompanies Dr. Attas on all her visits. She also has an arrangement with a hospital where she treats and admits serious cases. After the initial visit, pet owners do not even need to be home for Dr. Attas to perform her service. Her fee is $95, plus the cost of transportation to your apartment. Each additional pet is $65.

DR. GEORGE M. KORIN • (212) 838-2569 • (718) 349-6379

Dr. Korin can perform routine preventive care and treatment of minor problems and chronic old-age problems at the home. He brings a technician when it is necessary and can take blood, do a urinalysis, and do skin tests. Full medical and surgical services are available through the two animal hospitals that he is affiliated with. Dr. Korin will service clients South of 96th Street, on the East and West Side. His fees start at $65 (local midtown) for the house call and $56 per pet for the physical exam.

DOG LICENSES

Every dog must have one. It's the law.

BUREAU OF VETERINARY PUBLIC HEALTH SERVICES
(212) 676-2100

The license fee is $11.50; $8.50 if the dog is spayed or neutered. They will send you an application.

DOG RUNS

A great place for dogs to roam and owners to brag about their pet with other dog owners.

MANHATTAN

Battery Park City

West and West Thames Street

Carl Schurz Park

East End Avenue to East River from Gracie Square, East 84th to East 89th Street (one for big dogs; one for small dogs)

Dewitt Clinton Park

52nd Street and 11th Avenue

Fishbridge Park

Dover/Pearl Street and Water Street

J. Hood Wright Park

Fort Washington and Haven Avenues, West 173rd Street

Madison Square Park

Madison Avenue to Fifth Avenue, between East 23rd Street and East 26th Street

Peter Detmold Park

West of FDR Drive, between East 49th and East 51st Streets

Riverside Park

Riverside Drive to Hudson River, at West 87th Street and West 105th Street (two runs)

Robert Moses Park

First Avenue at 41st and 42nd Streets

Theodore Roosevelt Park

Central Park West to Columbus Avenue from West 77th to 81st Streets

Thomas F. Smith Park

11th Avenue, West 22nd to West 23rd Streets

AND IF A DOG RUN DOESN'T PROVIDE ENOUGH ENTERTAINMENT FOR YOU AND YOUR PET, VISIT THE FIRST DOG PLAYGROUND TO OPEN IN OR AROUND MANHATTAN, AT VAN CORTLANDT PARK IN THE BRONX. THE PLAY AREA EVEN HAS A FEW BENCHES FOR TIRED PET OWNERS.

"LOVE YOUR PET/ LOVE YOUR PARK" IS A BROCHURE WRITTEN BY THE DEPARTMENT OF PARKS & RECREATION. IT DISCUSSES WHY YOU SHOULD LEASH YOUR DOG, HOW TO KEEP YOUR PET HEALTHY, AND ALSO LISTS DOG RUNS AND SCENIC PARKS. THE BROCHURE IS GIVEN OUT AT ANNUAL PET EVENTS. YOU CAN ALSO ACCESS SOME OF THE INFORMATION AT WWW.NYCPARKS.ORG. FOR MORE INFORMATION, CONTACT THE PARKS DEPARTMENT AT (212) 360-8111.

Tompkins Square Park

Avenue A to Avenue B, from East 7th to 10th Streets

Union Square Park

15th Street and Union Square West

Washington Square Park

Fifth Avenue, Waverly Place, West 4th Street between MacDougal and Thompson Streets, south side of the park (behind the building)

GROOMING CARE

Routine grooming is the best way to keep your dog or cat's coat, nails, and teeth in healthy condition. Listed below are do-it-yourself as well as professional options.

BEVERLY HILL'S LAUNDERMUTT
45 Grove Street • (212) 691-7700 • $$

A do-it-yourself dog wash. For an extra fee, the staff will wash your dog for you.

CAMP CANINE
46 W. 73rd St. • (212) 787-3647

A personalized approach to grooming your special pet.

CANINE STYLES
830 Lexington Avenue (63rd & 64th Streets) (212) 751-4549 • $$$

One of the oldest grooming shops in the City with a loyal and high profile clientele.

DOGGIE-DO AND PUSSYCATS, TOO!
567 Third Avenue (37th & 38th Streets) • (212) 661-9111 • $$$

Dogs and cats that need a shampoo, cut, and blow-dry are entitled to this upscale shop's pick-up and delivery service at an additional fee.

KAREN'S FOR PEOPLE & PETS
1195 Lexington Avenue (at 81st Street) • (212) 472-9440 • $$$

They do an excellent job grooming any breed of dog.

LE CHIEN PET SALON
1044 Third Avenue (61st & 62nd Streets) • (212) 861-8100 • $$$

This shop is known for its exceptional grooming of small dogs.

NEW YORK SCHOOL OF DOG GROOMING
248 East 34th Street • (212) 685-3776 • $

Where it all begins! The only professional grooming school in
Manhattan, it offers complete grooming services as well.

PET ACCESSORIES & SUPPLIES

ALL CREATURES GREAT & SMALL
833 Lexington Avenue (63rd & 64th Streets)
(212) 754-6369 • $$$

They carry a wonderful selection of antique and collectible animal
items.

ANIMAL WORLD
219 East 26th Street • (212) 685-0027 • $$

The owners have been at this location for 15 years and are truly
knowledgeable about animals. They provide the customer with
excellent personalized attention and are happy to answer any ques-
tions about animals that you may have. They sell a varied selection
of food, accessories, vitamins, and shampoos, among other items.

DOGGIE-DO AND PUSSYCATS, TOO!
567 Third Avenue (37th and 38th Streets) • (212) 661-9111 • $$$

This boutique and grooming facility caters to the upscale dog and
cat owner—homemade cookies, sterling silver dog statues, and
custom-made dog coats—can be found here.

JB WHOLESALE PET SUPPLIES • By Mail: (800) 526-0388 • $

Within two days, you can receive wholesale vitamins, treats, toys,
grooming supplies, crates, and much more from their warehouse in
New Jersey.

JUST CATS
244 East 60th Street • (212) 888-2287 • $$

They sell everything for cats only—clothing, cat supplies, and
gourmet cat food. They also carry clothing, house-wares, jewelry,
and gift items for cat owners and lovers.

KAREN'S FOR PEOPLE & PETS
1195 Lexington Avenue (at 81st Street) • (212) 472-9440 • $$$

Karen's is the "Tiffany's" of pet items and accessories.
Designer/owner Karen offers her customers a fabulous selection of

unique, custom pet tags and accessories, with matching ensembles for owners. A full array of treats, toys, books, and food is available.

MR. B.'S PET DEPOT • (718) 423-0082 • $

Mr. B.'s is a delivery service for pet food at discount prices. The food is restocked frequently and is always fresh. The delivery turn-around time is generally two days. There is a $1 delivery fee.

PETCO
147 East 86th Street (at Lexington) • (212) 831-8001
860 Broadway (at 17th Street) • (212) 358-0692
560 2nd Avenue (at 31st Street) • (212) 779-4550

This chain store sells pet food, toys, bowls and other basic pet supplies. They also sell small animals such as reptiles, birds, and aquatic animals.

PET BOWL
440 Amsterdam Avenue (at 81st Street) • (212) 595-4200 • $$

400 varieties of cat and dog food can be found at Pet Bowl. They offer a "Reminder Call" delivery service, whereby you work out an order schedule with them and they will call to remind you that it's time for your new order, and will then deliver it to you. There is no commitment to purchase items when they call. If you do participate, you will receive an automatic 5 percent off food and litter and 10 percent off accessory purchases.

PET NECESSITIES • 236 East 75th Street • (212) 988-0769 • $$

They carry an excellent supply of food stuffs, collars, sweaters, and dog beds.

R.C. STEELE CATALOGUE • By Mail: (800) 872-3773 • $

A wholesale supply catalogue (no food). They deliver right to your door for half the price of New York stores.

WHISKERS • 235 East 9th Street • (212) 979-2532 • $$$

Besides providing holistic home cooked meals, this shop also sells natural brand dog foods, vitamins, supplements, herbs, natural remedies, and environmentally sound toys.

PHOTOGRAPHS/GALLERIES

PETOGRAPHY • 25 Central Park West • (212) 245-0914

Jim Dratfield travels all over the world to photograph his clients and their pets.

WILLIAM SECORD GALLERY
52 East 76th Street • (212) 249-0075

Wonderful gallery of 19th and 20th Century dog oil paintings.

TRAINING

When choosing a training program for yourself and your dog, ask about the instructor's methods. Seek a class or instructor with a positive training approach. Most importantly, watch a class before you enroll.

In addition to the trainers listed below, several animal adoption agencies also offer private and group lessons. Discounts are given to pets who were adopted from the agency.

AMERICAN DOG TRAINERS NETWORK
www.inch.com/~dogs

The Network's comprehensive web site offers an enormous variety of dog-related information, including articles on dog training, how to choose a dog trainer, pet safety tips, problem-solving techniques, and referrals for many other dog services.

ASPCA • 424 East 92nd Street • (212) 876-7700 • $$

The ASPCA offers quality dog training for all levels.

BASH DIBRA • (718) 796-4541 • $$$

Founder of the ASPCA's Woofstock and author of two obedience training manuals, Bash Dibra is trainer to the stars.

CITY DOG OBEDIENCE SCHOOL
158 West 23rd Street • (212) 255-3618 • $$

Here your dog can train in group classes, from a beginning level, to a competitive level.

FOLLOW MY LEAD • 117 West 74th Street • (212) 873-5511 • $$

Small classes with lots of personal attention can comfort and inspire first-time dog owners.

MANHATTAN BEHAVIORAL TRAINING
145 W. 18th Street • (212) 243-1199 • $$$

Group classes and puppy kindergarten are held at the New York Dog Spa & Hotel.

ROBIN KOVARY • (212) 243-5460 • $$

Robin has been a professional dog trainer and behavioral consultant for over 16 years. Her impressive credentials include being founder of the American Dog Trainers Network, certified as an Animal Assisted Therapy Evaluator, and currently, Director of the Canine Resource and Referral Help Line. Her at-home services comprise basic and advanced obedience, problem prevention, owner counseling, house-training, behavioral modification, and trick-training. Robin's emphasis is on positive motivational methods. You can visit Robin's web site at www.inch.com/~dogs/profile.html.

TRANSPORTING

Unlike Amtrak, pets are welcome on the Long Island Railroad and Metro North, as long as they are under 20 pounds and are in a carrier. New York City taxi drivers may refuse to pick up you and your furry friend without a carrier as well. Bus drivers will not let you enter the bus with your pet.

In a city with so many restrictions, a car service especially for pets is a welcome solution.

COSMOPOLITAN CANINE CARRIERS • (800) PET-RELO • $$

They are in the business of moving all kinds of pets. They are the only Interstate Commerce Commission licensed carrier of pets in the United States.

PET TAXI • (212) 755-1757 • $$$

Lawrence Reilly drives a yellow G.M. minivan adorned with black and white squares to mimic the look of the old Checker cabs. He drives only one pet customer at a time, and is available from 7:30 A.M. to 7:30 P.M., seven days a week. The fare is $20 each way anywhere in Manhattan, up to 60 blocks. For travel outside the City, Larry charges $30 per hour. Best of all, Larry is registered as an animal handler with the United States Department of Agriculture and has had a dog (or two) as a pet all his life. You can rest assured your pet will be well cared for on his journey. Larry also offers a twenty-four-hour emergency service for pets who need to be rushed to the hospital. He has a stretcher, gloves, and a muzzle in his van. The fee is $50 and up depending on the time of day.

WHEN YOU'RE AWAY FROM HOME — SITTING & WALKING/DOGGIE DAYCARE & BOARDING

There are so many pet care services available, you need not feel guilty about leaving your pet home alone. But choose wisely. Ask for a list of references and check them out. Hire a sitter that is insured and bonded.

PET SITTERS & DOG WALKERS

CAT-CARE EAST, INC. • (212) 838-2996 • $$

Since 1975, Lynda Fisher has run Cat-Care, a pet care service for cats and other small animals (birds, rabbits, turtles.) During the daytime hours, one of Lynda's sitters will come to your home once or twice a day to play with and feed your pet, as well as to clean up after them. They can also give medication to your pet if necessary. Visits last from 20 to 30 minutes. Lynda is a member of the National Association of Professional Pet Sitters. Cat-Care serves the East side of Manhattan only.

JIM BUCK • (212) 410-BUCK • $$

This is "the" dog-walking company on the Upper East Side. They will walk dogs in packs from 57th Street to 98th Street, Fifth Avenue to the River.

NOAH'S ARK PET CARE • (212) 255-8939 • $$

Geza Harasz runs this company, which specializes in the care of parrots and other varieties of birds, but will basically take on any type of pet client. A sitter will come to your home in the daytime and evening, but not overnight, to feed, play with, and walk your pet. Someone can visit your pet several times a day if necessary. Visits generally last from 15 to 45 minutes.

PAMPERED PETS • (212) 772-2181 • $$

Pampered Pets is an inclusive at-home pet care service. Employees of the company are licensed professionals who can take care of the needs of pets, whether it is walking, feeding, grooming, administering medicine or supplying affection.

PET PATROL • (212) 924-6319 • $$

Here you will find someone willing to walk your dog solo. Walks are forty-five minutes and cost $15.

TWO DOGS & A GOAT INCORPORATED
326 East 34th Street
(212) 631-1157 • $$

Director Charlotte Reed operates the most comprehensive and vet recommended pet care company in Manhattan. Services include dog walking, pet sitting, in-home grooming, and obedience training. The staff of pet care providers can walk your dog solo, dispense medicine and fluids to your animal if necessary, and will even take your dog to the vet. They can also keep your cat company ($15 per visit). Sleepover provisions can be arranged as well. A single dog walk costs $15; sleepovers cost $30. They are a member of PSI and the National Association of Professional Pet Sitters.

URBAN ANIMAL • (212) 969-8506 • $$

Ilene Richman owns and operates this walking service with a staff of 25 animal lovers. They walk one dog at a time, and cover Houston to 100th Street, on the east and west side. The cost is $12 per half hour. They will also pet sit at your home for a short or extended period.

DOGGIE DAYCARE & ANIMAL BOARDING FACILITIES

CAMP CANINE • 46 West 73rd Street • (212) 787-3647 • $$

Three indoor playrooms provide ample space for your pet. The

BOOKS ABOUT CARING FOR YOUR NEW YORK PET ARE VERY HELPFUL RESOURCES. SOME GREAT CHOICES: *DGNY*, A BI-MONTHLY GUIDE TO OWNING A DOG IN NEW YORK. FOR A SUBSCRIPTION AT $12 A YEAR, CALL (212) 832-2828; *THE GREAT NEW YORK DOG BOOK*, BY DEBORAH LOVEN. HARPERCOLLINS PUBLISHERS, INC., COPYRIGHT 1995; *THE NEW YORK CAT OWNERS GUIDE*, BY BILL DWORKIN. PUBLISHED BY CITY & COMPANY, COPYRIGHT 1995; AND *THE NEW YORK DOG OWNERS GUIDE*, BY MARTHA KAPLAN. PUBLISHED BY CITY & COMPANY, COPYRIGHT 1994.

campers' exercise regimen consists of chasing each other around the dog runs and fetching the balls and frisbees that the counselors use to play with them. Dogs are placed in crates for three hours a day for meals and rest. The daycare hours are from 7:00 A.M. to 9:30 P.M. Camp Canine also has provisions for overnight boarding.

CANINE COUNTRY
207 West 75th Street
(212) 877-7777 • $$

Canine Country has a big playroom for fun and exercise. Daycare hours are 7:00 A.M. to 10:00 P.M. The dogs are in cages when they eat, and in the evening when they sleep. They board dogs only, no cats, on an overnight basis.

THE NEW YORK DOG SPA & HOTEL
145 West 18th Street
(212) 243-1199 • $$$

Have a cup of joe in the lounge while your pooch is in daycare. At this center, dogs are separated by temperament and are walked in pairs three times a day. Your pet would be separated in a kennel run for eating and sleeping. The daycare hours are 7:00 A.M. to 10:00 P.M. There is also a vet and groomer on-site, and overnight boarding is available for dogs only.

THE PAWS INN
370 West 35th Street • (212) 736-7297 • $$
189 Ninth Avenue (between 21st & 22nd Streets) • (212) 645-7297

Big play zone with sloppy dog-friendly furniture. Upstairs "bedroom" where lots of snuggling and "Lassie" rerun watching goes on. Dogs are not caged, but are separated in rooms by size and disposition. Daycare hours are from 7:00 A.M. to 10:00 P.M. They will board dogs and cats on an overnight basis.

RUN SPOT RUN • 415 East 91st Street • (212) 996-6666 • $$

This facility has 5,000 square feet of space, divided into five separate play areas, depending on the size of the dog. They are open from 7:00 A.M. to 10:00 P.M. The dogs are placed in kennels for eating and sleeping. Run Spot Run will also board dogs and cats on an overnight basis.

SUTTON DOG PARLOUR & DAYCARE CENTER
311 East 60th Street
(212) 355-2850 • $$

Dogs have it made at the Sutton Dog Parlour which offers its "customers" indoor, as well as a 2,500 square foot, outdoor play area. Dogs are separated in a kennel run, each of which has a bed and a mat. The dogs are never caged. Hours of the daycare are 8:00 A.M. to 7:00 P.M. Overnight boarding is available for dogs, cats, and birds. They also offer grooming services.

YOU CAN ALSO ACCESS THE DOG LOVER'S BOOKSHOP ON LINE AT WWW.DOGBOOKS.COM.

YUPPIE PUPPY PET CARE
274 West 86th Street
(212) 877-2747 • $$$

The first daycare center for dogs anywhere, the Yuppie Puppy has a big playroom, and an outdoor plastic swimming pool for hot days. Dogs sleep in individual kennels in the evening. They do not board cats. The daycare center runs from 8:00 A.M. to 7:45 P.M.

NOT TO BE OVERLOOKED... RESTAURANTS THAT ALLOW DOGS

It is against New York State law to allow pets inside restaurants. However, there are several restaurants with outdoor seating throughout the City that will allow dogs to dine outside with their owners. Most of these restaurants offer water, biscuits, and table scraps to hungry dogs.

Chelsea

CHELSEA LOBSTER COMPANY
156 Seventh Avenue (19th Street) • (212) 243-5732

SUMO
106 Eighth Avenue (15th Street) • (212) 352-0911

East Village

CAFÉ PICK ME UP
145 Avenue A (Ninth Street) • (212) 673-7231

PISCES
95 Avenue A (Sixth Street) • (212) 260-6660

SIDEWALK
94 Avenue A (Sixth Street) • (212) 473-7373

THE BBB STATES THAT REPRESENTATIVES FROM ALL ASPECTS OF THE PET INDUSTRY ARE IN AGREEMENT THAT A CONSUMER SHOULD LOOK FOR THE FOLLOWING MINIMUM STANDARDS IN A GUARANTEE: THE PET RETAILER OR BREEDER SHOULD GIVE A FIVE DAY HEALTH GUARANTEE. THE GUARANTEE REQUIRES THAT THE PET BE EXAMINED BY A VETERINARIAN. ON WRITTEN REQUEST FROM THE VET, THE GUARANTEE PERIOD SHOULD BE EXTENDED AN ADDITIONAL FIVE DAYS. IF DURING THIS PERIOD, THE VET DEEMS THE ANIMAL UNSUITABLE FOR REASONS OF HEALTH, IT SHOULD BE EXCHANGEABLE FOR A SECOND ANIMAL. A RETAILER OR BREEDER SHOULD GRANT A 30-DAY EXTENDED EXCHANGE GUARANTEE FROM DATE OF PURCHASE, COVERING DISTEMPER, HEPATITIS, AND CONGENITAL DEFECTS. IF IT IS NECESSARY TO PROVIDE A REPLACEMENT, THE SELLER SHALL DO SO WITHIN 45 DAYS OF RETURN.

Flatiron District and Murray Hill

CHRISTINA'S
606 Second Avenue (34th Street)
889-5169

VERBENA
54 Irving Place (17th Street)
(212) 260-5454

Greenwich Village

CAFÉ SHA SHA
510 Hudson Street (Christopher Street)
(212) 242-3021

TIME CAFÉ
380 Lafayette (Great Jones Street)
(212) 533-7000

Upper East Side

GIRASOLE • 151 East 82nd Street
(212) 772-6690

VESPA CIBOBUONO
1625 Second Avenue (at 84th Street)
(212) 472-2050

ZOCALO • 174 East 82nd Street
(212) 717-7772

Upper West Side

BELLA LUNA
584 Columbus Avenue (88th Street)
(212) 877-2267

MERCHANTS, N.Y.
521 Columbus Avenue
(85th & 86th Streets) • (212) 721-3689

HOME SWEET HOME

FINDING A HOME IN NYC: A HIGH-STAKES GAME YOU CAN WIN

PERCEPTION VS. REALITY

1. Out of towners have heard that New Yorkers live in shoe boxes.

2. That whether you are trying to rent, buy or sell a home, you have never seen the real estate game played the NYC way. That in addition to the prohibitively high cost of apartments and the small spaces we are expected to call home, the playing field is never level: first, you have to try to find an apartment in a city that has no "multiple listing service"; second, the market seems to shift seismically favoring buyers, then sellers, renters, then landlords – every few years or so. In addition, the rules can be confusing, archaic, sometimes infuriating, even demoralizing. All true, but at the very least, you can do respectably well in this marketplace, if you get sufficiently educated first, and then make a strategic plan of attack. And we New Yorkers get a lot more than an apartment. Many residential buildings now come complete with rooftop decks, health clubs, party rooms and indoor playgrounds. And Manhattan itself is *everyones*' backyard!

SOLUTION:
IT'S IMPORTANT TO UNDERSTAND CURRENT MARKET CONDITIONS AND HOW THEY CAN AFFECT YOU

Rentals:

The rental market has never been tighter. There is a 2% vacancy rate and a line around the block for every apartment. Landlords are charging and getting obscene rents – you can't put your big toe into most "unregulated" studio apartments for less than $1,400 a month. One bedrooms start at $1,900, 2 bedrooms at $2,800.

There is a chance of finding one of NYC's coveted, "rent stabilized" below market-priced apartments that are still regulated by NY State; but it's about being in the right place at the right time, and it's almost impossible to accomplish without a real estate broker who will charge you 15% of the first year's rent to complete the task. Just a few years ago, landlords were offering "no (broker's) fee" apartments, sometimes even adding on a "first month free" enticement, and brokers were agreeing to any percentage just to get your business. Today, in order to find what you are looking for in this market, you first have to find the real estate brokers who specialize in the specific neighborhoods, apartment styles and price range you request...then get over the shock that 1/2 your furniture won't fit in such a small space...then convince the landlord that you're a more qualified tenant than the other 5 people lined up behind you. Your landlord may require you to have another qualified member "co-guarantee" your lease. Then empty your wallet of two months rent upfront and a broker's commission equal to 15% of the first year's rent.

Sales:

NYC is, for the first time since the mid 1980s, experiencing an overheated, seller's market. In the early '90s, due to a weak economy, everybody started renting, not buying, out of fear they would not be able to unload their apartments when it came time to sell. In particular, owners of studios, and the smaller, "cookie-cutter"one and two-bedroom apartments, became prisoners to homes they couldn't sell, or they took a huge financial bath. Now, the opposite is happening. In a "throw money out the window" rental market, people are buying again. Studios, and small, one and two bedroom apartments are selling at a rational price. After looking at the after-tax dollars, your monthly mortgage and maintenance payments can be less than your rental bill. The grander two-plus bedrooms, however, are going for exorbitant prices with multiple bids over the asking price! The word on the street is that the excesses of the 80's haven't just returned, they've exceeded themselves. In an extremely fickle market, smart buyers make sure that they increase their resale odds by purchasing a home that has stand-out qualities, a good layout, and is located in a desirable neighborhood.

**The sources you can use to help you
evaluate market conditions:**

- **Real estate brokers:** get several opinions
- **Real estate attorneys:** can offer an objective point of view
- **Trade publications:**
    - Real estate sections of local newspapers

- Quarterly market reports put out by the major real estate firms such as Feathered Nest for rentals and Douglas Elliman or Corcoran for sales
- **Real estate web sites:** Can be more helpful if you are buying than renting.

SOLUTION:
FIGURE OUT WHICH NYC HOUSING STYLE MOST SUITS YOU.

- **Brownstone or townhouse living:** built in the late 1800s or early 1900s, this style of living is known for charming details such as fireplaces, original moldings and details, gardens or back decks, and original hardwood floors. They might house a single family or be divided into individual apartments. Many have renovated kitchens and baths for modern living.

- **Walk-up buildings:** these are 4 to 5 stories without elevators. They have multiple dwellings and tend to have the least expensive housing in the city. They have a reputation for lacking charm, but the quality can vary a great deal. Some have been very nicely renovated.

- **Elevator buildings:** can be either pre-war or post-war. Non-doorman buildings from 6 - 20 stories, usually have voice and video intercom security systems for entry into the building.

- **Prewar buildings:** these buildings were constructed before WWII. Either doorman or non-doorman, these buildings have the feel of an earlier, more elegant era and feature high ceilings, original details, fireplaces, and grander, more classic layouts. Many of these apartments have been renovated with modern fixtures, but many have not.

- **Postwar buildings:** built between the late 40s and early 70s. Plain in style, they have simple white, brown or red brick facades, usually more boxy apartment layouts, but larger spaces. Most have doormen and/or a concierge desk, and tend to be the most affordable of the "full-service" buildings.

- **Luxury doorman buildings:** these are NYC's most contemporary high-rises with up to 50 stories, incredible views, modern layouts with Jacuzzis and granite counter tops, plenty of amenities including healthclubs, concierges, rooftop decks and so on. Many are condominiums, some are rentals.

- **Loft buildings:** these are warehouses and factories that have been converted into huge open spaces with very high ceilings.

They are located "downtown" in neighborhoods such as Greenwich Village, Soho, Chelsea and Tribeca. Many had originally been zoned exclusively for artist studios. They are coveted for their large, open, airy living space. In real estate ads you will see the term "loft-like" or "one-room apartment with a loft". These are not real lofts. These descriptions refer to an apartment that has an open, spacious feel or one that has a loft area, meaning a space built above the living area and accessible by ladder or stairs. People either use them for storage or sleeping.

SOLUTION:
CHOOSE THE NEIGHBORHOOD THAT FEELS MOST LIKE "HOME", BEFORE YOU BEGIN THE APARTMENT SEARCH — REMEMBER, LOCATION, LOCATION, LOCATION

New Yorkers are even more passionate about the neighborhoods in which they live, than their apartments. It's an important quality-of-life issue because each area has very different characteristics in terms of culture, politics, aesthetics, lifestyle and community. Make sure you pick the area that feels most like home to you by considering:

- **Curbside appeal:** do you like the look and feel of the area surrounding your building and street? Is the apartment on a busy avenue or a quiet, tree-lined street?

- **Neighborhood life:** do you prefer quiet and tranquility or hustle and bustle? Do you like having a neighborhood that is alive until all hours of the night or one that has more traditional hours. Do you prefer a population that is more diverse, or more homogeneous?

- **Commute:** How long, how easy, how comfortable? Would you have to take a subway, a bus, or both? Can you walk?

- **Amenities:** Does the neighborhood have all the local merchants, service-providers restaurants, and recreational opportunities you want to have close by? How important is it to be near a park, or within a few blocks of the office?

- **How secure do you feel:** You can call the local neighborhood precinct and ask the "community affairs officer" about safety issues in the neighborhood. Perception is just as important as reality, however, in terms of your sense of well being, so no matter what the police say, if it doesn't feel completely comfortable to you, it probably never will. We also recommend that you walk the neighborhood at night as well as during the day. Some neighborhoods feel dramatically different at night.

More and more professionals are choosing to live in boroughs other than Manhattan, because rents have forced them to look on the other side of the East and Hudson Rivers. It is no longer considered "uncool" to live in areas such as Queens, Brooklyn, and Hoboken, New Jersey. And in some cases you can get twice the apartment by just commuting an extra 15 minutes, and still be able to use Manhattan as your back yard! A sample to show you what we mean:

QUEENS — Astoria, Woodside, Sunnyside and Long Island City: Just on the other side of the East River from Manhattan, these neighborhoods are a 10-15 minute commute by subway from the East 50s in midtown. Traditionally blue collar and a virtual ethnic melting pot from Greek to Asian families, the neighborhood ambiance is global, friendly, safe and community oriented. There is lots of street life, great restaurants, major shopping avenues and apartments are available for often half the price in single family homes or modest apartment buildings. As these areas are being discovered by white collar professionals, more cosmopolitan and upscale high-rises and local amenities are coming into these neighborhoods.

> NEW YORKERS WITHOUT DEEP POCKETS, WHO STILL CHOOSE TO LIVE IN MANHATTAN, ARE PURPOSELY GIVING UP SQUARE FOOTAGE IN ORDER TO HAVE UNLIMITED ACCESS TO AN EXCLUSIVE CLUB — AND THAT CLUB IS "MANHATTAN" AND ALL THAT IS HAS TO OFFER IN TERMS OF SOPHISTICATION, INTERNATIONAL FLAVOR, CULTURE AND WORLD CLASS PURSUITS. IF SQUARE FOOTAGE AND IN-HOME AMENITIES IS MORE IMPORTANT, THEN YOU MIGHT PREFER TO LIVE "OFF ISLAND" AND JUST BE A WEEKEND VISITOR.

BROOKLYN — Park Slope, Williamsburg, Greenpoint: As historic Brooklyn Heights has become almost as expensive as Manhattan, professionals are looking another 20 minutes further into Brooklyn in neighborhoods like Park Slope for value. With classic brownstone living, pretty, tree-lined neighborhoods and nearby Prospect Park, you can get more for your money in an attractive, smaller city setting. Williamsburg and Greenpoint are just on the other side of the East River from the East 20s in Manhattan. These funky, somewhat gritty but "cool" neighborhoods are attracting alternative lifestylers such as artists, musicians and all kinds of creative types who want more "loft-style" living than they could ever afford otherwise.

NEW JERSEY — Hoboken, Jersey City: Just across the Hudson River from the World Trade Centers, Hoboken is small city living at its most intimate. It is an old, established, cozy six-square block neighborhood with extraordinary skyline views of Manhattan. You can ferry or subway it in a matter of minutes and live in a charming brownstone apartment for considerably less than living in Manhattan. If you want modern, dramatic and amenity-rich, you can rent or purchase in ultra-modern high-rise and low-rise complexes along the waterfronts in both Hoboken and Jersey City.

MANHATTAN — For those of you who wouldn't trade the Manhattan experience for all the bagels in New York City, there is a neighborhood for any lifestyle, any image. There's established residential on the Upper East Side; there's the trendy, vibrant Upper West Side; the walk-to-work hustle and bustle of Midtown, below Central Park; the glitzy new media scene downtown in the Flat Iron, Soho, and Tribeca neighborhoods as well as the legitimate funk of the East Village, Little Italy and Chinatown. All have similar apartment price ranges give or take a few small exclusive areas. Most are chocablock with local amenities, and all are considered viable for residential living. In general, one can expect to spend $1200 and more for a studio apartment, $1500 and up for a one-bedroom and $2500 and up for a two-bedroom.

THE INTREPID PAGES OF
NEIGHBORHOOD FACT-FINDING RESOURCES

THE MUSEUM OF THE CITY OF NEW YORK
(212) 534-1672, Ext. 206

The museum offers walking tours on most Saturdays that feature different neighborhoods and themes and last about four hours. The fee is $7 for museum members, $9 for nonmembers.

92ND STREET Y WALKING TOURS • (212) 415-5628

To find out more about their tours, call for a copy of The Y Catalog. On Sundays, they usually focus on a specific theme, and range from $15 to $35.

MICHELIN, NEW YORK CITY

A terrific overall guide to the City and its neighborhoods. It can be bought at any major bookstore.

NEW YORK ACCESS

This guidebook divides up the City by neighborhood. A great way to educate yourself!

LOCAL COMMUNITY BOARDS

They can provide you with neighborhood directories that tell you about the local churches and synagogues, community organizations, libraries, schools, social services, recreational areas, major attractions, local newspapers, etc. Depending on the community board, some directories are more up to date and complete than others. But, if you have any questions, someone will be happy to answer them. See the Assertiveness chapter for community board telephone numbers.

NEIGHBORHOOD ASSOCIATIONS AND LOCAL PRECINCTS

You can get an idea from these organizations about how safe the neighborhood is, what the community is like, what its problems and strengths are. You can find out the names of neighborhood associations by asking the community affairs officer of the precinct (see the Safety chapter for numbers), or the community board.

LOCAL COMMUNITY NEWSPAPERS

Again, once you have narrowed your search, look through the community's local newspapers. They can really give you an idea of what is going on in a community. Below are some community newspapers to read:

MANHATTAN PAPERS

The Chelsea And Clinton News • (212) 268-2552

Area covered: From 14th to 59th Streets on the West Side.

The Downtown Express • (212) 242-6162

Area covered: South of Canal to the tip of Manhattan including Battery Park City.

Downtown Resident • (212) 679-4970

Area covered: West 23rd Street to Battery Park City; West 14th Street to the Financial District.

Manhattan Spirit • (212) 268-8600

Area covered: Most of Manhattan.

Midtown Resident • (212) 679-4970

Area covered: 14th to 50th Streets east of Fifth Avenue.

New York Press • (212) 244-2282

Calendar of events, day-to-day listings.

Our Town • (212) 268-8600

Area covered: East Side from 14th to 96th Streets, Fifth Avenue to the East River including Roosevelt Island and Central Park.

Upper East Side Resident • (212) 679-1850

Area covered: 50th to 96th Streets east of Fifth Avenue.

Upper West Side Resident • (212) 679-1850

Area covered: 57th to 125th Streets west of Fifth Avenue.

The Villager • (212) 229-1890

Area covered: All of lower Manhattan, the East Village, West Village, SoHo, and Chelsea.

The Westsider • (212) 268-2552

Area covered: From 59th to 125th Streets on the West Side.

BROOKLYN PAPERS:

The Brooklyn Papers • (718) 834-9350

Area covered: They publish 12 papers covering all areas of Brooklyn

HOBOKEN PAPERS:

The Hoboken Reporter • (201) 653-8166

Area covered: Hoboken

STATEN ISLAND PAPERS:

The Staten Island Advance (718) 981-1234

Area covered: Staten Island

QUEENS PAPERS:

The Gazette • (718) 271-0091

Area covered: Astoria

The Tribune • (718) 357-7400

Area covered: whole borough

BRONX PAPERS:

The Bronx Press Review • (718) 543-5200

Area covered: Riverdale

Riverdale Review • (718) 543-5200

Area covered: Riverdale

SOLUTION:
IF YOU UNDERSTAND HOW APARTMENTS ARE BROKERED IN NYC, YOU'LL GREATLY INCREASE THE ODDS OF FINDING THE ONE YOU WANT.

NYC has no multiple listing service: this means that there is no commonly shared book of apartment listings. There are a few big real estate firms that cover larger portions of the market than others, but nobody covers all of it. This is especially true in the rental market, which is a specialty unto itself.

Many real estate brokers get around the lack of a multiple listing service by agreeing to operate as a "co brokerage" community. This means that real estate companies "co-broke"(share) listings to increase their inventory of apartments. The companies split the commission when the apartment sells or rents. Many will try to rent or sell one of their own exclusives first in order to keep the full commission. It is critical to ask your broker at the outset, in order to see as much inventory as possible, if you are being shown co-broked apartments.

There are literally 1000s of real estate agents to choose from: There are about 18,000 real estate agents in NYC! An alarming number are ethically "challenged", self-serving or just plain incompetent, and they hide in plain sight, even within the most reputable firms. And more agents than not will tell you they can knowledgeably handle "all areas of the market" in order to get your business, but it just isn't so.

As is standard everywhere, the seller pays the broker's commission. But in NYC, the renter pays the broker's commission, not the landlord. In a sale, the commission is typically 6% and can go higher, depending on how difficult the home is to sell. In a rental situation, the commission can be anywhere from 10 - 15% of the first year's rent, depending on how strong or weak the market. When the market is tight and demand far outweighs supply, brokers typically receive a 15% fee, or even more.

A skilled and reputable broker is worth his/her weight in gold. Their value is in their:

- "Quality of service means repeat business" professionalism
- "Co-broke immediately" mentality
- Willingness to educate themselves and do the legwork required to find you the right place
- Ability to finesse the approval process with a difficult landlord or co-op board of directors.
- Negotiating skills that can talk a landlord into better lease terms
- Ability to steer you away from a potentially shaky deal
- Ability to qualify you financially.

Winding up in the hands of an incompetent or unethical agent can spell disaster. Even a brokerage company that has a world-class reputation for listings and service can have incompetent or self-interested agents within. Most agents function as independent contractors who only make money when they close a deal. And when an unethical broker is a top earner, the company may choose to go deaf, dumb and blind to their indiscretions. Bottom line, NEVER pick an agent without a strong recommendation, because an incompetent or unethical agent can:

- Get you way in over your head financially by only showing you apartments outside your budget
- Lead you to believe that the apartment is yours, when it's not and never would have been
- Blow a deal on an apartment that should have been yours

- Waste days showing you apartments you don't want because they won't admit they don't have the type of inventory that you want
- Pull the bait and switch on you; entice you with listings that are too good to be true and then tell you those apartments just got taken

ABOUT 5 YEARS AGO, HERE AT HALSTEAD PROPERTY COMPANY, WE HAD AN INKLING THAT NEW YORKERS WERE BEGINNING TO THINK DIFFERENTLY ABOUT RAISING CHILDREN IN MANHATTAN. THERE WERE MANY CLUES THAT FAMILIES WERE NO LONGER PLANNING THEIR FLIGHT TO THE SUBURBS AS SOON AS THEIR FIRST CHILD WAS BORN, THUS THE MARKET FOR LARGER, FAMILY-SIZED APARTMENTS GREW TIGHTER. HERE WE ARE FIVE YEARS LATER AND THE TREND HAS NOT ONLY INCREASED, IT HAS TURNED INTO A VIRTUAL FLOOD OF INTEREST IN LARGER, FAMILY-SIZED APARTMENTS TO ACCOMMODATE FAMILIES' GROWING NEEDS. INDEED, NO CATEGORY OF RESIDENTIAL PROPERTY HAS SEEN PRICES ESCALATE FASTER OR EXPERIENCED GREATER DEMAND. THE LARGER PROPER-TIES ARE THERE TO BE FOUND, IF YOU KNOW WHERE—AND HOW—TO LOOK. THE FACT IS, THERE ARE STRATEGIES FOR FINDING AND GETTING WHAT YOU WANT EVEN IN THIS FAST MOVING MARKET. SOME BUYERS BEAT THE SHORTAGE BY PURCHASING AND COMBINING ADJACENT APART-MENTS. OTHERS LOOK IN LESS TRADITIONAL FAMILY NEIGHBORHOODS WHERE LOFTS PROVIDE GREAT SPACE AND FLEXIBILITY.

CLARK P HALSTEAD, CRB, AIA
FOUNDER & MANAGING
PARTNER
THE HALSTEAD PROPERTY
COMPANY

THE INTREPID PAGES OF

REAL ESTATE COMPANIES AND NEWSPAPER CLASSIFIEDS WITH ONLINE RESOURCES

There is no doubt that the web can provide some useful information for those in need of an apartment. But what you see in ads may not be close to what you get. The listing may be gone, if not, at least misleading. Having said that first, you can download the real estate classifieds from local newspapers. Second, you can visit a real estate company's web site and check out their listings. But never choose a broker based solely upon their web site. **REMEMBER WITH NO MULTIPLE LISTING SERVICE AND 18,000 BROKERS IN NYC, IT IS CRITICAL TO CHOOSE AGENTS WHO SPECIALIZE IN YOUR PRICE RANGE, NEIGHBORHOOD, AND STYLE OF HOUSING.**

THE CORCORAN GROUP: www.corcoran.com

One of the finest real estate firms in the city founded and run by THE guru of NY Real estate Barbara Corcoran.

DOUGLAS ELLIMAN: www.elliman.com

The Douglas Elliman site contains thousands of sale and rental listings in New York City, selected suburban locations, as well as properties in other U.S. locations and throughout the world.

GABRIEL'S GUIDE: www.gabriels.net

You can find Gabriel's real estate and neighborhood information on Digital City at AOL. Gabriel started by publishing Manhattan rental and buying guides and now has a very active on line company. www.gabriels.net

THE HALSTEAD PROPERTY COMPANY: www.halsteadproperty.com

Another blue chip real estate firm that publishes a shortened market summary.

HOMENET • (212) 474-6100 • www.homenet.com

HomeNet is a nationwide enterprise with online listings of real estate properties for sale and for rent around the country. You will have access to over 4,000 brokers, agents, and real estate-related companies by visiting their web site at www.homenet.com.

THE NEW YORK PRESS: www.adone.com/nypress/

This alternative weekly newspaper offers online users a web site of real estate listings. This information is the same as what is listed in its hard copy counterpart.

THE NEW YORK TIMES ONLINE: www.newyorktimes.com

The New York Times also has its own web site of real estate listings which is the equivalent of what you will find in the actual newspaper.

THE VILLAGE VOICE ONLINE: www.villagevoice.com

Similar to *The New York Press* and *The New York Times*, *The Village Voice* services online users with the same real estate listings available in the weekly newspaper.

THE INTREPID PAGES OF
ONLINE REAL ESTATE SERVICES

As we mentioned earlier, The Intrepid New Yorker has never had great success with online real estate services, but having said that, they cannot be ignored in today's Web environment. You might want to at least give them a try. There are several apartment referral services currently available to a potential renter. These referral services provide listings of no fee rental apartments for a onetime fee, ranging from $39.99 to $185. They get their information much the same way brokers do, from daily contact with management companies, landlords, and owners. They will fax or e-mail listings to you on a daily basis after you provide them with a profile of your budget, location, size, and amenity specifications. Unlike brokers, these referral services do not accompany you on your apartment search, nor do they assist you with the application process.

APARTMENT SOURCE, INC.
580 Broadway (Houston and Prince Streets) • (212) 343-8155

For a fee of $185, for four months; or $65 for one month, a licensed Realtor from Apartment Source will provide you with a daily listing of no-fee rental apartments that are available, via fax or e-mail. Each apartment listing has detailed information on its availability, address, apartment number, building amenities, and all pertinent information about who owns the available apartment, how to gain access, and how to apply. When you sign on with Apartment Source, you can receive special discounts from their sponsors. You can visit Apartment Source's web site at **www.apartmentsource.com**

THE APARTMENT STORE • 44 East 29th Street • (212) 545-1996

The Apartment Store has a database of over 2,800 properties with new listings updated on a daily basis. No fee apartment listings can be faxed or e-mailed to you for a onetime fee of $39.99 (which is for your credit report). Client contact is very important to owner Barry Feinsmith and his staff. If you do not find an apartment within two weeks, they will send you a notice to call them and discuss your progress. Before you register, you can preview your apartment search on their web site at **www.apartment-store.com**.

HOMELINE
444 Park Avenue South (30th and 31st Streets)
(212) 220-HOME

HOMEline sets up an INTELLImatch of available apartments based on your apartment rental requirements. Via fax or on line, the

INTELLImatch will consist of apartment addresses, contact names and phone numbers, as well as rents, sizes, amenities, and availability dates. Sponsors such as New York Sports Club and Time Warner Cable have made discounted services available to HOMEline users. HOMEline's onetime fee is $150 for three-month access to their rental sight and for six-month access to their sale sight. They have a mix of fee and non-fee apartments. Their web site address is www.220home.com.

SOLUTION:
TO RENTING SMART

There are three different types of rentals:

There are three types of buildings in which you can rent an apartment – a rental building, a condominium, and a cooperative, and they all have different requirements and regulations.

Rental buildings: the building is owned by a landlord who leases out apartments to tenants.

- **Lease terms:** A tenant can take out a one or two year lease with an option to renew at the end of each term.

- **Approval process:** Typically 1 or 2 days...occasionally, more. The landlord will conduct a credit check, verify your employment and occasionally ask for references from previous landlords and employers.

- **Date to start home search:** approximately 4 weeks prior to start of lease.

- **Funds required:** application fee for credit check ($25 - $50), first month's rent, security deposit equal to one month's rent and refundable at the end of the lease, and the broker's commission.

There are two types of rental units:

Rent stabilized apartments: based on rent regulation laws that are decades old, these are rentals that have limits on the amount that landlords can raise the rent for rent renewals or on vacated apartments. The increases are determined by the Rent Guidelines Board and usually average between 3-5% per annum. The increase is announced every July and put into effect in October. You can read about it in the local papers or you can call The Division of Housing and Community Renewal at 718-739-6400.

Non-stabilized (unregulated) apartments: the rent level is based on whatever the free market will bear. Landlords raise rents based purely on what they think they can attain. Unregulated apartments are far more typical than stabilized dwellings.

IN RENT-STABILIZED APARTMENTS, LANDLORDS ARE REQUIRED TO ATTACH TO APARTMENT LEASES THE FORMER RENT PAID, SO THAT THE NEW TENANT CAN DETERMINE IF HIS RENT IS LEGAL. NEW TENANTS WHO SUSPECT OVERCHARGING CAN FILE A CHALLENGE FORM WITH THE STATE DIVISION OF HOUSING AND COMMUNITY RENEWAL DISTRICT OFFICE. IF YOU AREN'T SURE WHAT CATEGORY OF BUILDING YOU ARE IN, WRITE TO THE DHCR DISTRICT OFFICE, GIVE YOUR NAME, DATE YOUR LEASE COMMENCED, ADDRESS AND APARTMENT NUMBER, AND ASK FOR THE STATUS OF YOUR APARTMENT. THEY WILL SEND YOU A FORM TO FILE.

— THE TENANT FACT BOOK OPEN HOUSING CENTER, NEW YORK CITY

Cooperative building: is owned by a corporation made up of tenant shareholders.

A tenant shareholder may wish to sublet his apartment to a subtenant - you - and in effect, become your landlord. Rental prices are determined by what the market will bear and are set by the apartment owner and you; the tenant shareholder must get permission from the Board of Directors of the cooperative to sublet the apartment, and follow the Board's rules on subleasing. The lease term is typically for one year only, with an option to renew for one more year, based upon Board approval. In most co-ops, apartment own-ers are not allowed to rent for more than a one, sometimes a two-year period.

- **Lease terms:** typically one to two years
- **Approval process:** can take as little as a few days, or up to 8 weeks. A board package has to be submitted to the Managing Agent of the co-op for review by the Board of Directors. You will be asked to submit financial statements, tax returns, and personal and business references. The board usually requires a face-to-face interview. And then there is still the risk that a prospective tenant will be rejected; if you cannot afford that risk, don't try to rent in a co-op.
- **Date to start home search:** at least six to eight weeks in advance of when you need to start the lease, due to the length of the co-op board approval process.
- **Funds required:** Co-ops can charge fees from $200 - $1,000 which go toward pro-cessing the application, as well as move-in/move-out charges which are typically refundable if you've left the common areas in good shape. Plus one month's rent, the security deposit and the bro-ker's commission.

Condominium:

A condominium is considered "real property" and is owned outright by an individual. The tenant leases the apartment directly from the owner and the terms for the price and the length of lease are negotiated between the two parties.

- **Lease terms:** There are few Board restrictions about how long the owner can sublet his/her apartment.

- **Approval process:** A Board meeting may or may not be required, and the process is typically much shorter than a co-op's, but varies building to building.

- **Date to start home search:** 4 to 6 weeks prior to the start of the lease.

- **Funds required:** first month's rent, security deposit, application fees, move-in/move out refundable fees, and the broker's commission.

Procedures for securing a rental:

Look at ads in the newspapers and on real estate web sites: Newspapers such as *The New York Times* and *The Village Voice* have 1000s of listings weekly from brokers and individual owners. If you see something that looks interesting, call and schedule an appointment to go see the apartment. In a market with a 2% vacancy rate, apartments are gone within hours, so be prepared to jump on something if you like it.

In a tight market you have to go out with the small "mom and pop" brokers as well as the big firms, in order to see a proper representation of inventory. Much of the rental market is in the hands of small shops that have a particular niche in the market place and don't share their listings. If you pick up the real estate section of *The New York Times* you will see 100s of "boutique" brokers with a few listings. Their specialty can be the luxury buildings on the Upper East Side, the Wall Street area, or brownstones on the Upper West Side. These brokers may handle $1,000 rent-stabilized studios, or nothing much below $2,000 a month. Most have exclusive relationships with a handful of small landlords...that means, there's plenty of inventory out there that the big real estate companies can never access.

IT'S A SMART IDEA TO OBTAIN YOUR CREDIT REPORT PRIOR TO YOUR APARTMENT SEARCH TO CHECK FOR ANY BLEMISHES THAT MIGHT INTERFERE WITH SECURING THE APARTMENT OF CHOICE. THERE ARE THREE NATIONAL CREDIT BUREAUS, TWO OF WHICH CHARGE $8.00 PER REQUEST: EQUIFAX - 1-800-685-1111 & TRANSUNION - 1-800-916-8800. TRW - 1-800-392-1122, WILL SEND YOU ONE FOR FREE. WRITE TO: TRW CREDIT INFORMATION, CONSUMER ASSISTANCE, P.O. BOX 2350, CHATSWORTH, CA. 91313-2350. INCLUDE ADDRESS, PROOF OF RESIDENCE, DATE OF BIRTH, AND SOCIAL SECURITY NUMBER.

You can secure a rental apartment without a broker, but with a 2% vacancy rate, it is mostly about luck and timing to find an affordable, workable space without the help of a specialist. If you go it alone, look for ads in the paper that say "by owner" or "no fee", and call them up yourself. Only a few years ago, they were the rule, now they're the exception. Many determined and tenacious apartment hunters take to the streets and walk into buildings unannounced to speak to the doorman or the on-sight superintendent to find out about vacancies. Sometimes, a good will fee is expected before passing on a lead. If there is no one to speak to, look for the plaque (in the lobby or on the outside of the building) that states the name and phone number of the managing agent of the building and call them directly. There are also a handful of large-landlords who have on-site agents who are happy to take your application without a broker's fee.

What you need to pass a landlord's scrutiny:

- Personal references
- A clean credit history
- Money order, certified check or wire transfer capabilities for the deposit
- A letter from your employer verifying your salary and employment
- Annual income that is equal to 40-50 times your monthly rent
- If inadequate funds, co-guarantor (co-signer) who resides within the tri-state area.

Non-refundable application fee for a credit check: Landlords in today's market will turn away any potential tenant if his/her credit history is not clean. If you find an apartment you like, you will fill out an

"MOST LANDLORDS REQUIRE A SECURITY DEPOSIT OF AT LEAST ONE MONTH'S RENT AGAINST THE POSSIBILITY OF THE TENANT MOVING OUT WITHOUT PAYING THE LAST MONTH'S RENT, OR DAMAGING THE PREMISES. BY NY STATE LAW, THIS MONEY MUST BE DEPOSITED IN AN INTEREST-BEARING ACCOUNT (UNLESS IT IS A CO-OP OR CONDO). FURTHER, THE OWNER MUST NOTIFY THE TENANT, IN WRITING, OF THE NAME AND ADDRESS OF THE BANK. THE INTEREST (MINUS 1% FOR ADMINISTRATIVE EXPENSES) IS PAYABLE TO THE TENANT NO LATER THAN ANNUALLY FROM THE DATE THE SECURITY DEPOSIT WAS ORIGINALLY PAID. IF YOUR LANDLORD FAILS TO PAY YOU, CONTACT THE CONSUMER PROTECTION BUREAU OF THE NEW YORK STATE ATTORNEY GENERAL'S OFFICE AT 212-416-8345."

-THE TENANT FACTBOOK, OPEN HOUSING CENTER, NEW YORK CITY

application and pay a non-refundable fee ($25 - 50) for a credit history report. This in effect puts you in first place for the apartment (assuming no one else has filled out an application before you). You are not obligated to the apartment if you decide not to take it.

Deposit to secure the apartment: If you do decide to take the apartment, you will be required to wire money immediately, or have on hand certified checks to pay for the equivalent of two month's rent. Half of that is a security deposit that you will get back at the end of your lease if you haven't damaged the apartment. On the day of lease signing, the broker's commission usually has to be paid.

Lease signing: Before signing, read every word. Make sure that you understand all the terms and agree with them. Make sure there is a clause indicating what appliances and fixtures stay in the apartment, and which repairs the landlord agreed to make before you take possession. If there are existing damages, make sure those are noted, so you aren't liable for the repairs yourself. If you are renting in a rental building, landlords are required to clean and paint the apartment, and at least buff the floors, before you move in; get that in writing too.

Subletting: If you decide to sublet from a rental tenant, that tenant cannot raise the rent unless the apartment is offered as a furnished sublet, and then an additional 10% can be charged monthly. Make sure you get a written agreement that states all terms and lists preexisting damages. The *New York Times* & *The Village Voice* are the best sources for sublets. If a real estate agent finds you a sublet with a lease for a year or more, she is due a commission from either you or the owner of

A LANDLORD CANNOT "UNREASONABLY WITHHOLD CONSENT" TO LET YOU SUBLET YOUR APARTMENT IN NYC. BUT THE TENANT MUST INFORM THE LANDLORD THIRTY DAYS IN ADVANCE BY REGISTERED MAIL. THE NOTICE MUST INCLUDE THE SUBLESSEE'S NAME, ADDRESS, TELEPHONE NUMBER, PLACE OF BUSINESS, OCCUPATION, AND INCOME. YOU MUST TELL THE LANDORD WHERE YOU ARE GOING, WHY, AND FOR HOW LONG. IN RENT STABILIZED APARTMENTS, YOU CANNOT SUBLEASE FOR MORE THAN TWO YEARS IN A FOUR-YEAR PERIOD. IF, HOWEVER, YOU HAVE NO INTENTION OF RETURNING TO THE PREMISES, AND PLAN TO RENEW THE SUBLEASE, THE LANDLORD CAN REGAIN POSSESSION BY A HOUSING COURT ACTION IF HE CAN PROVE THE APARTMENT IS NO LONGER YOUR PRIMARY RESIDENCE. IF YOU ARE THE "SUBLESSEE", MAKE SURE YOU HAVE A LEGAL RIGHT TO BE THERE.

— THE TENANT FACTBOOK, OPEN HOUSING CENTER, NEW YORK CITY

the apartment.

Roommates: If you are the sole leasor of an apartment, you have a legal right to a roommate. Make sure you get a written agreement with your roommate that states who has the rights to the apartment. You can find ads for roommate shares in *The New York Times* & *Village Voice,* or you can call one of the city's many roommate referral agencies.

Clauses to watch out for: A "lockout" – a landlord of a rental building cannot lock you out of your apartment or remove your belongings. They cannot disallow children or tell you who you can and cannot share the apartment with. An "exculpatory" clause – exempting a landlord from legal responsibility if you have an accident because of faulty maintenance is illegal. Landlords can disallow pets and subletting. They can require that a percentage of the apartment be carpeted. They can include a "defacing" clause stating that a tenant cannot alter the apartment without approval, and an "escalator" clause stating that if the building has unforeseen expenses, the rent can be raised.

Basic tenant rights in a rental building that by law are yours: Sufficient heat, well-maintained electricity and plumbing for your apartment and the building, installation of smoke detectors, and an adequately safe and secure building. If you think your rights have been violated, call the Conciliation and Appeals Board of NYC Rent Stabilization Office at 718-739-6400, or the Department of Housing, Preservation and Development at 212-863-5000.

THE INTREPID PAGES OF
ORGANIZATIONS TO HELP TENANTS

There are organizations in Manhattan that are set up specifically to offer you guidance and information about renting in New York as well as to help protect your rights as a tenant.

OPEN HOUSING CENTER
594 Broadway, Suite 608 • (212) 231-7080

Whether you are an owner or a renter, this nonprofit agency assists anyone who feels in seeking housing they are meeting discrimination based on race, color, creed, national origin, sex, children, or marital status. The center provides investigators and legal assistance to help secure the right of equal access to all available housing. There is no charge for these services.

NEW YORK STATE DIVISION OF HOUSING AND COMMUNITY RENEWAL (DHCR)
Office locations vary according to your neighborhood
(212) 961-8930 • Rent Hotline (718) 739-6400

All rent regulation programs, including rent control, are administered by DHCR. Tenants should contact their borough office branch with complaints and questions. They also have a list of thirty free fact sheets on everything you need to know about renting in New York City.

The following organizations provide written information, information clinics, telephone advice, and in some cases advocacy for individuals and tenant organizations needing help with landlord-related problems:

GOOD OLD LOWER EAST SIDE (GOLES)
525 East 6th Street • (212) 533-2541

LENOX HILL NEIGHBORHOOD
331 East 70th Street • (212) 744-5022

10:00 A.M. to 5:00 P.M. (telephone hours); Monday and Wednesday, 10:00 A.M. to Noon, and Thursday, 6:00 P.M. to 8:00 P.M. (walk-ins).

METROPOLITAN COUNCIL ON HOUSING
102 Fulton Street, Room 302 • (212) 693-0550

Calls taken on Monday, Wednesday, and Friday from 1:30 P.M. to 5:00 P.M.

NEW YORK STATE TENANT AND NEIGHBORHOOD COALITION
505 Eighth Avenue, Room 1805 (at 35th Street) • (212) 695-8922

WEST SIDE TENANTS UNION
200 West 72nd Street, Room 63 • (212) 595-1274

THE INTREPID PAGES OF
ROOMMATE REFERRAL AGENCIES

EASYROOMMATE • www.easyroommate.com

An online service helping to match your needs. A flat fee of $39.00 per month for access to their database. All match results are sent online automatically as they come in.

ROOMMATE FINDERS • 250 West 57th Street • (212) 489-6860

This company appears to be the largest roommate referral business in the City. Since 1979 they have helped over 217,000 people find roommates. There is a $200 one-year membership fee if you are looking for a roommate, 50 percent of which is refundable for the first 30 days if you are not happy. If you want to list your apartment there is a $25 fee. However, if you mention that you are an Intrepid New Yorker reader, Roommate Finders will waive the $25 fee.

SOLUTIONS:
BUYING AND SELLING

As we mentioned earlier, NYC is one of the few areas in the country that does not have a multiple listing service for the over 10,000 apartments that are typically available at any given time. If you are a buyer, that means that it's harder to find all the properties available for purchase; if you're a seller, it's harder to get your apartment exposed to all possible willing and able buyers. However, there are methods to ensure that almost all stones get unturned. And fortunately, most sales agents co-broke their listings, making the process work much more efficiently than the multi-broker search required in the rental market.

THE BUSINESS OF BROKERING:

In sales, there's a lot more co-brokering going on. There's much more sharing of listings in sales, making the process work much more efficiently than the multi-broker strategy required in the rental market. One skilled and service-oriented broker may be sufficient because he/she will

> MAKE ABSOLUTELY CERTAIN THAT IF YOU OFFER A BROKER THE EXCLUSIVE RIGHT TO LIST YOUR APARTMENT, HE/SHE AGREES TO CO-BROKE YOUR APARTMENT IMMEDIATELY. MAKE SURE YOU GET THE CO-BROKE AGREEMENT AND THE LENGTH OF THE EXCLUSIVE ARRANGEMENT IN WRITING.

make sure that if you are a buyer, you are seeing all the inventory that matches your requirements, and if you are the seller, your apartment is getting maximum exposure. But it's important to know that sales agents, like rental agents, have specialties too, in terms of neighborhoods and price ranges. Some may primarily handle multi-million dollar apartments in the most upscale neighborhoods, others may handle mostly loft spaces downtown. But as we've already told you, the really valuable brokers:

- know their market niche cold, and are honest about what they don't know
- co-broke immediately for maximum results
- steer you clear of raw deals
- are highly skilled negotiators who can handle buyers, sellers, co-op boards and lawyers, with equal grace
- know how to secure the best financing arrangement
- have a highly qualified list of accountants, lawyers and mortgage brokers
- won't ever be responsible for blowing a deal
- put a customer's interests above their own
- have expert knowledge about the buildings and apartments they show

Real estate sales jargon that explains the process:

An "exclusive": You, the seller, can give the exclusive right to one real estate agency to sell your apartment; they will still co-broke your listing with the brokerage community, but they will be guaranteed at least 1/2 the broker's commission. For the right to obtain an exclusive from you, this agency promises to put money into marketing and advertising your home, bring in all ready, willing and able buyers, be the on-sight broker for all showings of your apartment, and give you regular, updated reports on activity.

"Co-brokering": This is what happens when a real estate agent has the exclusive right to list and show your apartment, but makes the listing available to other real estate companies for maximum exposure. If the listing broker ultimately brings in the buyer, then he/she receives the entire commission. If a second broker from another company brings in the buyer, the commission is split between them.

"Open listing": You the seller can give your apartment's listing to as many real estate companies as you wish. The commission gets paid to the broker who brings in the buyer and closes the deal. The hitch for the seller is that you have to do all the work and manage the process yourself. That means getting the listing out to all the real estate companies, spending your own money on ads, and being onsite at your home for all showings. AND YOU PAY THE SAME COMMISSION FOR DOING ALL THE WORK.

CONDO VS. CO-OP.
DETERMINE WHICH BUILDING TYPE BEST MEETS YOUR NEEDS, BEFORE YOU BEGIN YOUR SEARCH.

Co-operatives: 85% of the apartments for sale in NYC are in co-op buildings, only 15% are in condominiums. Co-ops cost less than condos due to supply vs. demand, and purchase practices. Co-ops are owned by an apartment corporation. When you purchase an apartment in a co-op, you are actually buying a certain number of "shares" in the corporation and receiving a "proprietary lease" to the apartment. The corporation pays the total amount of the building's mortgage (a co-op may have an underlying mortgage on the entire building, whereas a condominium must be owned outright), real estate taxes, employee salaries, and other expenses for the upkeep of the building. Each tenant-owner, in turn, makes monthly payments on a percentage of all these expenses based on the number of shares the tenant owns in the corporation. Share amounts are usually dictated by apartment size and floor level.

Considerations when buying a co-op:

- **The tenant-owners have the right to approve or disapprove of any potential owner.** The building's Board of Directors, which is elected by all of the tenant-owners of the co-op, interview prospective owners. They have the responsibility of protecting the interests of their fellow tenant-owners by selecting well-qualified candidates.
  The Board of Directors maintains a high standard for the quality of the services and the building's security. This is administered by the management company that is hired to run the day to day operations.
  Portions of the monthly maintenance are tax deductible. Each building has its own tax structure, but all co-ops offer a tax advantage. Shareholders can deduct their portion of the building's real estate taxes as well as the interest on the building's mortgage.

- **The amount of money that may be financed is determined by each co-op.** Some buildings require substantial down payments. Generally speaking, in Manhattan, prospective purchasers should be prepared to put down at least 20 - 25% of the purchase price.

ACCORDING TO BRIAN KAPLAN, ESQ., OF GOLDBERG & KAPLAN, LLP, IT IS EXTREMELY IMPORTANT TO CONDUCT A THOROUGH INVESTIGATION (KNOWN AS DUE DILIGENCE) WHEN REPRESENTING THE PURCHASER. REVIEWING THE FINANCIALS IS NOT ENOUGH. IN A CO-OP THE BEST INFORMATION IS FOUND IN THE SHAREHOLDER MINUTES. THE BOARD OF DIRECTORS OF CO-OPS HAVE REGULARLY SCHEDULED MEETINGS AND THE MINUTES FROM THOSE MEETINGS CAN BE REVIEWED. A BUILDING CAN HAVE MONEY IN RESERVE; HOWEVER, ONE MAY FIND FROM THE MINUTES THAT ALL OF THE MONEY IS BEING USED FOR SOME PLANNED RENOVATIONS. FROM THE MINUTES YOU CAN FIND OUT HOW MANY SHAREHOLDERS ARE IN ARREARS, AND WHETHER THERE ARE ANY LAWSUITS INVOLVING THE BUILDING. YOU CAN ALSO FIND OUT WHO COMPRISES THE BOARD AND WHETHER THEY HAVE BEEN ACCEPTING OR REJECTING RECENT APPLICANTS. THE TRICK IS TO DO THIS DUE DILIGENCE QUICKLY SO AS NOT TO LOSE THE DEAL.

In some co-ops, the down payment can be much higher.

Condominiums: condos are rapidly growing, but are still a relatively new concept to NYC and represent only 15% of the real estate market. A condo apartment is real property. The buyer owns the apartment outright and gets a deed. Because condos are real property, there is a separate tax lot for each apartment. A condo owner pays his/her own real estate taxes as well as common charges, on a monthly basis. Common charges are similar to maintenance charges in a co-op, except that they do not include either the real estate taxes which are paid separately, or the building's mortgage because a condominium, by law, cannot have an underlying mortgage.

Considerations when buying a condominium vs. co-op:

- **Financing rules for the purchase of a condominium are much less rigid.** Generally, a buyer can finance up to 90% of the purchase price.

- **The application and approval process is not nearly as formal.** The likelihood of rejection is minimal. The board has the right of first refusal when reviewing a buyers application.

- **There is greater flexibility in sub-leasing your apartment.** This makes condominiums the choice for investment property and absentee owners who need to keep up payments.

- **Condos are the ideal choice for non-US citizens or those with their assets held outside the U.S.** Co-ops are unlikely to approve a buyer whose funds are not in the U.S.

- **Condos are more expensive than co-ops** because of the supply shortage in NYC, and the more flexible purchase procedures.

MAKE SURE YOU HAVE LINED UP THE RIGHT EXPERTS AT THE TIME YOU BEGIN YOUR HOME SEARCH SO THAT YOU CAN USE THEM AS ADVISORS ALONG THE WAY

Mortgage broker: whose job it is to preapprove and prequalify you so that you are a ready, willing, and able buyer by the time you actually want to purchase.

An accountant: to tell you what your financial limits are as a buyer, or how to manage a potential profit or loss if you are a seller...or if it's smarter to rent. Your accountant should run all the numbers before you begin the process. If you are thinking about buying in NYC's current market, but you plan to sell in a couple of years, make sure that, after broker commissions, lawyer's fees, accounting and closing costs, it isn't more cost-effective to rent.

Real estate attorney: Choose an attorney whose specialty is in the condo, co-op game. Your real estate attorney is responsible for conducting the due diligence required to ascertain the financial condition of the building, examine its by-laws, negotiate the best deal for you, and ultimately determine whether or not your purchase is a sound one. Inexperienced or lazy attorneys can blow a deal or miss opportunities for a much better one. Sometimes attorneys either over "nit pick" the issues, or drag out the process until a simple procedure can turn into a deal-breaking situation. Make sure they are performing their duties in a timely manner.

Real estate agent: we've already told you why they can be so critical to the process and the outcome.

DO YOUR HOMEWORK! YOUR LEVEL OF KNOWLEDGE WILL HAVE A GREAT EFFECT ON THE OUTCOME.

Keep asking questions until you are satisfied you really "get it". Check out the local bookstore for books on real estate. Get current

> IT IS IMPORTANT FOR SOMEONE RELOCATING TO NEW YORK TO BE WITH A MORTGAGE COMPANY THAT HAS RELATIONSHIPS WITH THE LOCAL LENDERS. THE MOST COMPETITIVE LENDERS IN THE NEW YORK MARKETPLACE ARE THE SMALLER LENDERS THAT ARE NOT THE "HOUSEHOLD NAMES" AND DO NOT ADVERTISE FOR BUSINESS. IN ADDITION, WHEN A BUYER COMES TO NEW YORK AND PURCHASES A COOPERATIVE — MANY OF THE "BIG BANKS" CHARGE PREMIUMS ON THIS TYPE OF HOUSING. CHOOSE A MORTGAGE COMPANY THAT DEALS WITH LOCAL LENDERS THAT WILL GIVE THE SAME GREAT RATES FOR CO-OPS AS THEY DO FOR CONDOS AND HOUSES.
>
> — MELISSA L. COHN; THE MANHATTAN MORTGAGE COMPANY

market reports and "how-to" advisories from the big real estate companies that print them. And then keep asking questions.

DOUGLAS ELLIMAN REAL ESTATE EXPLAINS WHAT YOU NEED TO KNOW ABOUT NYC PURCHASE PROCEDURES:

1. Offers are made orally in NYC. When you have found the right property, a bid or offer will be placed through your agent. They will convey your offer to either the seller's agent or to the seller directly.

2. The seller may "counter" your offer. This will begin a negotiation process that will eventually lead to a "meeting of the minds", at which point, price, terms and closing date will be agreed upon.

3. Contact a real estate attorney familiar with real estate in our area. The seller's attorney will begin preparation of a contract of sale, and during that time your attorney will begin to examine the financial condition of the building in which you wish to purchase.

4. After your lawyer concludes that the financial condition is satisfactory, that the by-laws of the building are acceptable to you, and that the contract of sale is also acceptable, your attorney will advise you to sign the contract. At that time you will usually be required to present a deposit of 10% of the purchase price. The contract will then be forwarded for signature by the seller along with the deposit. This money will be held in the seller's attorney's escrow account until closing.

5. If financing, you should move forward with your loan application.

6. You will, by now, have received from your real estate agent the board requirements and application materials. The application materials can be similar for a co-op and condo. However, the actual process is quite different. You will work to complete all of the required materials which typically include: an application, a financial statement signed by a CPA, all requisite support for your financial statement, three years of tax returns, bank statements, letters of personal and financial reference, letters of professional reference, the contract of sale, bank documents (if financing) indicating that your loan is in place, etc.

7. When your "package" is complete, it will be reviewed by one of the managers in your real estate broker's office, and then, assuming it is accurate, it will be forwarded to the managing agent for review. Upon determination that it is in order and that credit checks were acceptable, it will be forwarded to the Board of Directors. No applications will be accepted by a Managing Agent unless they are complete.

10 THINGS TO LOOK FOR IN A REAL ESTATE BROKER:

If you are selling your property, and before you sign an exclusive listing agreement:

1. Find a reputable real estate company. Ask around for recommendations.

2. Interview 2 to 3 agents. What's your "gut" comfortability level? Some of this involves marketing skill and some of it boils down to chemistry. Sometimes selecting a "newer" agent is not necessarily a bad thing - their energy and enthusiasm might be just what you need. On the other hand, you might feel more comfortable with a "seasoned pro".

3. Ask agents if they are members of the Board of Realtors. Do they adhere to its code of ethics?

4. Ask agents about their knowledge of co-ops, condos or townhouses. Do they understand the particulars of your property?

5. Ask agents what they plan to do for you. What's their marketing plan?

6. Ask yourself, "how can I help my agent?" What can I supply to aid in the marketing...floor plans, financial information, rules and regulations of the building, etc.

7. Ask agents how they arrived at the "asking price". What are the comparables? a note here...pricing is very important. Don't be flattered by the agent who suggests the highest price. Strive to understand the method behind the pricing.

   And please, remember that your improvements (the Greco Roman Fountain under the mirrored ceiling) do not always translate into something that a buyer is willing to pay for.

8. Ask agents if they will co-broke your listing. How can you know if you're getting the best price unless it's exposed to the entire marketplace by inviting other firms to "share" the listing?

9. Ask agents if they will be available to "show" the property. It may sound silly, but a lot of agents are simply not around. Does the agent have a partner, or an assistant who can step in when they're not available? By the same token, make it easy for the agent and potential buyers to view your home.

10. You get what you pay for. Commissions are not fixed, but you want to encourage the brokerage community to show and sell your property, and you want your own agent to work hard for you.

— *Paul Purcell, Chief Operating Officer, Douglas Elliman*

8. In the case of a co-op, if your application meets initial approval, you will be invited to be interviewed by the Board or by an interviewing committee. Please take this meeting seriously. It should be treated as a business meeting. This is the opportunity for the Board to determine whether or not you will be comfortable in their building and whether or not they will be comfortable having you as a neighbor. In the case of a condominium, there is generally no formal interview. Your application will be reviewed, and if all required materials are included and in order, an approval is typically granted. From the home search to closing, this process typically takes a minimum of 90 days.

9. After approval by the Board, you are ready to plan for the closing.

BUYER BEWARE CHECKLIST FOR NYC

The broker represents the seller when they are dealing with their own exclusive listing. This means that the agent must disclose what he/she knows about the buyer to the seller and work to get the best offer possible. However, above all, a broker has a responsibility to be truthful and honest to both buyer and seller at all times.

A successful resale has everything to do with accurate pricing, location, the uniqueness of the property and the financial health of the building: To determine resale value, you greatly increase your chances for success by picking a desirable location, an apartment that has standout characteristics and an appealing layout, and a building that is financially sound and well maintained.

Building's financial health: Examine the building's "financial statements" which tell you what the building's assets and liabilities are, what money has been spent on, and how large a fund is in reserve for repairs. Your building may look great on the outside but may be heading for bankruptcy internally. Without a properly anticipated reserve fund, the money may have to come out of each unit owner's own pocket. Your real estate attorney is the one who will ascertain the building's health.

Unresolved problems with the building: In addition to looking at the financial statements, ask to see the minutes of the board meetings to determine what problems are outstanding or likely to occur. Boards are not obligated to give out the minutes, but your attorney should always ask to go and read them.

Monthly maintenance charges: Determine as best you can what the scale of monthly maintenance charges will be one to ten years in the future. If you compare monthly maintenance fees from year to year, you can get a good idea of what trends have been.

THE INTREPID PAGES OF

INFORMATION SOURCES FOR APARTMENT BUYERS

Before buying, arm yourself with as much knowledge as possible. Here are some places to start.

BOLD PROPERTY INFORMATION SYSTEM, INC. • (212) 673-7700

BOLD can prepare a customized property-risk report on the apartment you are interested in buying. Drawing on its huge database, BOLD can tell you the quality of life in the particular building and neighborhood; plans, if any, for new construction in the area; and whether the neighborhood is home to noisy nightclubs, drug dealing, or homeless shelters. The fee is $95.

THE CORCORAN GROUP
660 Madison Avenue (59th and 60th Streets) • (212) 355-3550

They publish The Corcoran Report, which comes out twice a year and is a comprehensive study of the co-op and condo market trends in Manhattan. You can receive it by calling and putting your name on their mailing list.

DOMUS APPRAISALS, INC • (212) 629-4430

Kevin Kinney runs the business, and specializes in appraisals of co-ops and condos in Manhattan. Call Kevin to inspect the property in which you are interested in buying so that you can learn its true market value.

DOUGLAS ELLIMAN
575 Madison Avenue (56 - 57th St.)
212-891-7645 or 888-891-MOVE

Douglas Elliman publishes Buying and Renting Guides to New York City, which are informative overviews of the unique Manhattan purchase and rental process. The Buyer's Guides are published in English, Spanish, Portugese, Chinese, Russian, French and Japanese. Douglas Elliman is also the publisher of The Manhattan Market Report and The Manhattan Townhouse Report, the most extensive multi-year studies of the Manhattan residential real estate market available.

EMIGRANT MORTGAGE COMPANY
5 East 42nd Street • 212 850-4848

Emigrant is famous for some of its niche programs such as loans to foreigners on a no income, no asset and no credit basis; negative pledge mortgage for co-ops; true no income asset loans, as well as loaning 100% financing with securities pledge or blank mortgage against additional property.

FIRST UNION MORTGAGE COMPANY • 1-800-776-3396

First Union has gained a good reputation for customer care. They can provide mortgages for real property throughout the country. (They do not deal with co-ops).

GUARDHILL FINANCIAL CORPORATION
450 Park Avenue, Suite 2703 (56th and 57th Streets) (212) 688-9500

GuardHill Financial is a mortgage company which specializes in obtaining the most competitive interest rates and products currently available. They have expertise in dealing with difficult and time-sensitive transactions. The staff is knowledgeable, professional, and service-oriented.

HOMESHARK • www.homeshark.com

HomeShark is an online mortgage broker service that can help you better understand the mortgage process, and help you find a cheaper loan. You can even procure a mortgage online and complete everything short of signing the paperwork.

H S H ASSOCIATES • (800) UPDATES

H S H compiles mortgage rates and terms nationwide on a weekly basis. For a fee of $20 you can receive the home buyers mortgage kit, which is a printout of current rates and terms in your area and a booklet on how the mortgage process actually works. If you already know the process, you can just buy the printouts.

THE MANHATTAN MORTGAGE COMPANY
555 Madison Avenue • 212-318-9494

The guru of residential mortgages. Melissa Cohn runs a top-notch company known for getting the buyer the best deal in the market.

MERRILL LYNCH • 800-586-2494 or 212-338-6122

For creative home financing solutions, contact Kim and Dan Brenna, Financial consultants at Merrill Lynch. Merrill Lynch offers innovative mortgage programs such as 100 percent home financing and interest only mortgages.

MILLER SAMUEL Inc.
16 West 45th Street • 212-768-8100

Miller Samuel Inc. is a leading residential real estate appraisal and consulting firm. They publish an extensive quarterly and annual market report. They maintain one of the largest historical sales databases of coops, condos and townhouses.

MITCHELL, MAXWELL AND JACKSON, Inc.
645 Fifth Avenue • (212) 319-7300

Appraisers that have created an incredible database with quite an accurate performance record.

THE NEW YORK COOPERATOR NEWSPAPER
301 East 45th Street • (212) 683-5700

An information source for co-op or condo owners, The Cooperator is really in the business of publishing its monthly newspaper, but because they are experts in the field of co-ops, they are happy to try and answer any questions you might have about the co-op in which you live or in which you are thinking of buying. They also hold seminars to help teach and guide co-op boards and their members on how to run an efficient building.

SKYSCRAPER
555 Fifth Avenue (46th Street) (212) 490-1800

Neil Bader is the mortgage broker with whom you want to speak. This company obtains mortgages for homebuyers at no extra cost to the buyer. Rather than shopping around by yourself for the best deal, let Skyscraper do it for you.

"THE TWO BIGGEST MISTAKES A BUYER MAKES IS TO MAKE AN OFFENSIVELY LOW BID THAT ALIENATES THE SELLER AND LABELS HIMSELF A WISE GUY, AND FALLING PREY TO THE CLASSIC "BUYER'S REMORSE". MANY BUYERS, JUST BEFORE CLOSING A DEAL, HAVE THOUGHTS OF PULLING OUT BECAUSE THEY ALL OF A SUDDEN FEEL THEY ARE MISSING SOMETHING BETTER OUT THERE. WE RECOMMEND THAT, INSTEAD, THEY TAKE SOME TIME WITH THEIR BROKER TO TAKE ONE MORE LOOK AT OTHER APARTMENTS TO COMPARE. MORE OFTEN THAN NOT, THEY CLOSE ON THE DEAL."

— BARBARA CORCORAN, THE CORCORAN GROUP

"A COMMON MISTAKE MANY BUYERS MAKE IS NOT LOOKING INTO FIFTEEN TO TWENTY-YEAR MORTGAGES. THE MONTHLY PAYMENTS ARE NOT THAT MUCH HIGHER THAN ON A THIRTY-YEAR MORTGAGE, YET YOU WILL SAVE THOUSANDS IN INTEREST PAYMENTS. JUST HAVE YOUR ACCOUNTANT DO THE CALCULATION FOR YOU. YOU'LL BE AMAZED".

— ROBERT GOLDSTEIN, REAL ESTATE ATTORNEY, BERGER AND KRAMER

TO MAXIMIZING YOUR CHANCES TO SELL YOUR APARTMENT

Fix it up! The Corcoran Group, a well-known real estate company in NYC, offers the following advise for enhancing the appearance and value of your apartment before putting it on the market:

• Scrub everything until it sparkles

• Wash all the windows

• Remove and repair any signs of water damage, mildew, and other deterioration.

• Repair holes and cracks in walls and ceilings

• Repaint with a "commercial double coat" of flat white on walls, eggshell white on ceilings.

• Repair wallpaper

• Repair or restore floor surfaces

• Regrout wall tiles

• Clean floor-tile grout with a mild muriatic-acid solution

• Restore or repair bathroom fixtures

• Add new shower curtains, rods and hooks

• Repair kitchen cabinets, and make sure doors and drawers work

• Increase existing lighting. Replace old ceiling fixtures.

• Eliminate odors

• "Expand" bathroom size with visual ploys. Install a mirror opposite medicine chest.

• "Expand" closet size with visual ploys by thinning out clothes, reorganizing, etc.

• "Expand" size of other rooms, with mirrors at ends of hallways, in corners, adjacent to windows.

• Replace broken window panes and mirrors

Price to sell: Get estimates from at least three brokers. If your brokers are experienced, they should be able to give you an educated appraisal on the first visit. A price is determined by "comparables" - what equivalent apartments are going for within your building and in the neighborhood. Beware of the broker who tells you what you want to hear and basically lets you dictate the price. Also, a good broker will not let you take an inferior bid just to sell the apartment.

Give your broker all the facts: Never hide any obvious problems that exist in the building or the apartment. They will come up sooner or later, and if it's later, the buyer might pull out of the deal. The following is a list of questions your broker will most likely ask:

- Purchase date, condo or co-op, and who holds title?
- Is there a flip tax, how is it calculated, and who pays it?
- What is the maintenance? When was the last increase?
- What percentage of the maintenance is tax deductible?
- What is your board's current view regarding the percentage of financing they will allow a buyer?
- If there been a recent assessment of tenant shareholders, for what amount, and for what purpose?
- Are you aware of any significant proposals under review by your board?
- Why are you selling?
- At what price have other apartments in your line sold for?
- When do you have to move out?
- When is it most convenient to show your apartment?
- How quickly do you need/want to sell?
- What are your board's procedures for reviewing an application?
- Is there a written or unwritten net worth requirement for buyers?
- What types of board restrictions are heavily enforced?
- How long has your property been on the market? How do you want this broker to work differently?
- What special amenities enhance the property?
- What are the board policies about pets, renovations and so on?
- What kinds of services are provided by the building?
- Are there any fixtures you plan to take or furniture you plan to leave?
- Will you spend money to paint the apartment and do repairs?
- Why you chose to buy the apartment, what appealed to you?

Tips for someone trying to sell a small, inexpensive studio or one-bedroom.

- Offer a higher commission: Sellers who are having trouble selling studios or one bedrooms may need to offer incentives to a broker to work hard on the apartment by offering a higher commission...let's say up to 10%. Many brokers don't take the low-end-of-the-market apartments as exclusives because it's just not worth it for a 3 - 6% return.

- Try placing your own ads and put the commission back into your own pocket:
    - Make the ad so appealing that buyers have to check it out.
    - Spend the extra money for a larger, standout ad
    - A catchy headline is a must: "Room With A View" or "Country in the City"
    - Look at other ads and see what attracts you to certain ones
    - Be specific and colorful in the writing; instead of saying "lots of light", say, "floor to ceiling, sun flooded windows". "Country kitchen" sounds more interesting than eat-in kitchen, etc.
    - List major selling points.
    - Clarify what your apartment actually contains - full two bedrooms, 1-1/2 baths, etc., so you don't attract inappropriate buyers
    - If your apartment stays on the market for some time, change your ad so buyers don't wonder why you can't sell it.
    - Target your buyer: Think about the most likely buyer for your apartment and then advertise to attract them. Maybe post ads on the bulletin boards of local hospital, or graduate schools, or in your alma mater's newsletter

SOLUTIONS:
TO MOVING IN AND OUT OF NYC

Our tried and true checklist to follow in order to make moving day as painless as possible:

- Get at least three on-site estimates from movers.
- Always ask if they will put a cap on the estimate (a dollar figure that the estimate cannot exceed once the job is finished)
- Take pictures of important items before the move in case you need to prove damage occurred during the move.
- Decide if you want the movers to do all the packing and/or unpacking
- Boxes and wrapping materials should be dropped off by the movers
- Triple confirm the move date and agreements

- Treat the movers with kindness and offer them short breaks and snacks to keep them motivated
- One mover is the leader. Take your concerns to him.
- Make sure to notify your building in advance of the move so they have it scheduled.

"THERE ARE TWO BIG MISTAKES SELLERS MAKE. ONE IS OVERPRICING THEIR APARTMENT AND THEN NOT BRINGING IT DOWN FAST ENOUGH. THE OTHER IS NOT GOING WITH A REAL ESTATE FIRM THAT GUARANTEES MAXIMUM EXPOSURE."

— BARBARA CORCORAN, THE CORCORAN GROUP REAL ESTATE FIRM

THE INTREPID PAGES OF
RELIABLE MOVERS

Here are companies that The Intrepid New Yorker relies on for moving.

AUTO MOVERS

CERTIFIED AUTO RELOCATION & SERVICES • (732) 469-0010

Contact: Paul Batsarika

FINE ART MOVERS

JOHN HUGHES MOVING AND EXPRESS • (718) 786-7340

GENERAL MOVERS

ARTHUR WERNER • (718) 326-1000

Contact: Dana Bitton.

CAREFUL MOVERS • (718) 584-3542

Contact: Jim or Fred.

INTERNATIONAL MOVERS

MOVERS INTERNATIONAL • (888) 644-6673

Contact: Brian Ward

TRANSPORTATION WORLDWIDE, INC. • (800) 356-7723

Contact: Michael Ronan

VICTORY WORLDWIDE TRANSPORTATION • (800) 544-4310

Contact: Jim Simpson

PIANO MOVERS

BUN-RITE MOVERS • (718) 589-4662

THE INTREPID PAGES OF
STORAGE FACILITIES

MOVING COMPANIES THAT HAVE STORAGE

ARTHUR WERNER • (718) 326-1000

For storing your belongings out of Manhattan, Arthur Werner runs an efficient operation that is completely full service. (You are not meant to go in and out yourself). Cost is $80 per month for 330 cubic feet (about seven feet in each direction).

CIRKERS MOVING AND STORAGE
444 West 55th Street • (212) 484-0200

A clean, well-maintained, and well-run storage facility in a relatively convenient location. A first-class operation with more than accommodating personnel. Some of New York's celebrities use this place for storing both documents and excess belongings. You can either have your own bin or wall storage space and of course they pick up and pack. The smallest private space to store your belongings is five by seven feet. One month rental is $140.

WAREHOUSE STORAGE

MANHATTAN MINI STORAGE
(212) 255-0482 • Locations Throughout the City

These facilities are well-maintained and offer fairly good quality service. The security is good: computerized card access to automatic elevators and storage floors, closed-circuit TV surveillance, and on-premise management at all times when they are open. You bring your belongings and move them yourself. Smallest room space is five feet by five feet; cost is $93 a month. Smallest economy unit is a four-by-four-by-four-foot cube. Cost is $40. There are some twenty-four-hour locations.

STORAGE USA • 510 West 21st Street • (212) 924-5111

Storage USA is a clean, new facility from a national chain. The building is alarmed and they also have closed-circuit video surveillance. The staff is articulate and helpful. Rates are reasonable and no security deposit is required. The cost for the smallest space which is four-by-four-by-nine is $60 per month.

MAXIMIZING YOUR LIVING SPACE

PERCEPTION VS. REALITY

Yeah, it's another New York fact. We live in tiny spaces, where 1,200 square feet feels palatial. But New Yorkers have very creative ways to eke out extra square footage for storage, home offices and living space.

SOLUTION:
HOW TO MAXIMIZE MINUTE LIVING SPACES

Think vertically:

Make your wall space functional. Hang shelves and storage cabinets, not just pictures. Build vertically. When building wall units and shelving, take advantage of high ceilings and build up, not just horizontally. Think vertical furniture. Armoires for everything from clothes to entertainment and office centers go a long way in NYC apartments. And home furnishing stores have figured out that New Yorkers want something completely functional as well as beautiful to look at and sell all kinds of great looking beds, desks, coffee tables and benches with storage areas built in.

Build loft areas:

Many New York apartments have ceilings high enough to build a small space above a living area which can be used either as storage, an office area, or an extra sleeping loft.

Hire a closet organizer:

Hire a closet organizer who works vertically as well as horizontally. These experts are big business in NYC. You'll find custom closet stores all over the city. They will evaluate your closets and your needs and rework the space to make it far more functional, as well as dramatically increase storage potential.

Even if you are in a rental, it pays to have a professional come in and double your closet space. It will save you from spending every other weekend "redoing" your closets to make them work. And your landlord might be willing to share the cost because he can get a "renovation" rent increase when you vacate.

Hire a contractor to help you restructure your space:

It can be well worth the money to have an expert come in and help you figure out how to carve out an extra room or special area out of an underutilized living space.

Use it or lose it...or put it in storage.

New Yorkers rent out storage facilities as our "attics" and "garages". There are two kinds of facilities: Traditional storage warehouses where the operator accepts your goods under a storage contract and controls access to your goods, or self-storage (mini-storage), where you rent the space under an "occupancy agreement". In this case, you control access and are provided a key. The operator has limited responsibility for the goods. The Department of Consumer Affairs licenses the traditional storage warehouses and requires a $10,000 bond, but self-storage is not regulated. So, if you choose self storage, the DCA is limited in their ability to help you. Traditional storage warehouses that are licensed must by law:

- State in writing where your goods will be stored

- Give you a written contract for storage (look for DCA license number on it)

- At your request, prepare a written estimate of monthly charge

- Give you a written inventory of your goods at the time of storage

- Provide minimum valuation of $.30 per pound per item up to $2,000 for the goods, and offer to increase the valuation for an additional charge

- Provide you with its schedule of rates and charges, including packing, warehouse labor, and access to your goods

- A licensed warehouse operator must bill you within 5 business days after the arrival of your goods, and at least bi-monthly thereafter. The operator can't charge you for any services or expenses that do not appear on the written estimate.

- If you don't pay your bill, the operator may place a lien on your property and sell it to cover storage charges; however the operator must notify you in writing in advance and give you the opportunity for a hearing at the New York Better Business Bureau.

The Intrepid Pages of
Space-Organizing Companies & Suppliers

BETTER YOUR HOME • 103 West 96th Street • (212) 866-8700

Home furnishings! Housewares for your bathroom and kitchen, frames, racks, shades, and stools. You name it and they carry it.

CALIFORNIA CLOSET COMPANY
1625 York Avenue (85th & 86th Streets) • (212) 517-7877

A well-known closet company that knows what it is doing. Their work is clean and efficient and they have a good sense of design. They charge about $100 per linear foot when they organize your closet. There is a $500 work minimum. They sell a small assortment of do-it-yourself merchandise.

THE CLOSET FACTORY
32-45 Hunters Point Avenue, Queens • (800) 400-2673

If they can design a closet to accommodate a professional basketball player's 46-inch inseams, they can certainly create a closet that will best suit your needs. There is no charge for an in-home consultation. Prices start as low as $350. Delivery and installation take one to three weeks.

CLUTTERBUSTERS • (212) 362-9433

Laura LaKin is a professional organizer who specializes in straightening closets, making order in the kitchen, and setting up filing systems.

CREATIVE CLOSETS
364 Amsterdam Ave. (77nd St.) • (212) 496-2473

They provide full service closet organization from solid wood to wire shelving. Call for a free consultation.

GRACIOUS HOME
1220 Third Avenue (70th and 71st Streets) • (212) 517-6300

Once again a great place for hooks, hangers, shelves, brackets, pegboards, lazy susans, and the like. If you need something that they don't carry we will be surprised—but just in case they don't have it, they will tell you where to get it.

HOLD EVERYTHING • 104 7th Avenue • (212) 633-1674

Although they sell all over the United States, we are sure that the need for this store is greatest in New York City. Every conceivable device for storing and organizing your entire apartment. Sock dividers, shoe organizers, one-stop shopping for your desk-supply holders, bathroom shelving, hat boxes, and more.

INDIVIDUAL SOLUTIONS • (917) 954-0936

Shana is great at making everything fit in it's proper place. She will even help to design built-in's if it will help fit your needs. She also does a lot of work with newlyweds coping with their new homes and wedding gifts.

NEW YORK CLOSET COMPANY
1458 Third Avenue (82nd and 83rd Streets) • (212) 439-9500

The wonderful thing about this company is that they are owned and operated by a Manhattan couple who have to contend with space problems themselves. They have a good eye, excellent materials, and more than fair prices for this kind of work. Their shop is filled with do-it-yourself organizing merchandise.

PAPERCHASERS • (212) 721-4991

President Barbara Fredericks Fields and her staff can help you create organization systems which will make you more productive at home and/or the office. They will help you manage paper flow, set up filing systems, and establish work patterns for your office and each room of your home, wherever you need help organizing your space. They will even shop for organization supplies for or with you. PAPERCHASERS also provides personal services. They can help you coordinate a move, respond to mail, schedule appointments, and shop.

The Intrepid Pages of
Where to Sell
(Or Just Get Rid of)
Your Belongings

CHARITY AND THRIFT STORES

CALL AGAIN
1711 First Avenue (88th and 89th Streets) • (212) 831-0845

They have the capability to pick up if you have a lot. Items must be clean and in good condition. They list what you donated and you set the deduction.

IRVINGTON HOUSE
1534 Second Avenue (at 80th Street) (212) 879-4555

In Manhattan they pick up if you have at least three large cartons. Appointments are necessary if you need an appraisal.

> DRESS FOR SUCCESS NY, A NON-PROFIT ORGANIZATION, HELPS LOW INCOME WOMEN MAKE TRANSITIONS INTO THE WORKFORCE BY PROVIDING THEM WITH INTERVIEW APPROPRIATE CLOTHING.

MATERIALS FOR THE ARTS
410 West 16th Street • (212) 255-5924

Accepts undamaged furniture (no clothing). Donated items are placed in 1,200 cultural organizations, from the Met to Soho Repertory. They will pick up heavy items. You set the deduction amount.

MEMORIAL SLOAN-KETTERING THRIFT SHOP
1440 Third Avenue • (81st & 82nd Streets) • (212) 535-1250

Minimum amount for pick up is a lot (furniture, etc.). Items must be clean and in good condition. They set the deduction.

SALVATION ARMY
Locations Throughout the City • (212) 757-2311

No minimum amount needed for pick up. You set the deduction. Pick up service: 536 West 46th Street. For store locations see the white pages.

SPENCE CHAPIN
1473 Third Avenue (83rd Street) • (212) 737-8448

They will pick up heavy items, such as furniture. Light items you bring to them. They set the deduction. They send you an appraisal.

WHERE TO SELL BOOKS

ACADEMY • 10 West 18th Street • (212) 242-4848

They will not buy textbooks, technical, or paperback books. They will buy art, photography, and rare books.

ARGOSY BOOKS • 116 East 59th Street • (212) 753-4455

Here you can sell your older, rare books. They will not buy textbooks or, generally, books of this century.

BARNES & NOBLE
105 Fifth Avenue (at 18th Street) • (212) 675-5500

They buy current-edition textbooks, fiction, and trade. You must have student I.D. to sell textbooks. They will not buy hardcover fiction.

GRYPHON
2246 Broadway (80th and 81st Streets) • (212) 362-0706

They tend to purchase any good literature. They prefer art, history, science, philosophy, psychology, performing arts, music, and good cookbooks. They will not buy technical, computer, business, or textbooks.

STRAND • 828 Broadway (at 12th Street) • (212) 473-1452

They are interested in mostly hardcover books of all types. They generally do not take paperbacks. The books should be in good condition.

WHERE TO SELL CAMERAS

FOTO CARE • 132 West 21st • (212) 741-2990

Service is incredible and delivered from a knowledgeable and friendly staff. They buy and sell all sorts of equipment.

OLDEN • 1265 Broadway (31st and 32nd Streets) • (212) 725-1234

Bring in your camera and a technician will price it. Appointments are not necessary.

WILLOUGHBY'S PEERLESS CAMERA STORE
136 West 32nd Street • (212) 564-1600

Bring in your camera and they will give you a price. Appointments are not necessary.

WHERE TO SELL FURNITURE

BIG APPLE FURNITURE
430 East 188th Street, Bronx • (718) 220-4018

It can be hit or miss in terms of what they are buying when you are ready to sell. But if they won't take your item they might be able to tell you where to go.

CHRISTIE'S • 502 Park Avenue (at 59th Street) • (212) 636-2000

Deals with high-quality goods. They only work on consignment, and take commission on an inverse sliding scale—the higher the price, the less they take. You both decide the lowest price you would be willing to accept. If it does not sell you either take it back or put it up for auction again. They would need to see a photograph of the items first before they can be considered for auction.

SOTHEBY'S • 1334 York Avenue (at 72nd Street) • (212) 606-7000

Operates in a similar fashion to Christie's.

TEPPER • 110 East 25th Street • (212) 677-5300

Deals in solid furniture to antique pieces. It is necessary for you to first send a photograph of the furniture you wish to sell. Depending on the market, they will either purchase your item outright from you (they bring you a check and take the item away), or you give them your furniture to sell on consignment. In that case, you pay for trucking. They take 20 percent commission.

WILLIAM DOYLE GALLERIES, INC.
175 East 87th Street • (212) 427-2730

Speak to Gillian Ryan. They occasionally buy outright—depending on what condition the items are in. They only buy entire estates, not individual pieces. You must first bring in or send photos of the items that you want to sell. If they are interested, they will send someone to take a look. At auction they get 15 percent of the sale price below $50,000; 10 percent above $50,000.

WHERE TO SELL MAGAZINES/NEWSPAPERS

ABRAHAM'S MAGAZINE SERVICE
By Appointment: • (212) 777-4700

They buy only the more esoteric literary and artistic magazines.

JAY BEE MAGAZINE STORES, INC.
134 West 26th Street • (212) 675-1600

They purchase magazines such as *TV Guide, Life, People, Us, Vogue,* and other media trade magazines. You get about 10 cents a magazine.

WHERE TO SELL RECORDS

SECOND COMING RECORDS, INC.
235 Sullivan Street (Bleecker & West 3rd Streets)
(212) 228-1313

Depending on the market, they will purchase any kind of record.

SKYLINE • 13 WEST 18TH STREET • (212) 759-5463

They will buy all kinds of records, but specifically like 50's and 60's jazz and rhythm and blues. They will also buy hardcover books.

The Intrepid Pages of
Home Office Services

SOLUTION:
MAXIMIZE HOME OFFICE SPACES

More and more New Yorkers are working out of their homes, compounding the problem of how to eke out living vs. work space in confined quarters. The following are a list of home-office resources for maximizing office space as well as off-premises support services.

AUDIO & TELEPHONE SYSTEMS

E HOME • 718-459-0238

Ben Rosner is a genius. His expertise does not come cheap but if you need to install computers, stereo systems, TVs, etc. he knows all the latest equipment. And he takes care of all the design, planning and installation.

INNOVATIVE AUDIO VIDEO SHOWROOMS • (212) 634-4444

Innovative is a full-service operation that offers audio and video products with custom installation in the home and the boardroom. They offer everything from home theaters, music systems, and centralized lighting systems to video tele-conference centers. They provide seven-day-a-week in-home service and have a paging system for off-hours service.

BUSINESS COACH

PERSEPHONE ZILL • (914) 478-7661

Provides help to small businesses looking to expand or revamp their business.

COMPUTER HELP

COMPUTER TUTOR • (212) 787-6636

Here you can get all kinds of help, whether it be installation, software tutorials, navigation through the Internet, and/or advice on buying a computer.

COMPUTER GUYS, LLC • (212) 288-2416

This small, friendly company offers a wide range of personal and professional consulting services. Personal consulting services include on-site (yes, they do make house-calls!) hardware and software installation, hands-on tutorials, and troubleshooting. Professional services include the above, as well as networking services, software development, technical support, and a variety of Internet consulting services.

PRATT MANHATTAN • (212) 925-8481

Send your job request by fax to (212) 461-6026. Your request will be looked at by both students and professors.

COMPUTER RENTAL

Prices will vary depending on the type of computer, its features, and the length of the rental. Here are some options:

BUSINESS EQUIPMENT RENTAL
250 West 49th Street • (212) 582-2020

COMPUSTART
2058 Broadway (70th and 71st Streets) • (212) 873-0954

In addition to renting a computer from Compustart, you can also rent time on a computer in the store.

KINKO'S • Locations Throughout the City

Kinko's offers a large selection of state-of-the-art computers that you can rent time on twenty-four hours a day. They also have color laser printers.

CONFERENCE ROOM/OFFICE RENTAL

If you want to present a professional image to a client, you may want to consider renting an office or conference room.

THE OMNIOFFICES GROUP
90 Park Avenue (39th and 40th Streets) • (212) 984-0700

OmniOffices offers the privacy, prestige, and comfort of an executive office when you need it. They will work with you to develop an individual plan to meet your business needs, whether it be renting an office, conference room, or training room, or using their wide range of services. Services include but are not limited to: desktop publishing, videoconferencing, computers, scanners, laser and color printers, electronic mail, copier, and shipping services. A totally staffed facility, including a secretary, receptionist, switchboard operator, and office assistant can be provided if needed.

COPY/PRINTING SERVICES

KINKO'S • Locations Throughout the City

Kinko's provides copy and printing services twenty-four hours a day. They can help you with the printing of business stationery, flyers, and brochures. Some locations offer pick up and delivery service.

UNIQUE COPY CENTER
9 East 4th Street • (212) 777-5391
252 Greene Street • (212) 420-9198
74 Fifth Avenue (13th and 14th Streets) • (212) 924-9792

Unique is a full-service shop that offers high-quality printing and copy services. They also have a selection of self-service Macintosh and IBM-compatible PC stations and laser printers. Pick up and delivery are free with a $50 minimum order.

WESTPRINT
873 Washington (13th and 14th Streets) • (212) 989-2948

Tim Bissell owns the shop and caters to non-profit organizations and small businesses. He is known for his attention to detail, pleasant nature, and fair prices. He will take both small and large jobs. In addition to filling your printing, typesetting and graphic design needs, Westprint also offers mailing services, such as envelope addressing and stuffing. Tim suggests that you call first before coming to the shop so that someone is there to help you.

ERGONOMICALLY CORRECT OFFICE FURNITURE

Sitting at a desk, talking on the telephone, and using a computer can wreck havoc on the body. Purchasing comfortable office equipment can help take the strain off your body.

B.P. ASSOCIATES
200 Lexington Avenue (32nd & 33rd Streets) • (212) 679-0800

B.P. does not sell furniture directly, but they can provide you with a list of retailers who carry their lines. They do have a showroom where you can sample adjustable chairs, tables, and foot rests.

DIRECT POSITION • 225 West 86th Street • (212) 769-8779

Direct Position offers ergonomic education, software, and exercise equipment. Joel Kendall is very knowledgeable about the dynamics of improper body alignment. He can talk with you about what would work best for your situation and advise you on an appropriate course of action. You can access Direct Position's web site at www.directposition.com.

ERGONOMIC WORK SPACES • (718) 499-3577

Tricia Martin can work with you to purchase ergonomic office furniture. This company is not a retail store, but Tricia can provide you with literature and tell you where you can sample the items that interest you. After you have made a decision, you would then buy the items from Ergonomic Work Spaces.

GIRSBERGER OFFICE SEATING
150 East 58th Street • (212) 750-7760

Girsberger is a Swiss company that manufactures adjustable office chairs. You can sample the chairs in their showroom, and they will put you in touch with a Girsberger dealer.

OFFICE SUPPLIES & EQUIPMENT

STAPLES • Locations Throughout the City • (800) 333-3330

Every item you could possibly want for the home office. You buy items in bulk and save a lot of money. They also have a good selection of computers, printers, telephones, answering machines, fax machines, and other home office necessities. Staples also provides a copy service. There's a $10 delivery charge for orders under $50.

PUBLIC RELATIONS

RGN COMMUNICATIONS • (516) 773-0911

Robin Gorman Newman has extensive experience promoting companies and their products/services. She is a generalist, and has worked with a range of clients in the areas of fitness/health, beauty products, and sports, to name a few. In addition to running her thriving public relations business, Robin has also authored a book and written articles for major publications.

STATIONERY, INVITATIONS & ANNOUNCEMENTS

ANNA PINTO • (201) 656-7402

Anna is a calligrapher who creates very pretty scrolls, testimonials, awards, cards, and menus in many different lettering styles. Her work is clean and neat, two important features in a good calligrapher. She has designed a group of festive, contemporary decorated letters which can be used on note cards.

ELLEN WELDON DESIGN
273 Church Street (Franklin and White Streets) • (212) 925-4483

You have a lot of creative choices when you work with Ellen. Her calligraphy is just one of many personal touches that results in striking and personal invitations. Ellen also offers a wide range of paper options, several printing methods, and various fun ways to embellish the paper, like watercolor and ribbon ties. In addition to creating custom-made invitations, Ellen specializes in producing personal stationery, menu cards, seating cards, and testimonials.

The Intrepid Pages of
Where to Stay

SOLUTION:
PLACES TO STAY FOR FAMILY AND FRIENDS VISITING NEW YORK

For New Yorkers who don't have a pull-out couch, let alone a second bedroom, The Intrepid New Yorker has come up with a critical list of sanely priced places for family and friends to stay.

ABINGTON B & B
13 Eighth Avenue (at 12th Street) • (212) 243-5384

Located in the West Village, this small bed and breakfast is comprised of three rooms, and situated over a café. The rooms are decorated in an eclectic manner. One room, the Polo Room, is decorated with Ralph Lauren touches. Another room, the Shaker Room, is embellished with Shaker furniture. One room has its own bathroom, the other two rooms share one. Prices start at $95 and up, and depending on the day and season, there may be a minimum night stay required.

ABODE, LTD. • (212) 472-2000

Abode offers furnished, unhosted apartments throughout the City for use as bed and breakfasts. The apartment sizes range from studios to three bedrooms apartments. Some apartments are in brownstones, others in high-rise, doorman buildings. A good majority of the apartments have been recently renovated and decorated. There is a four night minimum stay.

BEACON HOTEL
2130 Broadway (at 75th Street) • (212) 787-1100

The Beacon Hotel has been in business for seven years and was formerly an apartment building. The hotel has 25 floors with 210 rooms, ranging from doubles to suites. This comfortable, informal hotel offers a TV and phone in each room, as well as a kitchenette in the smaller rooms and a kitchen in the suites. Prices start at $155 and up. No minimum night stay is required.

BED & BREAKFAST ON THE PARK
113 Prospect Park West • Park Slope, Brooklyn • (718) 499-6115

This landmark townhouse is lavishly decorated with art and Victorian antiques. The eight rooms offer city and park views. Room rates range from $125 to $275 including a full breakfast. There is a minimum stay of two nights, three nights over most holidays, although a one night stay might be available the day before.

BELVEDERE HOTEL
319 West 48th Street • (212) 245-7000

Located in the heart of the theater district, the Belvedere is appealing to theater-goers. The hotel was recently refurbished. Rooms come with an unequipped kitchenette with either a microwave or gas stove and cost $129.

BROADWAY INN B&B • 264 West 46th Street • (212) 997-9200

The Broadway Inn offers 40 simply designed rooms ranging from $105 to $135. Higher priced rooms have kitchenettes and microwaves. All rooms have private bathrooms.

CITY LIGHTS • (212) 737-7049

City Lights is an agency that scouts out potential homes for use as bed and breakfasts. They screen apartments for safety, privacy, and comfort. You give City Lights your requirements, such as location, budget, and hosted or unhosted, and they will recommend a bed and breakfast. The price they quote you includes a fee for their services.

COUNTRY IN THE CITY • 270 West 77th Street • (212) 580-4183

Country Inn is located in a charming 1891 four-and-a-half story restored limestone building. Each of the four furnished studio apartments is decorated in a country eclectic manner and comes with a TV, phone, and a refrigerator stocked with the basics. Rooms cost $145 per night, with a three-night minimum stay required. If you stay seven nights or more, you do not have to pay $8\frac{1}{4}$ percent sales tax. Smoking, pets, and children are not allowed.

EAST VILLAGE BED & BREAKFAST • 110 Avenue C • (212) 533-4175

If you are interested in staying in one of NY's up and coming "hot" neighborhoods, this is the place.

THE GRACIE INN • 502 East 81st Street • (212) 628-1700

Twelve rooms range in size from a small studio to a two bedroom penthouse suite with a roof terrace. Each room has a private bath, cable TV, VCR, telephone, and kitchenette. Rates vary according to day and length of stay, and include a continental breakfast.

HOTEL LUCERNE
201 West 79th Street • (212) 875-1000

Located close to Central Park, Hotel Lucerne is part of a chain of seven hotels, different in name, but similar in design, located in the City. The two-year old hotel has a total of 177 rooms, spread out over 12 floors. The ambiance is comfortable and intimate. Prices are fairly affordable, starting at $135 per night, with no minimum night stay required.

HOTEL SEVENTEEN • 225 East 17th Street • (212) 475-2845

This 150-room, century-old hotel offers modest room rates. Single rooms are $75; double rooms are $98 ($110 with TV). Bathrooms are shared.

THE INN AT IRVING PLACE
56 Irving Place (17th and 18th Streets) • (212) 533-4600

A charming inn located in residential Gramercy Park. The Inn has 12 rooms, seven of which are suites. Most rooms have decorative, non-working fireplaces, and all are adorned with period antiques. Children and pets are not allowed. There is no minimum stay required. Rates are $275 and up and include a continental breakfast.

INN NEW YORK CITY • 266 West 71st Street • (212) 580-1900

Situated in a late nineteenth century restored townhouse, this Inn is comprised of four suites, each with its own unique style. All rooms have a fully equipped kitchen, a washer/dryer, cable TV, a VCR, and other amenities. The Library Suite is the most spacious room, and features an extensive library. It is located on the top floor, and has high-beamed ceilings with abundant wood features and a fireplace. The Spa Suite is comprised of an entire floor. It comes with a spa room, a sauna, and a huge jacuzzi. The Opera Suite has a working fireplace, a private terrace, and a Jacuzzi. The Vermont Suite is a duplex with its own private entrance. Prices start at $250 and up and there is a two-night minimum stay required.

THE LARCHMONT • 27 West 11th Street • (212) 989-9333

The Larchmont houses 50 small rooms with many nice touches, including books in each room, a TV, air conditioner, desk, and good lighting. Bathrooms are shared. Prices are under $100 for a double.

MANHATTAN EAST SUITE HOTELS
500 West 37th Street • (212) 465-3690

This hotel chain is made up of nine hotels, eight of which are on the East side, from 30th to 70th Streets, and one on the West side. Manhattan East only offers suites, ranging in size from studios to two-bedrooms. All rooms have kitchenettes or full kitchens, phones and TVs. The hotels are medium-size, the smallest of which is 16 floors with 80 suites. The hotels are each designed a little differently, but are all decorated with contemporary furnishings. Prices start at $209 with no minimum night stay required.

THE MANSFIELD
12 West 44th Street • (212) 944-6050

Built in 1904, The Mansfield is one of the most attractive small hotels in the city. Rooms are small, but are elegantly designed and inviting. Rooms start at $175.

MILBURN HOTEL
242 West 76th Street • (212) 362-1006

Similar in ambiance to the Beacon Hotel with its quaint European charm, the Milburn is smaller than the Beacon and offers 100 rooms spread out over 16 floors. Studios and suites are available, each with a full bath and kitchenette. Rooms come complete with a TV and phone, and a VCR is available for rental. Studios cost $145 per night; one-bedroom suites are $185 per night. No minimum night stay is required.

92ND STREET Y
1395 Lexington Avenue (91st and 92nd Streets) • (212) 415-5650

The de Hirsch Residence at the 92nd Street Y has fully-furnished dormitory-style rooms available for short and long term stays. Short term stays must be for a minimum of three nights. Prices for single rooms are $53 per day; $38 per person, per day for a shared room. There are no bathrooms in the room; residents share a communal bathroom on the floor. Long-term stays require a minimum stay of two months; maximum stay of a year. You need to fill out an application and must work full time, go to school full time, or both. Single rooms cost $715 per month; $575 per person for a shared room. As a resident of the Y, you would receive free access to the health club and pool. Pets are not allowed.

63RD STREET WEST SIDE Y
5 West 63rd Street • (212) 875-4100

Single rooms are $69 per night and include a TV in the room. Double rooms have bunk beds and a bathroom in the room ($95 per night). Your room price includes free access to the gym and pool. There is no minimum night stay required. Pets are not allowed.

VANDERBILT YMCA • 224 East 47th Street • (212) 756-9600

This Y offers single rooms at $55 per night; double rooms are $68 per night. The rooms have a TV, but no bathroom (you share one with other residents on the floor). As a resident, you would have complimentary access to the gym and pool. No minimum night stay is required. Pets are not allowed.

IF YOU ARE A MEMBER OF A UNIVERSITY CLUB, YOU CAN TAKE ADVANTAGE OF THEIR LODGING ACCOMMODATIONS WHEN YOU TRAVEL. THE ROOM RATES ARE REASONABLE AND YOU WILL BE ENTITLED TO ALL YOUR MEMBER SERVICES, INCLUDING USE OF THEIR RESTAURANTS. SOME CLUBS ALSO HAVE A PRIVATE LIBRARY, GYM FACILITIES, AND OTHER AMENITIES.

WASHINGTON SQUARE HOTEL
103 Waverly Place • (212) 777-9515

The Washington Square Hotel offers affordable lodging right in the heart of Greenwich Village. 180 rooms make up this appealing European-style hotel. Rooms come with TVs and a phone, and most have bathrooms. There is also an exercise room in the building. A modest room with one single bed costs $110. A continental breakfast is included in the price of all rooms, and no minimum night stay is required.

FINDING A HANDYMAN YOU CAN TRUST

PERCEPTION VS. REALITY

New Yorkers, like everyone else, have to depend on local handymen, plumbers, electricians, and professional cleaners to keep their homes in day-to-day working order, but how do you find someone qualified and trustworthy? With no small town accountability, New Yorkers say it's trial and error. Yes, but not if you take the time to do proper due diligence.

SOLUTION:
FINDING LOCAL HANDYMEN YOU CAN TRUST

Word of mouth:

Tried and true. Ask friends, other local service providers and other experts. Example: If you are looking for a rug cleaner, call one of the better rug and carpet retailers and ask them who they use.

Be very critical in your search:

You want handymen you can trust so completely, that you wouldn't think twice about giving them access to your apartment when you can't be there. If you hire right, it should feel as though you have your very own home maintenance staff.

Conduct a thorough interview:

- How long have you been in business?
- What kind of work do you specialize in?
- Will you do the repairs yourself, or send in the second string?
- What do you charge and how do you expect to be paid?
- May I have three references?
- Is the work guaranteed?
- Are you bonded and insured?

Bonded means that the company has posted a bond with their surety company as a protection against a proven theft; theoretically,

KENNETH W. KAUFMAN, CHIEF EXECUTIVE OFFICER OF KEEVILY SPERO WHITELAW INC., AN INSURANCE COMPANY, STRESSES THE IMPORTANCE OF HIRING A COMPANY WITH INSURANCE. "IF THEY DO NOT HAVE INSURANCE EVIDENCE IN WRITING, THEN YOU ARE THE INSURANCE COMPANY. THE RESPONSIBILITY WILL FALL INTO YOUR LAP." KEN SUGGESTS AS AN ADDED PRECAUTION THAT YOU ASK TO BE NAMED AS ADDITIONAL INSURED ON THE COMPANY'S POLICY. IT DOES NOT COST THE CONTRACTOR EXTRA ON HIS INSURANCE PLAN, AND IT MAY PREVENT YOU FROM HAVING TO INVOLVE YOUR OWN INSURANCE COMPANY IN THE EVENT OF A LAWSUIT.

that means that if a worker steals something from your home you the client may have some protection.

Insured means that the company's insurance company protects you the client against property and bodily damage. The company should also have workers' compensation, in the event that a worker is injured on the job. The burden of proof ultimately falls on you, but if you have hired a reputable company in the first place, they will own up to an accident right away.

The Intrepid Pages of
"Down Home" Handymen

$ = inexpensive   **$$ = moderate**   **$$$ = expensive**

AIR CONDITIONER REPAIR
AA KOLD AIR, INC. • (718) 402-9400 • $

AA Kold Air has been in business for 30 years and services Manhattan and parts of the Bronx. They charge $48.71 for a service call (applied to the total cost of the repair), at which time they will discuss with you if it is cost-effective to repair your air conditioner. More complex problems will require them to service the air conditioner at their shop.

> CON EDISON OFFERS FREE AIR CONDITIONER ADVICE. THEY CAN TELL YOU WHAT FACTORS TO LOOK FOR WHEN PURCHASING AN AIR CONDITIONER, WHETHER IT IS COST EFFECTIVE TO HAVE A UNIT REPAIRED OR REPLACED, AS WELL AS PROVIDE HELPFUL INFORMATION ON ENERGY EFFICIENCY RATINGS. CALL (800) 343-4646 TO SPEAK WITH A REPRESENTATIVE.

ADVANTAGE AIR CONDITIONING
327 East 12th Street • (212) 598-0016 • $

Advantage will come to your home to determine the cause of the problem. A service call is $45, which will be applied to the total cost of the repair. Similar to AA Kold Air, if they can, they will repair the unit at your home. If not, they will bring it to their shop and deliver it back to you.

CARPET, FURNITURE, DRAPERIES, BLINDS & UPHOLSTERED WALL CLEANING

New York is a haven for dirt and soot. Don't think that your apartment is the only one in constant need of a good cleaning. White rugs—what a horror! Your carpets, upholstered furniture, window blinds, and draperies will last a lot longer if you take care of them.

ACTIVE VENETIAN BLIND LAUNDRY • (718) 392-7373 • $$

They will come to your home for a free estimate and to get measurements. There is a $40-$50 minimum charge which includes free pick up and delivery. They will also take down and re-hang your blinds at no extra charge. A job usually takes two days to complete.

CLEANTEX PROCESS CO. INC. • (212) 283-1200 • $$

They are the people to call to clean your drapes and curtains. The only company that truly knows how to deal with custom curtains and blinds. They do the removal and the installation. Also great for upholstered walls, wall-to-wall carpeting, and area rugs.

DELMONT CARPET CLEANING • (718) 531-4700 • $$

Reliable and accommodating. They do their best to give you the exact time they will arrive and if you are not satisfied with the job they will keep coming back at no extra charge until you are.

LONG ISLAND CARPET CLEANERS • (718) 383-7000 • $$

These cleaners offer dry cleaning or steam cleaning for your uphol-stered furniture. A technician will determine which service is best for your furniture. The cost to steam clean a sofa is $17 per square foot plus $3.50 per pillow. Dry cleaning is a little more. They can also clean your carpet and window treatments.

MAJESTIC RUG CLEANING COMPANY • (718) 542-7474 • $$$

Juan Carlos' crew is especially dependable and skilled at thoroughly cleaning carpets. The price to clean wall-to-wall carpets is a mini-mum of $59.95 for 300 square feet, and 20¢ per square foot there-after. Majestic also cleans area rugs (they pick up and deliver free of charge), upholstery and draperies.

NAPTHA RUG & CARPET CLEANING• (212) 686-6240 • $$

If you have very simple curtains (on pins) they do good work. Also available to clean rugs, carpets, and upholstered furniture. They specialize in oriental rug cleaning.

CHIMNEY SWEEP

D.W. KOLVENBACH • (212) 879-3035 • $$

Ask for Doug, a very nice person who does great work. If you want to make some changes to your fireplace, he will work with an installer on a consulting basis.

CLEANING SERVICES

There are several ways to find help: Ask any of the household help and employees in your building; ask your office cleaners; share your friend's.

DIRT BUSTERS • (212) 721-HELP • $$

David runs this very efficient and pleasant cleaning service. He is very flexible when it comes to trying to fill a request. He arranges for home and office cleaning, day or night.

MAIDS UNLIMITED • (212) 369-9100 • $$$

Mr. Marchesi is a smart businessman. He saw the need for someone to pool and supervise a crew of rotating cleaners. He can arrange to have someone come to you on a regular or onetime basis. For an extra fee, they can bring all the equipment too.

NEW YORK'S LITTLE ELVES • (212) 674-2629 • $$

This company employs a crew of about 35 people who aim to make your home spotless. They provide maid service to some very fussy people, including many interior decorators. Services include post-renovation cleaning, with the number of workers determined by the size of the mess you're in. The fee is $19.50 per hour, with a three-hour minimum.

SERGIO • (718) 562-4788 • $$

A real find in this city of grime. He is a fantastic cleaner who pays attention to all the details.

ELECTRICIAN

We suggest you ask your building super to recommend an electrician. Your local hardware store might refer someone to you for a small job. But, you do not want a bargain-basement technician when it comes to doing dangerous work.

THE ELECTRIC CONNECTION • (212) 629-5176 • $$$

Neil Fairey runs this company which specializes in small interior project work. They will hang lighting fixtures, ceiling fans, and chandeliers. They can also help with electronic wiring for your stereo and computer. They charge $75 for the first half hour, and then $65 per hour.

FGE ELECTRIC • (212) 966-0504 • $$

Frank, the owner, has been an electrician for twenty-two years. His company has been in business for twelve years. They work with both residential and commercial properties, and are happy to work on small jobs. They give free estimates, and are quick and efficient.

PLANT CARE/GARDENING

JANE GILL • (212) 316-6789 • $$$

Jane is a horticulturist with twenty years experience in the world of plants and flowers. Her specialty is big indoor trees, which she transplants, prunes, and trims. She can also diagnose what is wrong with a sick plant and advise you on a course of treatment. Jane will perform indoor maintenance on a case-by-case basis. Her true love is designing and installing large perennials gardens. Jane charges between $75 to $100 for house calls.

PLANT SPECIALISTS
(718) 392-9404 • $$

These indoor and outdoor plant experts will take good care of your greenery.

WILLOWTOWN GARDENS
(718) 243-1257 • $$

Catherine Fitzsimons can create a beautiful garden in your front or backyard, a terrace, or a window ledge. She is trained as a landscape garden designer and specializes in redesigning small city garden spaces. Catherine will select the site appropriate plants and flowers for the garden and help maintain them on a regular basis if necessary.

IF YOU WANT TO LEARN THE BASICS ON HOW TO CARE FOR YOUR INDOOR HOUSEPLANTS, CALL THE HORTICULTURAL SOCIETY OF NY. THEY TEACH A VARIETY OF CLASSES, SOME OF WHICH ARE ONLY ONE SESSION. THEY CAN BE REACHED AT (212) 757-0915.

WINDOW BOX • (212) 686-5382 • $$

Maggie Geiger has been digging up gardens around the City for twenty-four years. She is skilled at creating eye-pleasing gardens in a small or large space. Maggie will come to your home to create a garden in a window box, terrace, rooftop, or yard. She can also help you to maintain the garden on a weekly basis.

PLUMBER

To find a plumber, ask your building manager or call:

FRED SMITH PLUMBERS • (212) 744-1300 • $$$

Top notch plumbing company used by many buildings.

ROBERT McFARLAND, CO. • (718) 543-1232 • $$$

Robert is considered to be a very "wise guy". Clients swear by his expertise and reliability.

ROTO-ROOTER • (718) 849-2842 • $$

Excellent for stopped-up or clogged drains.

WINDOWS WASHED

EAST END WINDOW CLEANERS • (212) 879-5590 • $$

Mr. Kay has run this company for years. If you are persistent, he will narrow down the time that you will have to wait for your window washer.

FLAT IRON • (212) 876-1000 • $$

Another good choice. They clean windows from 55 Hudson Street to 96th Street.

PRESTIGE WINDOW CLEANING • (212) 517-0873 • $

Tom Lorenzo runs the company and does great work. He is thorough, reliable, and his prices are reasonable.

SHIELDS WINDOW CLEANING • (212) 929-5396 • $$

Pat Shields owns and runs this small residential window cleaning company. Pat will travel anywhere in the City, and won't balk at working on the weekend if he is available.

One last suggestion: If you are hiring a company for a big job, call the Better Business Bureau to find out if there are any complaints or liens against them. For public inquiries and complaints, their number is (212) 533-6200. (For extensive information about this bureau and how it operates see the Assertiveness Training chapter).

The Intrepid Pages of
Repair & Maintenance Services

We have never been stumped trying to find a reliable repair person and we have found that many of the better people run family businesses. They pass the trade on from generation to generation. Be precise about what is broken and get everything in writing. Most important, always appeal to someone's human side. Explain to them why you are desperate to have your camera back in one week in time to go on safari, why you need your word processor looked at today because you work out of your home as a free-lance writer, or why you need your dress mended for a big date you have on Saturday. People really do care.

BOOK BINDING

CAROLYN CHADWICK • By Appointment Only • (212) 865-5157

Carolyn repairs and rebinds old books. In some cases when rebinding may actually damage a book, she will make slip cases to protect them. Carolyn can use gold lettering, and binding is done with leather, paper, or a combination of both.

WEITZ, WEITZ, COLEMAN
1377 Lexington Avenue (90th and 91st Streets) • (212) 831-2213

Your books will be in good hands here. Old books can be worth a lot, so maintaining the bindings is quite important.

CAMERA REPAIR

MORMENDS
1228 Madison Avenue (88th & 89th Streets) • (212) 289-3978

They will send your camera back to the manufacturer and then inform you of the estimate. A trustworthy and timely shop.

PROFESSIONAL CAMERA REPAIR SERVICE
37 West 47th Street • (212) 382-0550

This shop appears to be one of the largest repair places in the City. They attempt to do repairs in their shop (and are often successful) but sometimes the camera must be sent back to the manufacturer. They work on still cameras from 35 mm and up.

CAMPING EQUIPMENT

DOWN EAST
50 Spring Street (Lafayette & Mulberry Streets)
(212) 925-2632

A great place to get your gear repaired, modified, or customized.

CARPET REPAIR

ABC CARPET & HOME • (212) 929-1275

Not all fine rug companies restore wall-to-wall carpeting, but ABC Carpet & Home, a repair arm of the furniture and rug store, does. They charge $100 for the first hour, and $80 each additional hour. You will be charged a $75 consultation fee if you decide not to have your carpet repaired. Their cleaning fee is 35¢ per square foot, with a $75 minimum.

BESHAR'S • 1513 First Avenue (at 79th Street) • (212) 288-1998

Beshar's has been cleaning and restoring fine carpets and rugs for almost a hundred years. New fringes can be added or existing ones protected; worn or moth-eaten spots are rewoven or re-piled, and bindings are restored. All repairs are preceded by cleaning, which costs from $2 to $3 a square foot. Ask for Mr. Barovan.

RESTORATION BY COSTIKYAN
28-13 14th Street, Long Island City • (718) 726-1090

If you own a true gem of a rug that needs repair, give it to Costikyan. They have been in business for 110 years, and specialize in the restoration of fine rugs. They can repair fringe, and can actually restore the color and design of a rug. Restoration is an expensive process, but it may be worth it if you own an heirloom rug that would cost a bundle to replace. Costikyan also cleans wall-to-wall carpets at $1 per square foot.

CHAIR CANING

VETERAN'S CANING SHOP, INC.
442 Tenth Avenue (34th and 35th Streets) • (212) 868-3244

Chair caning, rush seating, and splint seating—all can be done by this family-owned business (over ninety years in the business).

WEST SIDE CHAIR CANING AND FURNITURE REPAIR
371 Amsterdam Avenue (77th and 78th Streets) • (212) 724-4408

Jeffrey Weiss is an expert in caning and keeps very busy. His prices are reasonable but he does have limited hours.

CLOCK AND WATCH REPAIR

Fanelli Antique Timepiece, Ltd. • 790 Madison Avenue (66th & 67th Streets) Suite 202 • (212) 517-2300

Fanelli's cleans, repairs and restores antique timepieces. You can bring in your timepiece and leave it for an estimate. The shop is open Monday to Friday, 11-6, and Saturday 11-5.

CLOTHES REPAIR

ALICE ZOTTA • 2 West 45th Street, 17th Floor • (212) 840-7657

The mender of the impossible. She has been mending anything and everything for over thirty years. If it can be fixed, she can do it.

**EVELYN KENNEDY • By Mail: Sewtique
391 Long Hill Road, Groton, Connecticut 06340-1293
(860) 445-7320**

Evelyn restores vintage and contemporary textiles—from laces, linens, and quilts—to beaded dresses, baptismal and wedding gowns, furs, and leathers. You can send her your garment, and generally have it back in sixty days. Evelyn is licensed by the International Society of Appraisers to give insurance and estate appraisals, which costs about $100 an hour, her fee for house calls in the City.

FRENCH-AMERICAN RE-WEAVING
119 West 57th Street • (212) 765-4670

They repair both knit and woven garments. Ron Moore, who has been managing the store for over twenty-five years, is helpful and knowledgeable about whether an article can be fixed. If a jacket or pair of pants need to be repaired and they are part of a suit, Ron suggests that you bring in the entire suit. Most repairs take about two weeks.

COMPUTER REPAIR

**ABC COMPUTER SERVICES
375 Fifth Avenue (between 35th & 36th Streets)
Second Floor • (212) 725-3511**

ABC repairs PCs, Macs, printers and scanners. They charge $55 for in-shop repairs and $80 for on-site repairs.

**MACVISION COMPUTERS
210 East 6th Street (between Second & Third Avenues)
(212) 586-8445**

MacVision specializes in repairing Macs, and also repairs printers and scanners. They charge $50 for in-shop repairs and $85 for on-site repairs.

DOLL REPAIR
NEW YORK DOLL HOSPITAL
787 Lexington Avenue (61st and 62nd Streets) • (212) 838-7527

A family business that was started ninety-five years ago, they can repair, clean, and spruce up any doll. They don't take on any project that they can't do a good job on. Deposit required.

DOWN REPAIR

J. SCHACHTER • 5 Cook Street, Brooklyn • (212) 533-1150

Schachter is the place to go if your down pillows and comforters are looking less then plump and fluffy. Reconditioning entails dusting the inside free of decomposed down, sterilizing the remaining down, adding new down, and changing the fabric cover. Although this sounds like a lot of work, it can be cheaper than buying a new one.

WILLIAM ITZKOWITZ
174 Ludlow Street (Stanton & Houston Streets)
(212) 477-1788

Only in New York can you walk by a hole-in-the-wall store and see feathers flying around and know that it is a place to bring your down to get repaired and reconditioned. They also make new comforters, pillows, mattress covers, percales, and patch quilts.

FINE ART REPAIR
ALVAREZ FINE ART SERVICES, INC.
29 West 36th Street • (212) 244-5255

Antonio Alvarez has twenty-plus years experience repairing different types of art, from drawings and watercolors to manuscripts and prints. He dedicates the same skill and enthusiasm to items of purely sentimental value that he devotes to major museum commissions.

FURNITURE REPAIR
ANATOLI'S Restoration
555 Eighth Avenue, 23rd Floor (corner of 38th Street)
(212) 629-0071

Anatoli Lapushner repairs all types of furniture and also specializes in globe restoration. He also makes custom upholstery. His shop is open Monday to Friday, 9-5, and an appointment is necessary.

ANTIQUE FURNITURE WORKROOM
210 Eleventh Avenue (24th and 25th Streets) • (212) 683-0551

Keep in mind that this is mostly for repair of good-quality furniture and that a repair to keep the value of the piece does not come cheap. Their work as well as their attitude is beyond reproach.

PRECISION LEATHER CRAFTERS, INC.
73-34 Bell Boulevard, Queens • (718) 465-3661

Specialize in the cleaning, dyeing, and repair of leather and vinyl furniture. Cleaning prices start at $200. Refinishing (stripping and dyeing) a three-seat couch runs $600 and up. Emergency services are available.

INSTRUMENT REPAIR

BIASE & FANTONI RARE VIOLINS • (212) 840-8373

Established in 1935, Biase & Fantoni's is the city's longest-running fine instrument dealer and restorer in the City. Paul Biase, himself a former musician, takes great pride in repairing and tuning up broken string and bow instruments for musicians around the world. He is also a dealer and expert in fine, rare instruments.

JEWELRY REPAIR

For hooks, loose catches, and small problems.

ALEX'S JEWELRY
1157 Madison Avenue (85th and 86th Streets) • (212) 988-5135

Any repair; prompt, reliable, and honest.

EURO JEWELRY DESIGNS
1230 Lexington Avenue (83rd and 84th Streets) • (212) 734-5787

Fairly prompt. Good attention to detail when doing repairs.

MURREYS JEWELERS
1395 Third Avenue (79th and 80th Streets) • (212) 879-3690

This is a gem of a store; honest, trustworthy, and efficient.

KNIVES AND SCISSORS SHARPENED

FRED DECARLO • (201) 945-7609

He will come to your home and sharpen away.

HENRY WESTPFAL & CO. • 105 West 30th Street • (212) 563-5990

Henry Westpfal is a retail store that carries an extensive line of cutlery and scissors. A family business since 1874, they perform knife sharpening the old fashioned way. They sharpen knives with a spinning wheel, whereby the blade is pressed against the wheel and the wheel is lubricated with water. The use of water prevents the metal from burning. They can also sharpen scissors here.

LAMP REPAIR

Depending on the problem, you should first try your local hardware store. After that:

LEE'S STUDIO • 1755 Broadway (at 56th Street) • (212) 581-4400

Can only fix electric problems, not cosmetic ones.

RESTORATION & DESIGN STUDIO
249 East 77th Street • (212) 517-9742

Paul Karner can rewire complex lighting fixtures and repair a large variety of lamps.

LUGGAGE REPAIR

JOHN R. GERARDO, INC. • 30 West 31st Street • (212) 695-6955

This is the authorized repair service for Louis Vuitton and Gucci. Need we say more? Believe it or not, you can even take your Samsonite, because they repair everything—even your soft luggage.

LEXINGTON LUGGAGE
793 Lexington Avenue (61st and 62nd Streets) • (212) 223-0698

They can repair Hartman, American Tourister, Samsonite, and more. A repair takes usually less than a week and they always stand by their work.

PEN REPAIR

AUTHORIZED REPAIR SERVICE
30 West 57th Street • (212) 586-0947

Richard Weinstein and Vanessa Cardenas repair and sell new and vintage pens. To recondition an old pen, they will replace the fill system and adjust the ink flow to be compatible with modern inks. They will also clean and polish the pen.

FOUNTAIN PEN HOSPITAL
10 Warren Street (Church Street & Broadway) • (212) 964-0580

A family business started in 1946. They are the largest retailer and showroom of vintage pens in the country. Not only can they repair any broken pen, but they are experts in advising you as to what pen is right for you.

PIANO TUNER

To find a tuner we suggest you call:

JUILLIARD SCHOOL OF MUSIC • (212) 799-5000

TURTLE BAY SCHOOL OF MUSIC • (212) 753-8811

PHOTOGRAPH RESTORATION

ANA B. HOFMANN, INC.
145 Vail Lane (North Salem) • (914) 669-5915

Ana B. Hofmann, Inc. is a studio which specializes in the conservation of photographs. Ana will mend a tear in a fine art photograph or a hole in a precious family heirloom. Photographs can be shipped to the studio for evaluation. In-person consultations are by appointment.

POCKETBOOK REPAIR

A dingy, dirty, broken bag just isn't worth having.

ARTBAG CREATIONS
735 Madison Avenue (64th and 65th Streets) • (212) 744-2720

Bring your better bags here to be fixed and maintained. We have never heard the words "can't be done" when we have brought in a repair. With the high cost of pocketbooks, it makes sense to repair the old. They also carry a great selection of new bags.

KAY LEATHER GOODS REPAIR SERVICE
333 Fifth Avenue (at 33rd Street) • (212) 481-5579

Owner Jakov Dopter creatively and expertly repairs handbags, belts, and attaché cases.

MODERN LEATHER GOODS REPAIR SHOP
2 West 32nd Street • (212) 279-3263

Another fabulous source for bag repair, and they even pick up and deliver your goods for free. Once they have the item, they will give you an estimate over the phone, and if you decide not to use them, they will deliver the item back to you at no charge. Whether you need a needlepoint mounting, a good cleaning (suede, leather, or canvas), or just a repair, you can get it done here. They also repair luggage and leather accessories, such as wallets and belts.

RESTORATION

Repair and maintenance of porcelain, ceramics, lacquer, enamel, stone, glass, wood, and silver.

CENTER ART STUDIO • 250 West 54th Street • (212) 247-3881

Lancing Moore runs an impeccable repair and restoration shop. He concentrates on museum-quality pieces but that should not discourage you from making a phone call to see if he can accommodate you. This expertise does not come cheap but buying new pieces is much more.

GLASS RESTORATIONS
1597 York Avenue (84th and 85th Streets) • (212) 517-3287

Augustine Jochec works miracles on cracked crystal. Chips in faceted cut-glass edges are removed by regrinding, re-beveling, and polishing. At about $20 per glass, it's well worth it to repair that broken $50 Waterford wine glass. They also do copper wheel engraving. On objects with a floral or figural design, they seamlessly re-engrave the pattern after repairing the break.

HESS RESTORATIONS
200 Park Avenue South (at 17th Street) • (212) 260-2255

Hess works on ceramics, silver, ivory, lacquer, and more. Remember, restoration can be expensive but here you have two options: commercial-invisible restoration or museum-quality restoration. Commercial can run twice as much so be sure you know what you want.

RESTORATION & DESIGN STUDIO
249 East 77th Street • (212) 517-9742

Paul Karner, a craftsman with exquisite taste, can restore the impossible. He can hammer even the largest dents out of silver ewers, restore fireplace tools to their former glory, and rewire complex lighting fixtures.

THOME SILVERSMITHS • 49 West 37th Street • (212) 764-5426

This family business was started in 1931 and it is the place to go to restore, re-plate, and repair all your silver.

RETINNING AND COPPER REPAIR

RETINNING AND COPPER REPAIR, INC.
525 West 26th Street • (212) 244-4896

This is old New York. After you climb the four rickety flights (yes, they do have an industrial elevator) you enter New York of the early 1900s. Here you will find the art of retinning in action. So don't throw out your worn pots—they can be made to look like new. They can also clean up any brass or copper hardware.

SEWING MACHINE REPAIR

CROWN MACHINE SERVICE
2792 Broadway (107th and 108th Streets) • (212) 663-8968

Crown is the authorized service center for over fifty companies. Don't despair if you have an antique or computerized machine, because this is the place to repair those too. They also repair vacuums, VCRs, and typewriters. Best of all, house calls are provided, and they pick up and deliver as well.

SMALL APPLIANCE REPAIR

For phones, VCRs, toasters, TVs, etc. call the 800 number of the company manufacturing the product you want repaired. The customer service department will give you the authorized repair location closest to you. Anything and everything can be repaired in this city. Keep in mind: If the product is no longer covered under warranty, it might be more economical to buy a new one. Always get an estimate first.

ADVISORY RADIO & TV LABS OF AMERICA
175 Seventh Avenue (at 20th Street) • (212) 243-0786
1425 Lexington Avenue (at 93rd Street) • (212) 534-3800

They repair all leading brand names, including products under warranty. Their estimates of time and price are quite accurate. They will repair items at your home for an extra fee.

AMERICAN VIDEO SERVICE
516 Amsterdam Avenue (84th and 85th Streets) • (212) 724-4870

American Video services VCRs, stereos, CD players, tape decks, and even turntables. Free estimates are given, as is a 90 day warranty on labor and parts. There is no pick up or delivery service available.

BORGERS • 336 East 78th Street • (212) 744-4224

Thank goodness for Borgers because they make house calls! Has your VCR been unhooked for ages? Is your TV still on the blink? All because of lack of time and energy? Well, fret no longer.

GERMAN HI-FI CENTER • 247 East 94th Street • (212) 369-3366

A fifty-year old company that does honest and timely work. They repair all brands of audio and video equipment. For an extra fee, they will pick up and deliver your merchandise.

TYPEWRITER, WORD PROCESSOR, & CALCULATOR REPAIR

LINCOLN TYPEWRITERS AND COPY CENTER
111 West 68th Street • (212) 787-9397

A congenial store that has a free pickup and delivery service. It's a good bet that they can not only detect the problem, but can fix it as well. For a fee, they will make a service call to your home.

OSNER BUSINESS MACHINES
393 Amsterdam Avenue (78th and 79th Streets) • (212) 873-8734

Osner repairs manual, electric, and electronic typewriters. There is a $15 estimate fee to determine the problem which will be deducted from the cost of the repair should you decide to go through with it. They also carry typewriting ribbons and cartridges.

UMBRELLA REPAIR

Depending on how much your umbrella costs, it might make sense to get it repaired.

ZIP JACK
141 South Central Avenue, Route 9A, Elmsford, New York 10523
(914) 592-2000

If you send them your repair they will give you an estimate.

VACUUM REPAIR

ACTIVE VACUUM CLEANER COMPANY
2559 Broadway (at 98th Street) • (212) 663-1600
1594 York Avenue (at 84th Street) • (212) 663-1600

A great choice, and they also pick up and deliver.

DESCO VACUUM CLEANER COMPANY
1236 Lexington Avenue (83rd and 84th Streets) • (212) 879-1980

Here's a company that picks up and repairs your vacuum for a fair price when you know it is broken and you are just about to throw it out—what more needs to be said?

HOME IMPROVEMENTS... BE THE VICTOR, NOT THE VICTIM

PERCEPTION VS. REALTY

The New York Consumer Affairs Department says that the greatest number of incoming complaints are from consumers who have home improvement horror stories - costs that have escalated out of control, workers who skipped out on the job, and renovations filled with flaws. Disasters could be avoided if consumers would do their due diligence. Because incompetence and shady work ethics can elude quality control in a big city, there is only one way to go into a home improvement project – with eyes wide open, alert to the most common pitfalls, and fully informed about the process and the planned project.

SOLUTIONS:
MAKE SURE YOUR HOME IMPROVEMENT PAYS:

When you own: The National Association of Realtors maintains that if you plan to sell your home in the future, the amount you spend on remodeling added to the current market value of your home shouldn't exceed the value of the highest-valued homes in your neighborhood by more than 20 percent.

When you are selling: There are standard improvements that can enhance the value of your home before selling. The American Institute of Real Estate Appraisers says a cosmetic face-lift such as painting and wallpapering the walls, and refinishing the floors or putting down carpeting, can tip the balance into a sale. Renovated kitchens and bathrooms are also a major selling point. Last, a fresh coat of paint on the exterior will add to curb appeal.

When you are buying: Before you buy a home that needs a sub-stantial renovation, get a ball park idea of what it will cost. If it is going to cost a disproportionate amount compared to the overall value of the apartment, it might not be a smart investment. It's worth a small fee to have an architect, contractor, or interior designer give you an estimate, and their best advice.

When you rent: Even in a rental, it may be worth remodeling if you have an excellent deal financially and plan to make it home for a long time. Landlords are often very receptive to sharing the costs because they can add it proportionately to the future rental value of the apartment, when you vacate.

SOLUTION:
THE PRE-RENOVATION HIT LIST

Permits: Some renovations are extensive enough that they must pass local codes and regulations. And if you are planning a major renovation, the filing and approval of those plans can take weeks. We strongly recommend in that case that you hire a professional expeditor to facilitate the process. And if you are living in a co-op apartment, your plan also has to pass your co-op board of directors.

TAKE "BEFORE" RENOVATION PICTURES OF YOUR HOME AND KEEP ALL RECORDS AND RECEIPTS THAT DOCUMENT THE COST OF THE IMPROVEMENT. THE COST CAN BE ADDED TO THE PURCHASE PRICE OF YOUR HOME TO ARRIVE AT YOUR "BASIS". THE BASIS IS SUBTRACTED FROM THE SELLING PRICE TO DETERMINE YOUR CAPITAL GAIN. ALSO, WHEN DOING CAPITAL IMPROVEMENT WORK, MUCH OF IT WILL BE EXEMPT FROM SALES TAX SO BE SURE YOUR CONTRACTOR SUPPLIES YOU WITH A CAPITAL IMPROVEMENT SALES TAX EXEMPTION FORM.

Budget: Force yourself to come up with a realistic budget. If you waffle about your bottom line, or worse yet, don't have one, you run the serious risk of losing control of the project.

Your vision: You can make costly mistakes if you are unsure of what you want or can't completely visualize the end product. Educate yourself. Look at what's possible in design by looking at design showrooms, books and magazines. On the last pages of most design magazines there is a long list of how-to booklets that are available for a small fee. They include everything from do-it-yourself decorating tips to how to hire an architect.

The materials you plan to use: A formica countertop could cost you $600, a granite one, $3,000. Even faucets can vary by hundreds of dollars. Make sure you pick out your materials before the renovation begins! It is also important to understand that the slightest alteration can cost you dearly. One of our clients wanted to round out the edges on a square granite countertop she had purchased and it raised the cost another 20 percent!

The actual plan: This may be the most important piece of advice we give you. Having a plan from the start will prevent huge cost escalations due to day-to-day changes in the project. We recommend that you consider hiring an architect or designer and pay a one-time-only consulting fee to draw up detailed plans for you. It may save you thousands in the end.

The right laborers for the job: There are plenty of home improvement specialists out there but are they skilled in the type of improvement you are planning? Make sure you have the right guy for the job!

SOLUTION
KNOW WHO'S WHO IN HOME IMPROVEMENT

Architect: An architect has a degree from an architectural school and has to be licensed. An architect is an expert regarding special relationships and a building's internal plumbing and electrical systems. He/she designs and constructs new spaces and knows which laborers and materials are required.

Interior Designer: An interior designer is not licensed, but has graduated from an interior design school. In addition to being able to create a look, he/she can provide expertise on room layouts, living space blueprints and specifications, and the designer has a professional eye for structural changes.

Decorator: A decorator is not licensed and need not have completed any formal school training. A decorator's value lies in the cosmetic changes he/she can make by picking out coordinating fabrics, paint, wallpaper, furniture, rugs, and fixtures, and providing room layout expertise. Decorators also have access to the trade showrooms for some of the better materials that are not available to the consumer.

Contractor: A contractor must be licensed. He/she is the implementer of all the plans that have been put together by you and your architect or interior designer. A contractor will oversee the day-to-day task of

> "IT IS CRITICAL IN NEW YORK CITY TO HIRE CONTRACTORS, ARCHITECTS AND INTERIOR DESIGNERS WITH INTERPERSONAL SKILLS. THEY HAVE TO FINESSE ALL KINDS OF RELATIONSHIPS. STARTING WITH MAKING SURE THAT EVERYONE UNDERSTANDS THAT THE SUPERINTENDENT IS THE KEY PERSON IN ALL BUILDINGS."
>
> — BRETT BELDOCK
> BRETT DESIGNS

> CATCH A MISTAKE
> BEFORE IT GETS TOO BIG.
> INSPECT THE RENOVATION
> WORK EVERY DAY BEFORE THE
> WORKERS GO HOME.
> MAKE SURE YOU GET THE
> BEEPER NUMBERS OF
> ALL THE LABORERS;
> THEY ARE
> NOT EASY TO TRACK DOWN
> WITHOUT THEM.

> ANDREW BARTLE IS AN
> AMAZING FIND.
> HE HAS A GREAT EYE AND A
> WONDERFUL PERSONALITY —
>
> WHAT AN ARCHITECT!
> 212-206-8929

> IN APARTMENT BUILDINGS,
> MAKE SURE BEFORE
> PROCEEDING WITH A
> PLUMBING AND ELECTRICAL
> RENOVATION THAT
> YOUR BUILDING ISN'T
> ALREADY PLANNING AN
> OVERHAUL OF
> THESE SYSTEMS.

buying construction materials, hiring laborers, and getting the actual construction and installation completed. The better contractors can also have excellent design sense and can make recommendations in terms of ready-made versus custom work. He/she may subcontract out for laborers or have an in-house staff. A contractor who subcontracts out has the advantage of being able to pick and choose the workers. On the other hand, a contractor with his/her own staff can better control their work habits.

SOLUTION: WHEN AND HOW TO HIRE AN ARCHITECT

When: You hire an architect when you need to make structural changes to your home.

How: For help in finding an architect, call the American Institute of Architects at 212-683-0023. They have a directory of their members. You can go directly to them at 200 Lexington Avenue and spend time looking through the directory. All the architects who join AIA are fully licensed professionals. And as always, word of mouth and personal referrals are the best way to go. Make sure you see their work, and that you see eye-to-eye on the project, time frame and the budget.

SOLUTION: YOUR CONTRACTOR - GETTING THIS CRITICAL HIRE RIGHT.

The wrong contractor will blow the job: There is no more critical hire. He/she is the implementer of all the plans; if he can't implement them, they will remain on paper; if he can't motivate his sub contractors and workers, the job will never be completed; the contractor stays until the bitter end; if he skips out on the job, the punch list will never be crossed off.

Contractors have to be licensed: They have to be licensed by the New York City Department of Consumer Affairs. Call the DCA to make sure at 212-487-4444. Call the Better Business Bureau to make sure no significant complaints have been filed against them. Make a point to get four or five referrals on several different contractors and then go see their work.

Get at least three estimates: The law states that upon request, a contractor must furnish you with a written estimate of the work to be done. A low price might not necessarily mean a bargain. In fact, a big difference in estimates is a red flag. One builder may be planning to use lower-grade materials, or he may not have understood what you wanted, or he may have low balled you as an enticement to hire him. Ask for estimates that include materials to be used, all labor costs, and time of completion. Ask for detailed information about the materials including size, quantity, model and brand name. Some contractors charge for an estimate, some don't.

Don't hire a contractor without getting satisfactory answers to these questions:

1. How long have you been in business?

2. Is this the original company or did you buy the name?

3. Do you subcontract out all your crews or do you have your own staff laborers?

4. Do you have your own cabinet shop or do you contract that out too?

5. Do you carry insurance – Workman's Compensation and Liability? (Most apartment buildings require insurance certificates to be filed prior to the work commencing.)

MAKE SURE YOU ORDER ALL YOUR APPLIANCES AND CABINETS IN PLENTY OF TIME FOR THE INSTALLATION. WE HAVE HAD MANY A FRUSTRATED CLIENT WHOSE INSTALLERS SHOWED UP ON SCHEDULE, BUT THE MATERIALS WERE NOT READY.

DON'T EVER ASSUME YOUR PROJECT IS UNWORTHY OF AN ARCHITECT'S EXPERTISE OR INTEREST. AND PARTICULARLY WHEN THE HOUSING MARKET IS SOFT, THE BETTER ARCHITECTS ARE FAR MORE OPEN TO REDUCED FEES AND SMALL PROJECTS. SOME ARE WILLING TO BE HIRED ON A ONE-TIME-ONLY CONSULTING BASIS TO AT LEAST GIVE YOU SOME IDEAS AND GUIDANCE. IT REALLY PAYS TO ASK. JUST MAKE SURE YOU INTERVIEW TWO OR THREE, GET SEVERAL REFERRALS, AND SEVERAL ESTIMATES, BEFORE GOING AHEAD.

YOU WILL GET WHAT YOU PAY FOR. ONE MISTAKE THAT MANY PEOPLE MAKE IS THAT THEIR EXPECTATIONS ARE GREATER THAN THEIR BUDGETS. THAT IS ONE REASON WHY RELATIONSHIPS BETWEEN CLIENT AND LABORERS OFTEN TURN SOUR. YOU CAN AVOID THIS BY GOING INTO THE PROJECT KNOWING WHAT LABOR AND MATERIALS COST. YOU CANNOT TURN A HONDA INTO A ROLLS ROYCE.

6. Will you allow me to buy my own appliances? (Sometimes you can buy your own appliances more cheaply because your contractor may add on a markup for purchasing them for you).

7. Are the cabinets stock or custom made?

8. May I see some of your work?

9. May I have four or five references?

10. Are there any liens against you? (You can also call the BBB).

11. Do you specialize in the type of remodeling I am planning?

12. Can you really commit to my time frame for completing the job? (Make sure you find out from their references how reliable they were)

13. Who is actually overseeing the job and how often can I expect them to be on site? (You don't want them farming it out to subordinates.)

14. How long will it take to get an estimate? (It shouldn't take more than a week or so.)

15. Would you consider putting a cap on the estimate?

16. What is the payment schedule? What is the turnkey price? (Price of entire job.)

17. How will you charge for extras and changes? Will the fee include a penalty charge?

The Better Business Bureau's Home Improvement Report states that NY State law requires that contractors provide consumers with a complete, legible copy of the contract at the time it is signed by all parties, and before any work is started! And that it should include:

• Signatures and Date

• Contractors' company name, address, phone number and license number

• List of materials to be used, including brand names and model numbers

• Schedule of completion, including stages of completion- should have estimated dates for start and completion of project, including reasons why it might be delayed.

- A very detailed description of the work to be done. Be clear about the location of doors, windows, walls, plumbing and electrical outlets, the brand names and model numbers of appliances and materials to be used, and anything else required to complete the job. If possible, have all blueprints, photos, plans or sketches made part of the contract.

- Payment schedule that states how payment will be made and under what circumstances...if payment will correspond to completed work or be due on specific dates, etc.

- All verbal agreements

- Clause stating that the contractor will obtain all permits required by law

- Statement that contractor will be responsible for repairing mistakes and for cleaning the area after the job is finished

- Clauses stating that the contractor must provide proof of payment to subcontractors and supply houses and give the consumer permission to withhold final payment to the contractor until he or she provides such proof—otherwise, the subcontractors and suppliers can put a lien on the consumer's property if the contractor does not pay them.

- Statement of the consumer's right to cancel the home improvement contract within three business days of signing it, and a Notice of Cancellation which the consumer should use in that situation.

"Storefront" contractors are another way to go: Kitchen and bathroom design storefronts have their own in-house contractors. They will charge you a fee of about

> "IN A SMALL TOWN, A CONTRACTOR WILL NOT SURVIVE IF HE DOES INADEQUATE WORK. NEW YORK CITY, BY COMPARISON, IS A VAST GALAXY THAT CAN HIDE INCOMPETENCE. IT IS CRITICAL TO NOT ONLY GET FIVE OR SIX REFERRALS BEFORE SETTLING ON A CONTRACTOR, BUT TO GO AND ACTUALLY SEE THEIR WORK."
>
> — BROOKE LOENING CONTRACTING

> "A PROOF OF PAYMENT CLAUSE WILL PROTECT YOU IN THE EVENT THE CONTRACTOR FAILS TO PAY HIS SUBCONTRACTORS OR SUPPLIERS. WITH THIS CLAUSE, YOU CAN WITHHOLD PAYMENT UNTIL PROOF OF PAYMENT IS SUBMITTED TO YOU. WITHOUT THIS CLAUSE, THE SUBCONTRACTORS AND SUPPLIERS COULD PUT A LIEN ON YOUR HOME FOR THE AMOUNT DUE THEM."
>
> — DEPARTMENT OF CONSUMER AFFAIRS

$300 to come to your home, look at your kitchen space and do a design plan. That $300 is put toward the completion of the project, if you go forward. If you choose, you can take your design plan with you and continue to shop for a better price. The storefront contractor will do all the measuring and oversee the project through installation with a freelance team of plumbers, electricians, etc. These stores have a range of stock items for different needs and budgets, and they do custom work. If you were to buy 10 custom cabinets versus ten ready-made, the difference in cost would be about $2,000, which is going toward a perfect fit, better quality workmanship and a custom design. There are on-sight design planners to help you through the project.

SOLUTION: WHAT TO LOOK FOR IN A DECORATOR

- Hiring a decorator is a very personal choice based on compatible vision and taste. If you aren't sold on his/her portfolio, or don't feel simpatico, move on.

- If you want to go with a large, well-established design firm, make sure that the decorator you choose isn't planning to hand the work off to a subordinate.

- Make sure you and your decorator agree on the degree of commitment to the job, the time it will take to complete it, the design elements, as well as budget limitations.

- If you decide to go with a small outfit, make sure you really love the work they do. Your design options are pretty much limited to the vision and style of the one or two people who run it.

- Be sure you understand what percent commission the decorator will be charg-

THE BBB SAYS THAT NY STATE LAW REQUIRES THAT HOME IMPROVEMENT CONTRACTORS DEPOSIT ALL PAYMENTS RECEIVED PRIOR TO THE COMPLETION OF THE JOB INTO AN ESCROW ACCOUNT, TO BE WITHDRAWN ACCORDING TO THE SCHEDULE SET FORTH IN THE CONTRACT. THE AMOUNT OF PAYMENTS SHOULD BE APPROXIMATELY PROPORTIONAL TO THE AMOUNT OF WORK DONE AND MATERIALS NEEDED TO BE PURCHASED DURING EACH TIME PERIOD. THIS DEPOSIT REMAINS THE CONSUMER'S PROPERTY UNTIL THE FUNDS ARE USED IN ACCORDANCE WITH THE CONTRACT, OR THE HOME IMPROVEMENT JOB IS FINISHED, OR THE CONSUMER DEFAULTS, RELIEVING THE CONTRACTOR FROM HAVING TO FINISH THE CONTRACT.

THINK TWICE, MAKE THAT THREE TIMES, ABOUT HIRING A CONTRACTOR WHO IS LATE WITH AN ESTIMATE, WHO CAN'T ANSWER ALL YOUR QUESTIONS TO YOUR SATISFACTION, AND WHO IS HARD TO GET ON THE PHONE.

ing you for the materials he/she buys for you. On the low end, some decorators will only charge you 15 percent on top of the wholesale price, on the high end, 30 percent on top of the retail price.

The best ways to find a good decorator:

• Word of mouth. Always the best.

• Classified section of New York Magazine and design magazines: If you have a small job and limited budget, this is a great way to find an up-and-coming designer.

• New York School of Interior Design and Parsons School of Design: Their employment offices can help you find a graduate student, or teacher who might be right for the job

• Designer Showcases: Designers show off their abilities at special-ly planned showcases throughout the year. Local magazines and newspapers publish the dates and the place.

• The American Society of Interior Designers: This an organization that promotes design. You can go in and look at portfolios, and they will help you make the right match for your needs. You can call them at (877) ASK- ASID

SOLUTION:
THERE'S A METHOD FOR HIRING PAINTERS, TOO.

There are several categories of painters:

A handyman or building superintendent who can come in and put a fresh coat of paint on a five room rental apartment in a day. It may only cost you as little as $500 but there will be no attention to details and most likely the painter will not be insured.

A professional painter who will deliver a higher quality job which includes details such as taping the windows so the trim color does-n't bleed onto the walls, fixing cracks and crevices, painting the ceil-ing in a different color. And the older the building, the more compli-cated the expertise because layers of old paint might have to be removed, and walls may have to be replastered or recanvassed in order to make them smooth again. Depending on the degree of work and precision required, costs can start at $1,000 a room.

A painter whose expertise is artistic finishings. Specialists who cre-ate designs on top of your basic paint job. One type of work, called "sponging" or "ragging" gives texture and abstract design to your walls. Another, is the actual drawing on of designs or "scenes". This technique can be very expensive, but in NYC you can try to bypass the pros and go after artistic types who may want to do this as a sidebar hobby. One suggestion is to call schools such as Art

> THERE IS A PHRASE USED IN HOME IMPROVEMENT CALLED "PADDING THE BILL". THESE ARE MARKUPS THAT ARCHITECTS, DECORATORS, CONTRACTORS AND OTHERS MAY CHARGE THE CLIENT THAT ARE CONSIDERED COMPLETELY LEGITIMATE. THEY ARE CHARGING YOU MORE FOR THEIR TIME AND THE COST OF MATERIALS IN CASE THEY ENCOUNTER ANY UNFORESEEN PROBLEMS SUCH AS OVERTIME AND ITEM COST OVERRUNS. YOU SHOULD ASK THEM TO BREAK DOWN THE ESTIMATE FOR YOU. IT IS NOT INAPPROPRIATE FOR YOU TO ASK IF THERE IS ANY MONEY LEFT OVER AT THE END OF THE PROJECT

Students League, Parsons School of Design or the School of Visual Arts for leads.

SOLUTION: YOU CAN DO MANY SMALL PROJECTS YOURSELF AND SAVE A BUNDLE:

Expect markups for each expert you add to a project: If, for example, you hire a decorator to put in kitchen cabinets, she will call her carpenter. The carpenter takes measurements and drawings of the cabinets, counters, etc. to the wood shop, and the shop makes them. The wood shop charges the carpenter $400 for the items. The carpenter includes his markup and charges the decorator $500. The decorator includes her markup, a 20 percent commission, and you could owe as much as $720 for the work. Sometimes the decorator can deal directly with the shop, bypassing the carpenter, and sometimes she can get a break from the woodshop, but you are still paying more for her involvement.

If you don't hire a decorator, the costs can come way down: In this scenario, you select your own materials and choose a woodshop. You take the measurements and they build the cabinets. Cost to you is about $400. The downside is that it's your neck and pocketbook if the work isn't satisfactory. So, do your due diligence, and make sure the measurements are accurate, the materials are going to work, and that the woodshop has an unblemished track record.

Upholstering without a decorator: When recovering a few pieces of furniture, or making curtains, pillows, duvet covers, etc. you probably don't need a decorator if you hire a very good upholsterer. The better upholsters can guide you through the process, and they often know more about the practicality and workability of a particular fabric than a decorator. Also, your upholsterer can get you an entrée into the designer showrooms to pick out your fabric. He might charge you a percentage for the access, but it's still less than the markup decorators traditionally charge.

Buying fabric without a decorator: At one time, consumers couldn't find interesting selections of fabric unless they went through a decorator to access the design showrooms. Today, there are many more resources:

- Retail fabric boutiques such as Pierre Deux, Laura Ashley and Ralph Lauren where you can find the better fabrics as well as a sales staff that can help you plan a room.

- Discount fabric stores such as Silk Surplus, and The Rag Shop as well as those located in the wholesale fabric district on and around Grand Street on the lower East Side.

- Some of the exclusive mills that once only sold to designers now sell less expensive, unlabeled fabrics in bulk to huge discount fabric stores...so, if you don't care that much about labels and exclusivity, you can get excellent deals.

- Decorator and Design Building for fabrics:The Decorator and Design Building at 979 Third Avenue sells fabric wholesale to the trade. That's about 30 percent off the retail price. If you want to try to access it yourself, it will be up to the discretion of the individual showroom to let you in. Some will let you browse. Some might let you buy fabric too, especially when the design market is soft. These showrooms don't post prices. If they agree to sell to you, make sure you ask them if they are selling to you at the wholesale or retail price.

Buying furniture without a decorator:

- Retail furniture: it always goes on sale: It pays to wait.

- Consider buying furniture at auction. Many auction houses specialize in furniture sales. You can furnish homes at very discounted prices. See shopping chapter on how to work an auction.

- Dealer & Antique Shows that come into town: The shows are put together by Stella Management (212 255-0020), or Wendy Management (914 698-3442).

> TWO THINGS TO KEEP IN MIND WHEN RE-UPHOLSTERING: ASK THE UPHOLSTERER IF HE HAS ANY LEFT OVER FABRIC THAT HE WILL SELL TO YOU AT A DEEP DISCOUNT AND MAKE SURE THAT IT WILL NOT COST YOU MORE TO REUPHOLSTER YOUR OLD FURNITURE THAN IT WILL TO BUY PIECES.

> THERE IS A REASON WHY YOU CAN GO TO TWO DIFFERENT FABRIC SHOWROOMS AND SEE ALMOST THE SAME FABRIC AT VERY DIFFERENT PRICES. FABRIC COMPANIES CONTRACT WITH DIFFERENT MILLS TO HAVE THE FABRICS MADE AND THE PRICE IS AFFECTED BY THE COLORS AND MATERIALS, THE DETAIL OF THE DESIGN, AND THE EXCLUSIVITY OF THE LABEL. BE ADVISED THAT THE DURABILITY OF A FABRIC IS NOT NECESSARILY RELATED TO THE PRICE, BUT ON HOW MUCH WEAR AND TEAR THE FABRIC IS GOING TO GET, AND HOW WELL IT'S UPHOLSTERED, AND MAINTAINED.

DECORATORS GET TRADE DISCOUNTS ON ALL HOME FURNISHINGS FROM FABRICS TO ANTIQUES; THE SAVINGS ARE CONSIDERABLE. IF YOU HAVE A FRIEND WHO IS A DECORATOR, WHY NOT SUGGEST AN EQUITABLE ARRANGEMENT. MAYBE SHE CAN GET YOU INTO THE SHOWROOM TO GET THE DISCOUNT, AND YOU CAN OFFER HER A SMALL COMMISSION, OR BARTER YOUR OWN SERVICES FOR HERS.

THE YELLOW PAGES ARE LOADED WITH LISTINGS OF RENTAL FURNITURE SUPPLIERS, BECAUSE THERE IS SUCH A BIG DEMAND FOR SHORT-TERM HOUSING FOR CORPORATE TRANSFEREES. IT CAN BE A CONVENIENT AND COST EFFECTIVE APPROACH TO FURNISHING AN APARTMENT RIGHT DOWN TO THE BED COMFORTER AND CLOCK RADIO! THEY ARE ALSO WILLING TO SELL YOU THEIR USED RENTAL FURNITURE, FOR ALMOST NOTHING.

They run large adds in the papers or call to find when the shows will be.

- Upscale flea markets: NYC has great flea markets for furniture and room accessories. You want to get there either early in the morning before the dealers pick over the items or at the end of the day when they are dramatically reducing prices so they don't have to take the merchandise home. There is the Antique Center on 26th street between 6th and 7th Avenue and 67th between 1st and 2nd Avenue.

- Furniture designers that sell to the trade only, hold their own sample sales annually to sell leftover furniture. We suggest you call your favorite designer and ask when their sale is coming up or subscribe to the "s & b report". You will be paying wholesale prices or less. Always check the furniture for flaws.

- The Furniture Building: 200 Lexington...many showrooms will sell to the public and even take credit cards.

- Consult the Wholesale By Mail Catalog: How Consumers Can Shop By Mail or Telephone and Save 30% to 90% off List Price. Compiled by The Print Project, you can find it in any major bookstore. The key to shopping this way is to go to the retail showrooms first, pick out the brands you like, take down the style and models #s and then call the wholesalers, manufacturers, etc. that are in the book.

- Thrift shops: Do not discount the idea of buying some pieces from a thrift shop. New York is filled with people who donate great furniture to make room for their new pieces. For starters try the Irvington Institute at 80th street and Third Avenue or The Salvation Army at 44th between 10th and 11th Avenue.

HOME IMPROVEMENT SOURCES AND SERVICES

$ = inexpensive $$ = moderate $$$ = expensive

ARCHITECTS, INTERIOR DESIGNERS & DECORATORS

ASID: AMERICAN SOCIETY OF INTERIOR DESIGNERS (ASID) (877) ASK-ASID

They are the credential-granting agency to which many degreed designers belong. You specify your needs, taste, and budget on an application form. They will then recommend two choices. Most of these designers will not accept a job under $50,000. There is a $40 handling fee.

DESIGNER PREVIEWS • (212) 777-2966

Karen Fisher matches the right architect, designer, and landscaping expert to the client. She shows you slides of their work, answers your questions, and helps you select the best firms to interview in view of your personal style and priorities. Most of her designers won't do a job under $50,000. Her fee is $100.

FASHION INSTITUTE OF TECHNOLOGY • (212) 217-7999

The alumni job bank handles all inquiries for advanced students or graduates. Call April Kinser; she will recommend students who have graduated within the last five years. No fee.

INTERIOR OPTIONS • (212) 726-9708

Michael Love, ASID runs this designer referral service which allows consumers access to "to-the-trade-only" decorator showrooms. Located in the New York Design Center which houses over 50 furniture and fabric showrooms, one of Michael's designers will walk you through the showrooms that interest you and will assist you in your selection for a fee of $50 (credited toward anything you purchase). You also have the option to hire one of Michael's eight designers. The fee is $450 for a three-hour minimum design consultation. If you just need some basic questions answered, they charge $145 per hour for their time. These prices would be applied to the cost of the total project if you actually retain them.

NEW YORK SCHOOL OF INTERIOR DESIGN • 800-696-9743

Speak to Nina Bunchuk in the placement office. Over the phone she is more than happy to recommend professors and graduates who might be right for your job. There is no fee for this service.

PARSONS SCHOOL OF DESIGN • (212) 229-8940

Speak to the placement office. They will ask you to fax a job description which they will post for students and graduates. Students and alumni will call you directly. No fee.

The following professionals should be called during regular office hours.

BRETT DESIGN, INC. • (212) 987-8270

If you are planning a big decorating project and need some real expert help, call Brett Beldock. Her expertise lies in getting a job done by first determining exactly what her client's needs are and then implementing her own good taste and resources. If time allows, she may be hired for hourly consultations.

ELLEN S. BERNS DESIGN ASSOCIATES (212) 517-7155

Ellen Berns, ASID has over twenty-five years experience in contract/commercial and residential design. She has been listed in "Who's Who of Interior Design" for the past ten years, and taught design at Parsons School of Design for eleven years. Her skills range from complete kitchen-bath design and renovation, to private home exterior and complete interior/architectural requirements. Ellen's consultation fee is $350. Her design package which includes drawings and fabric selection runs $175 per hour. The price for Ellen to purchase items will vary depending on your needs.

KFD DESIGNS, LTD. • (212) 633-0660

Kimberley Fiterman, ASID specializes in space planning to help you maximize the use of your home or apartment. She focuses on residential interiors, including kitchens, baths, bedrooms, home office design, and storage needs. The initial consultation to view her portfolio is free. Her consulting fee is $125 an hour, or on a fee basis of 30 percent of the budget if you want her to design a room.

LIZA LERNER • (212) 888-2804

Liza runs a small firm that specializes in high-end design and decoration. They cover all phases of a project including renovations. Their style is eclectic in that they work with each client to achieve the best design for his/her individual needs. The smallest budget they are usually given is $150,000.

NEW YORK DESIGN ASSOCIATES, INC. ARCHITECTS/PLANNERS (212) 840-5599

New York Design Associates, Inc. is an interior design firm specializing in residential and commercial projects. The principal, George Feher, is a licensed architect with over twenty-five years of experience. NYDA has a flexible fee structure: generally 20 to 25 percent of the total cost of the job, depending on the complexity of the project. They do not frown upon small projects. Your initial consultation is free.

THE STUDIO OF SOPHIA GRUZDYS • (212) 252-0610

Here you can find licensed architects who specialize in renovation. They can help clients visualize fresh and innovative ideas quickly by providing them with 3-D sketches in a short period of time. Clients can then take these sketches to their contractors, or Sophia can provide you with a full set of services, including construction documents, bidding, filing with local authorities and construction supervision. They provide a free initial hour of design consultation, and bill $125 per hour thereafter. For more extensive services, they charge 15 percent of the estimated construction budget, at a minimum construction budget of $100,000.

CARPENTERS AND MORE

There are all different types of carpenters. We have discovered some who truly are craftsmen and artisans.

ALAN LAX STUDIO INC. • (516) 674-6183 • $$ • Insured

Alan can handle all types of woodwork jobs. He has expertise in lacquer, custom cabinet work, and more. His shop is located on Long Island, and he services the New York metro area. Estimates are free and his emphasis is on quality craftsmanship.

CARPISTRY • (212) 595-0028 • $$-$$$ • Insured

Robert Benes is a designer and craftsman. He prefers to design his own pieces that suit your needs, but he is more than capable of following other people's plans. He has designed and built art deco bedroom sets, entertainment units, and more.

FERNANDO MARTINEZ • (203) 532-9701 • $$-$$$ • Insured

Fernando, an interior designer by trade, can custom-make just about anything you can think of. He will come to your home to take measurements, offer suggestions and design the items you need, then build and install them. Fernando is known for his Misma Productions and Go To Your Room furniture lines. His showroom, which displays all of his handiwork, (none of which is for sale) is located in Byram, Connecticut. However, is not necessary for you to visit it. Fernando will come to you at a rate of $50 per hour, and will quote you a price for the job. Delivery is about $150 to Manhattan, unless you wish to pick the items up.

HENRY LEVINE • (718) 596-7323 • $$ • No Insurance

Henry can take on small carpentry jobs. He specializes in building and finishing walls.

JOHN FOWLER• (212) 686-2277 • $$-$$$ • No Insurance

John has been working in New York City for twenty-five years and is known both as a contractor and interior renovation expert. Talented as a carpenter and designer, he's an overall craftsperson. He has worked on everything from rooftop decks to kitchens to bathrooms. He holds a Masters degree in stage design.

THE LITTLE WOLF CABINET SHOP
1583 First Avenue
(82nd and 83rd Streets)
(212) 734-1116 • $$$ • Insured

John Wolf runs the business that his Dad started forty years ago. About half of their work is for designers and architects, the remaining half for individuals. They don't finish furniture here, but will recommend finishers who will work in your home. They also do formica work.

ALEXANDRA MUSE, AN ART CONSULTANT AND CURATOR, SAYS THAT ART IS PROBABLY THE MOST SUBJECTIVE PURCHASE YOU WILL MAKE FOR YOUR HOME. CHOOSE WORKS THAT YOU REACT TO AND THAT YOU CAN GROW WITH...ONES THAT GIVE YOU PLEASURE, THAT SEEM FRESH EACH TIME YOU LOOK AT THEM, AND THAT SET THE TONE YOU WANT IN YOUR HOME. DON'T EVER BUY SOMETHING JUST BECAUSE SOMEONE SAYS IT IS A GOOD INVESTMENT.

914-325-4237

RESTORATIONS BY PETER SCHICHTEL
(973) 605-8818 • $$ • Insured

Although the bread-and-butter business at RPS is the restoration and preservation of all types of antiques, they are woodworkers at heart, and jump at any excuse to pursue their craft.

CARPET INSTALLATION

ABC CARPET & HOME • 888 Broadway
(212) 473-3000

Call 212 929-1275 direct. Installation runs around $100 per hour and they have a great expertise in this area.

EINSTEIN MOOMJY • 150 East 58th
Street • (212) 758-0900

Before you go to this location call to make an appointment with Mark. He is one of the best salespeople in New York. Mark has a good understanding of which carpet is appropriate for what spaces. He does not try to oversell you or promise you something that they cannot deliver. Don't hesitate to call them even if you have your own carpet that needs laying.

CHILDREN'S CUSTOM ROOMS & FURNITURE

Both of these designers can help solve the small space restrictions we New Yorkers face, while still creating a children's room that even a suburban kid would love.

CHARM AND WHIMSY • (212) 683-7609

Esther Sadowsky, ASID has been transforming children's rooms for 13 years. She can assist you with standard decorating, like color, fabric selection, and furniture purchase, and she can also make artistic changes to a room. Esther specializes in the design and painting of children's' furniture, wall murals, and ceilings, and can create multi-functional pieces to save space. In one instance, Esther designed a doll's house bed for a child in a very small room. Toys were stowed in the house and the bed was on the roof, which was bordered with a picket fence guard rail. Her initial consultation fee of $150 includes two at-home visits in which Esther will measure the room(s), discuss custom furniture designs and fabric, and show you wall covering samples. You can also view her portfolio at this time. Esther also makes personalized baby gifts, such as painted footstools, pegboards, rocking chairs, and play tables.

FUNTASTIC INTERIORS, INC.
(212) 633-0660

Whether you want to add a room, divide a children's room, or furnish it, Kimberley Fiterman, ASID can meet your needs. She can create custom pieces, or transform one piece of furniture (a shelving unit) into another (a changing table). Kimberley also takes lighting and noise into consideration when designing a room. The initial consultation to view her portfolio is free. Her consulting fee is $125 an hour, or on a fee basis of 30 percent of the budget if you want her to design a room.

DECORATING DEPARTMENTS
IN MAJOR STORES

Big department stores often have in-store decorating services. It is a wonderful way for them to guarantee they will sell some of their furniture. Customers beware: This is only a good way to go if you like their furniture!

UNLIKE OTHER DESIGN BUILDINGS WHICH ARE CLOSED TO THE GENERAL PUBLIC, THE GREENPOINT MANUFACTURING AND DESIGN CENTER ALLOWS NON-DESIGNERS TO THEIR SITE. THE DESIGN CENTER HOUSES 400,000 SQUARE FEET OF SHOPS RANGING FROM FINE ARTS, CERAMICS, AND JEWELRY DESIGNERS, TO WOOD, METAL, AND GLASS ARTISANS, TO COUNTLESS OTHER CRAFTSMEN. THERE ARE NO READY-TO-BUY ITEMS HERE; ALL WORK IS CUSTOM-MADE. THEY CAN BE REACHED AT (718) 383-3935.

BLOOMINGDALE'S
1000 Third Avenue (at 59th Street) • (212) 705-2590

They have a staff of fully experienced interior designers. This is a comprehensive interior design service–they supply painters, wallpaper hangers, plumbers, etc. The fee is based on a sliding scale depending on how many rooms are being renovated. For one or two rooms the minimum you must spend is $10,000 (half of which must be spent at Bloomingdale's). First you make an appointment in the store with a designer at no fee. If you choose to continue, the designer comes to your home and creates a floor plan. There is a $750 fee for that. If you go ahead with the job a $500 refund of the floor-plan fee is applied to your final bill.

CRATE & BARREL • 650 Madison Avenue • (212) 308-0011

Not only do they have great furniture, but many of their sales staff are trained in drawing floor plans to scale. Make sure you call first to make an appointment with one of their trained sales professional. If you like their designs, it can be one stop shopping.

MACY'S • 151 West 34th Street • (212) 494-4154

They do not get involved with construction. They are more of a decorating service whose primary interests are finding you the right furniture, area rugs, upholstery, and fabrics. There is a $250 fee for drawing plans, which is reimbursed after delivery of $1,500 worth of items spent at Macy's.

DEMOLITION AND CARTING

Finding good people who will do demolition and/or carting away of debris is tough in this city.

PIERRE COBB • (212) 491-6970 • $ • No Insurance

Pierre is one of a kind. He can tackle any job that requires muscle, from helping you move your furniture around to breaking down cement walls. And best of all, he carts anything and everything away. He even works evenings. His only fault may be his timeliness; leave yourself some leeway when you make an appointment.

ELECTRICAL AND LIGHTING PEOPLE

CHRISTINE SCIULLI LIGHTING DESIGN
(212) 420-0151 • $$ • No Insurance

Light can evoke different feelings and change the overall impression of a space. Christine Sciulli will work with your architect or electrician to create and enhance the lighting of your home. She has expertise in different types of lighting – ambient, reading, the lighting of art, kitchen lighting, and exterior lighting, to name a few. Christine will meet with you at your home for an initial one to three hour consultation to determine your needs and to offer some solutions. She will then charge you a set fee for the entire project.

FGE ELECTRIC • (212) 966-0504 • $$
Insured

They work with both residential and commercial properties, and are happy to work on small jobs. They give free estimates, and are quick and efficient.

LIGHTING BY GREGORY
158 Bowery • (212) 226-1276 • $$
Insured

Cliff Starr, the lighting consultant at Lighting by Gregory, can come to your home to determine your lighting needs. Depending on your budget, he may advise you on using different bulbs or purchasing new lights and fixtures. Cliff will draw a lighting map and work directly with your electrician. A two to three hour consultation costs about $300, depending on where you live.

> YOU CAN FIND A REPUTABLE LIGHTING DESIGNER THROUGH THE INTERNATIONAL ASSOCIATION OF LIGHTING DESIGNERS AT (312) 527-3677.

LEE'S LIGHTING STUDIO
1069 Third Avenue (63rd) (212) 371-1122

Ray is a genius when it comes to installing any light fixtures. Call in advance because he does book quickly. They charge aprox. $100.00 per hour.

EXPEDITERS

New York is a jungle when trying to get renovation plans approved by the building department. Even most architects and designers don't attempt to process the plans themselves; they hire experts to do this. The experts are called expediters. If you want to file plans, you will need one too.

DAVID TRACHTENBERG • (212) 643-1797

David is an expert in filing architectural plans and pushing them through the buildings department.

FLOOR FINISHERS

Making a wood floor beautiful can be a tricky job but these people can handle it.

WOODCRAFT FLOORING• (718) 325-0666 • $$ • insured

Woodcraft is used by many NY contractors. Ask for Tony and you will get top notch service.

PEISER FLOORS • (212) 222-3424 • $$ • Insured

Ask for Barry–he will make an appointment for an estimate. They are still the best in the business.

FURNITURE REFINISHERS

Don't despair if you think your wood furniture is chipped, stained, or looks simply dismal. New York has some of the top refinishers. They can make your pieces look beautiful and even change their color. If you are worried about your furniture when it is out of the home, don't despair—many times your home owner's policy will cover you , so check.

JOHN BOSSONE • (718) 275-1721 • $$ • insured

John is used by many New York designers. For ten years, John and his staff has been doing amazing restoration as well as designing and making custom furniture. For a first class job, you must call them.

JOSEPH BIUNNO COMPANY
(212) 629-5630 • $$ • No Insurance

Joseph Biunno is the fourth generation of his family to work his magic on restoring, repairing, and refinishing antique to contemporary furniture. One of his specialties is making skeleton and barrel keys for antique pieces and furniture doors, and he makes house calls. Don't forget—an antique piece of furniture is worth more if it has an original working lock.

INTERIOR ART DESIGNS • (717) 620-7120 • $$$ • Insured

Tom Krause can restore fine furniture and antiques which are scratched, gouged, or water damaged. The refinishing is done at your home. He can also repair wooden wall panels.

RELIABLE FURNITURE • (718) 387-7308 • $$ • No Insurance

Sam Garachi is one of the best, an artisan from way back. We haven't run across any piece of furniture that Sam can't make look wonderful. He can either work in your home or bring your item to his studio. He works with a great cabinetmaker.

GENERAL CONTRACTORS

Be careful when hiring a contractor. Do your homework or call our picks. All joking aside, the state of the economy dictates the minimum job that each of these companies will accept. In a booming market, the minimum goes up. If you have a small job, try to be flexible and gracious. Most contractors are looking for high end work but if they think that you will be easy to work for, they may consider your job.

BARRY FISHELBERG INC. • (718) 658-0192 • $$ • Insured

Barry Fishelberg Inc. is a family who's been in business for over twenty-five years. Now his two sons have joined him. Their expertise lies in total and complete apartment renovations. Barry has a custom cabinet shop on the premises as well as a staff of laborers, tile people, an electrician, Formica specialists, painters, and wallpaper hangers.

BROOKE LOENING RENOVATIONS, INC.
(212) 517-5725 • $$ • Insured

A contracting company that has been in business for ten years. They have the capability to handle large or small jobs. They emphasize careful planning and execution of jobs with realistic budgets and time frames. Their interpersonal skills combined with their knowledge and expertise make them a good company to call.

BURR GRAAL GLASS • (212) 925-1016 • $$-$$$ • Insured

Howard Burr runs this quality, high-end contracting business. Burr specializes in bathroom and kitchen upgrades and renovations, painting, ceramic and marble work, floor scraping and refinishing. They are pleased to provide free estimates on any home improvement project.

HD CONTRACTING • (718) 331-2916 • $-$$ • Insured

Hector Diaz is a real find. He is talented, creative and timely. A few years from now he will be quite sought after so we suggest you hire him now.

RESHEFF INC. • (212) 533-3301 • $$ • Insured

Resheff is a family-owned husband and wife team that has been in business for 12 years. They do commercial and residential general construction, and work only on mid-to-larger sized projects. Resheff specializes in combining apartments, gut renovations, and kitchen and bath construction. What makes this an exceptional company is that the principals are very involved and detail-oriented. In fact, they visit the sites every day. They also give free estimates, complete projects on-time, and do not go over-budget.

RG RENOVATION SERVICES
(718) 972-7098 or Beep (917) 712-3471 • $$ • Insured

Ricardo Gomez's company performs quality custom work. They specialize in plastering, sheet rock, paint removal, wallpapering, floor scraping and refinishing, and tile installation.

SILVERLINING INTERIORS • (212) 496-7800 • $$ • Insured • $$$

Joshua Weiner has been provided top notch contracting services for over 13 years. He and his highly talented staff are reliable and talented. His work even comes with a one year guarantee. His minimum job truly depends upon how busy he is. Do not hesitate to call.

BARR JEFF COMPANY • (201) 436-4489

Jeff is a stand out among contractors. He is responsible, reliable and a perfectionist. In the ever-changing world of renovation, you can count on Jeff.

HEATING & AIR CONDITIONING

HAMILTON AIR • (212) 682-2710 • $$ • Insured

Always recommended by the large co-ops and condos in Manhattan. Call for your heating or air conditioning needs.

STANLEY RUTH COMPANY • (718) 993-4000 • $$• Insured

Experts in recommending and installing all types of air-conditioning and heating units.

KITCHEN/BATHROOM STOREFRONT DESIGN/CONTRACTORS

ELGOT
937 Lexington Avenue (68th and 69th Streets) • $$-$$$ (212) 879-1200 • Insured

Walk in off the street and take a look. They can do partial or total kitchen and bathroom renovations. They have on staff three kitchen/bath designers. There is no fee for their initial in-store con-sultation. If you want to go ahead they will come to your home and create a floor plan. The charge for the floor plan will be deducted off the price of the job.

HASTING
230 Park Avenue South (at 19th Street) • $$-$$$ (212) 674-9700 • Insured

Only do bathroom renovations. You can go to their storefront to speak with a designer. You will need to hire a contractor because they do not do installations.

ST. CHARLES KITCHENS
150 East 58th Street • $$-$$$ • (212) 838-2812 • Insured

St. Charles has been doing business for years and operates along the same lines as Elgot.

PAINTERS

New York is full of all types of painters–rental painters, co-op painters, artist painters – from which we provide a sampling. Be wary of the painter who says he can paint your two-bedroom apart-ment in one day.

GREGORY CRAMER • (914) 636-4393 • $-$$ • No Insurance

Gregory has a BFA from Carnegie-Mellon and specializes in painting murals and furniture. His enchanting Peter Rabbit and Alice in

Wonderland wall murals are simply the best and can often cost less than wallpaper. His work is not limited to children's designs only.

JEANNE MANZELLI • (860) 233-8777 • $-$$ • No Insurance

Jeanne is a fine artist painter and designer. She specializes in trompe l'oeil and mural painting for any type of apartment. Jeanne also does grain painting, marbleizing, and individually designed wall treatments. She is exceptionally talented in landscapes, animals, and whimsical designs. Jeanne usually charges by the job. Her first consultation is free, after which is a price structure. If you are interested, Jeanne can also teach you her technique

MARCO LUKSICH • (516) 883-4153 Beep: (917) 486-0437 • $-$$ • Insured

Marco is a warm, talented, and friendly house painter. He works mostly solo and his strength lies in clean, simple paint jobs.

MSR COLOR• (718) 384-5069 • $$• Insured

Mark Reynolds is a true artist at work. He has a great eye. If you are looking for wonderful artistic painting, he is your man.

ROBERTO MONTANO
(917) 748-1469 • (212) 722-0173 • $$$ • Insured

Roberto specializes in decorative and regular painting and wall paper. He also has a great eye for duplicating designs, and making your walls like new.

SMOLIN PAINTING CO., INC. • (212) 831-0205 • $$$ • Insured

Ira Smolin has been a residential painting contractor for 17 years. Known for his methodical and meticulous work, Ira will not look down on small jobs, like painting a single room or papering a bathroom. If you require decorative painting, his partner, Marat Kadyrov, does glazing, marbling, gold leafing, and trompe l'oeil.

PLUMBERS

Plumbing problems in New York can be a nightmare. These two companies have a good reputation and have the ability to respond quickly.

FRED SMITH • (212) 744-1300 • $$-$$$ • Insured

A reputable and large plumbing company, they handle the plumbing needs of many condos and co-ops in New York.

J. BARONE & CO. INC.
414 East 116th Street • (212) 722-4666 • $$-$$$ • Insured

They have been serving New York for over thirty years and do a good job.

PORCELAIN BATHROOM REFINISHER

One of the charms of New York is our prewar buildings with all their wonderful architectural detail and those fabulous old bathrooms. Well, sometimes those bathrooms need some sprucing up and it can be done simply and rather inexpensively.

DURA-GLOSS • (516) 225-7213 • $$ • Insured

Tom Peck started his company eight years ago. His reglazing process includes a chemical cleansing, acid wash, any minor repairs, three coats of primer, three coats of color, and two coats of clear finish. He gives a two-year unconditional guarantee.

NEW YORK PORCELAIN • (718) 380-8952 • $$ • Insured

They can repair and reglaze all the porcelain in your bathroom, including the bathtub, sink/vanity and tile. Their process is similar to that used by Dura-Gloss.

REFACING KITCHEN CABINETS

BARRY FISCSHELBERG • (718) 658-0192 • $$ • Insured

Not only is Barry a great contractor but he also has a cabinet shop on his premises. He has the ability to change your cabinets.

RE-FACE N.Y.
1645 First Avenue (85th and 86th Streets)
(212) 517-4200 • $ • Insured

This company specializes in kitchen cabinet refacing, and also works with counters, doors, tiles, floors and bathrooms. They supply and install materials and provide free in-home consultations. The owner, George, is very accommodating and easy to work with.

SEARS • (800) 888-0224 • $-$$ • Insured

A professional designer/consultant from Sears will come to you for a free hour to hour and a half at-home visit. They will take measurements and provide you with samples. Depending on material availability, jobs generally take no more than one week.

TILE AND MARBLE WORK

JOHN ADAMIA • (718) 531-8119 • $$ • Insured

Works on ceramic tile, marble, and granite. He does excellent work. Laying stone is quite difficult and if it is done poorly, it really looks bad. So hire John.

TONY GILBERTO • (212) 533-6315 • $$

Great sense of design. Beautiful work!

UPHOLSTERY AND WINDOW TREATMENTS

ABC CARPET AND HOME
888 Broadway (19th Street) • (212) 473-3000 • $$$ • Insured

ABC has an extensive selection of fabrics and drapery hardware. Although they offer no decorator advice, they will, for a fee, come to your home to take measurements. The price that they quote you for your window treatments includes fabric, labor, and installation.

DIAMANT
324 East 59th Street (First and Second)
(212) 754-1155 • $ Insured

They work with many designers and consistently produce high quality work. They also do upholstered headboards and slipcovers.

EMPIRE SEATING
79 Delancey Street (Orchard and Allen)
(718) 625-2993 • $$ • Insured

Empire can customize sofas, chairs, and other upholstered furniture according to your needs.

FORSYTH STREET DECORATORS
100 Forsyth Street • (212) 226-3624 • $$ • Insured

The workmanship is top-notch here. Katalin Spierer and her two sons can perform miracles with upholstery and window treatments for much less than you would pay elsewhere. They can upholster wicker furniture and make plasticized fabric seats for outdoor furniture; Naugahyde and vinyl seat covers and cushions are a subspecialty. They can also expertly mount needlepoint pillows.

GRACIOUS HOME
1217 Third Avenue (70th Street) • (212) 988-8990

Gracious Home offers ready-made curtain panels in a range of fabrics, as well as a custom department for style and fabric advice and installation. They also have an excellent assortment of drapery hardware and replacement parts.

LE DÉCOR FRANCAIS
1006 Lexington Avenue (72nd and 73rd Streets)
$$$ (212) 734-0032 • Insured

They use many fabrics from France and Italy. They will come to your home to give you an estimate regarding the project. They also do slipcovers.

MARTIN ALBERT • 9 East 19th Street • (212) 673-8000 • $$
Some of the best workmanship in the city. You cannot go wrong.

NO MORE EGGS
312 East Ninth Street • (212) 777-0393 • $ • Insured

Gale Kessler owns and runs this store filled with lovely home decor items, such as picture frames, vases, candleholders, decorative pillows—the list goes on and on. She is skilled at fashioning curtains and linens, and would be happy to customize simple tab or rod pocket curtains, a duvet cover, tablecloth, or throw pillows with your fabric or fabric from her store. Gale charges $50 for a two hour minimum consultation if you need her to come to your home.

RICHARDS INTERIOR DESIGN
1390 Lexington Avenue (91st and 92nd Streets)
(212) 831-9000 • $$ • Insured

They offer many fabric and style choices, and can upholster for all your needs.

VERSAILLES DRAPERY AND UPHOLSTERY
(212) 533-2059 • $$-$$$ • Insured

A family-run business for over thirty years. The finest custom upholstery work that we have seen in New York City. They have a wonderful eye for material, color, design, and fit. This expertise does not come cheap but when you have spent money on fabric you want the job to be done right and to last. They specialize in restoring eighteenth-century original furniture, as well as making any new piece of upholstered furniture you might want; and it does not cost as much as you might think.

WALLPAPER

JANE SILLERY • (212) 865-0846

One of the best in the city. She has a reputation for being able to match every seam and fit every corner.

WINDOWS

When walking down the street it seems that scaffolding is always over our heads, being set up for new window installation. New windows can dramatically cut down on the noise of the City.

PANORAMA WINDOW • (212) 489-6400 • $$ • Insured

Doug Simpson is a reliable, hardworking man who deals with the installation of one new window with the same diligence as he does for an entire building. He tells you all your realistic options, explaining the possible mess and repair work that you will encounter. He is also extremely aware if your new windows will not accommodate your existing window treatment.

WINDOW GLASS
ABALONE GLASS • (212) 744-0556 • $ • Insured
They work with all types of glass for table tops as well as windows.

HOME RENOVATING SOFTWARE PROGRAMS

The latest high-tech software programs will allow you to visualize a renovation of your home, and you don't even have to move one piece of furniture. You should find out the minimum system requirements of each software package before purchasing one. Some of the more sophisticated 3D programs run best on a fast Pentium machine. Prices will fluctuate depending on whether you purchase directly from the manufacturer or through a discount re-seller, but most run between $50 to $200.

Floor Plan Plus 3D
Turbo CAD • IMSI • (800) 833-4674

www.imsisoft.com

Key Cad Pro, Landscape Architect, My House
The Learning Company • (800) 227-5609

www.learningco.com

Land Designer • Sierra On-Line • (206) 649-9800

www.sierra.com

Landscape Design 3D, Quick and Easy CAD
Expert Software • (800) 759-2562

www.expertsoftware.com

The Reader's Digest Complete Do-It-Yourself Guide
The Reader's Digest Association • (800) 310-4361

www.readersdigest.com

Smart CAD • Wiz Technology Inc. • (714) 443-3000

www.wiztech.com

3D Home Architect • Broderbund Software Inc.• (415) 382-4400

www.broderbund.com

THE INTREPID PAGES OF
HOME RENOVATING/ REDECORATING STORES

APPLIANCES, MAJOR

It is possible to buy large appliances in the New York area for a discount, but it is not always a pleasant experience. So be sure that you know exactly what you want and that you get everything in writing. You can get an idea of what you want by looking at the more expensive stores.

CIRCUIT CITY • LOCATIONS THROUGHOUT

They have good prices on all major appliances, TV's, VCR, stereos and computers. They deliver and install.

DEMBITZER BROTHERS • 5 Essex Street • (212) 254-1310

A great discount shop that sells all major brand-name appliances. They do not install but will recommend a company that does.

ELGOT APPLIANCES
937 Lexington Avenue (67th and 68th St.)• (212) 879-1200

For full service shopping go to Elgot. Their storefront shop has a great display of most kitchen appliances. They deliver and install as well as maintain a good repair department.

HOME SALES DIAL-A-DISCOUNT • (212) 513-1513

All you have to do for this service is make a phone call. You need to know the exact make and model number of your item. You certainly should check the price here before you go elsewhere. They sell air conditioners, major kitchen appliances, trash compactors, TVs, and VCRs.

P.C. RICHARD
120 14th Street (at Union Square) • (212) 979-2600
205 East 86th Street (Second & Third Avenues) • (212) 348-1287

Great buys on small and large appliances. They will install the appliance and cart away the old one. The selection is good and the staff is very helpful. Delivery service is available.

ARCHITECTURAL DETAIL SHOPS

Even if you are renovating a modern apartment, you still have the option to add some old-world detail.

URBAN ARCHAEOLOGY
143 Franklin Street • (212) 431-4646 • 285 Lafayette Street (212) 431-6969

In this 50,000-square foot shop you will find items that date back 150 years. Because of the large space they have set up entire rooms filled with bookcases, fireplace mantels, pool tables, and even brick facing.

DECORATIVE HARDWARE

When renovating we find it can be the little "things" that are hard to find but that ultimately make a big aesthetic difference. You can find just the right doorknob, furniture handles, or closet pull if you know where to go.

THE BRASS CENTER • 248 East 58th Street • (212) 421-0090

Here you can find good quality door handles and knobs. Items are displayed on eye level sliding panels so it is easy to find what you are looking for.

GRACIOUS HOME
1220 Third Avenue (at 71st Street) • (212) 517-6300

Floor-to-ceiling display panels offers a huge choice of decorative hardware, including knobs and hooks in the shape of animals and period pieces, such as tiny porcelain tassel knobs.

KRAFT HARDWARE • 306 East 61st Street • (212) 838-2214

A wonderfully stocked, decorative supply store that deals mostly with the trade. They have an extensive selection of doorknobs, hinges, hooks, and handles, and don't forget to look at their display of faucets, shower heads, vanities, sinks, tubs, etc.

MACKENZIE-CHILDS LTD.
940 Madison Avenue (74th Street) • (212) 879-5178

This whimiscle store sells decorative hardware, ceramic bowls, platters and other tableware, kitchen and bath accessories such as tiles and sinks, unique furniture. It's well worth a visit!

SIMON'S HARDWARE & BATH
421 Third Avenue (29th and 30th Streets) • (212) 532-9220

They have a complete, extensive selection of decorative hardware such as doorknobs, handles, switch plates, house numbers, closet pulls, and decorative trim, as well as a commercial department that sells architectural hardware and equipment. Best of all, you will find many types of professional laborers who buy at Simon's. Don't be shy—get their card and check them out.

FLOOR COVERING
ABC CARPET AND HOME
888 Broadway (at 19th Street) • (212) 473-3000

We have looked around and when all is said and done, you really can't go wrong with ABC. Their prices and choices are good and if you appeal to their human side you can even get good service and samples. Remember: Some buildings in New York City require you to carpet a portion of your apartment.

EINSTEIN MOOMJY • 150 East 58th Street • (212) 758-0900

Einstein stocks a varied assortment of area rugs and wall-to-wall carpeting. The prices are not cheap, but the service is top-notch.

LANES FLOOR COVERING
2 Park Avenue South • (212) 532-5200

A full selection of floor covering including all resilient flooring. They also retain their own installers and thereby have total control over the installation.

TILES
A REFINED SELECTION • 42 West 15th Street • (212) 255-4450

Here you will probably find the largest selection of ceramic tile in New York City. They carry everything from plain, ordinary four-by-four-inch white tile to hand-painted tile from Europe. You can commission them to create any design you want.

COUNTRY FLOORS • 15 East 16th Street • (212) 627-8300

Here you will find a gorgeous selection of ceramic and terra-cotta tiles from all over the world. Their prices are high, but their selection is great. If you bring them a floor plan they can help you arrange a design. They don't install but they do provide you with a list of installers.

M&K TILES • (718) 388-4466

Custom tiles by design. If you are looking for the unique, you have found the source. They can custom design tiles for all your decorating needs.

FURNITURE

The following list is made up of furniture stores that are well-priced.

APARTMENT LIVING • 12 West 21st Street • (212) 260-5050

They stock the catalogues of all the major American furniture makers and encourage you to spend time looking through them. After that you should spend time in the major department stores looking at similar furniture. Once you see what you like go back to Apartment Living. They usually can beat any price you have seen.

They say they are not in the business of helping you decide, but our experience is that they are very helpful.

THE BOMBAY COMPANY
Locations Throughout the City • (800) 829-7789

If you are in search of furnishings that reflect your appreciation for the finer things in life, rather than your ability to spend money, go to The Bombay Company. There you will discover elegant furniture and accessories that are not expensive. They make wonderful reproductions and sell them at more than reasonable prices. Their furniture is shipped in a compact package and is easily assembled.

CRATE & BARREL • 650 Madison Avenue • (212) 308-0011

Where did we shop for furniture before Crate & Barrel came to town. Great designs, wonderful customer service and good prices.

FREDERICK BED CENTRAL • 107 East 31st Street • (212) 683-8322

FBC is the only custom bed-maker left in Manhattan. Go there to for a custom water bed, a custom-shaped bed, a new mattress and box spring for an antique or European bed frame, or a bed called the "short king," a popular model that fits into the average cramped City apartment. Prices are reasonable and the staff is courteous, friendly, and helpful.

IKEA
Elizabeth, New Jersey • (908) 289-4488
Hicksville, Long Island • (516) 681-4532 • Call for directions

We can't say enough about IKEA, the Swedish-owned chain. Not only have we used it in our office but also in our home. A "clean," inexpensive, and when not crowded a fairly painless approach to furnishings and cabinetry. The staff tries hard to be accommodating but they are not supposed to hold your hand every step of the way. They sell furniture and other merchandise such as fabric, dishes, sheets, flooring, and more. Be prepared to walk around with a pen, paper, and measuring tape because it is up to you to write down the order number, color, and measurements of each item that you want to buy. Delivery is available. Depending on where you live in Manhattan, the cost is about $90, and you can choose the day that you want (but of course not the time). They are equipped with a full restaurant, play area for children, and rest rooms. There are only two drawbacks: (1) locations—you must either go by car, by bus to New Jersey (leaves from the Port Authority), or by train to Long Island (leaves from Penn Station); and (2) assembly—if you really aren't good with your hands you will have to find someone to assemble your purchases. For help, look in our carpentry section.

THE PACE COLLECTION
11-11 34th Avenue (11th Street), Long Island City • (718) 721-8201

At this location which houses their executive offices, one floor has been turned into an outlet center. This is where the floor models usually end up, along with other samples and some damaged goods. You can find a good selection of furniture at the outlet, and the savings are worth the trip out of Manhattan. Delivery can be arranged.

THE POTTERY BARN • Locations through out

Pottery Barn has sure come a long way from selling great glass-ware and plates. They carry an upscale line of well priced furniture.

TECHLINE • 35 East 19th St. • 212 674-1813

If you are looking for a way to design tight living spaces, you must visit Techline. Their furniture systems work great for NY apartments.

FURNITURE AT AUCTION HOUSES

An offbeat, fun way to find truly unique pieces at affordable prices is to attend auctions. Here are some recommended auction houses outside of Manhattan. See the shopping chapter for those located in the City.

COLD SPRING GALLERIES
324 Main Street, Beacon, NY • (914) 831-6800

GEORGE COLE AUCTIONEERS & APPRAISERS
53 North Broadway, Suite 6, Red Hook, NY • (914) 876-5215

MARK VAIL AUCTION CO.
Kelly Avenue, Pine Bush, NY • (914) 744-2120

WILLIAM J. JENACK ESTATE APPRAISERS & AUCTIONEERS
37 Elkay Drive, Chester, NY • (914) 469-9095

RECOMMENDED PAPERS

ART & ANTIQUES NORTHEAST • (800) 274-7594

ANTIQUES & AUCTION NEWS • (717) 653-1833

ANTIQUES & THE ARTS WEEKLY • (203) 426-8036

THE HUDSON VALLEY ANTIQUER • (914) 876-8766

NEW ENGLAND ANTIQUES JOURNAL • (413) 967-3505

TREASURE CHEST • (212) 496-2234

THE WESTERN CONNECTICUT & WESTERN MASSACHUSETTS ANTIQUER • (800) 325-3854

FURNITURE RENTAL

If you find yourself in a temporary housing situation, it may pay for you to rent, instead of buy, furniture. These two rental facilities can outfit your entire apartment—whether it be a studio apartment or a deluxe Park Avenue townhouse—with furniture, electronics, pictures, rugs, and lamps. They both offer showroom quality, high-end items and impeccable service. The price of the rental will depend on the size of your home and the length of the rental period. Both have on sight designers to help you with floor plans and designs. If the items are in stock, delivery can be within 48 hours.

> FOR BUDGET SHOPPING, VISIT THE TINY SHOPS ON THE 300 BLOCK OF EAST NINTH STREET. HERE YOU CAN DISCOVER ALL TYPES OF FURNITURE, FROM 18TH CENTURY-STYLE, TO HAND-CANED CHAIRS. ALSO DO NOT MISS THE ARRAY OF SHOPS ON BRUCKNER BOULEVARD IN THE BRONX.

CORT-AFR FURNITURE RENTAL
711 Third Avenue (44th and 45th Streets) • (212) 867-2800

A well designed showroom filled with a wide range of choices.

INTERNATIONAL FURNITURE RENTALS
345 Park Avenue (51st Street) • (212) 421-0340

You can view their furniture on line at www.rent-ifr.com.

FURNITURE TOO BIG TO MOVE

Moving large pieces into an apartment with narrow hallways and doors can be a real problem. We have found some sources to help you.

AUER MOVING • (212) 427-7800

One of the few moving companies that can arrange to hoist your furniture through the window.

P. NATHAN CRAFTSMAN • 304 East 94th Street • (212) 722-3643

P. Nathan can make you a couch and best of all they might be able to cut yours in half to get it through the door.

TELESCA-HEYMAN • 304 East 94th Street • (212) 534-3442

If you have a piece of wooden furniture that is too large to fit either in the elevator or through your door call these people. They might be able to cut the piece and then reassemble it once it is inside your apartment.

KITCHEN SHELVING

EMPIRE RESTAURANT SUPPLY
114 Bowery (near Grand Street) • (212) 226-4447

Empire makes custom shelving and tables for many of the City's top restaurants, and will customize shelving for your kitchen as well.

Units can be precut to fit even the most irregular kitchen space. Empire quotes wholesale prices to anyone who walks in off the street.

LAMINATION

Sometimes it is a good idea to Scotchguard or laminate your fabric, especially if you have children.

CUSTOM LAMINATIONS
932 Market Street, Paterson, New Jersey • (201) 279-9174

They can laminate most types of fabric and it can all be done by mail.

LAMP SHADES

We found that a lamp shade can make all the difference in bringing out the beauty in a lamp.

JUST SHADES
21 Spring Street (at Elizabeth Street) • (212) 966-2757

A great selection of ready-made shades and if you can't find what you want they will make it for you.

RUTH VITOW INC. • 155 East 56th Street • (212) 355-6616

This company has been around for ages. All their shades are customized according to your needs. Because it is a "trade only" store, you must go there with a decorator or designer.

UNIQUE LAMPSHADES • 247 East 77th Street • (212) 472-1140

Ron has the best eye in New York for deciding what shade works with what lamp. Don't be surprised when sometimes a custom-made shade doesn't cost more than a ready-made one. For a small fee he will come to your home to inspect your lamps and shades.

LIGHTS AND LIGHT BULBS

Your best bet for both antique and contemporary fixtures is the lighting district on the Bowery. You won't be disappointed by the trip downtown because the selection is tremendous. Don't buy in the first place you visit and always bargain.

JUST BULBS
936 Broadway (21st and 22nd Streets) • (212) 228-7820

For the best selection of light bulbs.

LIGHTING BY GREGORY
158 Bowery (Delancey and Broome Streets) • (212) 226-1276

One of our favorites.

LUMBERYARDS

Many people seem surprised to find out that New York City has a number of lumberyards. If you're "handy" you can certainly save a bundle by doing any carpentry yourself. The best part about these yards is that they not only sell raw wood, but they can also get you all types of doors, shutters, and premade cabinets. By going straight to the yard you may be able to save money by cutting out the middleman. It's worth a try.

CITY LUMBER • 517 West 42nd Street • (212) 695-0380

Knowledgeable and friendly, they seem to know exactly what you need and the tools that will help you. A well-stocked yard with a delivery service.

DYKES LUMBER • 348 West 44th Street • (212) 246-6480

Dykes carries a wide range of decorative lumber supplies. If you are a novice in picking out the "right molding" they are quite helpful and will give you samples to take home. Delivery service is prompt.

LE NOBEL • 525 West 52nd Street • (212) 246-0050

This lumber yard caters to the movie business so along with the traditional supplies they carry a large variety of unusual foam, plywood, and woods.

PRINCE LUMBER
75 Ninth Avenue (15th and 16th Streets) • (212) 777-1150

Another excellent source for your wood needs. Some items such as shutters would need to be ordered, as they do not stock them there. Delivery service is available.

METAL PLATING

You would be surprised at how much better your hinges and doorknobs look when they have been treated and polished.

HYGRADE POLISHING & PLATING COMPANY • (718) 392-4082

MIRRORS, WINDOW SHADES, SHOWER DOORS

CENTURY MIRROR AND GLASS CORP.
213 Fordham Street, City Island • (718) 885-1666

This shop deals mostly with the trade, but sometimes they do work for the individual. They do incredible work with glass and mirrors. They can make everything from tables to countertops.

MANHATTAN SHADE & GLASS
1299 Third Avenue • (212) 288-5616

A great selection of hard and soft window treatment as well as glass and mirror work.

THE POOR TRASH DOOR & SASH CO. • (516) 862-6659

Steve Marsh makes distinctive, decorative windowpane mirrors made out of old window sashes, some of which come from Universal Studios' sets, given to Steve when he was a tour guide. The panes are replaced by glass, and the frames are finished to retain an authentic antique look. An 18"x22" frame costs $55. His less expensive line called "Great Panes" are designed with contemporary window panes. An 18"x22" frame sells for $35. Steve can customize a frame with artwork and a special finish. He also offers mirrors that are designed with shelves or window boxes.

STANLEY SCHOEN
1693 First Avenue (between 87th and 88th Streets)
(212) 369-0320

You can find cheaper places in town but certainly not better workmanship. They are reliable and accommodating. Mirrors installed, glass tabletops, or protective glass for your tables, tub enclosures, window shade treatments, picture framing, and more. Free estimates.

SUNDIAL SCHWARTZ
1582 First Avenue (82nd and 83rd Streets) • (212) 717-4207

A lot of their work is done with architects and contractors, but David Greenspan will consult with you in your home on wall mirrors, glass tops, mirrored bars, splash-backs, or any other mirror or glass use in the home. They can create a variety of design enhancements, such as antique finishes and floral patterns. They can install wall mirrors and replace medicine cabinet mirrors. Estimates are free.

NATURAL STONE YARD

New York does have everything—even a marble yard. If you are in the market to buy any natural stone you should always see the entire slab and not just one small piece. Stone varies widely in color, shade, and grain.

FORDHAM MARBLE
1931 West Farms Road, the Bronx • (718) 893-3380

It is a great place to go if you are buying stone. They show you all the slabs that are currently available and if you like one they reserve it for you. A full-service operation in that they give you advice, arrange for the floor plan, and do the installation.

PAINT STORES

Paint brands do differ so beware. We happen to like Benjamin Moore. Be careful when choosing a finish—make sure you understand what it will look like when it has dried.

DELMO PAINTS
1641 York Avenue (at 87th Street) • (212) 722-7797

A great small supplier of Benjamin Moore and Paragon paints. They have a good attitude and a great sense of color if you ask their opinion. Their computer seems to do a very accurate color mix. No minimum order is necessary for free same-day delivery up to 3:00 P.M.

JANOVIC/PLAZA
1150 Third Avenue (at 67th Street) • (212) 772-1400
Other Locations Throughout the City

They carry a wide selection of name brands as well as their own, and have a great selection of equipment that you will need if you are doing the painting. If you spend a minimum of $50, there is a $5 delivery charge. Delivery is next-day service.

PEARL PAINT
308 Canal Street (Broadway and Church Street) • (212) 431-7932

A large selection of paints and equipment. Free delivery service is available for orders over $200. For orders less than $200, they offer a $13.50 messenger service or the option to send your items via UPS.

PICTURE FRAMING

FILM AND FRAME CITY
6 Dorchester Avenue, New City • (212) 472-2781

Larry is one of the best kept secrets in New York. He never forgets a face or a frame. Although Larry's store is outside New York City, he will come to your apartment to determine what kind of frame you will need. This personal service is exceptional because not only can Larry see what needs to be framed, he can also see where the picture will be hung. Larry only manufactures custom frames; he does not supply stock frames. He also has a picture hanging service, and can restore old photographs and artwork

PLUMBING PARTS

NEW YORK REPLACEMENT PARTS
1464 Lexington Avenue (94th and 95th Streets) • (212) 534-0818

A real find in a city where your plumbing parts can take you back to early 1900's. Best bet is to bring in your old part and see if they can replace it. Also a wonderful source for contemporary fixtures.

UPHOLSTERY FABRIC

Fabrics vary greatly in color, style, quality, and price. Shop around before you make any decisions. You can find fabric for $3.99 a yard and you can find fabric for $399 a yard. We always advise our clients to think about how the furniture will be used. For example, if you have young children you might want to hold off on buying very expensive fabric until the kids are older. (Three stores, listed below, opened on Orchard Street in 1998 and offer an extensive selection of fabric at fairly reasonable prices, generally between $25 and $45 a yard.)

BARSOUV
91 Orchard Street (corner of Broome Street) • (212) 925-3400

Barsouv's specialty is exotic fabrics from Spain, Morocco, Egypt, and India. An upholsterer and drapery maker is on the premises and decorating house calls are free.

BECKENSTEIN FABRICS
130 Orchard Street (Delancey and Rivington) • (212) 475-4887

An ample collection of fabrics in an easy-to-see display can be found at Beckenstein.

HARRY ZARIN CO.
72 Allen Street (corner of Grand Street) • (212) 925-6112

Great buys on close-outs of designer fabrics. Though the store is well laid out you will have to spend some time looking through the thousands of yards of fabrics. The staff is well informed and helpful.

HERMES • 45 West 34th Street • (212) 947-1153

Leather abounds here! Great for covering walls, sofas, chairs, and more.

INTERCOASTAL TEXTILE CORPORATION
480 Broadway (Broome and Grand Streets) • (212) 925-9235

A great place to go for closeouts of designer decorative fabric. Bring your lunch and plan to spend some time looking around.

JOE'S FABRICS AND TRIMMINGS
102 Orchard Street (Delancey Street) • (212) 674-7089

This shop has 4,000 square feet of fabrics, trimmings, and tassels. It also has a warehouse shop next door.

LAURA ASHLEY
398 Columbus Avenue (at 79th Street) • (212) 496-5110

This location has both clothing and home furnishings—wallpapers, lamps, furniture, and fabrics. They do a great job coordinating everything.

LE DECOR FRANCAIS
1006 Lexington Avenue (72nd Street) • (212) 734-0032

If you want beautiful European fabrics and trim without going with a decorator you must go to Le Decor Francais. This is a full-service store; they will go to your home, look at your furniture, and then recommend fabric choices and design possibilities.

PIERRE DEUX
870 Madison Avenue (at 71st Street) • (212) 570-9343

French country fabrics and furniture. The fabrics have wonderful patterns and color. They also do upholstery.

THE RAG SHOP
200 Mill Creek Drive, Secaucus, New Jersey • (201) 867-5010

If you are looking for a primary source for first-quality decorative fabrics as well as trims and accessories at better than wholesale prices, this is the place. They sell Waverly, Woodridge, Concord, Covington, and more. Average price per yard is $12.99, and when on sale $9.75.

RALPH LAUREN
867 Madison Avenue (at 72nd Street) • (212) 606-2100

His complete line of fabrics can be ordered at this main store.

RICHARDS INTERIOR DESIGN
1390 Lexington Avenue (91st and 92nd Streets) • (212) 831-9000

They sell Robert Allen, Kravet, Waverly, and many more designer fabrics at a discount. A full-service store that can handle all your upholstery needs at a good price.

SILK SURPLUS • 235 East 58th Street • (212) 753-6511

This store is owned by Scalamandre and sells their discontinued fabrics to the retail customer. A great way to buy excellent-quality goods that the consumer normally could not get himself.

UPHOLSTERY/WINDOW DRESSING SUPPLIES

BZI DISTRIBUTORS CORP.
105 Eldridge Street (Grand and Broome Streets)
(212) 966-6690

Wonderful prices can be found in this friendly and accommodating store. They have a large selection of drapery hardware, upholstery supplies, trimmings, foam rubber, blinds, and more.

M & J TRIMMING CO.
1008 Avenue of the Americas (37th and 38th Streets)
(212) 391-9072

The best source for braid, rope, cord, and other ties that can be used on upholstered furniture and window treatments.

VAN WYCK WINDOW FASHIONS
21-27 Borden Avenue, Long Island City • (718) 482-6666

This is the store for the do-it-yourself person and the prices are great on tie backs, poles, finials, rods, and brackets. They will deliver to Manhattan if you set up an account.

WALLPAPER

Before you begin, don't forget you can be creative and use some floor covering for your walls. When looking for wallpaper, be aware that most of the time it must be ordered and that you need to know the amount of rolls that you need. We suggest you get an extra one or two rolls, just in case you have a leak or a rip. Kitchen paper should always be washable! Also bring any color swatches, fabric samples, etc. that you are trying to work with. At best, you will be able to tear off a small piece to bring home as a sample.

GLOBAL WALLCOVERING • By mail: (800) 521-0650

Call Global to check on the price. You need to know the title of the book, pattern/style number, retail price, and amount you need. They take credit cards over the phone.

GRACIOUS HOME
1217 Third Avenue (70th Street) • (212) 988-8990

This store operates in a similar way to Janovic, but does not stock wallpaper at the store.

JANOVIC/ PLAZA
1150 Third Avenue (at 67th Street) • (212) 772-1400
161 Sixth Avenue (at Spring Street) • (212) 627-1100
159 West 72nd Street • (212) 595-2500
Other Locations Throughout the City

They have many wallpaper books to look through so be prepared to spend some time browsing. They deal with various designer papers such as Schumacher, Waverly, Kinney, and more. If the paper is in stock at the manufacturer you should be able to get it in a few days. They do stock a good selection of wallpaper in the store at decent prices.

THE SUBURBS DECIPHERED

PERCEPTION VS. REALITY

The tri-state suburban areas of Connecticut, New York and New Jersey encompass a 75mile radius around Manhattan. Plain and simple, it's vast, and physically cut off from city limits by bridges, tunnels and highways. The commute "to and from" will take no less than ½ hour and up to 1¾ hours depending on how far out you live. Typically, New Yorkers don't move out to the suburbs until they have children, and are in need of more square footage and a back-yard, which creates distinct, family-focused culture. Our burbs are a combination of bedroom communities, charming villages and New England-style rural living. Because most of our communities were well established decades ago, new construction and development in most areas is sparse compared to other parts of the country. In terms of lifestyle, social focus and community feel—options are unlimited, literally. There is a neighborhood for new age artists as well as a society dame. Our communities are also some of the most culturally rich in the nation due to their proximity to NYC.

The sheer size of the tri-state area requires proper guidance, infor-mation and strategy for narrowing the field and zeroing in on these communities which are the best match for you, your family, your lifestyle, and your needs.

- **The first complication is choice**—three states and hundreds of viable suburbs in each that are all within commuting distance of the city.

- **The second complication is our high cost of living**—our housing and real estate taxes are some of the most expensive in the nation, particularly in those towns that have coveted public schools, a better commute, waterfront homes or a socially impor-tant "address".

- **The third are the dramatic variables, area to area,** in terms of cost of housing, taxes, quality of schools, length of the door-to-door commute, culture and social focus.

SOLUTIONS:

Our tri-state quality of life is very different from those in smaller cities such as Minneapolis or Dallas, for example; our housing is much more expensive, our suburbs more populated and the commute longer and more stressful. What we do share here is one of the most culturally fascinating metropolises in the world, with world class pursuits and opportunities, as well as a culturally and professionally diverse population. Those of us who have made trade-offs in order to incorporate that culture into our daily lives have done it with our eyes wide-open and without regret.

The most important first step is to make two separate lists:

Your wish list: for schools, ideal commute, style of housing, housing budget, lifestyle and community focus.

Your "must have" list, vs. what you are willing to trade-off list: This list will allow you to manage your own expectations for relocating to our suburbs, so you don't get stuck holding out for an impossible dream.

SOLUTIONS:
INFORMATION TO GUIDE YOU THROUGH
SOUTHERN CONNECTICUT

FAIRFIELD — THE COMMUTABLE COUNTY

Think New England - rolling hills, stone fences, charming villages, grand estates and antique colonials. Then, add lots of water - on Fairfield County's Eastern shore line— the Long Island Sound, a tributary of the Atlantic, creates a beach community and culture; inland, the Connecticut River meanders in and around homes and towns, and lakes and swimming holes seem to be everywhere. Think affluent. There are towns in which descendants of families from the Mayflower live in understated elegance, towns with a sophisticated, international population and towns for the "young and hip who commute to their jobs at New Media companies. Not least is the county's famous "Gold Coast," including Greenwich, Darien and New Canaan, in which Fortune 500 CEOs and celebrities reside.

Population: 829,800

Area: 659.1 square miles and 23 towns

Housing: Expensive; but some moderately priced communities are available. If you are looking for "address" in the Gold Coast, an above average, older, four bedroom home starts at $700,000. New construction starts at $1,000,000. If you want acreage, lots of square footage and the finest amenities, in the millions. However, there are wonderful communities such as Rowayton, Norwalk, Stamford, Trumbull and Danbury where properties can be found for substantially less—starting at about $350,000 and above.

Real estate taxes: High, but not as high as Westchester County, NY or Bergen County, NJ - $4,500-12,000

Commuting by car:

If you are going to drive into the city, you have a choice of two main highways — I 95 and The Merritt Parkway into the Hutchinson River Parkway to the East Side. But expect a 40-minute drive with no traffic, and 1 1/2 hours depending on rush hour traffic and how far north in the County you live.

Commuting by train:

The commuter train is called Metro North — The New Haven Line; it's air conditioned, comfortable and extremely efficient, especially if you live in a town that's on the line. It runs constantly to and from Grand Central Station which is located on Manhattan's eastside at 42nd street and Lexington Avenue. The initial hurdle is the potential waiting list for a parking slot at your station. For more information about Metro North, call 212-532-4900 or 800-METRO-INFO.

Schools – Private:

There are any number of excellent private and parochial schools to choose from. For some internationals, there is also "The German School" in Weston. Here's how to access the information:

Connecticut Association of Independent Schools (CAIS): Peter Tacy Is Executive Director and can answer your questions. They will also send you a booklet called *A Parents Guide To Independent Schools In Connecticut*. Call them at 860-572-2950.

The Independent Educational Consultants Association (IECA): If you are in need of a consultant, they provide a high quality service which is nationally recognized. 1-800-808-IECA

The Educational Records Bureau: The student testing center most used by private schools. They will also provide educational consulting for a free. Associated Director, Lucille Porter is happy to answer your questions. (212) 672 9800

One-stop shopping for independent school information on the web: EDUFAX: www.tiac.net/users/edufax/isl.state.AtoE.html

Schools – Public:

Most are good to nationally acclaimed, and part of a high-achieving system, and there are many ways to access the information you need:

Contact the local school district in which you have interest. They will send you general information about curriculum, statistics and state test results. In addition you can get the Connecticut State Department Of Education's Annual Strategic School District Profile (SSP Report) which includes Student/District Characteristics, School Resources, Facilities and Equipment and Student Performance.

Contact The State Of Connecticut PTA: Office Manager, Ida Carmichael, can refer you to the PTA heads in your district. 203-281-6617. Deborah Walsh is the state PTA Regional Coordinator for Fairfield County.

Contact The National School Reporting Service: For A $25 Annual Fee, the service will give you school district information such as demographics, class size, student/teacher ratio, specific strengths, and test scores. 1-800-229-4992.

Special Education:

"The Cooperative Educational Services" is a public school regional education center servicing districts In Fairfield County. The goal is to enhance the quality of special education in developmental learning, therapeutic day programs, preschool learning, and extended school day programs. They will evaluate your child and help identify appropriate programs. You can contact Anthony Maida, Director of Special Education. 203-365-8837. You can also contact IECA (above) for consultants who are skilled in special education needs.

One stop shopping for public school information on the web: CT Dept of Education website: www.state.ct.us.sde/strategicschoolprofiles

SCHOOLS – PAROCHIAL:

Connecticut—Fairfield

The Catholic Center • (203) 372-4301
Office of Education
Directory of Education Services
The Catholic Center
238 Jewett Avenue
Bridgeport, CT 06606
www.diobptctofe.com

Recreation:

From coastal to cultural, Fairfield County and environs has it all and they really know how to serve it up. Cultural opportunities from regional theatre and concerts to museums and performance art, the opportunities are world class. Connecticut towns particularly rich in offerings are Westport, Bridgeport, Norwalk and Stamford. And if you want to be physical, you don't have to join a club to kayak, hike, sail, fish, wind surf, play golf, play tennis, or ride horses. For more information and brochures:

The Coastal Fairfield County District Tourism Office: FAX 203-854-7825

The Fairfield Chamber of Commerce: 203-255-1011

Your local Department of Recreation, Chamber of Commerce, Town Hall, Library and YMCA

One-stop shopping web site: www.fairfieldweekly.com

Publications that can be found at the library, children's stores, YMCA's etc.:

Connecticut Family – free

Fairfield County Kids – free

Connecticut Magazine – Newsstands or $18 subscription

Eldercare resources:

There are a few key "help line" resources to access information about doctors, at-home care services, nursing homes, adult day care, physical therapy services, senior centers, even continuing education for seniors:

Infoline — www.ctunitedway.org – Connecticut's "First Call for Help". At 211 from Connecticut or (860) 571-7500, a free, round-the-clock, telephone information, referral, advocacy and crises helpline, which is a service of the Connecticut United Ways in partnership with the State of Connecticut. One of the many services for which they provide information is eldercare. A caseworker will take you through all options that might meet your needs.

Southwestern Connecticut Agency on Aging (SWCAA). Call Alice Deak, The Information Specialist for Fairfield County. 203-333-9288. A not-for-profit organization serving as a resource center for aging issues, including advocacy. The SWCAA is

TO FIND OUT ABOUT LICENSED FACILITIES, INSPECTIONS AND GENERAL DATA ON AT HOME ELDER CARE, NURSING HOMES, ETC, IN THE AREA, CALL THE CONNECTICUT DEPARTMENT OF PUBLIC HEALTH AT 1-800-509-7444. THEY CAN ALSO SEND YOU THE "CONNECTICUT NURSING HOME FACILITIES BOOK FOR $8, WHICH LISTS LICENSED HOMES AND PERTINENT INFORMATION ABOUT EACH. YOU CAN PURCHASE THEIR CONSUMER GUIDE LISTING THE AT-HOME AGENCIES AND THE SERVICES THEY PROVIDE FOR $4. FINALLY THE ACCREDITATION OF HEALTH CARE ORGANIZATIONS FOR CONNECTICUT ASSOCIATION OF HOME CARE AGENCIES AT 203-265-9931.

mandated by the federal government, and is responsible for developing and maintaining a comprehensive choice of services for the elderly. They can also provide counsel for health insurance issues.

Local Childcare resources:

Again, a few key resources to get you launched in the right direction:

Infoline — "Connecticut's "First Call for Help": 211 if in Connecticut or 860-571-7500. Shari Konn is the Child Care Coordinator for the infoline which provides referral, advocacy and a crises helpline.

Connecticut's Department of Public Health, Day Care Licensing Division: Janet Chisholm is the Program Supervisor in the Licensing Division. Call 800-439-0437 or 860-509-8045.

Babysitters: The best way to find them is word of mouth, by posting ads in town newspapers, the bulletin boards of schools, libraries, doctor's offices and universities.

SOLUTIONS:
INFORMATION TO GUIDE YOU THROUGH THE COMMUTABLE COUNTIES OF NEW JERSEY

New Jersey is a misunderstood state. In addition, it gets misrepresented, mostly by New Yorkers who have lived in either Westchester or Fairfield County most of their lives and don't really know much about it. They've heard it's industrial and anything but beaucolic; it's true that the industrial revolution began in New Jersey and that it continues to be a mecca for corporate and manufacturing centers, but with over 21 counties, 567 municipalities and 7,417 square miles, most of it is gorgeous park lands, lakes, forests and mountains, horse farms, quaint, established villages and sprawling suburbia...every bit as appealing as Westchester and Connecticut.

People also say that the commute into the city is significantly less convenient than from the suburbs of Westchester and Connecticut. That, in fact, is a true statement; driving can be the most stressful. Highways are congested during rush hours and a $1/2$ hour drive can take 1-1$1/2$ hours at peak times. Although commuter bus lines are highly efficient and go direct into midtown Manhattan, they too are at the mercy of traffic delays—no matter what, you must cross a bridge or tunnel. The commute by rail is problematic because it usually requires a change outside city limits to a subway line to take commuters into midtown or downtown Manhattan. Finally, the rail and bus systems all converge on the Westside of the city, so if you work on the Eastside, it is not a convenient entry point. The good news, however, is that the commuter rails are being upgraded, line by line with direct service to midtown Manhattan. So in some instances, commute time is being reduced by 20-30 minutes! A plus about living in New Jersey, at least until now, is that housing is less expensive due to commuting conditions; however, as direct rail service improves, housing prices will likely increase to match those of Westchester and Fairfield Counties.

Of the 21 counties, there are 13 that are considered within commuting distance of the city. Those that are furthest West of Manhattan are the most rural and scenic, and might take a solid 1-1½ hours in travel time. Those further East and closest to the Hudson River are obviously the easiest commute and the most populated. Northern New Jersey counties include Bergen, Essex, Hudson, Morris, Passaic, Sussex and Warren. In Central NJ - Hunterdon, Mercer, Middlesex, Monmouth, Somerset and Union Counties. The counties of Southern NJ are not considered as commutable to New York City.

NEW YORKERS HAVE ALWAYS TREATED NEW JERSEY SUBURBS AS THE TRI-STATE STEPCHILD, BECAUSE THE COMMUTE INTO THE CITY CAN BE A LOT MORE CUMBERSOME THAN THAT OF WESTCHESTER AND CONNECTICUT. THAT CAN BE SO, BUT IT TOTALLY DEPENDS ON YOUR TYPICAL COMMUTING HOURS AND WHERE YOU CHOOSE TO LIVE. FOR EXAMPLE, IN SHORT HILLS, NEW JERSEY, ONE OF THE MOST ATTRACTIVE AND DESIRABLE SUBURBS IN THE NE, THE COMMUTE IS NOT ONLY DIRECT BUT EXACTLY 1/2 HOUR ON THE COMMUTER TRAIN INTO PENN STATION IN MIDTOWN MANHATTAN.

Housing (costs): vary by town and county — range is from $250,000 to mega-millions.

Real Estate Taxes: Bergen and Morris Counties are higher and similar to LI and Westchester Counties, NY. Other counties are lower.

Commuting by car:

Major highways include The Garden State Parkway, New Jersey Turnpike, Route 78, and Route 80. If you plan to drive, you can get rush hour traffic information by calling 732-PARKWAY, NJ Turnpike 1-800-336-5875, 732-247-0900 or listening to WINS 1010 on your car radio. For additional information, call:

New Jersey Highway Authority 732-442-8600

New Jersey Department of Transportation 973-770-5000, 609-530-2000

Ride/Share: 800-245-7665

www.state.nj.us/transportation/www.state.nj.us/njcommuter/

Commuting by train:

Some rail lines are direct into Penn Station located on the Westside of Manhattan at 34th Street and 7th Avenue. Many are indirect, requiring a change to the Path Subway line or ferry service outside city limits in Newark, Hoboken or Jersey City. For more information:

Amtrak: 800-872-7245

N.J. Transit Bus & Rail: 973-762-5100

www.njtransit.state.nj.us/

PATH: 1-800-234-PATH

Ferry info: I-800-53-NY WATERWAY

www.nywaterway.com

Schools — Private:

Many excellent ones. For further information:

NJ State Department Of Education—Non Public School Info Center: 609-984-7814

Catholic Schools Office: 609-756-7900 Ext 6288

The Independent Educational Consultants Association: 800-808-IECA

New Jersey Assoc. of Independent Schools: 732-661-9000 www.njais.org/

ADVIS (Delaware Valley Indep. Schools Assoc. website: www.advis.org/

Schools — Public:

Again, like Westchester and Fairfield Counties, the commutable suburbs in New Jersey are very affluent and the public schools are mostly good to excellent.

For further information, contact your local school district:

Contact the state of New Jersey PTA 609-393-6709

Contact the NJ State Department of Education: 609-292-4469

Two great school resource sites on the web: www.state.nj.us/njded/directory/districts/index/html and

www.philly.com/packages/njschools/njs98.asp

Schools – Parochial:

The Catholic Center • 973-497-4000
171 Clifton Avenue
Newark, NJ 07104
www.arnewsos.impresso.com

Recreation:

New Jersey may be mostly landlocked but its mountains, lakes, forests and parklands provide high quality recreation for all. In addition, the famous Meadowlands Sports Complex provides stadiums for the NBA's "Nets", NHL's NJ Devils, and NY's Giants and Jets football teams. Finally, New Jersey is famous for its horse farms and equestrian activities and Jersey shore beaches. For all the information you need, call:

Meadowlands Sports Complex: 201-939-0707

Chambers of Commerce: 609-989-7888

Dept. of Tourism: 1-800-Jersey-7

Publications:

Jersey Journal

Newark Star Ledger

Bergen Record

Websites:

www.state.nj.us/index.htm and www.find=newjersey.com/

Eldercare Resources:

For information call:

NJ Self-Help Clearing House: 800-367-6274

Division of Senior Services: 201-646-2625

Local Childcare Resources:

For information call:

Youth & Family Services: 609-292-5100

Director of State Licensed Day Care Facilities: 609-292-1018

Community Coordinator Childcare (CCC): 973-923-1433

SOLUTIONS:
INFORMATION TO GUIDE YOU THROUGH LONG ISLAND

Long Island is divided into two counties - Nassau County which is closest to NYC, making it the most commutable, and Suffolk County. It may not be comparable to any other living experience in the country. It is basically a "one way on, one way off" peninsula that is 120 miles long, but only 12-16 miles wide; the Atlantic Ocean with its vast dune beaches, runs the entire length of its south shore, and the Long Island Sound the length of its north shore; lifestyles include suburban developments and shopping malls, farming and vineyard communities, funky beach bungalow villages, "Great Gatsby" inspired towns established by old wealth, and the famous celebrity Hamptons. With its extraordinary selection of past times and lifestyle choices, comes an island that is very pricey, highways and transit systems that have not been able to keep up with year-round commercial and residential development, and massive congestion in the summertime that can be a serious quality of life drawback.

It's a wonderful place to live, but it is essential that anyone who is thinking of making the move, determine which areas will meet their needs in terms of "real-time"commute, type of community and quality of life.

Population: 2.65 million

Area: Nassau County — 285.4 square miles;
Suffolk — 885.1 square miles

Note: The area code for Suffolk County is now 631, not 516.

Housing:

A wild cross section...from artists' hamlets, tract houses and middle class suburbia...to beach bungalows, vineyard farmhouses, major estates and beachfront McMansions. Depending on the area, houses can start at $150,000 and top off at the $15 million dollar range along the gold coasts.

Real Estate taxes: Relatively high—varies dramatically by town and county.

Commuting by car:

There are three major highways — The Long Island Expressway, and the Northern and Southern State Parkways. The L.I.E. has the dubious distinction of being called the "longest parking lot in the world". Figuring out which back roads will steer you around rush hour and summer traffic congestion continues to be topic "A" for island dwellers. Newly constructed HOV (high occupancy lanes ...for cars with more than 2 people) and "park and ride" lots are helping. For more information call 516-737-CARS.

Commuting by train:

The Long Island Railroad, the nation's oldest commuter line, gets as much bad press about it's performance as the L.I.E. Diesel trains, crowded platforms and indirect routes that force changes mid-commute are the norm; however, the transit system is inching its way into the 21st century with the introduction of electric bi-level trains on a few lines, as well as the addition of more direct routes to Penn Station in NYC. The Long Island RR has 10 branch lines that all converge at Penn Station, on the Westside of Manhattan at 34th Street and Eighth Avenue. For more information, call 718-217-5477; From Nassau 516-822-LIRR and from Suffolk 631-231-LIRR.

Schools – Private:

Most are good to excellent. For information call:

The Non-Public School Office within the NY State Department of Education at 518-474-3879, They publish a directory of non-public schools that they will send you ($5.00). You also can contact the New York State Association of Independent Schools at 518-274-0184 for information and to request a schools directory (with a Long Island section). The Independent Educational Consultants Association at 1-800-808-IECA can give you the name of a registered consultant on Long Island and they also publish a directory of consultants. Education Records Bureau, at 212-672-9800, is the testing organization for independent schools. You can call the independent school that interests you and inquire as to whether they require the ERBS.

The following web sites are also very informative:

www.newsday.com/az/prvrnk99.htm

Schools – Public:

Again, for the most part, good to nationally acclaimed. Contact the NY State Department of education. Their Office of Reporting and Technology at 518-474-7965 provides statistical information about public schools. You also can request their directory of Public Schools ($5.00). The Board Of Cooperative Education (BOCES) can also provide information; their number in Nassau County is 516-396-2207, Western Suffolk — 631-549-4900, Eastern Suffolk — 631-289-2200. You can also request school district reports by calling the School Reporting Service at 1-800-229-4992. The following web site is very useful:

www.nassauboces.com

www.newsday.com/az/99skuls.htm

Schools – Parochial:

The Catholic Center • 516-678-5800
The Catholic Schools Office
50 North Park Avenue
Rockville Center, New York 11570
www.edrvc.org

Recreation:

The sheer range of recreational and cultural activities is one of the primary reasons for its non-stop growth. The beaches alone make

L.I. the "Riviera" of the Northeast. The Long Island Sound has the busiest harbors in America. Its fishing, boating, state park systems, professional sports and arts programs are literally world class. For more information call the L.I. Convention and Visitor's Bureau at 877-FUN-ON-LI. For pro sports information call 718-293-6000.

Chamber of Commerce: 516-679-1875

Long Island's newspaper of record: *Newsday.*
Their web site address is: www.newsday.com

Eldercare Resources:

Useful resources:

Nassau Department for Senior Citizens: 516-571-5814

Suffolk Department for the Aging: 631-853-8201

Information: Long Term Care Booklet 516-571-5814; Nursing Home Guide — 516-571-5814; Directory of Services 516-571-5814 for assisted living in Nassau County.

Childcare Resources:

You can obtain information on Nassau County childcare program at 516-358-9250; Suffolk County 631-462-0303, 631-283-1838

SOLUTIONS:
INFORMATION TO GUIDE YOU THROUGH ROCKLAND COUNTY

The Hudson River Valley conjures up majestic cliffs, forested hillsides and deep river valleys as far as the eye can see. Rockland County is nestled quietly in the middle of it, and includes the dramatic Palisades, 30,000 acres of parkland, 600 lakes , seven golf courses, and of course, The Hudson River — all within 20 to 35 miles of New York City. With a mix of cultural and agricultural resources, Rockland's towns and villages are diverse - from the quaint antique shops and artisans of Nyack, farm stands and apple orchards to some of the finest and largest shopping malls.

Population: 265,475

Area: 176 square miles five towns and eighteen villages

Housing:

Reasonable to expensive, with the broadest spectrum on moderately priced communities. Housing choices are as diverse as the community options ranging from Victorians, old farmhouses, contemporaries, traditional colonials to many condominium complex options.

Pricing ranges from $150,000 to 1,000,000 + with the median range in the $350,000s. Depending upon the community, new construction begins at $350,000 or in the $500,000s.

Real Estate Taxes: Real estate taxes are proportionately high; but similar to Long Island, Westchester in New York and Bergen County in New Jersey, ranging from $3000 to $15,000.

Commuting by Car:

Driving to the city by car, you have many options—the two most popular choices are I87 over the Tappan Zee Bridge or the Palisades Parkway into New Jersey for the George Washington Bridge. Expect approximately a 55 minute to 75 minute commute, depending upon where in Rockland you start out and the time of day.

Commuting by public transportation:

Train lines are not readily available in Rockland County with the exception of the New Jersey Transit's Bergen Line from Suffern and the Pascack Valley Line which serves Pearl River, Nanuet and Spring Valley. Both these lines have PATH trains to mid-town and the World Trade Center. In addition, many commuters will travel to the Metro North stations at Croton-Harmon(via the Bear Mountain Bridge or water taxi) or Tarrytown (via the Tappan Zee Bridge or the TAPPANZEExpress buses which operate weekdays from Spring Valley and Nyack to the Tarrytown train station. In addition, the TAPPANZEExpress has added more buses to the White Plains transportation center.

The Red and Tan Line buses operates between Rockland and New York City commuter destinations such as the George Washington Bridge and the Port Authority Terminal. The Short Line service operates buses from Suffern and Sloatsburg to NYC.

For transportation information, call The Rockland County Department of Public Transportation at 914-364-3434 or Rockland Transit Information at 914-364-3333.

Schools – Private:

There are several private and sectarian schools to provide education choices and options which include the Green Meadow Waldorf School, the Cornerstone Christian School, Rockland County Country Day and the Blue Rock School. In addition, the county's Orthodox Jewish community has several yeshivas available. The Roman Catholic Church operates its own schools in Rockland, with Albertus Magnus High School receiving national awards and recognition.

Here's how to access information:

Website: http://www.co.rockland.ny.us/education/private.html

The Independent Educational Consultants Association (IECA): if you are in need of a consultant, they provide a high quality service which is nationally recognized. 1-800-808-IECA

Schools – Public:

There are eight individual school districts within the county, with two districts receiving national recognition. Here are some ways to access the information you may need:

Contact the local school district in which you have interest. They will send you general information about curriculum, statistics and state test results

Contact: BOCES (Board of Cooperative Educational Services). 914-623-3828

Contact The National School Reporting Service: for a $25 annual fee, the service will give you school district information such as demographics, class size, student/teacher ratio, specific strengths, and test scores. 1-800-229-4992.

Websites:
http://realestate.yahoo.com/realestate/schools/ny/rockland/index.html

http://www.co.rockland.ny.us/education/introed.html

Schools – Parochial:

The Catholic Center • 914-294-8735
Catholic Schools Office
John S. Burke H.S. Convent
Fletcher Street
Goshen, NY 10924

Recreation:

From agricultural fairs to arts and crafts festivals to a vast variety of cultural resources, Rockland has many diverse options for its residents. Being at the foothills of the Catskill Mountains and having 600 lakes, 30,000 acres of parkland and theHudson River, there is no shortage of outdoor opportunities—including skiing, horseback riding, fishing, apple-picking, hiking, boating and golfing. The cultural resources include an orchestra, opera company, puppet theater and many local playhouses.

For more information:

Rockland Economic Development Corporation: 914-735-7040
www.redc.org

Arts Council of Rockland: 914-426-3660

Rockland County Tourism: 800-295-5723

Publications:

Gannett *Journal News.*

Elder Care Resources:

There are any number of community services and resources. The following
resources can get you started:

The Rockland County Office for the Aging:
914-362-2110

You can call the Office for the Aging for
information and a copy of a directory of
services

Rockland Senior Centers: Local gathering
places with opportunities for day trips,
health screening, nutrition, recreation and
support services and a hot noon meal.
There are several located throughout
Rockland County. The Office for the Aging
will have each of the locations available.

> IT'S A CLASSIC STORY. NEW
> YORKERS MOVING TO THE
> SUBURBS VOW THEY WILL
> NEVER LOSE TOUCH WITH CITY
> LIFE, AND THEN REGRETFULLY,
> BEGIN TO TRADE CULTURE FOR A
> COMFORTABLE LAWN CHAIR;
> WE SUGGEST YOU CAN
> MAINTAIN THOSE CULTURAL
> TIES TO THE CITY BY
> PURCHASING ADVANCE TICKETS
> FOR THE YEAR COMING UP TO A
> CHERISHED PAST-TIME. IT GIVES
> YOU A HANDFUL OF PRE-PAID
> CITY ADVENTURES TO POINT
> TOWARD AND PLAN FOR.

Institute for Senior Education:
914-574-4739 Rockland Community College Institute for Senior
Education offers more than 100 classes and study circles, designed
to meet interests and needs of seniors.

Childcare Resources:

An excellent resource:

Child Care Resources of Rockland, Inc.: 914-425-0009
www.childcarerockland.org

SOLUTIONS:
INFORMATION TO GUIDE YOU THROUGH
WESTCHESTER COUNTY

New York State's most sophisticated and affluent suburb...no matter
what your politics, cultural interests, no matter whether you consider yourself an "alternative or traditional" lifestyle...you can find a
community that feels like home. The physical environment is just as
eclectic. The tiny towns that hug the hills overlooking Westchester's
majestic Hudson River, have housing styles from Mediterranean to
bungalow, and have been compared to Southern California living.
Up the landlocked middle of the county, there are a combination of
upscale, New England-style villages as well as larger towns/cities
that have grown up around the corporate headquarters of IBM,
Texaco, Pepsico and Mastercard. On its Eastern shore, along the

GRAND CENTRAL STATION ISN'T JUST A TRAIN DESTINATION ANYMORE. A MULTI-MILLION DOLLAR RESTORATION HAS TURNED IT INTO A TEMPLE TO THE TRAVELER, AND IT'S WORTHY OF ADDING TO YOUR LIST OF "MUST EXPLORES". ITS ARCHITECTURAL DETAILS AND CATHEDRAL-LIKE GRANDEUR TRANSPORT THE GAZER BACK TO A GLAMOROUS ERA LONG PAST. TO COMPLIMENT ITS MAJESTY, DOZENS OF VERY FINE BOUTIQUES, RESTUARANTS, WATERING HOLES AND FRESH PRODUCE STALLS HAVE BEEN ADDED TO KEEP YOU THOROUGHLY ENTERTAINED.

Long Island Sound, are affluent, established suburban beach communities. Of all three states, Southern Westchester County is the most accessible to the city. Even if you live in a town in Northern Westchester, your commute won't be more than fifty minutes.

Population: 80,000

Area: 450.5 square miles

Housing:

Moderate to expensive. On the high end, in the most exclusive communities, an above average house will start at $700,000 +. In a community that is more low key, you can find housing for $350,000+.

Real estate taxes: Some of the highest in the nation. $5,000 - $25,000.

Commuting by car:

Many more options than Connecticut, making rush hour much less stressful. Take your pick of the New York State Thruway (Interstate 87), Interstates 80, 78, 684 and 278 (Cross Westchester Expressway). Then, there's a network of county parkways such as The Hutchinson River, Saw Mill River, and the Taconic State Parkways. Parkways only permit cars.

Commuting by train:

Again, many more options. Metro North, running out of Grand Central Station has three lines running north and south throughout Westchester County. There's the Hudson River (Amtrak) line; the Harlem Line which runs up the middle, and New Haven Line running along the Long Island Sound. For more information, call Metro North at 212-532-4900. Toll free in 914 area code: 1-800-METRO-INFO.

Schools – Private:

Private American and International Schools: There are any number of superb private and parochial schools. For more information call the Non-Public School Office within the New York State Department of Education at 518-474-3879, as well as The Independent Educational Consultants Association and Education Records Bureau

212-672-9800. To accommodate a solid and still growing international community, the County has a number of culturally diverse institutions such as The German School in White Plains, The French-American School in Larchmont, and Keio Academy, a Japanese High School in Purchase, a Japanese Elementary School in Ardsley and Annexe d'Ardsley Lyceum Kennedy(French) in Ardsley.

Schools – Public:

Like Fairfield County, this affluent suburb has mostly good to nationally acclaimed public schools throughout the County, with several ranked in the top 12 nationally. Administration of Westchester's 18 school districts is conducted by county-level associations called "BOCES" (Board of Cooperative Educational Services). These BOCES provide instructional and administrative services to the local districts, and include on-going programs for special education.

Their Northern Westchester number is: 914-245-2700.
Southern Westchester: 914-937-3820.

Website: www.co.westchester.ny.us/ed

Schools – Parochial:

The Catholic Center • 914-946-7419
Westchester Catholic School Office
950 Mamaroneck Avenue
White Plaines, NT 10605

Recreation:

Like Fairfield County, the proximity to NYC allows for world class cultural opportunities, multi-star restaurants and the best in shopping. The cities of White Plains, New Rochelle and Mt. Kisco also provide city-like retail centers and shopping malls. Other towns along the Hudson River and Long Island Sound add many dimensions to outdoor activities through all four seasons. Add to that, great public golf courses, county parks, beaches, historic sites and seven nature preserves. For more information:

Westchester Chamber of Commerce: 914-948-2110 or www.westchesterny.com.

Westchester County's official website: www.co.westchester.ny.us/

The best in local and regional newspapers: include the Gannett *Journal News,* and *The Patent Trader.*

Elder Care Resources:

There are any number of community services. To get plugged in, the following resource will more than get you started:

Westchester County Office for the Aging: 914-665-5900

Childcare Resources:

An excellent resource to get you started:

Westchester County Child Care Council: 914-761-3456. Can provide you with information on licensed day care programs in the area.

NEW YORK, NEW JERSEY, CONNECTICUT UTILITIES

(Toll Free Area Codes include 800, 877, 888)

Utilities

With deregualtion and multiple choice options now available, permitting you the consumer to choose your electric and/or natural gas supplier, each state has created a state consumer assistance phone line and website.

New York: Public Service Commission toll free.........800-342-3377
www.dps.state.ny.us/energyguide.htm

CT: Dept. of Public Utility Control/Consumer Assistance
Toll free in CT 800-382-4586
Outside CT 860-827-2837
www.dpuc-electric-choice.com

New Jersey: New Jersey Energy Choice Hotline
Toll free 877-655-5678

Telephone Service: Major Service Suppliers

The comapnies that have provided the services for major regions include:

New Jersey: AT&T Toll free..800-222-0300
www.att.com

Bell AtlanticToll free 800-621-9900
www.ba.com

CT: SNET out-of-state Toll free 800-466-7638
In-state, just dial..811
www.snet.com

New York: AT&T Toll free..800-222-0300
www.att.com

Bell Atlantic toll free 800-698-3545
www.ba.com

MCI toll free 800-950-5555
www.mci.com

Sprint toll free...800-877-7746
www.sprint.com

Water

Is local and regional, or can be well water...you need to know each local community and how & by whom service is provided.

Oil Heat

Multiple service options, check around at local distributors and see what packages they offer. The larger your oil tank, the better the discount. There are also local clubs that purchase as a group for reduced rates.

Cable

Extremely regionalized — check your local directory.

WEB INFORMATION

For goverment motor vehicle and driver's licenses, passport, birth certificate, social security number, immigration and much more, the following addresses will be a great help:

NY State: www.state.ny.us

CT: www.state.ct.us

NJ: www.state.nj.us

For generalfederal government information assistance, the website is: http://fic.info.gov/

Phone number for any and all government information:

1-800-688-9889

Driver's License

CT DMV: to find the closest branch call toll free.....800-842-8222
http://dmvct.org

NJ DMV: to find the closest branch call
In-state toll free 888-343-5368
Out-of-state 609-292-6500
www.nj.us/mvs

NY DMV: to find the closest branch call toll free.....800-343-5368
(800-DIAL-DMV)
www.nydmv.state.ny.us

County Clerk Offices:

The best access is via the County Clerks in each region — many towns have town clerks; but here are the county options:

NJ – Bergen

Bergen County
County Clerk
Main & Essex Streets
Hackensack, NJ 07601

NJ – Hudson

County Clerk
595 Newark Avenue
Jersey City, NJ 07306
201-795-6600

CT – Fairfield

Vital Records
County Clerk
1061 Main Street
Bridgeport, CT 06604
203-579-6527

NY – Westchester

County Clerk
110 Martin Luther King Jr. Blvd.
White plains, NY 10601
914-285-3080

NY – Rockland

Vital Records Office
County Clerk
27 New Hempstead Road
New City, NY 10956
914-638-5070

NY – Nassau

County Clerk
1 West St.
Mineola, NY 11501-4812
516-535-2663

NY – Suffolk

County Clerk
Riverhead, NY 11901-3398
631-852-2000

PRECINCTS

There are county police, state police and town police:

For emergencies, call 911.

HOW TO OPERATE LIKE A VIP ON A POOR MAN'S BUDGET

PERCEPTIONS VS. REALITY

It's easy to feel like one of the "have nots" in a city swirling with celebrities, high society matrons, and fat-cat CEOs. The high-life is in our faces every day. Ivana lunching at her favorite four star restaurant, investment bankers limoing to work, Madison Avenue shoppers in their Chanels...buying more Chanels, celebrities jogging in Central Park with their personal trainers, *Daily News* gossip about who was at this $1000 a plate gala, and that premier. But there are many ways to defy the high cost of living well in New York and experience this city the way the "haves" do, just through a different door. It requires knowing that New York City has resources that exist in a parallel, less expensive universe, and using them.

SOLUTION: SHOPPING WHOLESALE FOR JEWELRY AND FURS

You can buy jewelry and furs at the whole-sale price while experiencing some of the finest, most luxurious, full-service shopping in the world. New Yorkers in the know have their own personal wholesaler for buying jewelry and furs. The key is to get formally introduced to a wholesaler who can be accessed only by referral and private appointment. These "haute" wholesalers sell only to the trade - dealers and retailers - never to a walk-in customer. If, however, an individual comes with an excellent reference, they are more than happy to be of service. They actually enjoy the repeat business of a quality customer who does not waste their time. Ask your friends and colleagues for a referral. Once the contact is made, and mutual trust established, this rela-

> THE ONLY REASON TO BUY FURS AND JEWELRY AT FULL RETAIL IS IF THE NAME IS MORE IMPORTANT THAN THE PRICE.

tionship can last a lifetime and get handed down through generations.

And for the same reason your wholesaler wants references, so should you! Never walk in off the street to a storefront jeweler or furrier who claims to sell wholesale, without a strong recommendation. Unless you are your own expert, chances are good you won't know when, how or if you've been "had".

About Fur Wholesalers

- Most fur wholesalers are located on Seventh Avenue in the West 30's.

- There is no reason to pay retail for a fur coat, unless it's important to you to have the designer label.

- A fine wholesaler will attend to all your needs and more. They will:
  - restore
  - repair
  - re-style your fur for a more updated look
  - let you "trade up" for a new coat

- Don't buy a fur from a wholesaler until you know what you are buying. Go to the top retailers, look at the fur collections and ask questions. Call the Fur Information Council of America (212) 564-5133. They answer consumer questions, and make available educational pamphlets about purchasing a fur. And, of course, your personal wholesaler is a great teacher. Just make sure you keep asking questions until you are comfortable that you are making an informed decision.

About Wholesale Jewelers

- Your wholesale jeweler will hunt for the perfect piece for you. Whether it's a particular type of stone or cut, or estate jewelry from a particular era...your jeweler will find it for you.

"EVERY WRITTEN APPRAISAL OF JEWELRY MUST STATE THE STANDARD OF MONETARY VALUE USED (I.E. RETAIL REPLACEMENT). PERSONS ENGAGED IN THE SALE OR APPRAISAL OF JEWELRY MAY NOT MISREPRESENT THE NATURE OF AN ARTICLE OF JEWELRY AND MUST DISCLOSE THAT JEWELRY APPRAISALS MAY VARY AS MUCH AS 25 PERCENT. FOR SALES OF MORE THAN $75, VERY DETAILED AND ACCURATE SALES SLIPS MUST BE GIVEN.
NOTE: "JEWELRY" MEANS UNSET RARE GEMS, PRECIOUS AND SEMIPRECIOUS STONES, AND ARTICLES FOR PERSONAL WEAR CONTAINING SUCH GEMS AND STONES. IT DOES NOT INCLUDE GOLD, SILVER, PLATINUM, OR OTHER PRECIOUS METALS."

—THE DEPARTMENT OF CONSUMER AFFAIRS

- Your jeweler is used to making house calls, and will come to you.
- Your jeweler will:
  - let you trade in or up for other pieces
  - allow you to sell a piece back to him
  - maintain, repair and restore precious pieces
  - restyle a piece into a new setting or create a new piece for alternative wear

TIFFANY & CO. OFFERS FREE BROCHURES ON "HOW TO BUY A DIAMOND" AND "A GUIDE TO TIFFANY PEARLS".

- Become an expert on the type of jewelry you are looking for. If it's stones, look at the stones in their settings at the top retailers first. Get an idea of what you want. Call Jewelers of America at (212) 768-8777 to get their pamphlets on what you need to know to be an informed consumer.
- Ask your wholesaler if the stone has been certified by the Gemological Institute of America, the last word on gems. If it hasn't, he will give you a letter of introduction to them so you can get the stone graded. Their number is (212) 944-5900.

The Intrepid Pages of
The Best Wholesale Jewelers & Furriers

"ONE REASON TO PAY RETAIL AT A SIGNATURE JEWELERS SUCH AS TIFFANY, HARRY WINSTON OR BULGARI IS THAT WHEN YOU SELL ONE OF THE PIECES YOU BOUGHT THERE, YOU MIGHT GET WHAT YOU PAID FOR IT, MAYBE EVEN A LITTLE MORE. EXAMPLE: YOU COULD BUY AN IMITATION OF THE CARTIER ROLLING RING FOR $100 WHOLESALE, BUT SELL IT BACK ONLY FOR THE SCRAP WEIGHT OF THE GOLD FOR ABOUT $55. HOWEVER, THE REAL CARTIER RING SELLS FOR ABOUT $500 TODAY. IF YOU HAD BOUGHT IT SOME YEARS BEFORE, LET'S SAY FOR $100, YOU COULD PROBABLY SELL IT TO A JEWELER TODAY FOR ABOUT $200. IF THE RING WAS DISCONTINUED, AND IS NOW CONSIDERED A COLLECTOR'S ITEM, YOU MIGHT SELL IT FOR CONSIDERABLY MORE THAN WHAT YOU PAID FOR IT".

—BRAD REH, WHOLESALE JEWELER

WHOLESALE JEWELERS
BRAD REH • (516) 476-9660

The premier expert of fine estate jewelry; specializing in pieces from the large European houses. But if you prefer something new don't hesitate to call. His selection of fine stones and gold is amazing and his prices are more than fair. One of the gems in the business. By appointment only.

FRIMAN & STEIN
589 Fifth Avenue (48th Street) (212) 308-6200

This is one of the finest family-run businesses on 48th Street. The quality of their goods, combined with their knowledge and expertise, is unmatchable. They are ostensibly "wholesale only," so be sure to call ahead to see if they can handle your request. By appointment only.

GRACE JEWELERS
(800) 484-1235 ext. 1723

One of the best ways to get personal service and an extraordinary selection of beautiful custom made pieces. And on the off chance that you do not find something you like, they can design and fabricate to your specifications. Do not be intimidated by such a "classy" way to shop; they have pieces that begin at a few hundred dollars. You will become a customer for life.

MURREY'S JEWELERS
1395 Third Avenue • (212) 879-3690

Earl and his father have been behind the counter of this shop for many years. If you were just passing by the window you might think that all they do is sell estate jewelry and perform repairs. Their best kept secret is their ability to copy and fabricate a piece from scratch at a fraction of what others charge. Top notch workmanship with great service. Many of the wealthiest New Yorkers have been shopping here for years.

WHOLESALE FURS

SMITH FURS
333 Seventh Avenue
(28th and 29th Streets) • (212) 736-2423

Gary Smith has a fabulous eye for helping you choose a coat that looks great on you and that suits all your needs. They have a good selection of furs and styles. By appointment only.

CHRISTIE BROTHERS
333 Seventh Avenue
(28th & 29th Streets) • (212) 736-6944

Longevity is the name of the game here. Five generations of the Christie family have made this one of the finest furriers in the country. You can be sure of getting exactly what you want—whether it is a traditional style or one that is more contemporary. By appointment only.

SOLUTION:
THE BACKDOOR ROUTES TO BUYING FASHION AVENUE'S DESIGNER CLOTHES AT HALF PRICE OR LESS.

Designer Sales

You've probably heard the terms "Fashion Avenue" and "The Garment Center" - it's the area in Manhattan that belongs to all the hot designer showrooms from Donna Karan to Calvin Klein and Prada. At the end of every season, designers have to unload leftover merchandise to make way for next season's clothes. To do it, they allow the public in and offer up their labels at 50-75% off. So for those of us who can't afford them, we still find a way to wear them! Here's the how, when and where:

UJA -FEDERATION'S ANNUAL BENEFIT SALE, "FASHION RESCUE," HELD DURING THANKSGIVING WEEK IS A FASHION FEAST FOR SHOPPERS IN THE KNOW. SPONSORED BY ONE OF NEW YORK'S LARGEST PHILANTHROPIES, THE SALE FEATURES NEW CLOTHING AND ACCESSORIES FOR MEN, WOMEN, AND CHILDREN, AND GREAT GIFTWARE BY OVER 700 LEADING DESIGNERS AND MANUFACTURERS AT PRICES WAY BELOW WHOLESALE. CLOTHES ARE RESTOCKED DAILY. PROCEEDS SUPPORT HUMAN SERVICES SPONSORED BY UJA-FEDERATION OF NEW YORK WITH SPECIAL FUNDS DESIGNATED FOR LOCAL AIDS AND CANCER PROGRAMS. FOR DETAILS, CALL (212) 836-1776.

S & B Report
56¹⁄₂ Queens St., Charleston, SC 29401 • (877) 579-0222

For a yearly subscription fee of $49, you can receive a monthly report of all sample/designer sales open to the public. A blackbelt subscription costs $104 and includes weekly sales updates.

New York Magazine

A weekly magazine that always includes a terrific section on all kinds of designer sample sales open to the public that week. You can find it at your local newsstand or you can subscribe.

Consignment Shops:

Only in New York would there be shops that specialize in reselling high society's once-worn haut couture castoffs!

These are the shops that society's well heeled take their once worn Versace's, Chanels, Ralph Laurens, because they can't bear to be seen in the same outfit twice. Most consignment shops have strict guidelines and only accept the very finest quality clothing in near-perfect condition. It's possible to find clothes that still have the original price tags on them. Items are usually sold at 30-75% off. For those of you who feel squeamish about wearing somebody else's clothes, you're likely to change your mind once you've browsed one of these shops. It's possible to find a Bob Mackie dress reduced from $3,000 to $500; a Ralph Lauren winter coat for $200; an Armani blouse for $75.

> IF YOU WANT A PRADA COAT, THEN YOU WILL HAVE TO BUY IT RETAIL;
> IF YOU DON'T CARE ABOUT THE LABEL, THEN YOU CAN GET A PRADA "KNOCK-OFF" MADE BY YOUR TAILOR.

The Intrepid Pages of
Clothing Consignment Shops

ALLAN & SUZI
416 Amsterdam (at 80th Street) • (212) 724-7445

A varied selection of vintage and couture clothing and accessories for men and women. Showy clothes that are not necessarily high end or new, but fun and certainly not run-of-the-mill. Some names to spot here include Helmut Lang, LaCroix, Gaultier, and Pucci.

BIS COLLECTIONS
1134 Madison Avenue (84th Street) • (212) 396-2760

Designer-wear at more than 50 percent off retail can be found at Bis. Names like Versace, Chanel, Donna Karan, and Fendi grace the shop. They also have an extensive selection of accessories—handbags, belts, scarves, and costume jewelry. Bis accepts designer merchandise in excellent condition.

COUTURE CLUB
789 Lexington Avenue (61st-62nd Streets) • (212) 421-8600

The Couture Club is an upscale resale designer shop for women's clothing. Because of their location, you can be sure to find some of the best labels.

DESIGNER RESALE • 324 East 81st Street • (212) 734-3639

Some of the best designer labels we came across in a small, manageable setting.

ENCORE
1132 Madison Avenue (at 84th Street) • (212) 879-2850

Encore has a well-deserved reputation for carrying designer label clothing for women. You can be sure to come across at least one Chanel every time you go.

EXCHANGE UNLIMITED
563 Second Avenue (at 31st Street) • (212) 889-3229

One of the only consignment shops that accepts men's clothing as well as women's. This shop has been in business for twenty years and has a good quantity and quality of merchandise.

GENTLEMEN'S RESALE • 303 East 81st Street • (212) 734-2739

Owner Gary Scheiner will take designer label men's clothing and accessories in excellent condition. If you covet a Hermes tie, look no further.

GOOD-BYES
By Appointment Only • 230 East 78th Street • (212) 794-2301

Good-Byes accepts infant and children's clothing to size 10, toys, infant equipment, and equipment accessories (stroller pad, crib bumper), books, even videos. Kids grow so fast, why not fill in with some bargains such as Ralph Lauren, Osh Kosh, etc., at below market prices.

INA
101 Thompson Street • (212) 941-4757
21 Prince Street • (212) 334-9048
INA MEN • 262 Mott Street • (212) 334-2210

Some of the more "trendy" clothing items can be found at INA.

KAVANAGH'S • 146 East 49th Street • (212) 702-0152

Very high-end designer clothing. Names like Chanel, Versace, and Armani abound here. A Chanel suit that would retail for $4,000 would be priced at $900 at Kavanagh's. Other designer suits would be priced at about $400.

MICHAEL'S
1041 Madison Avenue (79th and 80th Streets) • (212) 737-7273

A women's resale shop vying with Encore for the quality of its merchandise.

MOM'S NIGHT OUT
147 East 72nd Street
(212) 744-MOMS • By Appointment Only

Although Mom's Night Out is not a consignment shop, it is a store that can save you money if you are a pregnant woman in need of evening-wear. They carry stylish formal dresses for pregnant women at rental prices ranging from $110 to $225. All the dresses are their own designs. You must make an appointment at least a month in advance of needing your garment.

OUT OF OUR CLOSET • 136 West 18th Street • (212) 633-6965

Here you can find high-end/fashion-forward designers like Chanel, Dolce & Gabbana, and Richard Tyler. They also carry men's designer clothing.

RITZ THRIFT SHOP • 107 West 57th Street • (212) 265-4559

Ritz deals only in fur coats and they are quite selective in what they accept.

SECOND COUSIN
142 Seventh Avenue (10th and Charles Streets) • (212) 929-8048

Clothing for children under ten years old.

WHAT COMES AROUND GOES AROUND
351 West Broadway (Grand and Broome) • (212) 343-9303

Fine vintage clothing for men and women. Some business-wear, but more casual clothing. Suits range from $75 to $200; a cotton or polyester shirt for $25.

SOLUTION:
BUY CLOTHING, ACCESSORIES, AND NOVELTY ITEMS FROM UP-AND-COMING DESIGNERS

New York is also the home of struggling, up-and-coming designers and their cottage industries.

If there's a place for up-and-coming designers to "make it", it's the fashion capital - New York City. You'll find there are literally thousands of what we call "designer laboratories" - some flourish as cottage industries within loft spaces that double as design space, shop and home. Some have been given small display areas in established boutiques, and some manage tiny, shabby-chic storefronts in the off-beat nooks and crannies of Manhattan. Here you will find the future Elsa Perettis and Donna Karans. Once you've discovered them, they will gladly receive you, and sell what they have on display or make an original for you. There is nothing that will make you feel more luxurious or smug, than having your own personal designer...and at a fraction of the cost at the retail level. Now here's how to find them:

- At flea markets and upscale street fairs throughout the city. Designers who can't afford storefronts take booths at these markets to display and sell their designs. You can ask for their business card and make an appointment.

- Trade publications and local newspapers and magazines: *Women's Wear Daily* lists their "picks" of new designers. *The New York Times* has a column called "Stylemakers" which writes up interesting, new talent. *Time Out* and *New York* Magazines feature new designers regularly.

- The Fashion Institute of Technology has portfolios from which you can choose your very own personal designer. Call the Career Services Department at (212) 217-7654. You will fax your requirements, and they will do the matching.

- Specialty boutiques lease display space to favorite new designers. If you see something you like, ask the salesperson for the designer's name and whereabouts.

- Off-beat areas of the city: take a stroll down 9th Street in the East Village. You'll instantly understand what we mean.

The Intrepid Pages of
At-Home Designers

To meet with these designers, you must make an appointment.

IN NEW YORK CITY

CAROLYN CHADWICK • (212) 727-8842

Carolyn hand-makes lovely small and large notebooks and albums for a variety of purposes. She will create sketchbooks, journals, wedding albums, presentation books—you name it.

ELIZABETH CANNON COUTURE • (212) 929-8552

Elizabeth caters to a sophisticated, mostly arts-related clientele who seek understated elegance and extraordinary couture. Elizabeth works with the client to visualize a design, select fabric, create a pattern, and toil in the old European tradition. She will create a wedding or special occasion dress, as well as a multi-piece wardrobe which interchanges and suits the clients' particular lifestyle. Elizabeth also offers a selection of unique artist-painted silks and velvets from her atelier, "Ecole Martine." Prices start at $750 for evening dresses; $800 for suits; $240 for day-dresses. These prices do not include fabric.

HUT STUDIOS ARCHITECTURAL DECOUPAGE ART
(212) 628-8377

They make reproductions of buildings to suit your scale requirements — from miniatures to large, free-standing pieces. They are known for using beautiful woods, and for making exquisite pieces with great attention to color and other details.

KNOTTITUDE • (212) 239-4117

Valerie Mapp designs a line of women's resortwear inspired by Third-World traditional clothing. All items are put together with knots. Prices range from $25 to $110. You can get a four-piece outfit for under $250.

MALIA MILLS SWIM WEAR • (800) 685-3479

Malia creates signature swim wear designed to best flatter your figure. Her bathing suits are available in both one or two-pieces, in striking solids and prints. Malia's separates are made to mix and match so that you can combine a top and bottom in different sizes and build a swim wear wardrobe of interchangeable pieces. Her swimsuits sell for $135 and up and are available at Bloomingdale's, Barneys, Harvey Nichols, and through their catalog. They also schedule private fittings in their Manhattan studio.

MISS PYM • (212) 879-9530

High-end custom girls' special occasion clothing. Miss Pym special-izes in dresses, coats, and capes in velvets, silk, cotton, and wool. Lisa has a terrific trained eye for knowing just what fabric and design will look good on her clients. Dresses range from $200 to $300; capes and coats are $325 to $615. They also design head-pieces and crinolines. Special attention is given to handmade details. Several months are needed to complete a project so make sure you give yourself enough lead-time.

NOEL COPELAND • (718) 852-5487

Noel is a fine art sculptor and ceramist whose charming and whim-sical designs will brighten your home. His dinner plates, album cov-ers, paintings, huge three-dimensional sculptures and wall murals are painted with brilliant Caribbean-inspired colors; some have images of Rastafarians and narrative scenes. Plates that double as wall hangings are $32 to $100; triangular-shaped dreadlocked vases range from $42 to $300.

JABBOUR & SONS • (516) 674-9527

Mr. Jabbour knows that people still care about having beautiful housecoats, slips, and petticoats, embroidered bed linens, bath towels, and custom table linens. As a courtesy, he comes into New York City on Tuesdays and Thursdays and visits his customers at their homes. Call for prices.

SHIMODA ACCESSORIES • (212) 491-6726

Donna Emanuel creates interesting jewelry, mostly in the style of the Native American and African. Her materials include semi-precious stones, glass beads, and even bones. Price range—$15 to $600.

STUDIO 3 • (800) 803-4334

Sy Goldfond hand-paints beautiful terra cotta flower pots, galva-nized watering cans, planters, glass vases, and bottles. No two are exactly alike. He will also work with you to create one-of-a-kind cus-tom designs. Prices run $35 and up.

OUTSIDE NEW YORK CITY

All of these craftspeople will speak to you on the phone. Some have a catalogue that they can send to you, others will describe their goods over the phone. Most will sell directly to you. However, a few prefer that you buy from them when they are at a craft fair in New York City and will tell you the next time they will be in town.

ALISON PALMER • (914) 855-5493

Alison sells over 100 different spoon-rest designs. Her designs include: fried eggs, chickens, vegetables, fruits—all whimsical. Her price is about $25 per spoon rest.

BIG DIPPER CANDLES • (914) 469-9442

Jerome and Paula Spector make the most interesting array of hand-dipped, multi-colored candles. Their designs include a variety of sushi, long, delicate shapes, Hanukah candles, dinner tapers, and more. We're sure if the order is big enough they can be commissioned to make anything you want. Price range—$3 and up.

BOB MORRIS, TOYMAKER • (908) 522-1651

Bob makes the most charming and playful spinning wooden mobiles. His designs include Jack-in-the-boxes, clowns, and moon with stars, among others. Price range—$22 to $50.

THE CORDWAINER SHOP • (603) 463-7742

Paul Gordon Mathews designs handmade custom health footwear. They will send an illustrated brochure.

CORRIDOR CLAY STUDIO • (607) 587-9877

Four Alfred University graduates have formed a cooperative studio after receiving degrees from the New York State College of Ceramics. Their studio/display room is open by appointment or by chance and is located in the same building as the International Museum of Ceramic Art at Alfred. They will gladly sell to you over the phone. Robin Caster produces highly decorated, hand-built porcelain pottery; Karen Gringhuis creates brightly colored porcelain tableware; Michael Hagedorn makes bonsai containers, and cultivates his own collection of bonsai; and Linda Huey produces sculpture based on natural forms, plus smaller production items for a wholesale business.

DEEP SPRING STUDIO • (304) 257-4356

Collapsible wooden baskets are cut from a single piece of fine-quality exotic or domestic hardwood. The handle is cut integrally with the basket body to ensure proper fit when collapsed. It doubles as a trivet. Price range—$29 and up.

HEISE METAL SCULPTURE • (802) 862-8454

Bill Heise is a contemporary folk artist who creates shapes of birds, animals, and people indigenous to the hillsides of Vermont using discarded metal tools as his materials. The beauty of Bill's work is that he is able to animate old, rusty, and otherwise-useless objects. His work can be found in major stores and galleries in the United States. Price range: $85 and up.

LITTLE R&R WOODSHOP • (516) 593-8533

Robin and Rob Foreman hand-craft and hand-paint children's furniture and accessories—colorful picture frames, coat/hat peg boards and book ends, shaped like fish, bunny rabbits or moon and stars—among many other adorable designs.

THE MAINE COASTER • (207) 549-3932

Formerly creators of hand-crafted wooden rocking animals, the owners have shifted gears to manufacture glass coasters and paperweights. What makes these items unique is that they contain pressed and dried plant material that is wrapped in copper or silver and sealed. The final product is a beautiful, colorful flower/leaf arrangement sealed in glass. The coasters and paperweights can add a "beachy, outdoorsy" touch to the home. A set of four coasters is $30; paperweights are $10 each.

MELODIOUS • (207) 774-5519

Melodious music boxes present music and animation in irresistible combinations to delight music-box lovers of all ages. The size is approximately five by seven inches. They also have colorful musical picture frames. Average price is $42 for a music-box or musical picture frame. Music clocks sell for $60.

NANCY HOLLANDER-KOTARSKI • (203) 845-0835

Nancy makes desk accessories—notepads, picture frames, boxes, wastebaskets, blotters, pen holders, and more—all covered in beautiful Italian marbleized paper at half the cost you'd find in the City. Items start at $15.

PAMELA MORIN, INC./CONTEMPORARY PRIMITIVES (914) 831-2200

Pamela designs hand-painted accessories—wearables, clocks, furniture, and custom-interior pieces. Her style is that of whimsical contemporary primitives using bold, bright colors. All at moderate prices.

SWERVE DESIGN • (319) 895-8536

She hand-paints frames, furniture, mirrors, and more. Her finishes include a wide range of rich colors with impressionistic designs. A five-by-seven-inch frame sells for $15.

WHEEL WOODEN TOYS • (804) 295-0534

Robert Stroh designs these sturdy wooden objects for kids. Lamps that have dinosaurs or fish at the base, coat racks, counting beads that are held together with dinosaurs, and an animated assortment of pull toys. Price range—$6 and up.

The Intrepid Pages of
Design Collectors

There is a category of people who have a passion for collecting certain types of items—it could be anything from quilts to dried flowers—and sell them by appointment out of their home. Needless to say, they are hard to find because they don't advertise and they don't have storefronts, but we have been compiling a growing list.

JANE SYBILLA CROSLAND, F.R.H.S.
By Appointment: (212) 734-4216

Jane is a designer of 18th Century English Garden style true-to-life silk flower arrangements. You can buy already-made bouquets, or Jane will customize one for you. Price range—$200 and up.

JUDY CORMIER • By Appointment: (212) 517-3993

Judy specializes in antique decorative prints—book plates and copper-plate engravings. Designs include birds, flowers, and architectural and garden scenes. Price range—$98 to $5,000.

KAREN WARSHAW LTD. • 167 East 74th Street • (212) 439-7870

A 19th Century townhouse filled with English and French decorative antiques: furniture, paintings, accessories, mirrors, lamps, sconces, and porcelain. Just tell her what you are looking for and you can be sure she will eventually locate it for you. Her prices are reasonable and her turnover is frequent.

MRS. JOHN L. STRONG • By Appointment: (212) 838-3848

Here you will find some of the more expensive and nicest hand-engraved stationery and invitations.

PANTRY AND HEARTH • By Appointment: (212) 532-0535

At Gail Lettick's Georgian townhouse you will be able to browse through four floors of quality Americana and folk art. Her wonderful collection includes Pilgrim Era and 18th Century painted and high country furniture and decorative accessories. Price range—$25 and way up.

TROUVAILLE FRANCAISE • By Appointment: (212) 737-6015

Here you will find a large collection of antique and vintage lace goods—pillow shams, linen sheets, napkins, tablecloths, embroidered bedspreads, even baby clothes. Average price of a pillow sham is $75, other prices range from $12 to $550.

The Intrepid Pages of
Storefront Designer Labs

AMY DOWNS • 103 Stanton Street • (212) 598-4189

Amy designs free-form hats in bright colors. She is known as the "mad hatter". Price range is $40 to $120. She accepts only cash and personal checks.

BARNEYS New York • 660 Madison Avenue • (212) 826-8900
HENRI BENDEL • 712 Fifth Avenue • (212) 747-1100

Both like to discover young designers. Every now and then go and browse through the store; often they will have the designer there promoting and selling their designs.

BOMBALULU'S
101 West 10th Street • (212) 463-0897
332 Columbus Avenue (75th and 76th Streets) • (212) 501-8248

Hand-made children's clothing, all with original designs, for new-born babies to children 8 years old. Bombalulu's specializes in hand-painted 100 percent cotton T-shirts, hats, skirts, and jackets. They also sell high-quality toys. Prices range from $4 to $60.

BARBARA BUI
115 Wooster Street (Prince and Spring Streets) • (212) 625-1760

Barbara Bui, a French designer, is best known for her innovative use of material, including chenille, vinyl, and tapestry fabrics. Her large 9,000 square foot boutique houses an extensive selection of day-wear—separates such as skirts and trousers, as well as suits and dresses. Trousers average $250; dresses, $200 and up.

CALYPSO ENFANTS
284 Mulberry Street (Houston & Prince) • (212) 965-8910

This store carries imported French baby and toddler clothes. They are open Monday through Saturday, 11:00 A.M. to 7:00 P.M. and Sunday, 12 Noon to 7:00 P.M.

DAPHNE
467 Amsterdam Avenue (82nd and 83rd Streets) • (212) 877-5073

Daphne designs clothing, including lingerie, for the larger woman using a multitude of fabrics such as silk, wool, and rayon.

THE DRESS/MARY ADAMS • 159 Ludlow Street • (212) 473-0237

Mary Adams designs special occasion and bridal dresses—very feminine cotton dresses, princesslike silk organzas, layers of iridescent color. She works directly with the customer to design something dramatically special. Dresses—$275 to $800 (nonbridal); $950 to $4,500 (bridal). Bridal dresses by appointment only.

**EDDRIS SHOES
223 Seventh Avenue (3rd and 4th Streets), Park Slope, Brooklyn (718) 768-7172**

Eddy is the maker of these hand-made stylish, comfortable shoes for women only. Shoes are custom-made in sizes 4 to 11. There are also ready-to-wear shoes available. Prices range from $79 to $129 for ready-to-wear shoes. Customized shoes are $300 and up.

**GREGG WOLF BIJOUX COUTURE
346 East 9th Street • (212) 529-1784**

Gregg Wolf designs and manufactures exquisite sterling silver jewelry. His bold, handcrafted fashions are influenced by the ancient past. Prices start at $40.

JADED • 1048 Madison Avenue (at 80th Street) • (212) 288-6631

Jaded manufactures and designs contemporary jewelry, using coins and stones, which is sold throughout the country. They will accommodate all your needs. Prices start at $50.

JANE WILSON MARQUIS • 155 Prince Street • (212) 477-4408

Jane creates her own line of nontraditional bridal and evening wear that can be customized to accommodate your own style and taste. Her salon is the perfect place to go if you are searching for a period look or just something different.

**J. MORGAN PUETT
137 West Broadway • (212) 267-8004**

Morgan designs clothes for women, men, and children. The clothes are manufactured with natural hand-made fibers and are hand-dyed on the premises. Her pants and shirts are unisex and she designs two collections a year. Linen dresses: $200; jackets: $300; pants: $80; baby clothes: $50.

KATINKA • 303 East 9th Street • (212) 677-7897

Jane Williams works with materials that come from India. She designs shoes, vests, and sportswear. Her emphasis is not on customization, but she will do it. Prices start at $50.

LA LUMIA
253 Church Street (Leonard & Franklin Streets) • (212) 966-3923

Jackie Sencion is the owner and designer of this boutique that sells mostly contemporary casual clothing for women. She likes to use all types of fabrics. A dress runs about $100.

LOLA MILLINERY • 535 8th Avenue • (212) 279-9093

Lola can design anything from the classic to the funky. Her attention to detail in both her hats and her customers can't be beat. She can accommodate men looking for the offbeat. Average price is $185.

ONE OF A KIND BRIDE
89 Fifth Avenue (16th and 17th Streets) • (212) 645-7123
By Appointment

Candice Soloman designs a line of exquisite couture nontraditional wedding dresses that are sleek and high-end. She uses only the best European silk. Prices start at $3,500.

ONLY HEARTS
386 Columbus Avenue (78th and 79th Streets) • (212) 724-5608

Helena Stuart is the designer of this comfortable and fashionable line of lingerie and sleepwear. Most items are made from cotton or silk. Only Hearts is sold other places but this is the main outlet for her merchandise. Prices are moderate.

PALMA • 521 Broome Street • (212) 966-1722

Palma designs a line of women's clothing, but you can find other designer merchandise here. They also sell men's designer clothing. The store carries a varied selection of suits, shirts, jackets, sweaters, and sportswear. Palma can customize clothing for you or you can purchase garments off the rack. A Palma wool crepe lined suit sells for $500 to $600. They also have a gift section filled with lamps, keepsake boxes, and candlestick holders, among other items, and a costume jewelry section.

SERAFINA
29 East 19th Street • (212) 253-2754 • By Appointment

Here you can purchase ready-to-wear or custom-designed brides-maids' dresses fashionable and versatile enough to wear after the wedding. What makes these garments special is that they are available in long and short styles, with a choice of up to 100 colors, in a range of fabrics. Dresses cost between $250 and $400.

SEIZE SUR VINGT • 243 Elizabeth Street • (212) 343-0476

Beautifully made custom shirts and suits for men and women.

ST. REGIS DESIGNS
58 East 7th Street • (212) 533-7313

Andrij Pelensky started the business thirty years ago, and has been at this same location ever since. St. Regis hand-makes stylish all-leather handbags, purses, belts, wallets, and other accessories. Belts range from $30 to $120; small handbags are $50 to $170. You can buy items off the rack, or Andrij can custom-make an item for you.

TRACEY TOOKER HATS
1211 Lexington Avenue (at 82nd Street) (212) 472-9603

Tracey has a wonderful eye for designing traditional hats for all heads and occasions. She uses a wide variety of silk flowers and straw, and she does custom orders. Prices start at $125.

MOST UP AND COMING YOUNG DESIGNERS START WORKING OUT OF THEIR HOME AND GRADUATE TO A SMALL SHOP. DO NOT BE SURPRISED TO FIND ONLY A "FEW" ITEMS OF CLOTHING IN THEIR STORES. THEIR BUDGETS ONLY ALLOW THEM TO MAKE A *VERY* LIMITED SELECTION. FOR THE MOST "HIP" STORES TAKE A STROLL THROUGH LITTLE ITALY, CHINATOWN AND THE LOWER EAST SIDE. BY THE TIME THEY OPEN IN NOHO OR SOHO THEY HAVE "ARRIVED".

SOLUTION:
WHO SAYS YOU CAN'T AFFORD TO HAVE MARTHA STEWART CATER YOUR DINNER PARTY OR PETER DUCHIN PLAY AT YOUR WEDDING.

Many of the finest professional schools in the world are in NYC, and the most promising talents come here to pursue their dreams.

They enroll in famous schools such as Juillard, Parsons School of Design, School of Visual Arts, Peter Kump's Cooking School, and NYU Film School. We hire them before they become a household name, at a fraction of the cost. No matter how talented, these young professionals are still students, and they have to moonlight to support their education, not to mention, practice their craft. And all these schools are set up to help them. We've hired them all - young actors for kid's birthday parties, portrait photographers, computer programmers, even string quartets.

All the schools have temporary employment offices. They will ask you to fax your request and they will post it. It can take a few weeks to fulfill.

Be very explicit about what you need. Make sure the school feels confident that your request can be fulfilled. If you need the highest caliber talent, request one of their star, senior students or a teacher. Sometimes you will negotiate the price with the student, sometimes with the school.

The Intrepid Pages of
Professional Schools

The yellow pages has a section of schools arranged by subject. It's an excellent way to start looking for hired help, or call:

THE ART STUDENTS LEAGUE OF NEW YORK • (212) 247-4510

Here you can commission a student to paint, draw, or sculpt for you. Fax a job description to (212) 541-7024, Attn: Bulletin Board. Include a detailed job description, fee, and hours needed.

BARNARD COLLEGE • Career Services Office: (212) 854-2033

Mail your job description to Office of Career Development, Barnard College, 11 Milbank, 3009 Broadway, New York, NY 10027-6598, or fax it to (212) 854-7491, Attention: Office of Career Development. It will be posted and the fee is set between you and the student.

THE CHUBB INSTITUTE
Student Employment Office: (800) CHUBB-37

You can hire a computer programmer from this computer training school. Fax a job description with all the pertinent information to (212) 965-0206, Attn: Mr. Dante. The salary is negotiable.

COLUMBIA UNIVERSITY
Student Employment Office: (212) 854-2391

They will post the job description on their board. There is no set fee. You will negotiate that with the student you hire.

THE FRENCH CULINARY INSTITUTE
Student Employment Office • (212) 219-8890

Fax a detailed job description with the fee and hours needed to (212) 431-3054.

INTERNATIONAL BARTENDERS SCHOOL
Placement Office: (212) 239-4700

You can hire the instructors themselves; the students are a little cheaper. All are licensed by New York State for responsible service of alcohol, and are fully competent to help with liquor selection and setting up. They will also wear the standard uniform. The school will make sure you get the right person. The cost is $17.50 for a four-hour minimum booked at least a week in advance. The cost will be more with less lead time. The school also provides wine stewards and waiters.

INTERNATIONAL CENTER OF PHOTOGRAPHY • (212) 860-1777

Fax a detailed job description to (212) 722-3674 and they will then post it on their bulletin board. The salary can be negotiated between you and the student.

JEWELRY ARTS INSTITUTE • (212) 362-8633

If you send a job description, they will post it on their bulletin board. Their address is: 2180 Broadway, New York, NY 10024. The fee is negotiable between you and the student.

JUILLIARD SCHOOL OF MUSIC
Placement Office: (212) 799-5000, ext. 313

The director and associate director will find the right people for the job. The fee is set by the school.

KATHERINE GIBBS SECRETARIAL SCHOOL • (212) 973-4940

Ask for Julia Slick. She will post the job. The fee is set by you and the student.

NEW YORK RESTAURANT SCHOOL
Placement Office: (212) 226-5500, ext. 359

Your request gets reviewed, and Jane Miller makes sure the student or graduate will suit your needs. You will hear from students and graduates. The average salary is $15 an hour, negotiable.

NEW YORK SCHOOL OF INTERIOR DESIGN
Career Placement Office: • (212) 472-1500, ext. 34

The Career Placement Office can find you a graduate student to do anything from choosing paint colors to renovating an apartment. The fee is set between you and the student.

NEW YORK UNIVERSITY
Student Employment Office: (212) 998-4757

This student employment office handles staffing for the entire university, including their business and film schools. You can fax a job description to (212) 995-4197. You should include a job title, rate of compensation (set by you), skills needed, time needed, as well as your phone and fax. You can also list a job description online at www.nyu.edu/careerservices.

PARSONS SCHOOL OF DESIGN
Office of Career Services: (212) 229-8940

The school will check the student's portfolio to make sure he or she is well-suited for the job. You can tap into fashion designers, photographers, and interior decorators. The fee is set between you and the student.

PETER KUMP'S COOKING SCHOOL
Placement Office: (212) 847-0700

Tell the school exactly what you are looking for. The description is posted on the board, and postgrads and undergrads consult the board. You will set the fee with the student but the price averages about $15 to $20 an hour.

SCHOOL OF VISUAL ARTS
Office of Career Development: (212) 592-2370

The job description will go up on the board. You will have access to photographers, video experts, calligraphers, and graphic designers. The fee is negotiable.

SCREEN ACTORS GUILD • (212) 944-1030

You can fax a job description to (212) 944-6774, Attention: Bulletin Board. The job will be posted. It will cost you approximately $12 an hour.

SOLUTION:
ALL DRESSED UP
AND *ACTUALLY* SOMEPLACE TO GO.

It's no secret that New Yorkers pay a king's ransom for "stepping out" in style in this city. Those of us who can't pay $70 for a Broadway ticket, or $500 to a black tie benefit, can find creative ways to enjoy the same events, and sometimes from a more interesting vantage point.

Enjoy Cultural events the inexpensive way

Subscriptions and small donations can make the world of NYC culture, your oyster. By helping to support the arts, you will be treated as an insider. In addition, there are many ways to take advantage of reduced rates for first-class performances.

• **Amato Opera • 319 Bowery • (212) 228-8200** The Amato's have just celebrated their 15th year. This Italian couple still produces wonderful classical opera with the help of very talented Juilliard and Met students. You can avail yourself of this treat for about $20.00 a ticket.

• **Brooklyn Academy of the Arts • 30 Lafayette Street, Brooklyn (728) 636-4100** BAM has just celebrated its 140th birthday. One of New York's finest cultural meccas. It has an abundance of music, dance, and theater offerings. Do not overlook the new Rose Cinema, specializing in independent and foreign films.

- **The New York City Ballet and Opera:** For an annual guild membership fee of $70 to each, you can attend rehearsals and seminars, as well as receive newsletters, mailings, and shopping discounts. For more information, call the New York City Ballet at (212) 870-5677 and the New York City Opera at (212) 870-5626.

- **The Juilliard School:** holds free recitals in dance, music and drama throughout the year. A few cost about $10 and tickets can be bought the day of the performance. Call (212) 799-5000 for more information.

- **Lincoln Center Theatres:** A $35 annual membership entitles you to reserve any available seat for one of their productions for $25. These include the Vivian Beaumont, the Mitzi E. Newhouse, the Barrymore, and the Brooklyn Academy of Music. Call (212) 239-6277 for membership information. If you have difficulty gaining membership to Lincoln Center Theatres, you may want to try "Beaumont Plus." Beaumont Plus affords members tickets to productions at the Vivian Beaumont Theatre, or in a Broadway theatre, or to any production at the Mitzi E. Newhouse Theatre which extends beyond its original scheduled run. The annual fee is $20, and the ticket fee is $25. For more information, call (212) 239-6277.

- **A $60 annual membership to The Film Society of Lincoln Center.** (212) 875-5610, entitles you to advance mailings to events as well as *Film Comment* magazine. They hold three major events: the spring gala, the new directors and new films series, and the New York Film Festival.

- **The New York Philharmonic At Avery Fisher Hall** allows the public to attend open rehearsals. Rehearsals are held at 9:45 A.M. The cost of a ticket is $12. Call (212) 875-5656 for a calendar of upcoming rehearsals.

- **Join The Quicktix Line At The Joseph Papp Public Theater:** You can purchase discount tickets any time before 6:00 P.M. for evening performances and before 1:00 P.M. for matinees. They are sold a half-hour prior to performances on a first come, first served basis and cost $15. Call (212) 260-2400.

- **Audience Extras:** Join Audience Extras and receive tickets to off-Broadway shows, movie previews, cabarets, comedy clubs, dance and sporting events, and an occasional Broadway show. An annual membership is $85, and entitles you to choose from over a 1,000 different events a year. You only pay a mere $3 per ticket. Call (212) 989-9550 for more information.

- **Broadway and Off-Broadway Shows at a Reduced Rate:** Buy day-of-performance tickets at TKTS, West 47th Street and Broadway, 3:00-8:00 P.M. daily for evening performances; 10:00 A.M.-2:00 P.M. for Wednesday and Saturday matinees; 11:00 A.M. until closing for Sunday performances

  TKTS at 2 World Trade Center (mezzanine) is open Monday through Friday 11:00 A.M.-5:30 P.M.; Saturday 11:00 A.M.-3:30 P.M.; closed Sundays. Tickets to Wednesday, Saturday, and Sunday matinees can be purchased the day before the performances at this location.

  Both TKTS locations accept only cash and traveler's checks. For more information, call (212) 768-1818.

- **The Hit Show Club** is a free club that distributes "twofer" coupons for certain Broadway plays. These coupons should be brought to the particular box office and then you may purchase regular seats, two for the price of one. To join, send a self-addressed, stamped envelope for your first mailing to The Hit Show Club, 630 Ninth Avenue, New York, NY 10036, (212) 581-4211.

- **Theatre Development Fund:** By sending in $15 to the Theatre Development Fund, you will receive discounted tickets to Broadway and off-Broadway shows. Call (212) 221-0013 to be placed on the Fund's mailing list.

- **Buy Tickets At The Last Minute:** If you don't mind procrastinating, you could save yourself a bundle. Some theaters offer reduced rates on unsold tickets an hour before curtain time.

- **Museums:** Become a member of your favorite museum by donating $50 - $500 a year. As a card-carrying member, you are entitled to museum mailings such as newsletters and in-house magazines, private previews of new exhibits and invitations to black-tie openings, usually the turf of the rich and famous.

- **James Beard Foundation:** By becoming a member of the James Beard Foundation for a minimum of $125 per year, you will receive a free subscription to *The Beard House* magazine which discusses the latest gastronomy news and upcoming events. You will also receive *The James Beard Foundation Restaurant Guide,* an insider's guide that will help you find the best restaurants in the country; members enjoy special benefits when they dine at many of these restaurants. Foundation members can also savor the creations of both emerging and established chefs at the Beard House, and receive notices of culinary events happening in New York and throughout the country. Call (212) 675-4984 for additional membership information.

- **TV, Film & Radio at Inexpensive Prices:** Enjoy lectures and seminars presented by media experts at the American Museum of the Moving Image and the Museum of Television and Radio. Or, take advantage of the museums' vast collections of television and radio programs and films. If you wish to become a member, you will receive free admission to the museums, as well as priority registration and reduced rates on programs and special events. Call the American Museum of the Moving Image at (718) 784-0077 and the Museum of Television and Radio at (212) 621-6600 for membership information and a calendar of events.

- **The 92nd Street Y:** One of the best kept secrets in town. For $18 a ticket you can participate in lectures, panel discussions and interviews with the people of the moment. The Y attracts best-selling authors, world leaders, scientists, politicians, and comedians - the likes of Colin Powell, Marcia Clarke, Gorbachev, Dominic Dunne and Clint Eastwood. Call (212) 996-1100 for "The Y Catalog" of upcoming events, or go online at www.92ndsty.org.

- **St. John the Devine • 1047 Amsterdam Avenue • (212) 662-2133** One of the largest Gothic cathedrals in the world, seating over 3000 people. Aside from offering church services, the cathedral is used for wonderful concerts, seminars and childrens' activities.

World class outings, absolutely free!

- **New York City** sponsors countless free events throughout the year, usually held in one of the City's parks. You can bring a picnic and enjoy free concerts given by such luminaries as Paul Simon and Luciano Pavorotti. The Department of Parks & Recreation has a special events hot line which tells you all the free events that are taking place in the parks in the City. The number is (212) 360-3456.

- **Barnes & Noble:** New York City is a critical promotional stop for touring authors. Barnes and Noble stores all over Manhattan regularly host complimentary lectures, book signings and readings by the "authors du jour". Call your local bookstore for a schedule of special events.

- **The Metropolitan Opera** performs free concerts in each borough during the Summer. Call (212) 362-6000 for a list of upcoming events.

- **The New York Philharmonic** gives free performances in all the boroughs in the Summer. Call (212) 875-5000 for more information.

- **Carnegie Hall** sponsors the Carnegie Hall Neighborhood Concert Series from September through May. Call (212) 903-9741 to find out when a concert will be performed in your local community center, church, or library.

- **Free Summertime Movies And Concerts At Bryant Park:** During the week, at lunch-time and in the evening, Bryant Park offers free classical, jazz, and Broadway-theme concerts. On Monday evenings after sunset, HBO presents a classic film each week. Stop by Bryant Park for a calendar, or call (212) 391-4248.
- **Free Concerts, Dance, and Readings at Summerstage in Central Park:** At Summerstage, Rumsey Playfield, mid-Central Park at East 72nd Street (212) 360-2777, you can enjoy free performances from mid-June through early August.
- **Free Shakespeare In Central Park:** Joseph Papp's New York Shakespeare Festival presents free performances in Central Park at the Delacorte Theater during the summer. Call (212) 861-7277.
- **Lincoln Center's Out-of-Doors** offers an array of entertainment on its grand plaza and in Damrosch Park each August. Call (212) 875-5108.
- **Free Concerts At Public Spaces, Both Indoor and Outdoor:** Several public places throughout the City offer free concerts at lunchtime throughout the year — The Citicorp Center on 53rd and Lexington, South Street Seaport, The World Trade Center, The McGraw-Hill Building, The Exxon Building, and many more.
- **Washington Square Music Festival** offers free concerts during the summer. Call (212) 431-1088.
- **Partake in Music, Dance and Theater:** Visit the Winter Garden Plaza and Courtyard, at the World Financial Center in Battery Park City, where you will find shopping, dining and entertainment. It is open seven days a week. For further information, call (212) 945-0505, or look online at www.worldfinancialcenter.com.
- **View Special Exhibits:** Visit the New York Public Library. You can pick up a free calendar of cultural events at any public library branch, call the main branch at (212) 869-8089, or look online at www.nypl.org. Also visit the Forbes Magazine Gallery at 62 Fifth Avenue (12th Street). They are open to the public on Tuesdays, Wednesdays, Fridays and Saturdays, from 10:00 A.M. to 4:00 P.M. Call (212) 206-5548 for further information. As part of the Smithsonian Institution, the National Museum of the American Indian is also free to the public. Located in lower Manhattan at One Bowling Green, it is open seven days a week from 10:00 A.M. to 5:00 P.M., and until 8:00 P.M. on Thursdays. Call (212) 668-6624 for general information, and (212) 514-3888 for a recorded calendar of events.
- **Visit Spectacular Gardens:** Take a drive to the Queens Botanical Garden, located at 45-50 Main Street in Flushing, Queens. The

Botanical Garden is open year-round, Tuesday through Sunday, and offers workshops and special events for children and adults. Call (718) 886-3800 for further information.

- **Chelsea Piers,** a 30-acre sports village located at 23rd Street and the Hudson River, offers free sporting events open to the public. Pier Park, at Chelsea Piers, hosts free summertime concerts and community events. Call Chelsea Piers at (212) 336-6800 and Pier Park at (212) 336-6666 for more information.

Get free tickets to tapings of your favorite TV shows

- **The Rosie O'Donnell Show:** Tapings are generally Monday through Thursday at 10:00 A.M. and Wednesday at 2:00 P.M. Currently, there is a lottery for tickets for the 1999-2000 season. Send a postcard with your name, address, telephone number and number of tickets requested (no more than two) to: The Rosie O'Donnell Show, 30 Rockefeller Plaza, Suite 800E, New York, NY 10112. Standby tickets may be available. For further information, call (212) 506-3288.

- **Live With Regis and Kathie Lee:** Tapings are Monday through Friday at 9:00 A.M. Send a postcard with your name, address, telephone number and number of tickets requested (not to exceed four) to: Live Tickets, Ansonia Station, P.O. Box 777, New York, NY 10023-0777. Standby tickets also may be available at 8:00 A.M. at Columbus Avenue and 47th Street. Call (212) 456-2410 for further information.

- **The View:** Tapings are 11:00 A.M. Monday through Friday. Send a postcard with your name, address, phone number

THE NEW YORK CONVENTION & VISITORS BUREAU PRINTS A LIST OF "BIG APPLE BARGAINS" WHICH TELLS YOU WHERE FREE OR INEXPENSIVE HAPPENINGS ARE GOING ON IN THE CITY. PAST BULLETINS HAVE INCLUDED INFORMATION ON FREE MUSICAL AND DANCE PERFORMANCES AT THE WORLD TRADE CENTER AND FREE OPERA IN CENTRAL PARK. THE LISTING IS AVAILABLE TWICE A YEAR. CALL (212) 484-1244 TO RECEIVE A COPY, OR GO ONLINE: WWW.NYCVISIT.COM.

MANY THEATERS, OPERA HOUSES, AND PERFORMING ARTS CENTERS SELL STANDING-ROOM-ONLY TICKETS. JUST TO NAME A FEW — THE METROPOLITAN OPERA (212) 362-6000, THE NEW YORK STATE THEATER (212) 870-5570, THE JOSEPH PAPP PUBLIC THEATER (212) 260-2400, AND THE JOYCE THEATER (212) 242-0800. IF YOU BUY THEM, YOU MIGHT GET LUCKY AND BE ABLE TO SIT DOWN IN AN EMPTY SEAT.

MOST OF THE BROADWAY AND OFF-BROADWAY THEATERS HAVE SOMETHING CALLED HOUSE SEATS. THESE ARE SEATS THAT ARE RESERVED FOR FRIENDS OF THE CAST, DIRECTOR, PRODUCER, OR OTHERS IN THE BUSINESS. OFTEN PEOPLE DO RESERVE THESE SEATS BUT DO NOT SHOW UP FOR THE PERFORMANCE. WE SUGGEST YOU PICK THREE SOLD-OUT SHOWS THAT YOU WANT TO SEE, AND A HALF-HOUR BEFORE SHOWTIME, GO TO THE THEATER AND ASK IF THE HOUSE SEATS HAVE BEEN USED. IF NOT, THEY WILL SELL THEM TO YOU. MOST LIKELY YOU WILL GET INTO ONE OF THEM. THESE SEATS ARE SOLD AT NORMAL BOX OFFICE PRICES.

MOST MAJOR MUSEUMS SUSPEND THEIR USUAL ADMISSION FEES AT SOME POINT DURING THE WEEK. CALL SOME OF YOUR FAVORITES TO FIND OUT WHEN.

and number of tickets requested (no more than two) to: The View, 320 West 66th Street, New York, NY 10023. Call the ABC Studios at (212) 456-1000 for further information.

- **Late Show with David Letterman:** Tapings are Monday through Thursday at 5:30 P.M. with a second show taped on Thursdays at 8:00 P.M. Send a postcard with your name, address, telephone number and number of tickets requested (no more than two) to: Late Show Tickets, c/o Ed Sullivan Theater, 1697 Broadway, New York, NY 10019. Standby tickets may be available on the day of the show. Call (212) 975-5853 for further information.

- **Saturday Night Live:** Tapings are Saturdays at 11:30 P.M. Send a postcard with your name, address, telephone number, and the number of tickets requested (no more than two) to: 30 Rockefeller Plaza, New York, NY 10112. Standby tickets may also be available the day of the show. Call (212) 664-3056 for further information.

Enjoy behind-the-scenes tours

- **Lincoln Center for the Performing Arts – Metropolitan Opera House:** The Backstage Tour includes dressing rooms, costume areas and set construction areas. Tours are 90 minutes and are scheduled for most weekdays at 3:45 P.M. and Saturdays at 10:00 A.M., from October through June. Tickets cost $8.00 for adults and $4.00 for children and students. Lincoln Center is located on Broadway between 62nd and 65th Streets. Call (212) 769-7020 for further information and to make a reservation.

- **Radio City Music Hall:** The Grand Tour is offered Monday through Saturday, 10:00 A.M. to 5:00 P.M. and Sundays from

11:00 A.M. to 5:00 P.M. The tour commences approximately every hour at 1260 Avenue of the Americas between 50th and 51st Streets. Tickets cost $13.50 for adults and $9.00 for children 12 and under and are available on a first-come, first-served basis. Call (212) 632-4041 for further information.

Enjoy Drinks and Ambiance

- **Drinks Atop The Roof Garden At The Metropolitan Museum of Art:** In the Spring and Summer, you can sip a drink and enjoy the splendor of the Met's sculpture garden. In the colder months, the balcony overlooking the main entrance at 82nd Street is open for drinks and viewing. Call (212) 535-7710.

- **Drinks at the Finest Restaurants in the City:** You can experience the ambiance and luxury of the most expensive restaurants in Manhattan without ordering a meal. Restaurants such as The Rainbow Room, (212) 632-5000, Windows On The World, (212) 938-1111, The Four Seasons, (212) 754-9494, and Lutece (212) 752-2225 allow you to simply order cocktails at their bar.

- **High Tea At Manhattan's Finest Hotels:** Instead of emptying your wallet for a gourmet meal in one of the City's five-star hotels, you can feel like royalty as you enjoy Earl Grey Tea and cucumber sandwiches at high-tea. Most, if not all of the five-star hotels, offer high tea at fairly reasonable prices. The Pierre, (212) 838-8000, The Four Seasons, (212) 758-5700, and the Plaza (212) 546-5350 are just a sampling.

SOLUTION: YOUR OWN PERSONAL SHOPPER AT NO EXTRA CHARGE.

Department store personal shoppers:

There are few things left in life that are free. Department Store Personal Shoppers are one, but for some reason people either still don't know about them, or they don't feel they purchase enough to deserve them. Fact is, department stores created the personal shopper to bring in business, no matter how small, and they are there at your pleasure. It's not only a great time saver, and a luxurious experience, you also get free shopping advice from an expert. Here's what they can do for you:

Wardrobe shopping: You make the call, tell them what you are looking for, and your shopper will do the legwork, pulling all the pieces together. It will all be waiting for you in the private "Personal Shoppers Department" which has fitting rooms, phones for your use, and a pot of coffee brewing.

Wardrobe consulting: Most personal shoppers are very fashion savvy and also know how to mix-and-match outfits to give you a versatile wardrobe within your budget, steering you clear of impulse purchases.

Gift shopping: Whether you have to buy for one or a dozen, call in your list of ideas, and who the gifts are for and your shopper will do the rest. And if you don't know what to give the boss who has everything, your personal shopper will because she's been down this road a million times. If you can't get to the store, she'll be happy to bring the items to you.

Personal care and attention: Like wholesale furriers and jewelers, relationships with personal shoppers can span generations...they get to know you so well that they will spot items for you and put them aside, whether you've asked for them or not; if you need an emergency pair of hose, they will messenger them.

The Intrepid Pages of
Personal Shoppers

BERGDORF GOODMAN
754 Fifth Avenue (at 58th Street)
(212) 872-8812

Bergdorf's personal shopping department has several people who can assist you. It's best to make an appointment about two to three days in advance. You should plan to spend at least one hour there.

BLOOMINGDALE'S
1000 Third Avenue (at 59th Street)

Bloomingdale's has various departments of personal shoppers:

- At His Service (for Men): (212) 705-3030
- At Your Service (Women's Clothing): (212) 705-3135
- Corporate Gifts: (212) 705-3550
- Household Merchandise: (212) 705-2240
- Women's Clothing and Gifts: (212) 705-3375

Make an appointment one week in advance and plan to spend at least one hour in the store.

LORD & TAYLOR
424 Fifth Avenue (38th and 39th St.s)
Women's Personal Fashions:
(212) 391-3519
Men's Fashion Advisor: (212) 382-7607

Their personal shopping office is on the third floor. They are happy to consult with you on the phone. To make an appointment call one week in advance and plan to spend at least one hour in the store.

MACY'S • 151 West 34th Street • (212) 494-4181

"Macy's by Appointment" is organized slightly differently from the other stores. You call and tell them your requirements and then they have a personal shopper call you back to make arrangements with you. You are assigned to a specific consultant who will take care of your every need.

IF YOU REALLY CAN'T AFFORD A WARDROBE CONSULTANT, BUT NEED HELP PUTTING TOGETHER OUTFITS, CONSIDER HIRING A "STYLIST". A STYLIST IS A PROFESSIONAL WHOSE JOB IS TO FIND CLOTHES AND ACCESSORIES FOR PERFORMERS IN COMMERCIALS. MANY MOONLIGHT WHEN THEY AREN'T WORKING. TO FIND ONE, PLACE AN AD IN THEIR UNION'S MONTHLY NEWSLETTER. WRITE TO:
LOCAL 829
16 WEST 61ST STREET
11TH FLOOR
NEW YORK, NY 10023
(212) 581-0300.
ATTENTION: MONTHLY NEWSLETTER.

SAKS FIFTH AVENUE
611 Fifth Avenue (49th and 50th Streets) • (212) 940-4145
Saks for Men: (212) 940-4059

The name of Sak's general personal shopping department is One on One. They have their own private fitting rooms located on the fifth floor. Men and women are both welcome. Call ahead for an appointment and plan to spend one hour.

Independent personal shoppers:

You hire an independent shopper in order to access the designer showrooms and wholesale prices. These shoppers' livelyhoods are made on the relationships they develop with certain designers who give them entree. Most require a minimum order and about a 20% commission, but you still come out ahead because you're buying at the wholesale level. Here's what you need to know about them:

• **Some take you into the showrooms before the clothes hit the retail stores:** That means, for example, that you will buy your fall clothes in June. You get to see the entire line and get first picks. The disadvantage is that you usually can't try on the clothes. Professional shoppers, however, have a good eye for what will fit you or require a slight alteration. You must pay by check and there are no returns.

• **Some do the shopping for you:** After you've tried the clothes on in the retail stores, they will take your list of designers, sizes and style numbers of the clothes you want, and get them for you wholesale. The downside is that because the line is already out, the designer may not have your items in stock anymore.

• **These independents can only be found through the grape vine:** Because they are in direct competition with department stores and boutiques, they prefer to remain anonymous. The only way to access them is through word of mouth. If you call the Intrepid New Yorker, we will give you a few names.

Wardrobe and image consultants:

It would be a serious stretch to say that there is no extra charge for the services of wardrobe consultants, but it can be a very worthwhile one-time-only expense that, in the long run, will save you piles of money. If you are someone who has yet to discover a style to call your own, and who has a closest full of clothes, half of which you never wear, you are a potential candidate. They look at the clothes you have and tell you what to get rid of, paring your wardrobe down to the items that can be worked into outfits. The consultant then strategically purchases the remaining items you need to complete a spare but versatile wardrobe, for every season.

They will put together a wardrobe chart of styles, colors, and mixing-and-matching possibilities that you can work from yourself, from then on. The savings come in the versatility and real usefulness of your wardrobe, as well as the built-in control over impulse buying.

The Intrepid Pages of
Wardrobe & Image Consultants

ACCENT ON IMAGE • By Appointment: (212) 868-0536

Laura Lopata knows how to make people feel good about the way they look. Her talent lies in creating a wardrobe that will reflect your own personal style and most effectively meet your lifestyle needs. It all starts with an at-home consultation where Laura will go through your closet, rearrange your garments to make getting dressed easier, and offer advice on what to buy. She then takes you shopping. Laura keeps a file on each client of every garment he/she owns. A client can then call Laura for advice on what to wear to a special occasion, a business presentation, or dinner with a special someone. Laura's fee is $150 per hour.

CAROLYN GUSTAFSON, INC./
IMAGE STRATEGIES FOR MEN & WOMEN
By Appointment: (212) 755-4456

Carolyn is a former model and actress who knows how to dress and where to go to buy clothes. She is great at accommodating your needs and budget. Carolyn specializes in image evaluation, color analysis, hair/makeup advice, wardrobe evaluation and planning, personal shopping, and communication skills coaching. She works on an hourly basis, which means that she does not have a vested interest in seeing you spend thousands of dollars. Her fee for your first two-hour consultation is $500. Each additional hour is $150. She is well worth it.

PHYLLIS FINKEL/PERSONAL SHOPPER
By Appointment: (212) 860-0718

Phyllis will take you directly to the designer showrooms to purchase European and American collections, ranging from sportswear to black tie, or to have items customized. Remember: Although you will be privy to designer garments at half the price of what they sell for at Bergdorf, Saks, and Barneys, the items are still couture— expensive and ultra high-end. Phyllis' fee is 20% of your total purchase price.

SUCCESSFUL WAYS AND MEANS
By Appointment: (212) 877-1417

Susan Dresner has been in business for 17 years, and knows the in's and out's of the wardrobe/image consulting industry. She charges a yearly membership of $255 and provides her clients with their own personal profile, plus body analysis, color and wardrobe analysis, yearly budget, and referrals for shopping services during the year should the client suddenly need a special pair of shoes or an evening dress. Susan charges $95 an hour to take you shopping. A special feature of Susan's services is that she hosts trunk shows for members, in which designers from all over the world showcase their work. In addition to buying directly from the designers without paying a middleman, they will customize the clothing to meet your specific requirements.

SOLUTION:
HOW TO AFFORD CLOTHES THAT ARE MADE TO ORDER.

Most of us believe that having clothes made to order is so out of our league that we wouldn't even consider it. At face value, it would appear to be true. But if you are very selective about how and when to spend that kind of money, the long term savings will ultimately greatly outweigh the upfront financial hit. Here's what we mean:

> "IF YOU BUY THE BETTER DESIGNER LABELS AND THEIR SUPERIOR FABRICS, YOU SHOULD CONSIDER HAVING YOUR CLOTHES MADE. IT WILL ACTUALLY COST YOU LESS TO HAVE THEM MADE THAN TO BUY CLOTHES AT THAT PRICE OFF THE RACK."
>
> —ARIEL LAWRENCE, CUSTOM DRESSMAKING CONSULTANT

- It's a smart shopper that buys a few classic wardrobe staples that will not only last decades but make you look like a million bucks. In other words, you are paying for a lifetime guarantee, a piece that is beautifully made, fits perfectly to your body, and looks great no matter what the trends. The key is to have classic pieces made that can be mixed and matched over the years with trendier pieces.

- You are ordering a piece of clothing exactly the way you want it, and that can be altered to reflect current fashion styles. A man's suit, for example can have thin or wide lapels, cuffs or not, slit or flapped pockets. For a woman, just the right style of sleeve or collar, or flared, narrow or pleated skirt. Ask your tailor to make sure there is enough "play" in the fabric to make style or weight alterations throughout the life of the item.

- There are a few extra tricks to adding value. When having a suit made, get an extra pair of pants made, and perhaps in a different style. It not only gives you a more versatile wardrobe, it extends the life of the suit.

"BUILDING A WARDROBE AROUND CUSTOM-MADE CLOTHING AFFORDS YOU THE OPTION OF ACCENTUATING YOUR BEST FIGURE ASSETS ALL THE TIME. FOR INSTANCE, IF YOU FIND A SUIT THAT WORKS FOR YOU, YOU CAN REMAKE IT IN SEVERAL COLORS, AND BY USING DIFFERENT FABRICS, BUTTONS, AND TRIM YOU COME OUT WITH SEVERAL TERRIFIC SUITS THAT CAN BE MIXED AND MATCHED ALL YEAR LONG."

— ARIEL LAWRENCE, CUSTOM DRESSMAKING CONSULTANT

Tips for finding a tailor or seamstress:

- Word of mouth is the only way to go. You want a true craftsman. Never go in blind. The high end fabric stores usually have a list of quality clothes makers.

- Some may specialize more in sportswear, evening clothes or suits.

- Get references and interview the candidate in person. Look at samples of his/her work.

- Find out if the tailor helps customers choose fabrics and patterns, and if there is an extra charge for that. Is there an extra cost for purchasing thread, lining, interfacing.

- Get all price ranges depending on the quality of the fabric and difficulty of the pattern.

- Get several estimates. The same quality of work can vary greatly in charges.

The Intrepid Pages of
Dressmakers & Tailors

DRESSMAKING CONSULTANT
ARIEL LAWRENCE
526 East 5th Street • By Appointment (212) 529-2889

Ariel is the link between you and the dressmaker/tailor. If you don't have time or are not confident about your color or design choice, Ariel is the person you need. She has impeccable taste and has a background in design. Ariel will meet with you at your home or office, and will discuss styles and fabric choices to fit into your lifestyle and needs. She then finds the appropriate dressmaker or tailor. She "holds your hand" the entire way. All compliments, complaints, and payment are made to her. For this hassle-free approach to getting your clothes made you will pay more, but it is sure worth it.

DRESSMAKERS

ANDERKO - CUSTOM CLOTHIER
(212) 289-2988 • By Appointment

Deborah offers a full range of professional alterations for ladies and men. She specializes in custom bridal and wedding party wear. Custom dressmaking by way of duplicating those favorite items in your closet is a valuable service. Fabric shopping services, swatching, and home visits are available at an additional fee.

THE BLOUSE SHOP
1224 Lexington Avenue (82nd and 83rd Streets)
(212) 879-6094 • By Appointment

A shop that caters to women who want custom-made silk blouses. You can bring in your own fabric, or choose from over 100 shades on their color chart. A range of style options are available. You will pay about $250 for this service.

EVA DEVECSERY • 201 East 61st Street • (212) 751-6091

You can expect expert craftsmanship at Eva's studio, which is why many of the elite and well-to-do from as far away as Europe have garments designed there. The large staff consists of five tailors and five dressmakers who can design both day and evening wear.

Although most of their work is custom-made, each season they do have some garments you can buy off the rack, as well as others that serve as samples of frequently ordered standards. They also stock imported fabrics from Europe, and have fabric books on-hand. Prices for silk blouses start at about $280 (with their fabric); simple dresses at about $400. Eva only alters garments for regular customers on the items her dressmakers have designed.

HOLLY KRüEGER
28 Bethune Street (Washington and Greenwich)
(917) 862-9132

Holly fashions a line of suits and dresses each season which you can have custom-made to your specifications. Holly's aim is to translate the attributes of men's tailoring into the clothes she designs for women. She uses imported fabrics and each item is hand-tailored in the Old World tradition. A jacket and trousers cost around $1,500; $1,000 for a dress. Garments take four to six weeks.

ROSETTE COUTURIERE
160 West 71st Street • (212) 877-3372 • By Appointment

Brenda Barmore runs the shop and creates stylish custom garments, and does some copying and interpretation, as well as alterations. She is known for her honest, innovative, and timely work. Charges for repairs are fairly modest. Custom-made nine-to-five suits start at $550 (prices do not include fabric); dinner suits, at $650; trousers, at $175. Brenda is also skilled at renovating vintage clothing.

SURANG YAMNARM'S
767 Lexington Avenue (at 60th Street) • (212) 371-4842

Surang does both creating and copying. She gets calls from all over the United States so be sure to make an appointment well in advance. She can copy a Chanel as well as judge what original creation will look good on you. Her prices are moderate.

TAILORS & MADE-TO-MEASURE

BESPOKE ENTERPRISES
200 Central Park South (at 59th Street) • (212) 581-9003

Jack Simpson runs this spacious space, where men can shop for made-to-measure clothing. The suits, which are actually constructed at a well-respected shop in Brooklyn, are crafted with the finest fabrics. If you wish, Jack will advise you on your current wardrobe and tell you what to add and what to get rid of. Custom-made suits start at $1,200; shirts are $195 and up; ties range from $85 to $125.

DYNASTY TAILOR • 6 East 38th Street • (212) 679-1075

Although Hong Kong is far away, some of their best tailors are here. Joseph is one of them. He has an incredible understanding of fabric and style and his prices are reasonable. Don't be afraid to have him copy your favorite suit. He can also make you an original. They are happy to alter both men's and women's clothing.

L.N.C. CUSTOM TAILOR COMPANY, INC.
83 Baxter Street (near Centre Street)
(212) 406-9527

This tiny shop on a small street does fabulous custom tailoring at moderate prices. Their attention to detail, style, and timeliness is impeccable. Their fabric selection is excellent and they do their best to explain to you all your options. They will alter both men's and women's garments.

MID CITY TAILOR
28 West 44th Street • (212) 719-2215

The entire fashion industry seems to use these old-world tailors who cater to both men and women. Their alterations are done promptly, accurately, and inexpensively. Best of all they don't try to over-alter your clothes.

TOM JAMES OF MANHATTAN
(212) 973-0384, extension 21

Tom James Company is the largest manufacturer and retailer of tailored men's clothing in the world. What sets them apart from other clothiers is that they cater to busy clients by coming directly to the home or office. All purchases and fittings are made in your home or office, at your convenience. The company has thousands of fabrics and hundreds of styles from which to choose. The clothiers are trained in image consulting and can advise you on colors, patterns, and styles. Ted Fisher, Executive Clothier, is especially helpful and knowledgeable. Custom suits are $575 and up; off-the-rack suits start at $350.

CUSTOM NECKTIES

ROSA CUSTOM TIES • 30 West 57th Street • (212) 245-2191

An inexpensive way to express a man's individuality and to spruce up a wardrobe. A hand-stitched Rosa tie, at $95 to $125, can be created from a selection of 5,000-plus Italian silks. A paper pattern is cut and kept on file for each customer. There is no minimum order required. Turnaround time is one week to ten days.

CUSTOM SHIRTS

There is nothing that fits better, wears better, or looks better than a custom-made man's shirt.

CEGO CUSTOM SHIRTMAKER
174 Fifth Avenue (22nd and 23rd Streets) • (212) 620-4512
By Appointment Only

Carl Goldberg owns and runs Cego, which has been in business for fifteen years. Custom shirts range from $75 to $135, depending on the fabric. A cotton pinpoint shirt is $85 and an ultra cotton pinpoint is $100. They require that you purchase two shirts at your first fitting, and usually require a four shirt minimum thereafter. Delivery is within three weeks.

NICKY BELLANI
72 Narrows Road South (Staten Island) • (718) 447-7653

Nick's craftsmanship is excellent and his prices are reasonable. Polyester and cotton shirts are $55 per shirt (minimum order five shirts); Egyptian cotton, $68 per shirt (minimum order five shirts); Sea Island cotton, $75 per shirt (minimum order five shirts); $3 per shirt for a monogram. Shirts take about four weeks to make, so order early.

THE SHIRT STORE
51 East 44th Street (at Vanderbilt) • (800) 289-2744

Here you can have a shirt customized, or you can purchase ready-to-wear styles. A custom cotton pinpoint shirt is $115; ready-to-wear—$52.50. A customized Egyptian cotton shirt costs $125; ready-to-wear—$62.50. All custom orders require a minimum of 4 shirts. Made-to-measure (by machine) custom shirts take 4 to 6 weeks. Hand-made shirts take 8 to 10 weeks. Prices are comparable for machine and hand customization.

CUSTOM WOMEN'S JEANS

LEVI STRAUSS & CO.
3 East 57th Street • (212) 838-2125

Wouldn't it be great to own a pair of jeans that fit your figure like they were made for you? Levi's "Personal Pair Jeans" is the answer. All you do is have your measurements taken at the store. The data is fed into a computer which suggests a pair of prototype jeans. You will need to try on a few prototypes to determine exactly what fits you the best. Then you will choose a style and color. The price is $65, only about $15 more than a pair of non-custom Levi's jeans. Delivery is within ten to fifteen days. To make ordering new jeans more convenient, your jeans will be fitted with an individual bar code number so you do not have to go through the fitting process again.

The Intrepid Pages of
Fabric Stores for Clothes

BANKSVILLE DESIGNER FABRICS • Norwalk, CT • (203) 846-1333

Here they buy the best of the designer leftover fabrics, in all natural fiber. All fabrics are labeled by designer and content and they are about one-third less than the price in New York fabric stores.

B & J FABRIC • 263 West 40th Street • (212) 354-8150

If you are looking for a specific color and fabric go to B & J first. Their prices are reasonable and the selection is good.

PARON FABRICS • 56 West 57th Street • (212) 247-6451

Paron sells a good selection of fabrics at reasonable prices. They buy designer fabrics from jobbers.

STORES ON 40TH STREET
BETWEEN SEVENTH AND EIGHTH AVENUES

There are many stores that sell silks, wool gabardine, and wool crêpe in a tremendous array of colors.

The Intrepid Pages of
Trim Stores

GORDON BUTTON COMPANY, INC.
222 West 38th Street • (212) 921-1684

Incredible selection.

K TRIMMING & ZIPPERS
519 Broadway (Spring and Broome Streets) • (212) 431-8929

Trimmings as well as hundreds of buttons. You must have an idea of what you want; otherwise you will be overwhelmed.

M & J TRIMMING COMPANY
1008 Sixth Avenue (37th and 38th Streets) • (212) 391-9072

Everything you need to trim your outfit—beading, shoulder pads, feathers, patches, and much, much more.

TENDER BUTTONS • 143 East 62nd Street • (212) 758-7004

Non-New Yorkers would never believe that a salesperson will happily search for just the right button for you, even if you are only spending 15 cents. And you are bound to find what you need.

SOLUTIONS:
AUCTIONS 'R US.

Most auctions are mom and pop affairs, not the Sotheby's spectacles of Van Gogh and Jackie O sales.

There are many more small estate sales that are accessible throughout the tri-state area. And most are very affordable. It's a great way to buy one-of-a-kind treasures and home furnishings that on a retail level, would be way out of your budget. And it's a shopping method that is fun, and not the least bit intimidating once you get the hang of it:

- **Find out about upcoming auctions by looking in the local newspapers:** Every Friday, notices about estate sales throughout the NYC tri-state region are posted.

- **Auction houses hold exhibit days:** Prior to the auction, exhibit times are held to allow the public to inspect the items that will be auctioned. In-house experts are there to answer any questions, educate you and tell you about the "resale condition" of the item. You have all the time in the world to look over the selection and decide which items you really want to buy.

- **Auction houses offer catalogs featuring a detailed description, picture and estimated cost of every item up for sale:** The auction house experts set an estimated price range they believe the item will sell for, based on what they believe the piece is worth. In reality the item could go for much less or more, depending on the bidding activity.

- **The day of the auction:** Having been thoroughly educated by the advance exhibit, catalogs and staff experts, and knowing what items you plan to bid for, you have eliminated any chance for trial and error or unexpected surprise. At this point your focus needs to be on what your budget limit is, no matter how badly you want a particular piece.

The Intrepid Pages
of Auctions

SCHOOL AUCTIONS

Some of the auctions that are the most fun and have the best buys are held at fund-raising benefits for the various private and public schools throughout the City. The PTA of each school works for close to a year getting individuals and companies to donate cars, vacations, classes, merchandise, weekends away, professional services, summer camp fees, hot-air balloon rides, art work, and whatever else they can drum up. Ask your friends if their child's school has such a benefit. You can pick up great deals and give money to a good cause all at the same time.

YOU CAN NOW BID ONLINE. WWW.AUCTIONSON-LINE.COM OFFERS A COMPREHENSIVE LIST OF SECOND-TIER AUCTION HOUSES WITH ADDRESSES, TELEPHONE NUMBERS, AND LINKS TO INDIVIDUAL WEB SITES.

YOU CAN USE EBAY.COM TO BUY AND SELL ITEMS IN MORE THAN 1,000 CATEGORIES, INCLUDING ANTIQUES, COINS AND STAMPS, COLLECTIBLES, DOLLS, JEWELRY, SPORTS MEMORABILIA AND TOYS. TOUTED AS THE WORLD'S LARGEST PERSONAL ONLINE TRADING COMMUNITY, WWW.EBAY.COM OFFERS ONE-TO-ONE TRADING IN AN AUCTION FORMAT.

AUCTION HOUSES

CHRISTIE'S
20 Rockefeller Plaza • (212) 636-2000

High-end merchandise that usually sets the tone for what is considered to be valuable. Call for information on upcoming auctions.

CHRISTIE'S EAST
219 East 67th Street • (212) 606-0400

There are more affordable buys here. Call to see what the next auction offers.

GUERNSEY'S
108 East 73rd Street • (212) 794-2280

Guernsey's holds auctions about every three months. They are considered to be a leader in auctioning mass 20th Century Popular Culture items, such as Walt Disney and Rock 'n Roll memorabilia. They also auction the unique and unusual, like wooden carvings, carnival and sports memorabilia, and even antique cars.

PHILLIPS
406 East 79th Street • (212) 570-4830

Founded in 1796, Phillips is the largest privately-owned auction house in the world. Their gallery holds sales of antique and modern jewelry and watches, impressionist, modern, and contemporary art, furniture and decorations, 20th Century decorative arts, fine Judaica, Hebrew books and works of art, natural history, fine and rare wines, and golfing memorabilia. Whether you are interested in buying or selling at auction, or receiving a professional valuation, Phillips' expert and friendly staff can help.

SOTHEBY'S • 1334 York Avenue (at 72nd Street) • (212) 606-7000

Sotheby's is considered to be the most powerful and influential auction house in the world. Call for upcoming auction dates.

SOTHEBY'S ARCADE
1334 York Avenue (at 72nd Street) • (212) 606-7409

At the arcade you will find some less expensive and valuable collectibles as well as merchandise that wasn't exclusive enough to make it into their specialized sales.

TEPPER GALLERIES • 110 East 25th Street • (212) 677-5300

Tepper handles estates of all sizes and quality as well as individual pieces. You can find jewelry, lamps, furniture, and paintings. Prices can go high but they do start fairly low. Auctions are held every other Saturday.

THE TREASURE AUCTION
(Next door to William Doyle Galleries) • (212) 427-2314

Doyle operates a perpetual tag sale of goods from estate sales that could not sell at auction. A fun place to browse and buy.

WILLIAM DOYLE GALLERIES
175 East 87th Street • (212) 427-2730

William Doyle appears to fall in the middle of the auction houses. Their goods tend not to compete with Christie's and Sotheby's yet they seem more discerning than Tepper. Auctions are usually held on Wednesday's.

The Intrepid Pages
of Flea Markets

YOU CAN ACCESS A LIST OF UPCOMING STREET FAIRS ON LINE AT:
WWW.CI.NYC.NY.US/HTML/CAU/ HTML/EVENTS.HTML

ANNEX ANTIQUES FAIR AND FLEA MARKET
Sixth Avenue between 24th and 26th Streets • (212) 243-5343
Saturday and Sunday, 9:00 A.M. to 5:00 P.M.
Admission: $1

IS 44 FLEA MARKET
Columbus Avenue (at 77th Street) • (212) 721-0900
Sunday, 10:00 A.M. to 6:00 P.M.
(Outside as well as inside)

PS 183 FLEA MARKET
419 East 66th Street • (212) 721-0900
Saturday, 6:00 A.M. to 6:00 P.M.

YORKVILLE FLEA MARKET • 351 East 74th Street • (212) 535-5235
Saturday, 6:00 A.M. to 4:00 P.M.

SOLUTIONS:
NYC IS A RESOURCE "PHENOM"

NEW YORKERS IN THE KNOW USE THESE RESOURCES TO GET WHAT THEY WANT, EXACTLY THE WAY THEY WANT IT.

There are more specialty stores and services, cultural institutions, exotic products, self-help support organizations, universities, professions, craftsmen, hotlines, publications, experts, academics and advanced technology under one skyline than anywhere else in the world—and they lead New Yorkers to exactly what they need. Don't know where to begin? Use your logic and common sense to take you directly to the source. Some examples of what we mean:

Take advantage of the foreign embassies, consulates and associations, located here in NYC:

A client came to us at a loss as to how to find antique French china called Compare. She was trying to replenish a set that had been broken over the years but had had no luck via the French antique store route. We suggested she call NYC's French Bureau of Trade; they in turn gave her a list of merchants and organizations most likely to be of help. One was Brodean Fine Dining, a service that actually conducts searches for discontinued lines. Another was Replacements Limited at 800-562-4462, which for a small fee does a complete search.

Professional and vocational schools can help you find just about anything:

"I needed a bridesmaid dress but hated everything I saw on the rack. I called The Fashion Institute, a world-renowned school for fashion designing in NYC. As it turns out they have a Career Services Department, and they gave me a list of three or four graduate designers to call. The designer I picked invited me into her home, let me pick out materials, colors and the style I wanted, and made a dress to order that was way below retail prices."

Finding the right academic or professional niche for that obscure skill or unique expertise:

A client of mine was being relocated to New York, and her husband was going to transfer with her. The problem was that he needed to find a job in his field - a complex and obscure area in environmental and chemical engineering - and wanted to know if I could help. Knowing that New York City can accommodate just about any type of job seeker, I hit Barnes & Noble for resources. Sure enough, in the New York City section where there were over 500 titles, I found a huge encyclopedia called *The New York Job Book*. And within it, there were lists and lists of organizations, companies and academic institutions related to his area of expertise.

SOLUTIONS:
PICK ONE PASSION OR INDULGENCE AND FEED IT

No matter what kind of budget restrictions you have, give in to one indulgence; do whatever you have to do to have mad money left over at the end of the month to splurge on something that really makes a difference to you and your quality of life. We guarantee you will stop feeling like one of those "have-nots".

A few magnificent indulgences to whet your appetite:

Take a class from a famous person:

New York has many of the finest universities and professional schools anywhere in the world. It is conceivable to take a course or hear a lecture from George Stephanopolis at Columbia on political science; from Julia Child at the James Beard Foundation, from Al Pacino at NYU film school.

Car Services:

You can reserve a chauffeured luxury town car from one of dozens of car services in New York and be picked up and driven to your appointments for not much more than a taxi, and sometimes for less. When we have a full errand and shopping day, we hire one for several hours at $20 an hour; they drive us, wait for us, keep our packages and coats for us, and we probably save 3 hours in hassle and headache lugging packages on and off public transportation. If it still doesn't feel like a bargain, schedule the shopping day with a friend and share the cost.

Dine in a world renowned restaurant:

The 4 and 5-star restaurants can be widely expensive — the trick to being able to partake in the experience is to go for lunch. *All* the top restaurants have a prix-fix lunch that average $35 per person. A far cry from the $100 plus it might cost you at dinner.

Indulgence:

Treat yourself to one delicious, luxurious accessory. It can have the effect of turning the ordinary into the extraordinary. Purchase a Pashmina scarf or a Hermes tie. Whenever you wear it, you will feel, look and behave like a member of the Fifth Avenue set.

Pampering:

If pampering makes you feel rich, go world class with your favorite way to relax. Whether you love getting your hair cut, or having a pedicure, or perhaps getting a backrub, become a well-known regular at a salon with a world class staff, a world class environment, and world class service. There is no surer way to feel from the manor born.

FOR THOSE
SPECIAL INDULGENCES,
SEE THE NEXT CHAPTER —
THE BEST OF THE BEST

The Best of the Best

MYSTERY BOOKSHOP:
THE BLACK ORCHID BOOKSHOP
303 East 81st Street • (212) 734-5980
MURDER INK
2486 Broadway (92nd St) • (212) 362-8905

COOKING BOOKSHOP:
KITCHEN ARTS & LETTERS
1435 Lexington Avenue (93rd St) • (212) 876-3584

CHILDREN'S BOOKSHOP:
BOOKS OF WONDER
16 West 18th Street • (212) 989-3270

CHILDREN'S TUTORS:
ELIZABETH MAYER • (212) 423-5407
CRAIG EHRLICH • (914) 954-1332
STAMFORD COACHING • (212) 245-3888

AFTER SCHOOL EDUCATION:
SCORES
412 Columbus Avenue (80th St) • (212) 579-9066

BREAD BAKERY:
ECCE PANIS BAKERY
1260 Madison Avenue (90th Street) • (212) 348-0040
1120 Third Avenue (65th and 66th Streets) • (212) 535-2099
282 Columbus Avenue (73rd and 74th Streets) • (212) 362-7189

OLD FASHIONED DESERTS:
THE MAGNOLIA BAKERY
401 Bleecker Street (West 11th Street) • (212) 462-2572

EUROPEAN CHOCOLATES:
NEUHAUS INC.
922 Madison Avenue (73rd and 74th Streets) • (212) 861-2800

SMOKED FISH:
SABLE'S SMOKED FISH
1489 Second Avenue (77th and 78th Streets) (212) 249-6177

MILK IN A BOTTLE:
RONNYBROOK FARM (518) 772-milk

MASSAGE STUDIOS:
CARAPAN • 5 West 16th Street • (212) 633-6220
THE STRESS LESS STEP • (212) 826-6222

DAY SPAS:
BLISS 568 Broadway • (212) 219-8970
AVON • Trump Tower • (212) 755-2866

CATERER:
AS YOU LIKE IT • (212) 260-9888

PARTY PLANNER:
BARBARA ESSES • (212) 744-8136

ICE DELIVERY:
CASA MASINA • (212) 355-3734

WAITERS FOR HIRE:
THE GOODKIND ASSOCIATES • (212) 378-0700

PARTY RENTAL EQUIPMENT:
PARTY RENTALS OF NEW YORK • (212) 288-7384

FLOWER ARRANGER:
DOROTHY WAKO BEAUTIFUL FLOWERS • (212) 686-5569

DECORATED CAKES:
CAKES & SUGAR OBJECTS BY MARGARET BRAUN
(212) 929-1582

COSTUMES:
ABRACADABRA
10 Christopher Street • (212) 627-5745

DATING:
IT'S JUST LUNCH
120 East 56th Street • (212) 750-8899

BAKING SUPPLIES:
NY CAKE & BAKING DISTRIBUTORS
56 West 22nd Street • (212) 675-2253

NEWSPAPER DELIVER SERVICE:
MITCHEL'S • (212) 594-6426

EYE GLASS STORE:
20/20 EYEWEAR
57 East 8th Street • (212) 228-2192
150 East 86th Street • (212) 876-7676

MENTALIST FOR HIRE:
GERARD SENEHI (917) 405-7331

PORTRAIT PHOTOGRAPHER:
BEN ASEN (212) 348-0496

LITERARY AGENT:
CYNTHIA CANNELL (212) 737-7251

DRIVER AND CAR FOR HIRE:
MOHAMMAD • (917) 776-3686

VINTAGE CAR FOR HIRE:
(718) 748-6707

LIBRARY:
THE NEW YORK SOCIETY LIBRARY • (212) 288-6900

JAPANESE ART GALLERY:
THE RONIN ART GALLERY • (212) 688-0188

MOST ACCOMPLISHED UP & COMING ARTIST:
REINER GROSS • (212) 477-3859

PARTY VAN FOR HIRE:
MR. C'S TRANSPORTATION • (718) 370-7780

PIANO TEACHER:
LES HORAN • (212) 580-4837

GUITAR TEACHER:
DAN EMORY • (212) 642-5294

FINANCIAL PRINTER:
GLOBAL PRINTING • (212) 414-7300

BARBER:
KIM AT PAUL MOLE • (212) 988-9176

WAXING:
PAULA ZDOVC • 20 E. 68th St. • (212) 535-6878

ACUPUNCTURE:
DR. CHAN • (212) 661-6888

FRESH FISH:
JOY FISH MARKET • (212) 535-2256

INFORMATION ON PARTY SPACES:
THE BOOK PLACES • (212) 737-7536

GYM EQUIPMENT:
THE GYM SOURCE
40 East 52nd Street (Park & Madison) • (212) 688-4222

WATER SKI LESSONS:
COPAKE BOAT & SKI • (518) 325-5464

GIFTS THAT IMPRESS NEW YORKERS:
ANY ITEM FROM HERMES, CARTIER OR TIFFANY
(they all have at least one gift under $50.00)

MUSEUM MEMBERSHIPS

THEATER & CONCERT TICKETS

DONATIONS TO CHARITIES

STRESS RELIEVING SERVICES

OUTDOOR FUN WITH KID'S: (under $2.00 per child)
TRAM RIDE TO ROOSEVELT ISLAND

SOUTH STREET SEAPORT

CHINATOWN

FERRY TO STATEN ISLAND

THE CAROUSEL IN CENTRAL PARK

THE CLOCK TOWER

INDOOR FUN WITH KIDS'S:
STU LEONARD'S FOOD MARKET IN YONKERS

CHILDREN'S MUSEUM • (212) 721-1234

FAO SCHWARZ • (212) 644-9400

NYC PUBLIC LIBRARIES

BARNES & NOBLE FOR KIDS

SPORTS WORLD IN NEW JERSEY • (201) 262-1717

CHELSEA PIERS

VIDEO GAMES & SOFTWARE:
ELECTRONIC'S BOUTIQUE
(212) 879-9544

Software & Electronic Games. Great return policy.

GOOD CUSTOMER SERVICE:
THE GAP, BANANA REPUBLIC, CITERELLA, ANN TAYLOR

GIFT BASKETS:
FUN BY THE BASKET • (212) 534-5060

PILATES:
POWER PILATES
136 East 57th Street (Lexington/3rd Ave.) • (212) 371-0700

PERFUMERS:
PENHALIGON'S
870 Madison Avenue (70/71 St.) • (212) 287-8410

FRESH
1061 Madison Avenue (80/81 St.) • (212) 396-0344

SMOKE SHOPS:
DAVIDOFF OF GENEVA INC.
535 Madison (E.54/55th St.) • (212) 751-9060

PAPER STORE:
KATE'S PAPERIE
561 Broadway (Spring/Prince St.)
8 West 13th Street (5th/6th Ave.)
1282 Third Avenue (73rd/74th St.)
941-9816

CAPPACINO:
SAINT AMBROEUS
1000 Madison Avenue (near 77th Street) • (212) 570-2211

CHOCOLATE MOOSE:
PAYARD PATISSERIE
1032 Lexington Avenue (74th Street) • (212)717-5252

TOY STORE:
MARY ARNOLD• 1010 Lexington (72nd st) • (212) 744-8510

ASTROLOGER:
MAXINE ALBERT • (212) 877-5291

BUTCHERS:
LOBEL'S PRIME MEATS
1096 Madison Avenue (83nd & 83rd Streets) • (212) 737-1373

LES HALLES
411 Park Avenue South (28th & 29th Streets) • (212) 679-4111

DIVORCE ATTORNEY:
BERNARD CLAIR (Partner)
ROSENMAN & COLIN
Lynn Amari & Karen Golden (Associates)
570 Madison Avenue • (212) 940-8800

KITCHEN/COOKING EQUIPMENT:
BRIDGE KITCHENWARE
214 East 52nd Street (2nd & 3rd Avenues) • (212) 688-4220

EXOTIC BIRDS:
THE URBAN BIRD
200 Church Street (Duane/Thomas St.) • (212) 0791-3177

MOZZARELLA:
JOE'S DAIRY
156 Sullivan (Houston & Prince) • (212) 677-8780

CAVIAR:
CAVIARTERIA
SOHO Grand Hotel • 310 West B-way (Canal & Grand Street)

HOTEL DELMONICO • 502 Park Avenue (59th Street)

GRAND CENTRAL TERMINAL
lower level - (42nd Street at Park Avenue) • 800-422-8427

ACCOUNTANT:
MR. STEPHEN SEGER
Poper & Seger & Popper
192 Lexington Avenue (between 31-32nd) • (212) 686-4700

BEAUTY SUPPLIES:
BOYDS
655 Madison Avenue (60-61st) • (212) 838-6558

CAR REPAIR:
MANHATTAN EAST AUTO REPAIR
324 East 95th Street (1st & 2nd Aves) • (212) 831-4300

BASIC KIDS CLOTHING:
MORRIS BROTHERS
2322 Broadway (83rd St) • (212)724-9000

CUSTOM GLOVES:
LACRAISA GLOVES
304 Fifth Avenue (31st Street) • (212) 594-2223

TERRACE GARDENS LANDSCAPING:
DIMITRI'S NURSERIES
1992 2nd Ave. • (212) 831-2810

OFFICE SUPPLIES & EQUIPMENT:
MEL EHRLICH • (212) 687-5885 ext. 240

ONE ON ONE TRAINING GYMS:
CASA
48 East 73rd St (Between Park & Madison) • (212) 717-1998

SHAVING PRODUCTS:
THE ART OF SHAVING
141 East 62nd Street • (212) 317-8436

WROUGHT IRON FURNITURE:
MORGICK COMPANY
20 West 20th Street • (212) 463-0304

REPUTABLE REAL ESTATE BROKER
DANIEL SEGAL • (212) 541-5522 ext. 45
A.J. CLARK REAL ESTATE

CARDS: COLLECTABLE:
ALEX'S MVP
256 East 89th Street • (212) 831-2273

HAIR COLORIST:
DOUG
MANARDI SALON • 29 EAST 61ST • (212) 308-1711

PRIX FIX LUNCH:
LA CÔTE BASQUE • 60 WEST 55 STREET • (212) 688-6525

GRAPHIC DESIGN FOR WEB AND PRINT:
mike@stuntmonkey.com
www.stuntmonkey.com/portfolio

RELOCATION COMPANY:
THE INTREPID NEW YORKER • (212) 534-5071

Index